Convergence and Diversity in the Governance of Higher Education

Comparative Perspectives

For several decades, higher education systems have undergone continuous waves of reform, driven by a combination of concerns about the changing labour needs of the economy, competition within the global-knowledge economy, and nationally competitive positioning strategies to enhance the performance of higher education systems. Yet, despite far-ranging international pressures – including the emergence of an international higher education market, enormous growth in cross-border student mobility, and pressures to achieve universities of world-class standing, boost research productivity and impact, and compete in global league tables – the suites of policy, policy designs, and sector outcomes continue to be marked as much by hybridity as they are by similarity or convergence. This volume explores these complex governance outcomes from a theoretical and empirical comparative perspective, addressing those vectors precipitating change in the modalities and instruments of governance, and how they interface at the systemic and institutional levels and across geographic regions.

GILIBERTO CAPANO is Professor of Political Science and Public Policy at the University of Bologna. He has been member of the Executive Committee of the International Political Science Association, the co-founder of the International Public Policy Association, and a member of the Executive Committee of the European Consortium of Political Research. He has extensively written on public policy, policy change, administrative reforms, policy design and instruments, and comparative governance in higher education. His recent publications include *Making Policies Work* (with M. Howlett, M. Ramesh, and A. Virani, 2019) and *Changing Governance in Universities: Italian Higher Education in Comparative Perspective* (with M. Regini and M. Turri, 2016).

DARRYL S. L. JARVIS is Professor in the Department of Asian and Policy Studies, Faculty of Liberal Arts and Social Sciences, at the Education University of Hong Kong. His recent publications include *Transformations in Higher Education Governance in Asia: Policy, Politics and Progress* (with J. Ka-ho Mok; 2019); *Institutional Entrepreneurship and Policy Change: Theoretical and Empirical Explorations* (with C. Bakir, 2018); *Asia After the Developmental State: Disembedding Autonomy* (with T. Carroll, 2017); *Markets and Development: Civil Society, Citizens and the Politics of Neoliberalism* (with T. Carroll, 2018); *Financialisation and Development in Asia* (with T. Carroll, 2018); and *The Politics of Marketizing Asia* (with T. Carroll, 2014).

Cambridge Studies in Comparative Public Policy

The **Cambridge Studies in Comparative Public Policy** series was established to promote and disseminate comparative research in public policy. The objective of the series is to advance the understanding of public policies through the publication of the results of comparative research into the nature, dynamics and contexts of major policy challenges and responses to them. Works in the series will draw critical insights that enhance policy learning and are generalizable beyond specific policy contexts, sectors and time periods. Such works will also compare the development and application of public policy theory across institutional and cultural settings and examine how policy ideas, institutions and practices shape policies and their outcomes. Manuscripts comparing public policies in two or more cases as well as theoretically informed critical case studies which test more general theories are encouraged. Studies comparing policy development over time are also welcomed.

General Editors M. Ramesh, *National University of Singapore*; Xun Wu, *Hong Kong University of Science and Technology*; Michael Howlett, *Simon Fraser University, British Columbia and National University of Singapore*

Convergence and Diversity in the Governance of Higher Education

Comparative Perspectives

Edited by

GILIBERTO CAPANO
University of Bologna
DARRYL S. L. JARVIS
The Education University of Hong Kong

CAMBRIDGE
UNIVERSITY PRESS

CAMBRIDGE
UNIVERSITY PRESS

Shaftesbury Road, Cambridge CB2 8EA, United Kingdom

One Liberty Plaza, 20th Floor, New York, NY 10006, USA

477 Williamstown Road, Port Melbourne, VIC 3207, Australia

314–321, 3rd Floor, Plot 3, Splendor Forum, Jasola District Centre, New Delhi – 110025, India

103 Penang Road, #05–06/07, Visioncrest Commercial, Singapore 238467

Cambridge University Press is part of Cambridge University Press & Assessment, a department of the University of Cambridge.

We share the University's mission to contribute to society through the pursuit of education, learning and research at the highest international levels of excellence.

www.cambridge.org
Information on this title: www.cambridge.org/9781009380331

DOI: 10.1017/9781108669429

© Cambridge University Press & Assessment 2020

First published 2020
First paperback edition 2023

A catalogue record for this publication is available from the British Library

Library of Congress Cataloging-in-Publication data
Names: Capano, Giliberto, 1960– author. | Jarvis,D. S. L. (Darryl S. L.), 1963– author.
Title: Convergence and diversity in the governance of higher education : comparative perspectives / edited by Giliberto Capano, Darryl S.L. Jarvis.
Description: Cambridge ; New York, NY : Cambridge University Press, 2020. |
Series: Cambridge studies in comparative public policy | Includes bibliographical references and index.
Identifiers: LCCN 2020011087 (print) | LCCN 2020011088 (ebook) | ISBN 9781108483964 (hardback) | ISBN 9781108669429 (ebook)
Subjects: LCSH: Higher education and state. | Education, Higher – Administration. | Universities and colleges – Administration. | Transnational education – Government policy. | Education and globalization.
Classification: LCC LC171 .C37 2020 (print) | LCC LC171 (ebook) | DDC379–dc23
LC record available at https://lccn.loc.gov/2020011087
LC ebook record available at https://lccn.loc.gov/2020011088

ISBN   978-1-108-48396-4   Hardback
ISBN   978-1-009-38033-1   Paperback

For mum, Jean Jarvis
DSLJ
For my mamma, Melina
Giliberto

Contents

Figures

Tables

Notes on Contributors

Editors

Giliberto Capano is Professor of Public Policy at the University of Bologna, Italy. He is the director of the Italian Centre for Research on Universities and Higher Education Systems and co-editor of the journals *Policy & Society* and the *Journal of Comparative Policy Analysis*. He specializes in public administration, public policy analysis, and comparative higher education. His research focuses on governance dynamics and performance in higher education and education, policy design and policy change, policy instruments' impact, the social role of political science, and leadership as an embedded function of policy making.

His works on higher education have been published in various international journals, including *Higher Education, Higher Education Policy, South European Society & Politics, Journal of Legislative Studies, Public Administration, Journal of Comparative Policy Analysis, Journal of European Public Policy, Comparative Education Review, European Political Science, Policy Sciences, Policy and Society, European Policy Analysis, Journal of Public Policy,* and *Regulation & Governance*. He has recently published *Varieties of Governance* (co-edited with M. Howlett and M. Ramesh; Palgrave, 2015) and *Changing Governance in Universities: Italian Higher Education in Comparative Perspective* (co-authored with M. Regini and M. Turri; Palgrave, 2016).

Darryl S. L. Jarvis is Professor in the Department of Asian and Policy Studies, Faculty of Liberal Arts and Social Sciences at The Education University of Hong Kong (formally the Hong Kong Institute of Education). He previously held positions at the National University of Singapore and the University of Sydney, Australia. He has published widely in the areas of comparative political economy and comparative public policy. His publications include *Asia After the Developmental*

State: Disembedding Autonomy (with Toby Carroll; Cambridge University Press, 2017), *Transformations in Higher Education Governance in Asia: Policy, Politics and Progress* (with Joshua Ka Ho Mok; Springer, 2019), *Institutional Entrepreneurship and Policy Change: Theoretical and Empirical Explorations* (with Caner Bakir; Macmillan, 2018), *Markets and Development: Civil Society, Citizens and the Politics of Neoliberalism* (with Toby Carroll; Routledge, 2015), *Financialisation and Development in Asia* (with Toby Carroll; Routledge, 2015), *The Politics of Marketizing Asia* (with Toby Carroll; Palgrave Macmillan, 2014), *ASEAN Industries and the Challenge from China* (with Anthony Welch; Palgrave Macmillan, 2011), *Infrastructure Regulation: What Works, Why, and How Do We Know? Lessons from Asia and Beyond* (with Ed Araral, M. Ramesh, and Wu Xun; World Scientific, 2011), *International Business Risk: A Handbook of the Asia-Pacific Region* (Cambridge University Press, 2011), *International Relations and the Challenge of Postmodernism: Defending the Discipline* (University of South Carolina Press, 2000), *International Relations. Still an American Social Science? Toward Diversity in International Thought* (with R. M. Crawford; State University of New York Press, 2001), and *Post-modernism and Its Critics: International Relations and the Third Debate* (Praeger, 2002).

Contributors
Germán Álvarez-Mendiola received his undergraduate diploma in Sociology from the National Autonomous University of Mexico, and Master's and Doctoral Degrees in Educational Research from the Centre for Advanced Research and Studies in Mexico. From 2002 to 2004 he was a Postdoctoral Fellow at the University of British Columbia. Since 1993, he has worked for the Department of Educational Research at the Centre for Advanced Research UNAM, and is currently Head of the Department. He has extensive experience as a teacher at secondary and high school levels, and as a professor at undergraduate and graduate levels. His research interests focus on public policies and organizational change in higher education, private higher education, life-long learning policies and institutions, and adult learners in higher education. He coordinates the book series *Higher Education Library* of the National Association of Universities and Higher Education Institutions (the Rector's association in Mexico).

He is a member of the International Committee of the International Workshops on Higher Education annual series.

Rose Amazan is a lecturer in the School of Education, University of New England, Australia. Rose's research and teaching is in the area of international and developmental education. She has extensive experience in many countries and has contributed to numerous analyses of issues such as female skilled migration, diaspora mobility, and gender and higher education in Africa and African university partnerships. Her current research project explores the issues surrounding the position of women in Ethiopian society, particularly in relation to their increased participation as students and teachers in higher education. She is also examining the outcomes of Australian scholarships for Africans, including re-integration, development of networks of practice among returnees, and gender implications.

Kassahun Kebede Dawo is Director of the Quality Audit and Enhancement Directorate in the Ethiopian Higher Education Relevance and Quality Agency. He has participated in various national and international trainings on higher education quality assurance. He has served in the Ethiopian education system in various capacities, including teaching English in two high schools, leading the Department of Professional Science, and lecturing on education courses in Hosanna College of Teacher Education from 2001–2005. He also briefly lectured in Dilla University, one of the new universities in Ethiopia. Kassahun received his PhD in International and Comparative Education.

Harry F. de Boer is a senior research associate at the Center for Higher Education Policy Studies, University of Twente, the Netherlands. Within the field of higher education studies, he specializes in government–university relationships, steering models, policy analysis, institutional governance, leadership and management, and strategic planning. In his field of expertise, he participated in many national and international studies and research-based consultancy projects, and has published many edited books, book chapters, journal articles, and reports on the aforementioned topics. He has lectured several higher education and public administration courses at the University of Twente, as well as international programmes. He is on the editorial board of *Higher Education Quarterly*. In 2015, he was one of the editors of and contributors to *The Palgrave International Handbook of Higher Education Policy and Governance* and to the book *Policy Analysis of Structural Reforms in Higher Education* (Springer).

Michael Dobbins studied political science and Slavic studies at the Universities of Konstanz, Warsaw, and Rutgers. He completed his doctoral dissertation in Konstanz, which dealt with comparative higher education policies in post-communist Central and Eastern Europe. In 2013 Michael was appointed Assistant Professor for policy analysis at Goethe University Frankfurt. His main areas of research are higher education policy, secondary education policy, policy making in the EU, policy making in the USA, and transformation processes in Central and Eastern Europe as well as the Caucasus countries.

His education research deals specifically with issues of governance, the impact of internationalization, and partisan politics. Most recently, he has focused on issues of school autonomy and educational decentralization and the influence of teachers' unions on educational governance. He is also highly involved in teacher training as part of the new educational science study programmes in Germany.

Miguel Alejandro González-Ledesma holds a PhD in Political Science from the Scuola Normale Superior de Pisa, Italy. Since 2016 he has held a postdoctoral position at the Research Institute on University and Education of the National Autonomous University in Mexico. He is also a lecturer on Geopolitics at the School of Philosophy and Literature. His research interests lie in the area of Higher Education studies, particularly governance, funding, quality assurance, and student movements.

Åse Gornitzka holds a doctoral degree from the Faculty of Public Administration, University of Twente, the Netherlands. She was previously a senior researcher at the Norwegian Institute for Studies in Research and Higher Education and at the Center for Higher Education Policy Studies at the University of Twente. Gornitzka's main fields of academic interest are the transformation and sustainability of the European political order in the area of education and research policy, the dynamics of European-level governance sites, the role of expertise in EU policy making, and the domestic impact of the EU's soft modes of governance.

Jeroen Huisman is Professor of Higher Education at the Centre for Higher Education Governance of Ghent University, Belgium. He was a researcher at the Center for Higher Education Policy Studies at the University of Twente, the Netherlands (1991–2005) and Professor of Higher Education Management at the University of Bath (2005–2013). He is editor of the journal *Higher Education Policy*, co-editor of the SRHE/Routledge book series, and co-editor of the Emerald series *Theory and Method in Higher Education Research*. He is also a member of editorial boards of various higher education journals and a member of the Executive Committee of EAIR, a European society for linking policy, research, and practice in higher education.

Kanishka Jayasuriya is Professor of Politics and International Studies, Discipline Leader of the politics group, and Fellow of the Asia Research Centre at Murdoch University, Western Australia. Prior to his current appointment, in 2016 he was Professor of International Politics, Director of the Indo-Pacific Governance Research Centre, and Professor of International Politics at the University of Adelaide. He obtained his PhD from the Australian National University and served as a postdoctoral fellow at Griffith University. He has held teaching and research appointments in several Australian and overseas universities, including the Australian National University, the University of Sydney, Murdoch University, the National University of Singapore, and City University of Hong Kong, China.

His research interests lie mainly in the areas of international and comparative political economy. He has worked extensively on issues of regulation, rule of law, and regional governance with reference to Asia. His research focuses on the relationship between globalization and the transformation of state structures, including in the areas of social policy and higher education. He is also working on the dynamics of capitalist crisis and democracy with particular reference to Asia.

Jens Jungblut is Associate Professor of Public Policy and Public Administration at the Department of Political Science at the University of Oslo. Prior to this he held postdoctoral positions at the Scandinavian Consortium for Organizational Research at Stanford University and the International Centre for Higher Education

Research at the University of Kassel. He received his PhD from the University of Oslo. Jens serves as a member of the steering committee of the Standing Group on 'Politics of Higher Education, Research, and Innovation' at the European Consortium for Political Research. His main research interests include comparative higher education policy, policy making and governance in higher education, and healthcare, political parties and party politics, and organizational change of higher education institutions. He has published several peer-reviewed articles on topics relating to higher education policy, governance in higher education, institutional change of higher education institutions, and the role of student unions.

Renze Kolster is a research associate at the Center for Higher Education Policy Studies of the University of Twente, the Netherlands, where he mainly researches topics related to the internationalization of higher education, higher education relevance, excellence in higher education, and graduate employability. Recent publications include 'Introducing Excellence in Higher Education. Honours Programmes in the Netherlands and Students' Preferences' (with R. L. Dijk and B. Jongbloed; *Journal of the European Higher Education Area*, 2016), 'Study Success in Higher Education' (with F. Kaiser; *Global Challenges, National Initiatives, and Institutional Responses*, Sense Publishers, 2016), and 'Academic Attractiveness of Countries: A Possible Benchmark Strategy Applied to the Netherlands' (*European Journal of Higher Education*, 2014).

Jenny M. Lewis is Professor of Public Policy in the School of Social and Political Sciences, and Associate Dean of Research for the Faculty of Arts at The University of Melbourne. She is also the founding Director of the Policy Lab. Jenny is a public policy expert, with particular interests in governance, the policy-making process, policy influence, public sector innovation, and networks. She has published widely in a range of international journals, is the author of six books (including *Academic Governance: Disciplines and Policy*; Routledge, 2013), and has been awarded American, European, and Australian research prizes. Jenny spent nearly three years as a professor in Denmark before returning to Australia as an Australian Research Council Future Fellow in 2013. She is the President of the International Research Society for Public Management, and a past President of the Australian Political Studies Association.

Peter Maassen is a professor of Higher Education Studies and deputy head/research coordinator at the Department for Educational Research, Faculty of Education, University of Oslo, Norway, where he is also the academic coordinator of an Erasmus Mundus joint master's degree programme. Previously, he was the director of the Center for Higher Education Policy Studies, University of Twente, the Netherlands (1997–2000). His areas of academic specialization include public governance (including policy reform and institutional change) of higher education, university leadership and management, organizational change in higher education, and the economic role of higher education institutions in OECD countries as well as in Sub-Saharan Africa. He is a member of the Executive Board of the University College Oslo (Høyskole i Oslo), and of the Board of the Centrum für Hochschulentwicklung. He was a member of the international panel evaluating the Danish university reforms (2009), and of the Norwegian governmental commission on higher education (Stjernø Commission – 2007/08), as well as of the OECD review teams for Japan and Finland.

Greg McCarthy is Professor and BHP Chair of Australian Politics at Peking University, China. He also holds the Chair of Australian Politics at the University of Western Australia. His main research interests and extensive publications are on Australian politics and political culture. His long-standing research focuses on transitional change within and between nations. Recently, he has written on the internationalization of Australian higher education governance, and the political implications of the conversion of Australian higher education from an elite to a mass and internationalized education system. In addition, he has investigated the international relationship between Australia and China as read through the policies of contemporary Australian governments.

Robin Middlehurst is Professor of Higher Education and External Policy Adviser in the Vice Chancellor's Office, Kingston University, London. She also serves as a policy adviser to the Higher Education Academy, is a trustee of the British Accreditation Council, and is an Advisory Board member of the Observatory on Borderless Higher Education. Robin's research includes borderless education and internationalization, governance and leadership, and quality assurance and enhancement in higher education. Her abiding interest is in 'higher education futures'. Her previous roles include Director of Strategy, Research and International at the Leadership Foundation, United Kingdom, co-designing and co-directing the UK's Top Management Programme for Higher Education; Director of the Quality Enhancement Group of the Higher Education Quality Council (and Director of Development at QAA), United Kingdom; and academic posts at the University of Surrey and the Institute of Education, London, England. Professor Middlehurst has published extensively on higher education policy, leadership, and governance, both nationally and internationally, and acts as a consultant for governments and higher education agencies in the United Kingdom and overseas.

Marino Regini is Professor Emeritus of Economic Sociology at the University of Milan, Italy, where he has served as Dean and Vice-Rector. He has been a visiting professor at several universities, including Harvard, MIT, Johns Hopkins, and Duke. He has also served as the President of the Society for the Advancement of Socio-Economics, of which he is an honorary fellow; as President of the Research Committee 44 of the International Sociological Association; and as a member of the editorial boards of several journals, including *Socio-Economic Review*, *European Sociological Review*, and *European Journal of Industrial Relations*. Among his major books are *Uncertain Boundaries: The Social and Political Construction of European Economies* (Cambridge University Press, 1995), *From Tellers to Sellers: Changing Employment Relations in Banks* (with J. Kitay and M. Baethge; MIT Press, 1999), *Why Deregulate Labour Markets?* (with G. Esping-Andersen; Oxford University Press, 2000), *European Universities and the Challenge of the Market. A Comparative Analysis* (Elgar, 2011), and *Changing Governance in Universities* (with Giliberto Capano and M. Turri; Palgrave Macmillan, 2016).

Julie Rowlands is a senior lecturer in education leadership within the School of Education at Deakin University, Australia, and a member of the strategic research centre, Research for Education Impact. Julie researches in the areas of governance, higher education systems, academic quality assurance, leadership, academic work, and organizational change, taking a feminist, critical sociology of education perspective. She is passionately interested in the role and place of universities within social relations, and in the creation and maintenance of power within and by universities, and at what cost. Julie's work has led to governance reform at a number of universities in Australia and abroad. Her writing has been published in international journals, including the *British Journal of Sociology of Education, Critical Studies in Education, Studies in Higher Education, Higher Education Research*, and *Development and Discourse*. Julie's monograph *Academic Governance in Contemporary Universities: Perspectives from Anglophone Nations* was published by Springer in 2017, and she co-edited and contributed to the edited volume *Practice Theory and Education: Diffractive Readings in Professional Practice* (Routledge, 2017).

Xianlin Song is Associate Professor in the Department of Asian Studies at the University of Western Australia. Her research focuses on the current cultural transition and gender issues in contemporary China, and more recently on international higher education. Her recent publications include *Women Writers in Post Socialist China* (co-authored with Kay Schaffer; Routledge, 2014), *Bridging Transcultural Divides: Teaching Asian Languages and Cultures in a Globalising Academy* (co-edited with Kate Cadman; University of Adelaide Press, 2012), and *Transcultural Encounters in Knowledge Production and Consumption* (co-edited with Youzhong Sun; Springer and Higher Education Press, 2018).

Bjørn Stensaker is Professor of Higher Education at the University of Oslo, and a research professor at the Nordic Institute for Studies in Innovation, Research and Education in Oslo, Norway. He has a special interest in studies of governance and change in higher education, including studies of how external and internal quality assurance impacts the higher education sector. He has published widely on these issues in a range of international journals and books. Professor Stensaker holds a master's degree in Political Science from the University of Oslo and a PhD from the Center for Higher Education Policy Studies at the University of Twente, the Netherlands. He is currently a member of the Danish Accreditation Council, and a member of the International Advisory Board of A3ES (the Portuguese Quality Assurance Agency). He is also the current President of EAIR (the European Higher Education Society). His latest book is *Strengthening Teaching and Learning in Research Universities. Strategies and*

Initiatives for Institutional Change (co-edited with G. T. Bilbow, L. Breslow, and R. Van der Vaart; Palgrave MacMillan, 2017).

Pedro N. Teixeira is Vice-Rector for Academic Affairs and Associate Professor of the Faculty of Economics at the University of Porto, Portugal. He is also Director of CIPES (the Center for Research in Higher Education Policies). He has been a member of Portugal's National Council of Education since 2014, and has served as an adviser on higher education to the President of Portugal since April 2016. He has also served on the evaluation panels for the European University Association and the European Association for Quality Assurance in Higher Education, on the Board of the BIAL Foundation since 2015, and as a member of the Education Advisory Board of the Foundation Francisco Manuel dos Santos, Lisbon.

He has published widely on higher education policy in a broad range of scientific journals, and is the editor of *Human Capital: Critical Concepts in Economics*, 4 vols. (with Christine Musselin; Routledge, 2014), *Policy Design and Implementation in Higher Education* (Springer, 2013), and *Public Vices, Private Virtues? Assessing the Effects of Marketization in Higher Education* (with David Dill; Sense Publishers, 2011). He is also the editor of *The Changing Public–Private Mix in Higher Education – Patterns, Rationales and Challenges* (Sense, 2017) and *The International Encyclopedia of Higher Education* (4 vols, with Jung Sheol Chin; Springer, 2018). He is a member of the Editorial Boards of *Higher Education*, the *European Journal of Higher Education*, the *Journal of the European Higher Education Area*, and of *OEconomia: History/Methodology/Philosophy*. He is also a member of the Board of Governors and Secretary General of the Consortium of Higher Education Researchers, a Research Fellow at the Institute for the Study of Labor, and a member of the Scientific Committee of the Réseau d'Etudes sur l'Enseignement Supérieur and the European Network of Higher Education Doctoral Students.

Anthony Welch is Professor of Education at the University of Sydney, Australia. His numerous publications address education reforms, principally within Australia, and the Asia-Pacific. He has advised state, national, and international agencies, and governments, institutions, and foundations, in Australia, Asia, and the USA. Project experience includes East and South-East Asia, particularly in higher education. His work has been translated into numerous languages, and he has been Visiting Professor in the USA, the United Kingdom, Germany, France, Japan, Malaysia, and Hong Kong (China).

A *Fulbright New Century Scholar* (2007–2008), *DAAD Scholar*, and *Haiwai Mingshi* awardee, his recent books include *The Professoriate: Profile of a Profession* (Springer, 2005), *Education, Change and Society* (4th ed.; Oxford, 2017), *ASEAN Industries and the Challenge from China* (with Darryl S. L. Jarvis; Palgrave, 2011), and *Higher Education in South East Asia* (Routledge, 2011). He was a consultant to the ADB project *Higher Education in Dynamic Asia*, and directed the ARC project *The Chinese Knowledge Diaspora* (with Rui Yang).

Don F. Westerheijden is a senior research associate at the Center for Higher Education Policy Studies at the University of Twente, the Netherlands, where he coordinates research on quality management. Don mostly studies quality assurance and accreditation in higher education in the Netherlands and Europe and its impacts, as well as university rankings. Policy evaluation is another area of research interest. Since 1993 he has co-developed the CRE/EUA Institutional Evaluation Programme. He led the independent assessment of the Bologna Process in 2009/2010. He was a member of the team that developed U-Multirank, the online, multidimensional worldwide university ranking. He is a member of the editorial board of the journal *Quality in Higher Education*, and serves on international boards of quality assurance agencies in Portugal and Hong Kong. His publications include *Policy Analysis of Structural Reforms in Higher Education: Processes and Outcomes* (with H. de Boer, J. File, J. Huisman, M. Seeber, M. Vukasović, and D. F. Westerheijden; Springer, 2017) and 'Next Generations, Catwalks, Random Walks and Arms Races: Conceptualising the Development of Quality Assurance Schemes' (with D. F. Westerheijden, B. Stensaker, M. J. Rosa, and A. Corbett; *European Journal of Education*, 2014).

Jun Jie Woo is Assistant Professor in the Department of Asian and Policy Studies, Faculty of Liberal Arts and Social Sciences, the Education University of Hong Kong, and was previously Assistant Professor in the School of Humanities and Social Sciences, Nanyang Technological University, Singapore. He received his PhD from the Lee

Kuan Yew School of Public Policy, National University of Singapore, and holds a Master of Science in International Political Economy from the S. Rajaratnam School of International Studies, Nanyang Technological University. Prior to his current appointment, Dr Woo was a Postdoctoral Research Fellow at the Lee Kuan Yew Centre for Innovative Cities, Singapore University of Technology and Design. He also serves as assistant editor for *Policy & Society*, an interdisciplinary journal of policy research.

Preface

For historians, the rise and fall of civilizations have been relatively contiguous exercises in force projection, colonization, economic aggrandizement, overextension, exhaustion, and collapse, where the competition for territory, markets, and physical and economic resources has defined the ebbs and flows of history, explaining why 'some parts of the world have grown rich and others have lagged behind' (Kennedy, 1989; Maddison, 2007, p. 1).

In the twenty-first century, the wealth of nations continues to rest on trade and commerce, to be sure, but much less so on territory, extra-territorial wealth extraction, mercantilist trade practices, or resource competition. Ever-increasing amounts of wealth derive from knowledge, information, and technology – commodities that defy the confines of national borders or their amassing through military acquisition. The rise of the fourth industrial revolution (i.e., the nexus of technologies situated between the physical, digital, and biological spheres and represented by fields such as artificial intelligence, biotechnology, robotics, nanotechnology, and informatics) is largely supplanting industrial and manufacturing-based economic activity as core drivers of growth, employment, and national wealth (Klaus, 2017). While in 1917, for example, the largest economic enterprises (by share value) listed on the New York Stock Exchange were energy, steel, manufacturing, and resource-based firms, by 2017 it was knowledge and technology firms – the likes of Apple Inc., Alphabet Inc. (Google), Amazon, Facebook, Microsoft, financial services, biotechnology, and pharmaceutical firms. Indeed, just 2 firms (AT&T and General Electric) listed in the top 50 firms on the New York bourse in 1917 remain there today, with the rest either delisted, acquired by larger conglomerates, or having ceased trading (Kauflin, 2017).

This transformation from industrial-manufacturing to knowledge-based economic power is no better personified than by Apple and the iPhone. The value-capture in the development, manufacture, and assembly of the iPhone accrues disproportionately to the knowledge-ownership of the technology rather than the physical production and assembly of the hardware itself. As Gereffi demonstrates, assembled entirely in China (via a Taiwanese firm, Foxconn), with a per unit export value of $194.41, the value actually captured by China is a mere $6.54. If the costs per unit of technology imports required to assemble the iPhone are taken into account, then China's share is dwarfed by Korea at $80.85, Germany at $16.08, and by the rest of the world at $62.79 (Gereffi, 2014, pp. 20–21). By far the greatest value per iPhone produced accrues to Apple Inc., which retails the phone for approximately $700 and uses the platform to generate stream revenues through app and content sales, making Apple the most valuable publically traded company in the world (Carroll and Jarvis, 2017, pp. 27–28; Feiner, 2019; Gereffi, 2014, pp. 20–21). Brains, not industrial brawn, are what drive modern-day economic dynamism.

Little wonder that moving 'up the value chain' and positioning economies in knowledge-based activities has become the dominant policy mantra of the contemporary era. It also explains the ever-increasing interest in and emphasis on the 'knowledge factories' of the twenty-first century: higher education systems which collectively produce the human capital and know-how that nurtures creativity, innovation, and technological discovery – the *zeitgeist* of national economic competitive advantage (Marton, 2006; Raunig, 2013). If there are contemporary 'empires' they increasingly nestle around those spaces where the metabolic rate of creativity is most intensive: the 'silicone valleys' and hinterlands of commerce that leverage off higher education systems and the complex, myriad talent networks that arise. Richard Florida labels this the location geographies of creative classes; or, in more formulaic policy terms, it is what Etzkowitz and Leydesdorff term the triple helix paradigm – the interface between universities, government, and industry (Etzkowitz and Leydesdorff, 1995; Etzkowitz and Zhou, 2009; Florida, 2002, 2005). Regardless of the nomenclature employed, the point is clear: universities and higher education systems are the pillars that make possible the knowledge economy of the twenty-first century and the economic rewards that flow from it. They sit at the centre of modern-day economic empires.

This reality has made higher education fertile ground for policy reform as governments the world over seek to create universities of 'world class standing' and make higher education systems 'fit for purpose' (Gleason, 2018a, 2018b; Slaughter and Rhoades, 2004). Transforming higher education has become de rigueur, with higher education policy 'being "done" in new locations, on different scales, and by new actors and organizations' as never before (Jules and Jefferson, 2017, p. 124). The introduction of new forms of managerialism, regulation, accreditation, sector financing, institutional reporting and accountability regimes, metrics-driven performance assessment of institutional and sector outcomes, national and international rankings and benchmarking practices, and performance-based remuneration are recasting higher educational landscapes and the mechanisms by which they are governed.

But if the policy reform mantra surrounding higher education appears universally singular, it would be wrong to conclude a form of policy convergence, or, indeed, convergent trajectories or sector outcomes. Any rudimentary survey of the landscapes of higher education systems globally reveals contradictory realities – processes of both convergence and divergence. Indeed, despite far-ranging international pressures, the emergence of an international market in higher education and enormous growth in cross-border student mobility, pressures to achieve universities of world-class standing, recruit high-calibre international academic talent, boost research productivity and impact, or compete in global league tables, the suites of policy, policy designs, and sector outcomes are as much marked by hybridity as they are of similarity (King, 2010).

This volume grapples with this conundrum. It focuses on the governance of higher education, exploring those vectors precipitating change in the modalities and instruments of governance, and how they interface at the systemic and institutional levels, and across geographic regions.

By its very nature, however, focusing on governance is a necessarily amorphic activity, composed of both inductive and deductive forms of investigation. There is no settled analytical lens able to stabilize the language of governance or explicate and fix the parameters of its dimensions in a way that cartographers are able to map and reference points in geographic space. As a conceptual rubric, governance remains intellectually incongruent. While it is not the intention of this volume to grapple with these larger meta-theoretical and conceptual issues, the practical orientation of policy studies does require the emplacement of ordering devices, or at least frameworks, that permit the comparative application of the concept (Brennan, 2007, p. 168). To that end, this volume approaches governance in higher education across two interrelated spectrums, each broken down into their constituent parts. In Part II, governance is treated *analytically* and broken down into sub-categories such as regulation (the tools and instruments of governance, including quality assurance, accountability, and management), system or structural elements of governance (the composition and institutional design of the sector, including the public–private mix), sub-structural elements of governance (organizations and institutional-level decision making), and meta-structural elements (internationalization). In Part III, the governance of higher education is explored *geographically*, addressing regional variations and similarities in the case of Europe, North America, Asia, Africa, and South America. The volume is thus designed to facilitate a thematic analysis of specific elements of governance, but referenced more generally in relation to governance trends globally.

Ultimately, of course, no analysis of the governance of higher education, especially viewed macroscopically and comparatively, can hope to be exhaustive. Despite the increasing prevalence of relatively uniform, meta-structural forces impacting national systems of higher education, the manner in which these articulate and traverse institutional settings and socio-political and economic national contexts makes for a series of empirically rich landscapes. That said, it is also the case that reform and transformations in the governance of higher education have never been so intense and far reaching, impacting not just the competitive dynamics of how higher education systems are positioned, but the treatment of academic labour and the opportunities for participation.

We hope this volume contributes to a deeper understanding of those forces impacting and transforming the governance of higher education.

Giliberto Capano and Darryl S. L. Jarvis

References

Brennan, J. (2007) On researching ourselves: The difficult case of autonomy in researching higher education. In C. Kayrooz, G. Akerlind, and M. Tight (Eds), *Autonomy in social science university research – The view from the UK and Australian universities*, pp. 167–182. London: Elsevier.

Carroll, T., and Jarvis, D. S. L. (2017) Disembedding autonomy: Asia after the developmental state. In T. Carroll and D. S. L. Jarvis (Eds), *Asia after the developmental state: Disembedding autonomy*, pp. 3–50. Cambridge: Cambridge University Press.

Etzkowitz, H., and Leydesdorff, L. A. (1995) The triple helix – University-industry-government relations: A laboratory for knowledge based economic development. *EASST Review*, 14(1), 14–19.

Etzkowitz, H., and Zhou, C. (2009) Evolution of the university's role in innovation and the new Asian model. In J. A. Douglas, C. J. King, and I. Fekker (Eds), *Globalization's muse: Universities and higher education systems in a changing world*, pp. 229–247. Berkeley: Berkeley Public Policy Press.

Feiner, L. (2019) Apple is once again the most valuable public company in the world. www.cnbc.com/2019/02/06/apple-is-once-again-the-most-valuable-public-company-in-the-world.html

Florida, R. L. (2002) *The rise of the creative class and how it's transforming work, leisure, community and everyday life.* New York: Basic Books.

Florida, R. L. (2005) *Cities and the creative class.* New York; London: Routledge.

Gereffi, G. (2014) Global value chains in a post-Washington consensus world. *Review of International Political Economy*, 21(1), 9–37. doi:10.1080/09692290.2012.756414

Gleason, N. W. (2018a). Introduction. In N. W. Gleason (Ed.), *Higher education in the era of the fourth industrial revolution*, pp. 1–12. Singapore: Springer; Palgrave Macmillan.

Gleason, N. W. (Ed.) (2018b). *Higher education in the era of the fourth industrial revolution.* Singapore: Springer; Palgrave Macmillan.

Jules, T. D., and Jefferson, S. S. (2017) The next educational bubble – educational brokers and education governance mechanisms: Who governs what! In T. D. Jules (Ed.), *The global educational policy environment in the fourth industrial revolution: Gated, regulated and governed*, pp. 123–147. Bingley: Emerald.

Kauflin, J. (2017) America's top 50 companies 1917–2017. *Forbes.* www.forbes.com/sites/jeffkauflin/2017/09/19/americas-top-50-companies-1917-2017/#37a343b41629

Kennedy, P. M. (1989) *The rise and fall of the great powers: Economic change and military conflict from 1500–2000.* London: Fontana Press.

King, R. (2010) Policy internationalization, national variety and governance: Global models and network power in higher education states. *Higher Education: The International Journal of Higher Education and Educational Planning*, 60(6), 583–594.

Klaus, S. (2017) *The fourth industrial revolution*. New York: Crown Business.

Maddison, A. (2007) *Contours of the world economy, 1–2030 AD: Essays in macro-economic history*. Oxford: Oxford University Press.

Marton, S. (2006) Education policy. In B. G. Peters and J. Pierre (Eds), *Handbook of public policy*, pp. 231–248. London; Thousand Oaks: Sage Publications.

Raunig, G. (2013) *Factories of knowledge, industries of creativity*. Los Angeles/Cambridge, MA: Semiotexte.

Slaughter, S., and Rhoades, G. (2004) *Academic capitalism and the new economy: Markets, state, and higher education*. London/Baltimore: Johns Hopkins University Press.

Abbreviations

AACU	Association of American Colleges and Universities
AAU	Association of American Universities
AASCU	American Association of State Colleges and Universities
ACCT	Association of Community College Trustees
ACU	American Capital University
AERES	Agence de l'évaluation de la recherche et de l'enseigne-ment supérieur
AIU	Asian International University
ARACIS	Agenția Română de Asigurare a Calității în Învățământul Superior
ASEAN	Association of South East Asian Nations
BAN	Badan Akredtitasi Nasional
BFUG	Bologna Follow-Up Group
BHMN	Badan Hukum Milik Negera
CAE	Crédito con Aval del Estado
CAP	changing academic profession
CAS	Chinese Academy of Sciences
CCDI	Central Commission for Discipline Inspection
CCP	Chinese Communist Party
CEI	International Campus of Excellence
CEO	chief executive officer
CEQ	Course Experience Questionnaire
CHEA	Council for Higher Education Accreditation
CIC	Council of Independent Colleges
CMEC	Council of Ministers of Education, Canada
CNE	Comité National d'Evaluation
CNRS	Centre national de la recherche scientifique
CPI	Corruption Perception Index
DAAD	Deutscher Akademischer Austauschdienst
E4	ENQA, EUA, ESU, and EURASHE
EEA	European Economic Area

EMBA	executive master of business administration
ENQA	European Association for Quality Assurance in Higher Education
EPRDF	Ethiopia Peoples' Revolutionary Democratic Front
ERA	Excellence in Research for Australia
EROD	Education Resource Organizations Directory
ESC	Education Strategy Centre
ESG	European Standards and Guidelines for Quality Assurance
ESIB	now known as ESU
ESU	European Students' Union
ETP	Education and Training Policy
EU	European Union
EUA	European University Association
EURASHE	European Association of Institutions for Higher Education
FARC	Fuerzas Armadas Revolucionarias de Colombia
FDRE	Federal Democratic Republic of Ethiopia
FTE	full-time equivalent
GDP	gross domestic product
HE	higher education
HEI	higher education institution
HEP	Higher Education Proclamation
HERQA	Higher Education Relevance and Quality Agency
HEs	higher education system
IHE	international higher education
IIEP	International Institute for Educational Planning
ILO	International Labour Organization
IPB	Institut Pertanian Bogor
ISCED	International Standard Classification of Education
ITB	Institut Teknologi Bandung
IUCEA	Inter-University Council for East Africa
KEJN	Komitet Ewaluacji Jednostek Naukowych
KKN	Korupsi, Kolusi, Nepotisme
KNOW	Krajowe Naukowe Ośrodki Wiodące
KRASP	Polish Rectors Conference
LOLF	Loi organique relative aux lois de finance
MBA	master of business administration
MoE	Ministry of Education

MOET	Ministry of Education and Training
NAICU	National Association of Independent Colleges and Universities
NASULGC	National Association of State Universities and Land-Grant College
NCBR	Narodowe Centrum Badań i Rozwoju
NCCC	National Counter Corruption Commission
NCN	Narodowe Centrum Nauki
NGO	non-governmental organization
NPM	New Public Management
OECD	Organisation for Economic Co-operation and Development
ONESQA	Office for National Education Standards and Quality Assessment
PRC	People's Republic of China
PRHEI	private higher education institutions
PTP	Perguruan Tinggi yang Diselenggarakan Pemerintah
QA	quality assurance
REF	Research Excellence Framework
SAP	Structural Adjustment Programme
SHEEO	State Higher Education Executive Officer Network
SSA	Sub-Saharan African
(S)SCI	(Social) Science Citation Index
STEM	Science, Technology, Engineering, and Medicine
TI	Transparency International
TNE	transnational education
TVET	technical and vocational training
UMcedel	Universiti Malaya's Centre for Democracy and Elections
UMNO	United Malays National Organisation
UNDP	United Nations Development Programme
UNESCO	United Nations Educational, Scientific and Cultural Organization
UNICEF	United Nations Children's Fund
VC	Vice Chancellor
VPAR	Academic Vice President
VPN	virtual private network

PART I

Theorizing Governance in Higher Education

1 Theorizing the Governance of Higher Education

Beyond the 'Republic of Scholars' Ontology

GILIBERTO CAPANO AND DARRYL S. L. JARVIS

1.1 Introduction

Theorizing the governance of higher education is a fraught business. Not only can the experience of everyday interaction with the university get in the way of 'wider empirically informed theorizing about university systems', but the dominance of particular theoretical traditions can cast a long shadow over how actors, systems and the governance of higher education is studied (Brennan, 2007, 2010, p. 231). Scholarship on higher education has long been dominated by organizational and functionalist literatures, with universities understood as atomized organizational actors, each with discrete cultures and characteristics, and analysed in relation to their functional attributes (teaching, research, funding, recruitment), organizational composition (structure, management, decision making), and the articulation of sub-organizational interests (the professoriate, disciplines, students, administrators).

Burton Clark's influential analysis, *The Higher Education System* (1983), epitomized such approaches, drawing on organizational sociology as a key medium of inquiry and prism for theory building. Cross-national variation in higher education systems, for example, Clark situated in the distribution of authority across organizational sociologies and the degree to which they enjoyed autonomy relative to the state. Continental European higher education systems Clark characterized as neo-Weberian, hierarchal, bureaucratized, and centrally coordinated, with institutional autonomy constrained and academic matters dominated by academic guilds. The British system, by contrast, was more diffuse, characterized by state steering, with government overseeing funding and sector composition but otherwise devolving operating autonomy to universities, and institutional governance characterized by academic collegiality and loose patterns of academic

3

organization. The American model, on the other hand, was fundamentally diffuse. Institutional autonomy was procedurally ingrained but accountable to multiple external stakeholders through public monitoring of quality, outputs, and market needs, while institutional governance was bifurcated between professional university/college administrators who set strategic directions and academics exercising autonomy over recruitment and academic matters in strongly organized disciplinary contexts (Capano, 2011 Clark, 1983).

A central preoccupation of scholarship has thus concerned organizational forms and the interplay between authority and interests: how these shape organizational, systemic and social-political environments, and how they fundamentally impact or distort disciplinary authority and professional autonomy.[1] For a generation of scholars, institutional interest articulation has thus dominated intellectual inquiry, informed by a combination of institutionalist/neo-institutionalist perspectives (March and Olsen, 1989; Olsen, 2007; Peters, 2001), the sociology of organizations literature (Bowey, 1976; DiMaggio and Powell, 1983; Eldridge, 1974; Silverman, 1970), neo-managerialist and public sector management perspectives (Öberg and Bringselius, 2014; Reed, 2002; Smeenk et al., 2009), and organizational/practitioner literatures in leadership studies and human resource management (Brennan, 2007, p. 171; Pusser, 2015, p. 61).

1.2 The 'Republic of Scholars' Ontology: Methodological Upwardness, Downwardness, and Inwardness

This legacy of organizationally focused frameworks and questions of disciplinary authority continues to cast a long shadow over contemporary scholarship – much, if not most, preoccupied with mapping changes in the locus of authority and its impact on the 'republic of scholars' (Bleiklie and Kogan, 2007). King (2007, 2009, 2010), Deem (2010), Deem and Brehony (2005), Waks (2007), Morrissey (2013), Enders, Kehm, and Schimank (2015), Lucas (2014), McCarthy, Song, and Jayasuriya (2017), Miller (2014), and Dill (1997, 1998), for example, explore the assault on disciplinary authority and the subjugation of academic labour through processes of university corporatization, the rise of managerialism, and the encroaching dominance of market rationality. Slaughter, Rhoades, and Leslie (1997, 2004), Cantwell and Kauppinen (2014), Fischer and Mandell (2018) and Mandell (2018) address the rise of 'academic capitalism': the repurposing of universities as commercially driven/market responsive (entrepreneurial) enterprises and how this impacts professional autonomy, the organizational sanctity of disciplines and academic leadership in organizational management.

Ball (2010), Cloete (2006), Mok (2010), Mok and Cheung (2011), Marginson (2007), and Sam and Sijde (2014) focus on the systemic disruptions of globalization and the emergence of an international market for higher education: how this drives institutional transformation and traditions of collegiate governance, and repositions authority within management and dynamic international market forces. Douglass (2009, 2012), Douglass, King, and Feller (2009), Jayasuriya (2001, 2010, 2015a, 2015b), and Sandel (2012) similarly address the sublimation of the 'publicness' of universities with the rise of regulatory capitalism, the commodification of knowledge and the repurposing of the university towards instrumental ends driven by the interests of capital and the state, and which collectively discipline academic labour (see also Castells and Cloete, 2017). Musselin (2012), Bleiklie and Kogan (2007), Bladh (2007), Enders, de Boer, and Weyer (2013), Enders, Kehm, and Schimank (2015), Rip and Kulati (2015), Taylor, Webber, and Jacobs (2013) and Gumport and Snydman (2006) concern themselves with mapping the directionalities of change rather than attributing causality, identifying relatively uniform cross-national challenges to academic autonomy, including the rise of managerialism, metrics-based performance management of academic labour, competitive rankings and impact dynamics, and the extensive introduction of market- or quasi-market-based governance tools.

While it would be wrong to suggest such scholarship simply grapples with the same sets of issues as did Clark and his contemporaries, they are nevertheless clearly informed by the same ontological disciplinary standpoint and 'triangle of coordination' framework, where competitive interest articulation between the state, market and discipline defines the research landscape and outer analytical markers of intellectual inquiry (see Figure 1.1) (Dill, 2014). Much contemporary research, for example, continues the tradition of Cartesian *triangulation*, positioning higher education systems within a three-dimensional geometry in order to characterize governance types, hybridity, directionalities of change, and the extent of organizational and disciplinary autonomy – a model that otherwise serves as the episteme of

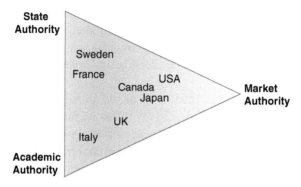

Figure 1.1 Triangle of coordination model: higher education systems
Source: Adopted from Clark (1983), p. 143.

comparative higher education studies (Becher, 1989; Clark, 1983b; Dobbins et al., 2011; Jürgen Enders et al., 2013; Goedegebuure and van Vught, 1996; Kosmützky and Krücken, 2014; Lapworth, 2004; Teichler, 1996, 2014). As Jessop observes, research effort has tended to focus on the rise of managerialism and 'shifts in internal management organization and capabilities', knowledge commodification and 'fit for purpose' market logics that reward commercializable research effort and the 'training' needs of the economy, the 'introduction of internal markets and quasi-markets', and the collective impact of these on academic labour, 'differentiated career tracks and growing [work] precarity' (Jessop, 2018, p. 105). Triangulation and empirical mapping of the academic guild, in other words, has often triumphed over broader and more sustained theoretical efforts focused on explanatory causality.

Part of the reason for this doubtless lies in the aetiology of (academic) guildism and how scholarship has investigated the professions. As Musselin observes, 'academics have always developed their activities in organizational structures called universities', producing a 'mix between professional power and autonomy on the one hand and bureaucratic features on the other' (Musselin, 2012, p. 26). This has lent itself to studies exploring the sociology of professions, including professional autonomy, practices of self-regulation, the construction of group identity and the management of group membership through specialist language, knowledge skills, processes of accreditation and, in turn, how these manifest as barriers to control by the state and market (see, for example, Freidson, 2001). When situated within an organizational matrix, guildism has fused with Weberian analytical tomes focused on organizational hierarchies, bureaucratization, power, and interest articulation in intra- and extra-organizational contexts to inform much, if not most, scholarship on higher education (Donaldson, 2010; Musselin, 2014). Doubtless, too, this has been amplified by a professional preoccupation with self-comparison. Academic fraternities like to compare. Questions of working conditions, salaries, research expectations, career progression, research support, academic autonomy, organizational and managerial cultures, existential threats (organizational and discipline restructuring) and resource issues tend to inform conversations and the 'data points' of comparative assessment, reinforcing the 'republic of scholars' ontology as the key prism of inquiry (Becher, 1989; Sultana, 2012, p. 353).

The result, we argue, has tended to entrench scholarship in relatively narrow, somewhat insular, typically descriptive *a*theoretical terrains, reflecting four interrelated and self-reinforcing methodological tendencies – and which operate largely without acknowledgement or critical scrutiny. First, what we term an implicit and overreaching *standpoint-guildism*, in which the ontological centrality of the discipline and of disciplinary authority serves as a kind of Rawlsian original position or referent point, and from which change or, inter alia, 'deviation' is plotted, measured and assessed (Rawls, 1999). Second, and because of this, a tendency to *exogenize agency* responsible for change – that is, change to the standing of disciplinary authority is nearly always assumed to emanate from outside the academy/discipline, with organic or internal disciplinary agency conceptually confined to group issues of fidelity and protection. And third, because of the legacy of sociological-organizational Weberian-informed scholarship, a tendency to locate explanatory causality engendering change in mechanistic institutional-group processes that are seen to emanate from above, external to the organization, morph internally into the organization, cascading downwards and inwards to the discipline – methodological *upwardness, downwardness* and *inwardness*. Fourth, *methodological nationalism*, in which the locus of governance, its apparatus (laws, rules, methods, tools, instruments) and geographic scope is predominantly confined to sub-state and state localities – a tendency to 'focus on internal institutional processes and influences (e.g., faculty senate, shared governance, administration, governing boards), and when external issues are examined' the tendency to situate these within national methodological containers, largely refracting the influence of supra-national causalities of change through state and sub-state institutional actors (Shahjahan and Kezar, 2013, p. 25).

These methodological fiats have been far reaching, shunting research into common thinking spaces and engendering relatively uniform conclusions about the causes and directionalities of change in higher education systems globally. As Figure 1.2 depicts, by far the dominant mode of conceptualization of higher education environments is of increasingly complex, multilevel, multi-stakeholder governance mechanisms, predominantly formal in nature but also situated among informal cascading environmental norms/pressures, some international in scope, that shape the operating environments of universities and influence/steer decision making at the university/institutional level, with consequential outcomes for organizational/disciplinary authority and the structure of higher education systems – with most intellectual effort focused on levels B and C and emblematic of a pervasive methodological nationalism (Bleiklie and Kogan, 2007; Shahjahan and Kezar, 2013 Sultana, 2012).

If there has been a shift in research effort and focus in the last few decades, then clearly this has resided in level A-type scholarship, with a growing number of studies examining the rise of international influences and how these create coercive pressures that informally/formally reorient and reshape organizational level–outcomes and national higher education systems. Erkkilä and Piironen's study of the emergence of de facto global policy instruments in knowledge governance – such as international university rankings and research impact metrics, for example – suggests their increasingly pervasive influence in governing the 'conduct and policies of individuals and organizations', steering national research production and knowledge dissemination, and defining policy thinking about how to assess (measure) the performance and competitiveness of higher education institutions/systems (Erkkilä and Piironen, 2018, pp. 19, 83, 123; see also Espeland and Sauder, 2012, pp. 100–107; Hazelkorn, 2011, 2014, 2017; Zlatkin-Troitschanskaia et al., 2015). Relatedly, work focusing on regulatory regionalism (Jayasuriya, 2008, 2009; Jayasuriya and Robertson, 2010; Nelson, 2013; Robertson, 2010; Robertson et al., 2016) has likewise highlighted the increasingly pervasive influence of regional governance regimes (the Bologna Process, the MERCOSUR-Educativo and the

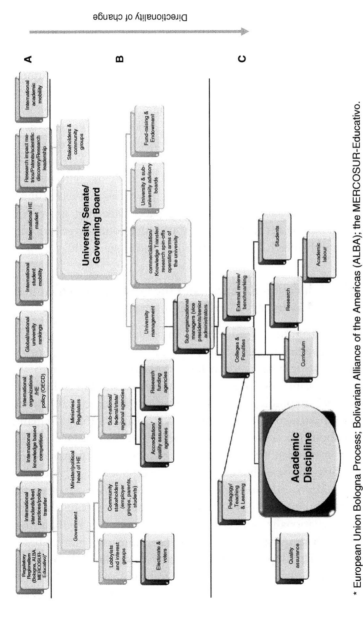

Directionality of change

A

B

C

* European Union Bologna Process; Bolivarian Alliance of the Americas (ALBA); the MERCOSUR-Educativo.

Figure 1.2 Research schema of scholarship on higher education

* European Union Bologna Process; Bolivarian Alliance of the Americas (ALBA); the MERCOSUR-Educativo.

Bolivarian Alliance of the Americas) on domestic systems of higher education governance, including standards, accreditation, skills recognition and comparability (EHEA, n.d.; Elken, 2017; Gornitzka and Stensaker, 2014; Jayasuriya and Robertson, 2010, p. 2; Magalhães et al., 2013).

Importantly, however, we argue that the increasing volume of level A-type scholarship has not so much disrupted organizationally focused or 'triangle of coordination' frameworks as added another 'influencing' layer, ensconcing the same methodological fiats previously identified. The directionalities of influence (Figure 1.2), for example, continue to be viewed through methodologically national lenses and studied predominantly in relation to their modality of articulation *downwards* in national, organizational/disciplinary/academic labour contexts.

In essence, scholarship on higher education has thus proceeded uninterrupted, keeping intact the 'republic of scholars' ontology but in the current context subject to influencing processes that increasingly emanate from international and other spaces reflecting growth in multi-stakeholder constituencies and thus more complex governance environments (Figure 1.2, level A) (Bleiklie and Kogan, 2007).

1.3 Higher Education Research and the Governance Dilemma: Convergence, Divergence, Variegation, or Hybridity?

Despite its contribution to a booming and voluminous literature, the 'republic of scholars' ontology has proven a far from adequate prism for theory development or deepening explanatory insight into the changing dimensions of governance in higher education. Indeed, we argue that such an ontology has contributed to theoretical paucity and confusion. In particular, the 'republic of scholars' ontology remains conflicted about the degree of homogeneity and convergence around what are typically identified as a narrowing range of policy approaches, the forces driving these changes and the governance trajectories that result. Methodological fiats such as *standpoint-guildism*, for example, are used to remonstrate against the rise of academic capitalism by mapping internationalization, efficiency and effectiveness metricization (performance-based management, rankings, impact), market-based intrusion and the adoption of instrumental rationalities (knowledge-based economic activity) into an ever-widening number of jurisdictions – on the one hand stressing their encroaching international omnipresence and the uniformity of the outcomes that result, on the other highlighting their localized modalities of articulation in discrete national/institutional contexts (see, for example, Benavides et al., 2019; Croucher and Woelert, 2016; Espinoza, 2017; Huang et al., 2018; Kail, 2011; Provini, 2018; Thorkelson, 2019; Westerheijden, 2018). Sameness and difference are venerated simultaneously, producing contradictory empirical observations but without theoretical explanation. As Taylor et al. (2013) observe, while higher education institutions, individuals, and countries face unique issues – indeed, display national and institutional specificity – many of these are in fact the same throughout the world, producing policy convergence and 'globalizing models' of higher education (Jarvis, 2017; King, 2007, 2010; Pilkington, 2014; Taylor et al., 2013).

Such observations are generally explained with reference to exogenous agency – in particular, structuralist and policy learning literatures. Structuralist accounts, for example, emphasizing the increasingly pervasive imperatives of competitive international dynamics (rankings, internationalization, and growth in the global higher education market – now worth an estimated USD1.9 trillion), are seen as coercive, producing convergence in higher education governance trajectories because of common sets of structural constraints that impact *all* nation states (Jürgen Enders, 2004; King, 2009, 2010; Marginson, 2014). Similarly, learning literatures, emphasizing policy transfer (or diffusion), where national decision makers and policy practitioners learn through peer-to-peer interaction in discrete policy communities, or adopt specific policy designs as a result of international benchmarking, the standard-setting activities of international organizations (e.g., OECD, EU), or gravitate towards the adoption of 'best practice' frameworks reflecting the dominant ideational values of international policy communities, are likewise seen as conspiring to produce convergence, or at least reducing diversity in the composition, structure and governance of higher education systems (Blanco et al., 2011; Busch and Jörgens, 2005; Cao, 2012; Fawcett and Daugbjerg, 2012; Howlett and Ramesh, 2002; Jarvis, 2014; Jayasuriya, 2001; Marsh and Sharman, 2009; Obinger et al., 2013; Peck, 2011).

Theoretical indeterminacy and explanatory paucity have thus been the hallmarks of the 'republic of scholars' ontology – an inability to explain divergence, variegation, hybridity or, indeed, coextensive processes of convergence and divergence.[2] Despite the oft-heralded advent of governance convergence around New Public Management (NPM) approaches, or more broadly of liberalization, privatization, deregulation, and marketization a quick survey of Australasian, European, North American, or Asian states, for example, reveals vast and continuing differences in the degree to which these new governance modes have been deployed – if at all (Capano, 2011; Goldfinch and Wallis, 2010). While liberalization is evident in some West European states (England, Netherlands), Australia, and New Zealand, where reforms have transformed universities into corporate actors and constructed governance mechanisms to foster institutional competition in resource allocation, identifying these same governance modalities in countries such as Germany, Italy, Finland, and France, for example, proves more difficult. Equally, the sense in which we can talk about the emergence of a ubiquitous approach to sector governance across Asia, or convergence in institutional forms, regulatory systems, or even of similar national/institutional responses to the emergence of global rankings and increasing international student mobility, overstates the degree to which *convergence* as opposed to *divergence* epitomizes the governance of higher education (Jarvis and Mok, 2019).

These same observations apply to sector financing and the spread of marketization, where higher education systems are typically characterized as experiencing a general diminution in the degree to which governments fund the sector relative to the rise of fee-for-service and user-pays financing models. As Table 1.1 highlights, these changes have been less than might be supposed. Indeed, the percentage of private expenditure on higher education has increased in some countries, remained static in others, and in some countries declined. While the OECD average level of private expenditure on higher education increased from 24.3 per cent in 2000 to 30.1 per cent in 2016, the composite differences between countries such as Finland, Germany, and Belgium compared to Korea, the United States, and the United Kingdom is stark. As Figure 1.1 demonstrates, the mix of public versus private sector financing displays continued variation rather than convergence around a market–private funding financing norm.

While this is not to dismiss the emergence of important cross-national governance trends or growth in global systemic forces impacting national higher education systems, it does suggest that cultures of governance continue to display national specificity and

Table 1.1 *Spending on tertiary education: private/public percentage of education spending, 2000–2016*

Country	2000	2007	2013	2016
Chile	80.5	85.6	62.5	67.5
Korea	76.7	79.3	67.5	63.8
United States	68.9	67.4	63.7	64.7
United Kingdom	32.3	64.2	42.7	71.4
Australia	50.4	55.7	57.5	62.1
Israel	43.5	48.4	49.7	41.6
Canada	39.0	43.4	n/a	50.6
New Zealand	–	34.3	48.1	48.4
Italy	22.5	30.1	32.8	35.3
OECD Average	23.4	30.9	n/a	30.1
Portugal	7.5	30.0	41.9	31.5
Mexico	20.6	28.6	32.2	29.1
Poland	33.4	28.5	19.6	16.1
Netherlands	23.5	28.5	29.7	29.2
Slovak Republic	8.8	23.8	24.5	19.7
Spain	25.6	21.0	30.7	31.7
Czech Republic	14.6	16.2	23.0	19.9
France	15.6	15.5	21.1	20.3
Germany	11.8	15.3	14.4	15.2
Austria	3.7	14.6	5.4	6.2
Ireland	20.8	14.6	22.3	26.3
Sweden	8.7	10.7	10.5	11.2
Belgium	8.5	9.7	10.7	14.2
Iceland	8.2	9.0	8.8	8.2
Finland	2.8	4.3	3.9	3.4

Source: OECD (2019).

that there are limits, or at least differences, in the degree to which internationalizing forces or 'globalizing models' impact national contexts. More obviously, it also highlights the continuing problem of theory development, the limitations of *standpoint-guildism* and the 'republic of scholars' ontology as analytical vantage points able to adequately explain international/national governance trajectories or, more fundamentally, whether the 'triangle of coordination model' remains fit for purpose.

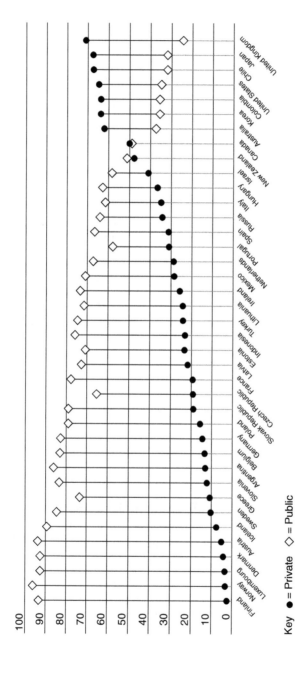

Key ● = Private ◇ = Public

Figure 1.3 Spending on tertiary education: private/public percentage of education spending 2016
Source: OECD (2019).

1.4 Beyond the Republic of Scholars Ontology: Theorizing Convergence and Diversity in the Governance of Higher Education

In this section we suggest the need to move beyond the 'republic of scholars' ontology: in part as a corrective to the methodological fiats associated with it, in part to support serious theory-building efforts able to adequately account for contradictory governance patterns across higher education systems. To do so we suggest three elemental but necessary correctives to the analytical focal plane that has traditionally informed studies of higher education governance. First, abandoning *standpoint-guildism* and adopting political economy and market segmentation lenses of inquiry. Second, abandoning methods of inquiry that situate the locus of change predominantly in mechanistic institutional-group processes and adopting instead frameworks that focus on the sociology of goods, their classification and value construction (esteem, reputation) as central drivers in market stratification and coextensive processes of divergence and convergence. And third, adopting more analytically rigorous conceptions of convergence and governance as a means of overcoming what we term is a false empiricism – that is, the tendency to conflate policy labels and political rhetoric with policy instruments and governance tools to produce overly inflated images of convergent governance trajectories. As the core object of inquiry, we argue, *governance* needs greater analytical precision and should be understood as constituted by three interrelated, yet distinctive elements which are nearly always in tension with one another: *politics*, *polity* and *policy* (Treib, Bähr, and Falkner, 2007). We explore each of these issues in turn.

1.4.1 Political Economy and Market Segmentation

As noted, the countervailing forces of internationalization and national specificity have been a persistent theoretical black hole for scholars concerned with the governance of higher education – that is, observations about ever-greater levels of convergence around 'globalizing models' but set amid continuing national distinctions. As also noted, in part this has arisen as a result of scholars mapping the impact of what have been seen as international structural forces encroaching into domestic governance contexts, with variation and diversity explained in relation to residual (institutional and national) path dependencies

(Berger and Dore, 1996; Brenner, Peck, and Theodore, 2010; Peck and Theodore, 2015). Such approaches, we contend, are methodologically flawed since they assume international structural forces (benchmarking, rankings, league tables, internationalization, etc.) to be relatively uniform and spatially ubiquitous – again, in part reflecting methodological fiats such as *standpoint-guildism*, the propensity to identify and locate agency-effecting change in exogenous processes because of methodological *upwardness, downwardness,* and *inwardness,* and to analyse these processes predominantly through methodologically national lenses producing contradictory empirical observations about convergence and diversity.

In contrast, we suggest that notions of structural or internationally coercive pressures need to be understood not by their ubiquity across national spaces but by their spatial unevenness. Here, we look outside higher education studies to other disciplines for appropriate analytical frameworks. Borrowing spatial concepts from economic geography provides a particularly useful means of disaggregating notions of globalization, 'globalizing models', or an 'international market place' for higher education and thus the supposed pressures of league tables, student mobility, global knowledge competition, or international benchmarking practices as omnipresent structural forces shaping the policy choices of countries in essentially similar ways. Christaller's place theory (Christaller and Baskin, 1966), for example, explains urban/market hierarchies as a function of their spatial and intrinsic *in*equalities. These result as a consequence of the differing efficiencies/qualities/technicalities to which goods/services can be supplied to markets relative to the distance that consumers need to travel to acquire them. In Christaller's thesis, goods have differing 'thresholds': the higher the value of the good, the higher the 'range' or maximum distance consumers will travel to acquire the good and the higher the price they are willing to pay for that good/service. This inverse relationship between the 'threshold' of goods and the 'range' tolerance for purchasing them thus produces a spatial configuration of urban centres, dispersing them hierarchically relative to the value order of the goods and services they produce. This creates distinctive spatial patterns with a relatively small number of large urban centres producing higher-order goods and services separated by large distances (specialist financial services, for example, in New York and London), while numerous smaller urban centres produce lower-order goods and services which are separated by smaller distances (printing, computer repair, or diagnostic services, for example) (Jarvis, 2011; Neal, 2008).

Christaller's conceptualization helps us differentiate between markets and the discrete spaces within which specific goods and services compete. For example, if we take the threshold of financial services produced in London or New York and attempt to identify the market space these occupy relative to competitor financial centres, it would obviously be inaccurate to view Manila's or Managua's financial services sector as competitor cities producing similar goods and services with similar thresholds. Rather, London and New York compete in highly discrete market spaces reflecting a complex series of specialist capacities and financial technologies that are not spatially dispersed but highly concentrated – that is, dense networks of financial knowledge, large capital markets, specialist systems of valuation, clearance and settlement, risk products and underwriting (derivatives markets), international debt securities, global insurance underwriting, and specific regulatory systems and practices. By contrast, Jakarta's and Malaysia's financial services sectors operate in more circumspect market spaces, including Islamic banking, insurance, back office treasury processing, and, in the case of Labuan (an offshore financial facility in Malaysia), ship registration, commodity trading, and wealth management, competing with financial centres such as Dubai rather than London, New York, Singapore or Hong Kong (Gipouloux, 2011; Woo, 2016).

We can apply place theory and this same logic to higher education and assumptions about an 'international market for higher education' or processes of internationalization and 'global knowledge competition'. Different countries and HEIs compete in distinct markets, and not necessarily in a unified or vertically integrated global higher education market. This reflects the different thresholds of educational services produced in, say, the United States compared to Malawi, to use an extreme example; or by Harvard University compared to Southern Arkansas University: Harvard University has a global market threshold, while the market threshold for Southern Arkansas University is predominantly local and regional.

Figures 1.4 and 1.5 attempt to depict the idea of market segmentation and that different countries and HEIs have different market thresholds (real or perceived) for the educational services and research they produce. As Figure 1.4 also suggests, assumptions that competition between countries and among HEIs is distributed uniformly, or that in

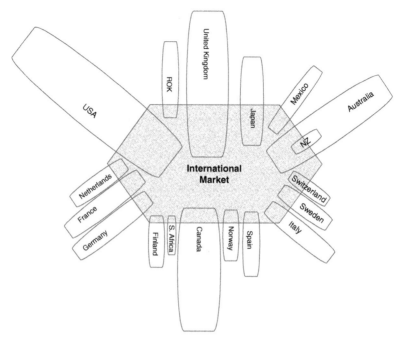

Figure 1.4 Global and national markets for higher education*
* This figure attempts to represent the relative spatial thresholds of countries participating in what might be termed a 'global' higher education market relative to the size of their higher education sectors. Nominally, this reflects the number of inbound international students relative to domestic students. Further, the figure also attempts to represent the number of HEIs as a proportion of the total HEIs in that country ranking highly in international league/reputational tables. The idea is to depict the greater weight, exposure or leadership in higher education that some countries enjoy relative to others, and thus the highly uneven segmentation and spatial distribution of centres (countries and HEIs) of higher education.

the case of 'global knowledge competition' Spain, the United States, Japan, or Mexico compete in the same sets of research domains and with the same coextensive sets of commercial–industry research collaborations, research impact, or research networks, is clearly inaccurate. The composite endowments of higher education systems in the United States, United Kingdom, Canada, Australia, and some Western European states, for example, are manifest in terms of research leadership, the number of international students they attract, levels of academic mobility, scientific patents, and investment in research infrastructure – and are non-comparable to countries in the Global South, the Middle East, or South America. Similarly, within countries such as the United States, United Kingdom, Canada, or Australia, market segmentation is institutionally stratified, with only some HEIs competing in certain international research spaces (or producing educational services or research outputs with similar thresholds), while others compete in more circumscribed, domestically focused domains specializing in vocational training or liberal arts education, for example.

Added to these processes, we can also observe religious and language segmentation as well as the existence of regional education markets (see Figure 1.5). In Southeast Asia, for example, the emergence of Islamic higher education services, most recently in Malaysia and Indonesia, has

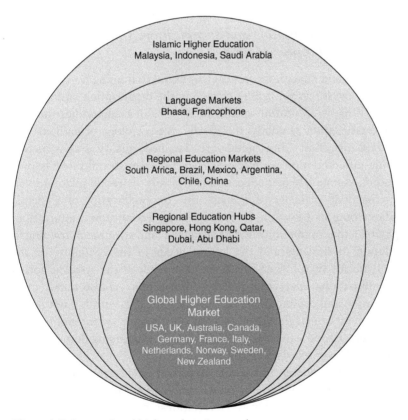

Figure 1.5 International higher education markets

seen enormous growth in inbound international students from the Middle East and Africa, while Singapore and Hong Kong's education hubs compete predominantly for Asian students – in the case of the former, predominantly for students from ASEAN (Association of Southeast Asian Nations) countries, and in the case of the latter, overwhelmingly for students from mainland China (Jarvis and Mok, 2019; Welch, 2017).

The point, obviously, is that notions of globalization, internationalization, or top-down systemic 'global' forces impacting countries and HEIs in broadly similar ways are anomalous in contexts of deep market segmentation. Indeed, market segmentation is the principal driver precipitating divergence in the governance trajectories of higher education systems, and it explains why structural or 'global' pressures are necessarily uneven in their distribution and impact on countries and HEIs.

1.4.2 Commodification and Stratification: The Sociology of Higher Education Markets

A second, and related, theoretical lens useful to framing how we might explore the forces propelling change in the organization and governance of higher education relates to notions of commodification and the classification of goods: specifically, the sociology of markets and market operation – how goods are classified, quality is constructed, value differentiation is determined, and market stratification is produced. As noted, higher education is typically viewed in relation to an encroaching 'academic capitalism': the commodification of academic labour outputs (research, knowledge commercialization, innovation, patents), the commodification of academic (and vocational) training in relation to students and the labour needs of the economy, or the reorganization of higher education as a result of the systemic forces of international market/knowledge competition. As also noted, marketization and commodification have become the central, if not dominant, motifs through which assaults on disciplinary autonomy have been understood – in part a reflection of the continuing dominance of the 'republic of scholars' ontology.

Strangely, however, this scholarship has been less than insightful in terms of the workings or actualization of marketization and commodification in higher education and its relationship to governance transformation, sector organization, or processes of differentiation among higher education systems (nationally and institutionally). Too little work, for example, has explored the sociology of markets in relation to value construction or how higher education goods become classified – processes that are necessary to both market formation and operation, but also instrumental to segmentation and product differentiation. Much scholarship on higher education, for example, explores the 'international market' for higher education (Davis, 2016; Gachon, 2013), often in reference to increasing international student mobility, and often in relation to the greater value now placed on higher education in terms of access, participation, social mobility, and competitiveness. Virtually absent from such perspectives, however, has been any examination or theoretical explication of what the international or national 'market' for higher education is: how goods are delineated, prices determined, demand distributed, and value apportioned – in essence, the social demand drivers which influence how governments and institutional actors respond to and organize governance of the sector or, more fundamentally, how institutional power, prestige, networks of influence and the management of access (the creation of product/access scarcity) creates supply-driven demand (Musselin, 2010).

In part this is not the fault of scholars of higher education, but reflects a deeper intellectual neglect among economists more generally. As Lie notes, while the 'market' is a central category in economics, it 'receives virtually no extended discussion in most works of economic theory or history' (Lie, 1997, p. 342). Instead, the 'market' is typically denoted by abstraction: price uniformity within specific categories of goods or areas, market clearance when the supply of goods matches demand, and transactional relationships in the supply and consumption of goods and services – what Lie terms an 'ontological indeterminacy' which allows for the universal application of the 'market' concept (Lie, 1997, p. 342).

This is also true of its usage among scholars of higher education, where the 'market' is treated as a central variable in terms of its role in structurally ordering, or at least strongly influencing, the supply of products relative to the demand of consumers (students, business, governments, the economy) and institutional decisions in terms of resource allocation, hiring, and planning. In doing so, however, the 'market' concept is reduced to a set of demand-driven externalities that create incentives to which governments and organizational actors are seen to respond – a highly reductive 'exchange economy' framework that is ill-equipped to capture the complex decisions of how institutions/higher education systems are valued relative to others, or how agential decisions about value and the selection of programmes, institutions, and countries occurs in the absence of information transparency given the ethereal nature of the educational services 'consumers' are 'purchasing'. Most 'consumers' (students, parents, the public – indeed, academic labour), for example, are ill-equipped to assess quality or understand the product on offer, the value of the product once conferred (in terms of impact on opportunities, life-time earnings, career progression and, more broadly, social mobility), or the tangible skills/knowledge that will be 'delivered' upon purchase. At the same time, as DiMaggio notes, for the 'market' concept to work and have theoretical veracity, common categories and understandings must operate, since they are what enable economic actors to make decisions and engage in 'economic action' (as quoted in Beckert and Musselin, 2013, p. 5). Attempting to explain higher education governance exclusively in relation to the market concept and an exchange economy framework thus remains problematic, especially in the absence of common market categories or understandings and in a context where market opacity and deep information asymmetries tend to typify the sector.

Similar examples of theoretical indeterminacy in the application of the market concept are also displayed in recent research on rankings (see Figure 1.2; Erkkilä and Piironen, 2018; Espeland and Sauder, 2012; Hazelkorn, 2011, 2017; Marginson, 2014), which evolved ostensibly to overcome information asymmetries and provide consumers with a means of mapping the global and national markets of higher education in terms of institutional quality (measured against specific performance metrics and reputational esteem measures). Yet much of the research focus has concerned itself with addressing the utility of rankings: how the information they generate is used in terms of institutional strategic positioning strategies, or how they impact policy making and the perceptions of decision makers in terms of sector performance. Scholarship has thus far failed to appreciably integrate rankings into fuller theoretical explanations in ways that are able to situate their role in mediating governance outcomes or the 'structural' role they play in determining national governance practices and sector organization.

Noticeably absent too from research on rankings are discussions about the construction of quality, reputation, and the emergence of market classification regimes. The construction of quality is not a socially or politically benign process. Classification regimes are, by definition, reflexive – they reflect specific values. More obviously, they also reflect power relations, the distribution of materiality (resources), influence, and the institutional reproduction of 'prestige' through credentialism, hierarchies and access to networks (i.e., elite 'club' goods) (Jessop, 2018, p. 104). Intrinsically, rankings reflect inequalities, how certain institutional actors possess specific traits relative to others, or how they confer on those who access those institutions specific advantages relative to others (Beckert and Musselin, 2013; Fligstein, 2001; Jessop, 2017).

Critical research frameworks around rankings, however, have gained little traction, failing to feature as part of a broader theoretical attempt to explain the spatially uneven distribution of 'quality' and 'esteem', the persistence of dense networks of research concentration in relatively few geographic/institutional locations, or the apparent embeddedness of institutional esteem within relatively few countries/institutions and which changes seemingly very little over time. Absent from such perspectives, for example, has been any sustained theoretical analysis of how higher education goods and the markets for them evolve, why certain higher education markets display relative consistency or equilibrium in the distribution of institutional forms, specializations and esteem measures, why others fail, or how markets (especially around issues such as reputation) consolidate and dominate.

In highlighting these perspectives, we are not suggesting their adoption as the primary lens for exploring the governance of higher education. Rather, we note them insofar as they are significant because of their absence and because of the potential theoretical pathways they offer for more powerful explanatory accounts of governance patterns in higher education.

1.4.3 Convergence and Governance: Definition and Exposition

A third and necessary corrective to conceptualizing and theorizing the governance of higher education rests in definitional precision, particularly in the deployment of key variables such as *convergence* and *governance*. Both concepts have tended to be employed intuitively, often without analytical exploration, in the process obviating their explanatory veracity and hindering theory development. As Pollit (2001) notes, as an analytical concept convergence is conceptually fungible and highly fragile, and typically operationalized in ways that are unable to capture the complexity of processes that occur at multiple levels (government, civil service, organization, sector), through multiple filters and actors, and across national and institutional spaces which produce a spectrum of convergent and divergent outcomes. In the context of higher education these observations are particularly cogent. While institutional isomorphism and changes in higher education governance are often characterized as systemic, exogenous, hierarchical, and top down (methodological *upwardness, downwardness,* and *inwardness*), such changes often have less to do with the 'dictates of the global economy or the functional necessity of increased efficiency' as with the local and national contexts within which political symbolism, governance fashions and the rhetoric of political discourse manifests. Policy transfer and the language of convergence, in other words, often conceal ideological-political agendas, with agential actors seeking to preserve or advance particular interests. The language of reform, increased efficiency, deregulation, or marketization, for example, might often be present but absent an 'equivalent amount of action' in terms of implementation of these practices, or they may be embraced and celebrated in the rhetorical sense as political agendas to press for or resist change. Indeed, what might seem like the adoption of a similar institutional or policy design may in practice conceal fundamentally divergent on-the-ground institutional/system norms (Pollitt, 2001, p. 934).

Goldfinch and Wallis (2010) take this analogy further, stratifying the notion of convergence along a continuum: the convergence of ideas (including paradigms, models, values, and interpretations of policy approaches in terms of the relationship between state and market, the role of government and the mechanisms of governance); convergence around 'policy rhetoric', in which buzzwords, clichés, and a specific language becomes the dominant discourse; convergence in legislation, organizational/institutional structures and policy design, in which organizational characteristics might be copied or transferred; and convergence around policy practice and implementation, in which styles of decision making, the methods of framing policy choices, and the ideas and values that inform them might be emulated and executed (Goldfinch and Wallis, 2010, pp. 1101–1102). The point, of course, is that each type of potential convergence is subject to variation reflecting

agential authority and interests, organizational and institutional sociologies, the socio-political environment, resource capacities, institutional legacies, and the socio-legal context – and which collectively
produce inherent diversity (or what might be termed 'hybridity'; n2)
in how policy ideas are translated into practice and deployed in specific
organizational and institutional contexts. As Goldfinch and Wallis
note, 'structures that seem similar at a distance may vary widely in
practice' (2010, p. 1102).

Holzinger and Knill (2005) have also attempted to address what they
perceive as 'theoretical deficits in the study of convergence', in part by
expanding the theoretical and analytical scope of the concept in order to
understand both its multi-causality and the varying forms of convergence that may obtain. Specifically, they differentiate between (a) the
degree, (b) the *direction* and (c) the *scope* of convergence. The *degree* of
convergence refers to the similarity of policy outputs (the policies
adopted by a government) and policy outcomes (the actual effects of
a policy in terms of goal achievement). In higher education, policy outputs might include certain governance arrangements, policy instruments,
and the policy solutions adopted for specific issues or goal attainment
(funding, student grants, internationalization). Policy outcomes refer to
the results achieved in respect of various internationally recognized
indicators, such as higher education participation rates; the percentage
of citizens with a tertiary degree in a specific age cohort; the percentage of
students getting the degree in a specific time period; research productivity
in terms of patents, impact, or quantum; equality (i.e., the level of social
mobility ensured by the HE system); or the number of foreign students
enrolled in the higher education system – among others.

The *direction* of convergence, by contrast, indicates the extent to
which convergence coincides with an upward or downward shift of
the mean from time t1 to t2. The mean can refer to both policy outputs
and policy outcomes. Finally, the *scope* of convergence focuses on
the absolute number of policy domains that are actually affected by
a certain convergence mechanism(s): for example, the total number
of countries and policy areas which demonstrate some form of
convergence.

In Holzinger and Knill's schema, convergence is thus disaggregated,
such that the adoption of similar policy instruments designed to realize
specific goals may appear broadly similar across multiple domains,
while the policy outputs (i.e., the actual achievements or attainment

of the policy goals) may show substantial variation. At one and the same time, convergence and divergence can thus inform the outcomes in particular policy domains (Knill, 2005).

Goldfinch and Wallis', Pollitt's, and Holzinger and Knill's theoretical schemas thus suggest the need for greater caution in making definitive observations about convergent governance trends or assuming decreasing diversity in in the governance of higher education as a result of structural or 'globalizing' forces. Rather, their approaches highlight the more complex, dynamic, and often contradictory mechanisms at play in governance, whether from the perspective of agential interests, ideational formation, or the political ends to which governance approaches and tools are adopted and deployed, and how. Taking such perspectives seriously, we suggest, and operationalizing them in scholarship on higher education is necessary if theory development is to be realized and transformations in the governance of higher education more adequately explained in both national and comparative contexts.

Finally, we note similar observations in relation to *governance*: a core concept employed in countless studies – indeed, the undergirding intellectual rationale of comparative higher education scholarship – but typically invoked absent definition or analytical dissection. Too often, governance is conflated with government and, in turn, with public management and administration, or in other contexts serves as a proxy for empirical/historical description of sectoral/system composition or reductive institutional mapping of higher education systems and their regulatory/institutional frameworks. Largely absent from scholarship on higher education governance, for example, have been attempts to break down governance into distinctive analytical components in order to facilitate more nuanced research supporting theory development. A useful approach pioneered by Treib et al. (2007), for example, disaggregates governance into three interrelated dimensions: *politics*, *polity*, and *policy* – each necessary to the other, but in ways that are often in tension. In Treib's schema, for example, *politics* reflects the ways and means by which the myriad preferences of public and private interests are accommodated within policy choices and modulated into specific actions, and how political processes are deployed to achieve enforcement of these actions. Political governance is understood along a continuum of two opposing ideal types: (1) a decision-making system where only public actors are involved; and (2) a decision-making system where only private actors are involved.

Obviously, these ideal types rarely obtain in practice, and thus politics is constituted by myriad forms of hybridity (n2). The *polity* dimension, on the other hand, considers the institutional architecture and the constellation of authority and its location in relation to decision making and implementation (concentrated, hierarchical, or diffuse), and whether authority is highly institutionalized or informal, inclusive, or exclusive. And finally, the *policy* dimension refers to the 'mode of political steering' in terms of the instruments present: the nature of legal 'bindingness' or hard versus soft law, ridged versus soft approaches to policy implementation, directed versus consultative (suggestive), standards versus procedurally based, sanctions versus incentive based (Tollefson et al., 2012; Treib et al., 2007, pp. 5–11).

Again, we highlight this scholarship not as a definitive account or settlement of the analytical constitution of *governance*, which remains a vexed and highly contested theoretical concept (Bevir, 2013; Bevir and Krupicka, 2011; Peters, 2012; Voegelin, 2003). Rather, we do so as a means of suggesting the need for greater analytical rigour in the deployment of the concept if the problem of false empiricism and the endless, and analytically non-grounded, observations about governance, governance trajectories, and governance convergence in higher education are to be overcome. To paraphrase Fligstein and Dauter, because so many scholars use the same or similar concepts but ascribe to them different meanings and apply them in different contexts, conceptual clarity and theory development become at best muddied and at worst impossible (Fligstein and Dauter, 2007, p. 106). Analytical precision remains key to theory building and enhancing explanatory power and insight.

1.5 Conclusion

The predominance of the republic of scholars ontology arises in part because of its institutive appeal. As we have argued in this chapter, however, it is also theoretically problematic, limiting the prospects for theory development because of the methodological fiats associated with it – in particular, the tendency to explain governance in relation to mechanistic group processes mediated by standpoint-guildist perspectives and viewed predominantly through the sociology of organizations and methodologically national lenses. To be sure, we are not suggesting that such perspectives are entirely without merit. Rather, we

suggest that much of the research produced has tended to be empirically descriptive as opposed to analytically explanatory, and tends to
produce circular and inconclusive perspectives that generate often
contradictory observations about the drivers and pathways of governance in higher education.

The three potential research domains we have identified suggest a
possible way forward. They offer the possibility of theoretical
accommodation in explaining the twin realities of heterogeneity
and convergence in the governance patterns of higher education,
and simultaneously of overcoming methodological nationalism and
organizational sociologies as the dominant vantage points for
explaining governance types. In highlighting these perspectives,
however, we are not proscribing their necessary adoption as the
sole or primary frameworks through which theory development
must proceed. There are many other potentially useful frameworks
that could be explored (see, for example, Capano et al., 2015; Jones,
2010; Parreira Do Amaral, 2010; Peters, 2011; Wiseman et al.,
2010). Rather, our motivation has been more circumspect – an
attempt to highlight the methodological tropes that have accompanied a style of scholarship that has dominated in the field for the last
several decades – and diagnostic, in the sense of attempting to outline how these have in turn limited the potential for theory building.
From our perspective, theory development rests first in a wide-
ranging analysis of the limitations of our achievements and why
this has been the case, and second in commencing a far-reaching
exploration beyond the narrow confines of higher education studies
for analytical and theoretical frameworks on which research can
proceed.

Notes

1. Indeed, for Clark, disciplinary authority was the ontological starting
   point, shaping everything else of importance and exemplified in his five
   key framing questions: how is work in the university arranged, how are
   group (discipline) beliefs sustained, how is authority distributed, how are
   systems integrated, and how does change take place? (Amaral and
   Magalhães, 2013; Brennan, 2010, p. 231; Clark, 1983; Etzioni, 1966;
   Williams, 2010).

2. We define variegation and hybridity as distinctive categories: variegation refers to a coextensive set of policy or governance instruments premised on a single policy ideal/design, e.g., marketization, but where marketization can assume various forms – e.g., privatization, the introduction of user-pays tuition fees, market-based pricing for specific courses, degrees, or the use of market or quasi-market instruments in resource allocation; hybridity refers to two or more distinctive policy designs that are mixed – e.g., marketization and centralized planning – producing a distinctive governance model.

References

Amaral, A., and Magalhães, A. (2013) Higher education research between policy and practice. In B. M. Kehm and C. Musselin (Eds), *The development of higher education research in Europe: 25 years of CHER* (pp. 43–59). Rotterdam: Sense Publishers.

Ball, S. J. (2010) Global education, heterarchies, and hybrid organizations. In K. H. Mok (Ed.), *The search for new governance in higher education in Asia* (pp. 13–28). New York: Palgrave Macmillan.

Becher, T. (1989) *Academic tribes and territories: Intellectual enquiry and the cultures of disciplines*. Bristol: Open University Press.

Beckert, J., and Musselin, C. (2013) Introduction. In J. Beckert and C. Musselin (Eds), *Constructing quality: The classification of goods in markets* (pp. 1–28). Oxford and New York: Oxford University Press.

Benavides, M., Arellano, A., and Zárate Vásquez, J. (2019) Market- and government-based higher education reforms in Latin America: The cases of Peru and Ecuador, 2008–2016. *Higher Education*, 77(6), 1015–1030. doi:10.1007/s10734-018-0317-3

Berger, S., and Dore, R. P. (1996) *National diversity and global capitalism*. Ithaca: Cornell University Press.

Bevir, M. (2013) *A theory of governance*. Berkeley: University of California.

Bevir, M., and Krupicka, B. (2011) On two types of governance theory. A response to B. Guy Peters. *Critical Policy Studies*, 5(4), 450–453. doi:10.1080/19460171.2011.628069

Bladh, A. (2007) Institutional autonomy with increasing dependency on outside actors. *Higher Education Policy*, 20(3), 243–259. doi:10.1057/palgrave.hep.8300161

Blanco, I., Lowndes, V., and Pratchett, L. (2011) Policy networks and governance networks: Towards greater conceptual clarity. *Political Studies Review*, 9(3), 297–308. doi:10.1111/j.1478-9302.2011.00239.x

Bleiklie, I., and Kogan, M. (2007). Organization and governance of universities. *Higher Education Policy*, 20, 477–493. doi:10.1057/palgrave. hep.8300167

Bowey, A. (1976) *The sociology of organisations*. London: Hodder and Stoughton.

Brennan, J. (2007) On researching ourselves: The difficult case of autonomy in researching higher education. In C. Kayrooz, G. Akerlind, and M. Tight (Eds), *Autonomy in social science university research: The view from the UK and Australian universities* (pp. 167–182). London: Elsevier.

Brennan, J. (2010) Burton Clark's the higher education system: Academic organization in cross-national perspective. *London Review of Education*, 8(3), 229–237. doi:10.1080/14748460.2010.515122

Brenner, N., Peck, J., and Theodore, N. (2010) Variegated neoliberalization: Geographies, modalities, pathways. *Global Networks*, 10(2), 182–222. doi:10.1111/j.1471-0374.2009.00277.x

Busch, P.-O., and Jörgens, H. (2005) The international sources of policy convergence: Explaining the spread of environmental policy innovations. *Journal of European Public Policy*, 12(5), 860–884. doi:10.1080/13501760500161514

Cantwell, B., and Kauppinen, I. (2014) *Academic capitalism in the age of globalization*: Baltimore: Johns Hopkins University Press.

Cao, X. (2012) Global networks and domestic policy convergence: A network explanation of policy changes. *World Politics*, 64(3), 375–425. doi:10.1017/S0043887112000081

Capano, G. (2011) Government continues to do its job: A comparative study of governance shifts in the higher education sector. *Public Administration*, 89(4), 1622–1642. doi:10.1111/j.1467-9299.2011.01936.x

Capano, G., Howlett, M., and Ramesh, M. (Eds). (2015) *Varieties of governance: Dynamics, strategies, capacities*. Houndmills and New York: Palgrave Macmillan.

Castells, M., and Cloete, N. (2017) Universities as dynamic systems of contradictory functions. In J. Muller (Ed.), *Castells in Africa: Universities and development*. (pp. 206–223). Oxford: African Books Collective: African Books Collective.

Christaller, W., and Baskin, C. W. (1966) *Central places in southern Germany*. Englewood Cliffs: Prentice-Hall.

Clark, B. R. (1983) *The higher education system: Academic organization in cross-national perspective*. Berkeley: University of California Press.

Cloete, N. (2006) *Transformation in higher education: Global pressures and local realities*: Dordrecht: Springer.

Croucher, G., and Woelert, P. (2016) Institutional isomorphism and the creation of the unified national system of higher education in Australia:

An empirical analysis. *Higher Education*, 71(4), 439–453. doi:10.1007/s10734-015-9914-6

Davis, J. (2016) *The market oriented university transforming higher education*. Northampton: Edward Elgar.

Deem, R. (2010) Globalisation, new managerialism, academic capitalism and entrepreneurialism in universities: Is the local dimension still important? *Comparative Education*, 37(1), 7–20. doi:10.1080/03050060020020408.

Deem, R., and Brehony, K. J. (2005) Management as ideology: The case of 'new managerialism' in higher education. *Oxford Review of Education*, 31(2), 217–235. doi:10.1080/03054980500117827

Dill, D. (1997) Higher education markets and public policy. *Higher Education Policy*, 10(3/4), 167–186.

Dill, D. (1998) Evaluating the 'evaluative state': Implications for research in higher education. *European Journal of Education*, 33(3), 361–377.

Dill, D. (2014) Public policy design and university reform: Insights into academic change. In C. Musselin and P. N. Teixeira (Eds), *Reforming higher education: Public policy design and implementation* (pp. 21–37). Dordrecht: Springer Netherlands.

DiMaggio, P. J., and Powell, W. W. (1983) The iron cage revisited: Institutional isomorphism and collective rationality in organizational fields. *American Sociological Review*, 48(2), 147–160. doi:10.2307/2095101

Dobbins, M., Knill, C., and Vögtle, E. M. (2011) An analytical framework for the cross-country comparison of higher education governance. *Higher Education*, 62(5), 665–683. doi:10.1007/s10734-011-9412-4

Donaldson, L. (2010) Organisational sociology. In C. Crothers (Ed.), *Historical developments and theoretical approaches in sociology* (Vol. II, pp. 32–46). Oxford: EOLSS Publishers.

Douglass, J. A. (2009) *Higher education's new global order: How and why governments are creating structured opportunity markets. Research & Occasional Paper Series: CSHE.10.09.* http://0-search.ebscohost.com.edlis.ied.edu.hk/login.aspx?direct=true&db=eric&AN=ED511958&site=eds-live&scope=site&groupid=Test

Douglass, J. A. (2012) The rise of the for-profit sector in US higher education and the Brazilian effect. *European Journal of Education*, 47(2), 242–259. doi:10.1111/j.1465-3435.2012.01521.x

Douglass, J. A., King, C. J., and Feller, I. (2009) A room with a view: Globalizations, universities, and the imperative of a broader US perspective. In J. A. Douglass, C. J. King, and I. Feller (Eds), *Globalization's muse: Universities and higher education systems in a changing world* (pp. 1–14). Berkeley: Berkeley Public Policy Press.

EHEA. (n.d.) *The Bologna Process: European Higher Education Arena (EHEA)*: www.ehea.info/.

Eldridge, J. E. T. (1974) *A sociology of organisations*. London: Allen and Unwin.

Elken, M. (2017) Standardization of (higher) education in Europe – policy coordination 2.0? *Policy and Society*, 36(1), 127–142. doi:10.1080/14494035.2017.1278873

Enders, J. (2004) Higher education, internationalisation, and the nation-state: Recent developments and challenges to governance theory. *Higher Education*, 47(3), 361–382. doi:10.1023/b:high.0000016461.98676.30

Enders, J., de Boer, H., and Weyer, E. (2013) Regulatory autonomy and performance: The reform of higher education re-visited. *Higher Education: The International Journal of Higher Education and Educational Planning*, 65(1), 5–23. doi:10.1007/s10734-012-9578-4

Enders, J., Kehm, B. M., and Schimank, U. (2015) Turning universities into actors on quasi-markets: How new public management reforms affect academic research. In D. Jansen and I. Pruisken (Eds), *The changing governance of higher education and research: Multilevel perspectives* (pp. 89–103). Cham: Springer International Publishing.

Erkkilä, T., and Piironen, O. (2018) *Rankings and global knowledge governance: Higher education, innovation and competitiveness*. Cham: Springer, Palgrave Macmillan.

Espeland, W. N., and Sauder, M. (2012) The dynamism of indicators. In Kevin Davis, Angelina Fisher, Benedict Kingsbury, and Sally Engle Merry (Eds), *Governance by indicators: Global power through quantification and rankings* (pp. 86–109). Oxford: Oxford University Press.

Espinoza, O. (2017) Paulo Freire's ideas as an alternative to higher education neo-liberal reforms in Latin America. *Journal of Moral Education*, 46(4), 435–448. doi:10.1080/03057240.2017.1363601

Etzioni, A. (1966) *Studies in social change*. New York/London: Holt, Rinehart & Winston.

Fawcett, P., and Daugbjerg, C. (2012) Explaining governance outcomes: Epistemology, network governance and policy network analysis. *Political Studies Review*, 10(2), 195–207. doi:10.1111/j.1478-9302.2012.00257.x

Fischer, F., and Mandell, A. (2018) The neo-liberal transformation of the university. *Critical Policy Studies*, 12(1), 103. doi:10.1080/19460171.2018.1441942

Fligstein, N. (2001). *The architecture of markets: An economic sociology of twenty-first century capitalist societies*. Princeton: Princeton University Press.

Fligstein, N., and Dauter, L. (2007) The sociology of markets. *Annual Review of Sociology*, 33(1), 105–128. doi:10.1146/annurev.soc.33.040406.131736

Freidson, E. (2001) *Professionalism: The third logic.* Cambridge: Polity Press; Blackwell Publishers.

Gachon, N. (2013) Model convergence and the global higher education market: The challenge to US exceptionalism. *Dimensión empresarial,* 11(1), 11–22.

Gipouloux, F. (2011) *Gateways to globalisation: Asia's international trading and finance centres.* Cheltenham: Edward Elgar.

Goedegebuure, L., and Van Vught, F. (1996) Comparative higher education studies: The perspective from the policy sciences. *Higher Education,* 32(4), 371–394. doi:10.1007/BF00133253

Goldfinch, S., and Wallis, J. (2010) Two myths of convergence in public management reform. *Public Administration,* 88(4), 1099–1115.

Gornitzka, Å., and Stensaker, B. (2014) The dynamics of European regulatory regimes in higher education – challenged prerogatives and evolutionary change. *Policy and Society,* 33(3), 177–188.

Gumport, P. J., and Snydman, S. K. (2006) Higher education evolving forms and emerging markets. In W. W. Powell and R. Steinberg (Eds), *The nonprofit sector* (pp. 462–484). New Haven: Yale University Press.

Hazelkorn, E. (2011) *Rankings and the reshaping of higher education: The battle for world-class excellence.* Houndmills; New York: Palgrave Macmillan.

Hazelkorn, E. (2014) Reflections on a decade of global rankings: What we've learned and outstanding issues. *European Journal of Education,* 49(1), 12–28. doi:10.1111/ejed.12059

Hazelkorn, E. (2017) *Global rankings and the geopolitics of higher education: Understanding the influence and impact of rankings on higher education, policy and society.* London/New York: Routledge.

Holzinger, K., and Knill, C. (2005) Causes and conditions of cross-national policy convergence. *Journal of European Public Policy,* 12(5), 775–796. doi:10.1080/13501760500161357

Howlett, M., and Ramesh, M. (2002) The policy effects of internationalization: A subsystem adjustment analysis of policy change. *Journal of Comparative Policy Analysis,* 4(1), 31–50. doi:10.1023/A:1014971422239

Huang, Y., Pang, S.-K., and Yu, S. (2018) Academic identities and university faculty responses to new managerialist reforms: experiences from China. *Studies in Higher Education,* 43(1), 154–172. doi:10.1080/03075079.2016.1157860

Jarvis, D. S. L. (2011) Race for the money: International financial centres in Asia. *Journal of International Relations & Development,* 14(1), 60–95.

Jarvis, D. S. L. (2014) Policy transfer, neo-liberalism or coercive institutional isomorphism? Explaining the emergence of a regulatory regime for quality assurance in the Hong Kong higher education sector. *Policy and Society*, 33(3), 237–257.

Jarvis, D. S. L. (2017) Exogeneity and convergence in policy formulation: Contested theories, approaches and perspectives. In M. Howlett and I. Mukherjee (Eds), *Elgar handbook of policy formulation* (pp. 394–409). Cheshire: Edward Elgar.

Jarvis, D. S. L., and Mok, K. H. (2019) The political economy of higher education governance in Asia: Challenges, trends and trajectories. In D. S. L. Jarvis and K. H. Mok (Eds), *Transformations in higher education governance in Asia: Policy, politics and progress* (pp. 1–46). Singapore: Springer.

Jayasuriya, K. (2001) Globalization and the changing architecture of the state: The regulatory state and the politics of negative co-ordination. *Journal of European Public Policy*, 8(1), 101–123.

Jayasuriya, K. (2008) Regionalising the state: Political topography of regulatory regionalism. *Contemporary Politics*, 14(1), 21–35. doi:10.1080/13569770801933270

Jayasuriya, K. (2009) Learning by the market: Regulatory regionalism, Bologna, and accountability communities. *Conference Papers – International Studies Association*, New York, 15–19 February, 1–24.

Jayasuriya, K. (2015a) Constituting market citizenship: Regulatory state, market making and higher education. *Higher Education*, 70(6), 1–13. doi:10.1007/s10734-015-9879-5

Jayasuriya, K. (2015b) Transforming the public university: Market citizenship and higher education regulatory projects. In M. Thorton (Ed.), *Through a glass darkly: The social sciences look at the neoliberal university* (pp. 89–102). Canberra: ANU Press.

Jayasuriya, K., and Robertson, S. L. (2010) Regulatory regionalism and the governance of higher education. *Globalisation, Societies & Education*, 8(1), 1–6. doi:10.1080/14767720903573993

Jessop, B. (2017) Varieties of academic capitalism and entrepreneurial universities. *Higher Education*, 73(6), 853–870. doi:10.1007/s10734-017-0120-6

Jessop, B. (2018) On academic capitalism. *Critical Policy Studies*, 12(1), 104–109. doi:10.1080/19460171.2017.1403342

Jones, P. (2010) Cultural political economy and the international governance of education: A theoretical framework. *International Perspectives on Education and Society*, 12, 19–56. doi:10.1108/S1479-3679(2010)0000012005

Kail, M. (2011) The university reform movement in France: A failure in terms of any immediate political effectiveness. *L'Homme et la société*, 178(4), 85–119. doi:10.3917/lhs.178.art07

King, R. (2007) *The regulatory state in an age of governance: Soft words and big sticks.* Houndmills/New York: Palgrave Macmillan.

King, R. (2009) *Governing universities globally: Organizations, regulation and rankings.* Cheltenham: Edward Elgar.

King, R. (2010) Policy internationalization, national variety and governance: Global models and network power in higher education states. *Higher Education: The International Journal of Higher Education and Educational Planning*, 60(6), 583–594.

Knill, C. (2005) Introduction: Cross-national policy convergence: concepts, approaches and explanatory factors. *Journal of European Public Policy*, 12(5), 764–774. doi:10.1080/13501760500161332

Kosmützky, A., and Krücken, G. (2014) Growth or steady state? A bibliometric focus on international comparative higher education research. *Higher Education*, 67(4), 457–472. doi:10.1007/s10734-013-9694-9

Lapworth, S. (2004) Arresting decline in shared governance: Towards a flexible model for academic participation. *Higher Education Quarterly*, 58(4), 299–314. doi:10.1111/j.1468-2273.2004.00275.x

Lie, J. (1997) Sociology of markets. *Annual Review of Sociology*, 23(1), 341–360. doi:10.1146/annurev.soc.23.1.341

Lucas, L. (2014) Academic resistance in the UK: Challenging quality assurance processes in higher education. *Policy and Society*, 33(3), 215–224.

Magalhães, A., Veiga, A., Ribeiro, F. M., Sousa, S., and Santiago, R. (2013) Creating a common grammar for European higher education governance. *Higher Education: The International Journal of Higher Education and Educational Planning*, 65(1), 95–112. doi:10.1007/s10734-012-9583-7

Mandell, A. (2018) Tensions within the neoliberal university: Sources of change and hope. *Critical Policy Studies*, 12(1), 116–120. doi:10.1080/19460171.2017.1403344

March, J. G., and Olsen, J. P. (1989) *Rediscovering institutions. The organizational basis of politics.* New York: The Free Press.

Marginson, S. (2007) *Prospects of higher education: Globalization, market competition, public goods and the future of the university.* Rotterdam: Sense Publishers.

Marginson, S. (2014) University rankings and social science. *European Journal of Education*, 49(1), 45–59. doi:10.1111/ejed.12061

Marsh, D., and Sharman, J. C. (2009) Policy diffusion and policy transfer. *Policy Studies*, 30(3), 269–288. doi:10.1080/01442870902863851

McCarthy, G., Song, X., and Jayasuriya, K. (2017) The proletarianisation of academic labour in Australia. *Higher Education Research and Development*, 36(5), 1017–1030. doi:10.1080/07294360.2016.1263936

Miller, B. (2014) Free to manage? A neo-liberal defence of academic freedom in British higher education. *Journal of Higher Education Policy & Management*, 36(2), 143–154. doi:10.1080/1360080X.2013.861055

Mok, K.-H. (2010) *The search for new governance of higher education in Asia* (1st ed.). New York: Palgrave Macmillan.

Mok, K. H., and Cheung, A. B. L. (2011) Global aspirations and strategising for world-class status: New form of politics in higher education governance in Hong Kong. *Journal of Higher Education Policy & Management*, 33(3), 231–251. doi:10.1080/1360080X.2011.564998

Morrissey, J. (2013) Governing the academic subject: Foucault, governmentality and the performing university. *Oxford Review of Education*, 39(6), 797–810. doi:10.1080/03054985.2013.860891

Musselin, C. (2010) Universities and pricing on higher education markets. In D. Mattheou (Ed.), *Changing educational landscapes: Educational policies, schooling systems and higher education – a comparative perspective* (pp. 75–90), Dordrecht: Springer.

Musselin, C. (2012) Redefinition of the relationships between academics and their university. *Higher Education*, 65(1), 25–37. doi:10.1007/s10734-012-9579-3

Musselin, C. (2014) Research issues and institutional prospects for higher education studies. *Studies in Higher Education*, 39(8), 1369–1380. doi:10.1080/03075079.2014.950449

Neal, Z. P. (2008) *From central places to network bases: A transition in the US urban hierarchy, 1900–2000.* GaWC Research Bulletin 267: www.lboro.ac.uk/gawc/rb/rb281.html.

Nelson, A. R. (2013) Regionalisation and internationalisation in higher education and development: A historical perspective, c. 1950–1970. *Journal of Higher Education Policy & Management*, 35(3), 238–248. doi:10.1080/1360080X.2013.786858

Öberg, S. A., and Bringselius, L. (2014) Professionalism and organizational performance in the wake of new managerialism. *European Political Science Review*, 7(4), 499–523. doi:10.1017/S1755773914000307

Obinger, H., Schmitt, C., and Starke, P. (2013) Policy diffusion and policy transfer in comparative welfare state research. *Social Policy and Administration*, 47(1), 111–129. doi:10.1111/spol.12003

OECD (2019) Spending on tertiary education (indicator). doi:10.1787/a3523185-en.https://data.oecd.org/eduresource/spending-on-tertiary-education.htm#indicator-chart.

Olsen, J. P. (2007) The institutional dynamics of the European university. In P. Maassen and J. P. Olsen (Eds), *University dynamics and European integration* (pp. 25–54). Dordrecht: Springer.

Parreira Do Amaral, M. (2010) Regime theory and educational governance: The emergence of an international education regime. *International Perspectives on Education and Society*, 12, 57–78. doi:10.1108/S1479-3679(2010)0000012006

Peck, J. (2011) Geographies of policy: From transfer-diffusion to mobility-mutation. *Progress in Human Geography*, 35(6), 773–797. doi:10.1177/0309132510394010

Peck, J., and Theodore, N. (2015) Geographies of policy. In J. Peck and N. Theodore (Eds), *Fast policy* (pp. 3–29). Minneapolis: University of Minnesota Press.

Peters, B. G. (2001) *Institutional theory in political science: The new institutionalism*. London and New York: Continuum.

Peters, B. G. (2011) Governance as political theory. *Critical Policy Studies*, 5 (1), 63–72. doi:10.1080/19460171.2011.555683

Peters, B. G. (2012) *Institutional theory in political science: The new institutionalism* (3rd ed.). New York: Continuum.

Pilkington, M. (2014) Converging higher education systems in a global setting: The example of France and India. *European Journal of Education*, 49(1), 113–126. doi:10.1111/ejed.12057

Pollitt, C. (2001) Convergence: The useful myth? *Public Administration*, 79 (4), 933–947. doi:10.1111/1467-9299.00287

Provini, O. (2018) Negotiating higher education policies in East Africa: Experiences from Tanzania and Kenya. *Higher Education*, 77, 323–342.

Pusser, B. (2015) A critical approach to power in higher education. In A. M. Martínez-Alemán, B. Pusser, and E. M. Bensimon (Eds), *Critical approaches to the study of higher education: A practical introduction* (pp. 59–79). Baltimore: Johns Hopkins University Press.

Rawls, J. (1999) *A theory of justice* (Rev. ed.). Cambridge, MA: Belknap; Harvard University Press.

Reed, M. (2002) New managerialism, professional power and organisational governance in UK universities: A review and assessment. In A. Amaral, G. A. Jones, and B. Karseth (Eds), *Governing higher education: National perspectives on institutional governance* (pp. 163–186). Dordrecht: Kluwer Press.

Rip, A., and Kulati, T. (2015) Multilevel dynamics in universities in changing research landscapes. In D. Jansen and I. Pruisken (Eds), *The changing governance of higher education and research: Multilevel perspectives* (pp. 105–115). Cham: Springer International Publishing.

Robertson, S. L. (2010) The EU, 'regulatory state regionalism' and new modes of higher education governance. *Globalisation, Societies and Education*, 8(1), 23–37. doi:10.1080/14767720903574033

Robertson, S. L., Olds, K., Dang, Q. A., and Dale, R. (2016) *Global regionalisms and higher education: Projects, processes, politics*. Northampton: Edward Elgar.

Sam, C., and Sijde, P. (2014) Understanding the concept of the entrepreneurial university from the perspective of higher education models. *Higher Education*, 68(6), 891–908. doi:10.1007/s10734-014-9750-0

Sandel, M. J. (2012) *What money can't buy: The moral limits of markets*. New York: Farrar, Straus and Giroux.

Shahjahan, R. A., and Kezar, A. J. (2013) Beyond the 'national container': Addressing methodological nationalism in higher education research. *Educational Researcher*, 42(1), 20–29.

Silverman, D. (1970) *Theory of organisations: A sociological framework*. London: Heinemann Educational.

Slaughter, S., and Leslie, L. L. (1997) *Academic capitalism: Politics, policies, and the entrepreneurial university*. Baltimore: Johns Hopkins University Press.

Slaughter, S., and Rhoades, G. (2004) *Academic capitalism and the new economy: Markets, state, and higher education*. Baltimore: Johns Hopkins University Press.

Smeenk, S., Teelken, C., Eisinga, R., and Doorewaard, H. (2009) Managerialism, organizational commitment, and quality of job performances among European university employees. *Research in Higher Education*, 50(6), 589–607. doi:10.1007/s11162-009-9132-0

Sultana, R. G. (2012) Higher education governance: A critical mapping of key themes and issues. *European Journal of Higher Education*, 2(4), 345–369. doi:10.1080/21568235.2012.719672

Taylor, B. J., Webber, K. L., and Jacobs, G. J. (2013) Institutional research in light of internationalization, growth, and competition. *New Directions for Institutional Research*, 2013(157), 5–22. doi:10.1002/ir.20036

Teichler, U. (1996) Comparative higher education: Potentials and limits. *Higher Education*, 32(4), 431–465. doi:10.1007/BF00133257

Teichler, U. (2014) Opportunities and problems of comparative higher education research: The daily life of research. *Higher Education*, 67(4), 393–408. doi:10.1007/s10734-013-9682-0

Thorkelson, E. (2019) A campus fractured: Neoliberalization and the clash of academic democracies in France. *Anthropology and Education Quarterly*, 50(1), 97–113. doi:10.1111/aeq.12279

Tollefson, C., Zito, A. R., and Gale, F. (2012) Symposium overview: Conceptualizing new governance arrangements. *Public Administration*, 90(1), 3–18. doi:10.1111/j.1467-9299.2011.02003.x

Treib, O., Bähr, H., and Falkner, G. (2007) Modes of governance: Towards a conceptual clarification. *Journal of European Public Policy*, 14(1), 1–20. doi:10.1080/13501760606106107140

Voegelin, E. (2003) *The theory of governance and other miscellaneous papers, 1921–1938*. Columbia and London: University of Missouri Press.

Waks, L. J. (2007) In the shadow of the Runis: Globalisation and the rise of corporate universities. In S. Marginson (Ed.), *Prospects for higher education: Globalisation, market competition, public goods and the future of the university* (pp. 101–120). Rotterdam/Taipei: Sense Publishers.

Welch, A. (2017) Higher education and the developmental state: The view from the East and South East Asia. In T. Carroll and D. S. L. Jarvis (Eds), *Asia after the developmental state: Disembedding autonomy* (pp. 359–387). Cambridge and New York: Cambridge University Press.

Westerheijden, D. F. (2018) University governance in the United Kingdom, the Netherlands and Japan: Autonomy and shared governance after new public management reforms. *Nagoya Journal of Higher Education*, 18, 199–220.

Williams, G. (2010) Perspectives on higher education after a quarter of a century. *London Review of Education*, 8(3), 239–249. doi:10.1080/14748460.2010.515123

Wiseman, A. W., Pilton, J., and Lowe, J. C. (2010) International educational governance models and national policy convergence. *International Perspectives on Education and Society*, 12, 3–18. doi:10.1108/S1479-3679(2010)0000012004

Woo, J. J. (2016) *Singapore as an international financial centre: History, policy and politics*. London: Palgrave Macmillan.

Zlatkin-Troitschanskaia, O., Shavelson, R. J., and Kuhn, C. (2015) The international state of research on measurement of competency in higher education. *Studies in Higher Education*, 40(3), 393–411. doi:10.1080/03075079.2015.1004241

PART II

Systems, Processes, and Dynamics of Governance in Higher Education

2 | *The Regulatory State and the Labour Process*

KANISHKA JAYASURIYA, GREG MCCARTHY,
AND XIANLIN SONG

2.1 Introduction

This chapter argues that changes to the academic labour process have
fundamentally deskilled or deprofessionalized academic labour over
recent decades. The chapter is based on a neo-Marxist appraisal of the
proletarianization of academic labour. We argue, firstly, that universities in Anglosphere countries have become commodified due to the
privatization of their funding. Secondly, the decline in public funding
and its replacement by student fees has resulted in the decomposition of
academic labour so as to minimize costs and increase the surplus from
student fees. Thirdly, the capacity of the state and universities to break
down the skills of academic labour is enhanced and then restructured in
terms of market veridiction; in the process, universities become corporatized and locked into a state regulatory regime that interpellates
(Althusser, 1971) and cajoles academics into that market-driven mission. Lastly, the chapter contends that academics are alienated from
their labour and proletarianized in the process, although they do show
forms of resistance which can be regarded as 'weapons of the weak'
(Scott, 1985) to counterattack the commodification process, and they
rely on the remnants of professionalism to defend their conditions. In
terms of the framework outlined by the introductory chapter to this
volume, we focus on the way changing politics – that is, mode of
governance – has played out in the reconstitution of academic labour.
We suggest that the politics – the reconstitution of authority – is
reflected in the way academic labour is governed and regulated. This
regulation of academic labour in turn profoundly changes the relation
and allocation of authority at the 'shop floor' level of the university.

Using Australia as a case study, we examine this deprofessionalizing
process at close quarters, maintaining that the privatization of university funds drives a market model to extract surplus values out of student

fees, and that this, combined with the commodification of the degree, brings universities into the process of uneven and combined development. Once part of the commodification system, Australian universities are corporatized and integrated into a market verification model orchestrated by state regulatory agencies. To achieve commodity relations, the state and university management dissect and then appropriate the skills of the academics – a deskilling process which has in effect proletarianized academic labour in Australia.

2.2 Commodifying Universities and Proletarianizing Academic Labour

The chapter contends that the commodity form enters universities and subsumes their management structures in order to extend the reach of commodity relations throughout society. As Harootunian (2015) points out, commodification creates uneven and combined development between and within national territories, but in an innovative twist this also includes the combined development of different temporalities. In the higher education sector this combined development of temporalities is reflected in the tension between commodification and pure knowledge production. That is, universities have existed within capitalism yet retained a unique structure and culture; however, as commodification spreads, universities become vulnerable to full integration into the market. In the past, universities have been afforded some protection from marketization by their role in nation building, which requires knowledge and expertise that cannot always be in the service of commodity production. However, when the state comes to regard universities as principally serving the market, as it did in Australia, then such protection is lost. The first step towards marketization in Australia was the privatization of university financing, which meant that students rather than the public became the major source of Australian university funds. The second step was to divest university life of its traditional, almost feudal, trappings, in which the professoriate ran the court, and to corporatize universities according to industry templates, with vice chancellors becoming CEOs. The third step was to bring universities under a state regulatory system that imposed market tests on what was taught and researched. To achieve that end, academic labour was dissected through quantification, measurement, and comparison within the university and across the sector, so the skills of academics were laid open to appropriation by management and the state. The court of the professoriate became divided, with some seeing material benefits in joining the corporate model and others bemoaning the changing times. Australian universities exhibit elements of combined and uneven development: while gowns at graduation ceremonies bear the hallmark of feudal trappings, the degree parchment and what it stands for carry the trademarks of commodity production.

Graduation ceremonies provide a good example of what Balibar (2010) terms the fabrication of myths to produce the illusion of shared historical universality, which we see as responding to the ambiguity caused by the universities' uneven absorption into commodity production. Universities continually create and promote myths of heritage in order to assert continuity even when the university has been essentially divided and commodified. For Balibar (2010), universality must include liberty and equality; however, following Marx, he recognizes that the universality of commodity production provides an ontological basis of labour that appears equal but embodies unequal exchange relations. Chakrabarty (2000) makes a similar point when he depicts equivalence or commensurability to labour value as a dominant form, which as a meta-narrative disguises the untranslatable, the contradictions of inequality and authoritarianism in universal myths and practices. Here Chakrabarty alerts us to how forms of authoritarian rule in democracies involve Foucault's procedures of control with vicarious forms of coercion, which are colonial in their roots. This phenomenon is clearly evident in the casualization of academic labour into a subaltern caste: one that cannot speak, in Spivak's (1988) sense of not being heard. Similarly, Butler and Athanasiou (2013) regard academic casual labour as the extension of precarious work into universities, carrying with it the unequal character of excessive vulnerability associated with oppressed minorities.

In analysing the roots of capitalist industrialization in Britain, Marx depicted capitalist industries as producing not just commodities but different kinds of humans, via an extremely forceful process. He described how industrialization is transformed as soon as surplus value is no longer conceived as compatible with equal human values but, rather, in terms of disciplining the body and the worker's psychology of self. Industrialization, in Marx's depiction, was brutal and violent; what is occurring in universities is more civil but just as effective in shaping academic psychology. Similar to the transformation of craft workers into a proletariat, as analysed by Braverman (1974), the commodification of academic labour has led to the loss of professional autonomy and control in way that is akin to the real subsumption of labour to capital. This transition remains somewhat partial and contingent given the still strong presence of notions of professionalism within the academic labour process – what Foucault (2002) would see as anti-conduct of conduct, or what Balibar (2015) terms the 'heresy' in Foucault's theory of subjectivity. In our formulation, the real subordination of academic labour takes place with the quantification of professional skills and the regulation of work intensity. This deprofessionalization is crucial to the development of a form – in the Marxian sense – of abstract labour that is transforming the nature of the academic labour process. Here, abstract labour becomes divorced from the concrete conditions and processes so that it is equalized in the social division of labour through the equal valuing of commodities on the market (Rubin, 1972).

For Marx, this duality between concrete and abstract labour was crucial to the production of the commodity form. This logic has now overtaken universities, as evidenced by shifts in the academic labour process. An important dimension of this process of abstraction is the social validation of this labour through various forms of measurement and quantification of the activities of academic labour. This does not mean that concrete activity disappears, but rather that abstract labour is materialized in the concrete activities of academics. It is this process of validation, which we describe as the loss of academic control over the products of labour, that leads to a fundamental change in the labour process. The distinctive characteristics of this process are, first, the way in which the attributes of academic labour are subject to quantification and, second, the way the products of this academic labour are then 'equalized' through various forms of measurement. In this way, the labour process within universities becomes the economic validation and measurement of academic labour. What is measured is no longer transference of knowledge per se, but knowledge for market capitalism.

Under this commodity form, there occurs a loss of control over the coordination, planning, and allocation of academic work (research or teaching) – in other words, the expropriation of the 'skills' of the academic and the power over their working conditions by management. One manifestation of this is the segmentation of academic skills, most noticeably in casual contracts but also in the proliferation of teaching-only academics. The shift in academic labour has so segmented academics' skills that it has caused deprofessionalization. Such deprofessionalization is an example of what Harootunian (2015, p. 9) regards as the 'remnant' or 'archaic' elements within the broader commodification of academic labour. In general, academics no longer have the ultimate say over their labour; this has been abrogated to 'central' management, overseen by regulations that flow down to the academic 'periphery' (Fitzgerald et al., 2012), causing the deskilling of academics. The remnants of the older semi-feudal university model of research for research's sake endure in abstract knowledge production; however, this is continually being sub-limated to the imperatives of the market in both teaching and in research.

The transformation in academic labour, Harvey argues, is a general trend under late capitalism: '[w]hat is on capital's agenda is not the eradication of skills per se but the abolition of monopolisable skills' (Harvey, 2014, p. 120). Harvey asserts that in the current era of globalization, the segments of labour with monopoly skills are an impediment to profits, so there is a perpetual process to break down these skills (Harvey, 2014, p. 120). For Harvey, 'capital logic' enters the public sphere to deskill labour so that the labourer is disempowered by decisions taken within the 'managerial machine' (Harvey, 2010, p. 103). Macfarlane (2011) argues that the 'proletarianization' of aca-demic labour is based on the deskilling of the 'all-round' academic, so that their skills are controlled by others or jettisoned altogether. Similarly, Barry et al. (2001) use a Taylorist metaphor to depict aca-demics as assembly line workers with targets to meet and where teach-ing is a standardized product. This subsumption of labour has paradoxically intensified state regulations over universities, which direct teaching to serve the market at the expense of academic auton-omy (Willmott, 2011). Likewise, in research, academics now have their skills regulated by market imperatives which are deeply embedded in the university global ranking status. For academics, this involves a loss of control over work practices in a highly structured, regulated, and managed environment (Roberts and Peters, 2008).

2.3 The Regulatory State

The transformation of academic labour is the result of deskilling, and it is essential to note that regulatory governance reinforces this process.

This creates an 'accountability architecture' that makes universities accountable to the market (Jayasuriya 2015). Under this state regulatory framework, universities are obligated to develop regulatory compliance units, instruments, and managers, to ensure that the student and research production processes fully accord with the logic of capital. A whole new layer of senior managers act as regulatory intermediaries, policing academics to conform to the market discourse (Forsyth, 2014). The role of these intermediary regulators is to respond to the auditing culture imposed by the state. Indeed, Anderson argues that this is the very essence of the 'audit culture' which has emerged in Australia, the United Kingdom and New Zealand for regulating academics. This auditing culture places universities under extreme pressure to standardize academic teaching to ensure student-customer satisfaction (Anderson, 2006).

One of the consequences of the higher education regulatory framework is that it reaches deep into the administrative structures and everyday interactions within universities, turning them into localized sites of regulation. Within these sites, centrally defined objectives and benchmarks are implemented through more specific local regulatory tools and accountability architectures. The analysis of the emergence of the enterprise university by Marginson and Considine (2000) perceptively explored the shifts of power and resources in the unification era of Australian higher education, which mirrored what had occurred in the United Kingdom. But the power shifts over the last decade have been even more substantial, with interventions in what Black (2002) calls 'regulatory conversations' – the processes of interaction over externally defined quality or research performance benchmarks – which have shaped the narrative through which administrative interaction takes place within the university. It is via these regulatory conversations that it is possible to see the constitution of a distinctive local regulatory site within the university which empowers new actors, identities, and forms of authority over academics. These local institutions are critical spaces within a larger regulatory geography that links higher education sites to broader national and even global systems of regulatory governance.

Academic labour is most readily managed by controlling its visible elements – that is, teaching and research – while invisible elements, such as service to students or the community, are secreted away, treated as non-important remnants of academic practice. Jayasuriya (2015) asserts that these visible aspects are those directly related to market citizenship – for instance, the employability of students and the global marketing of the university. Shore (2008) observes that managerial power over academics has been greatly enhanced by reducing academic labour to mathematical scorecards to establish a university-wide standard which is applied irrespective of discipline-specific expertise. The application of this standard is part of the interlocutory function of the regulatory state and its intermediaries for regulating academic practices. However, Shore contends that what is measured 'at a distance' by the state is not the 'archaic' Harootunian (2015) norm of 'critical intellectual skills' but the 'marketable skills' of the students (Shore, 2008, p. 289). Shore and Wright (2015) extend this argument to stress that the audit culture alters universities fundamentally and changes the way people think within them – from being collegial with the sense of a civic purpose, to being nothing more than cogs in the machinery of production. In her survey of academic reaction to the regulatory culture, Cheng (2011) finds that it was regarded as highly corrosive of academic professionalism and was coercively reinforced. She notes that academics were obliged to accept the top-down regulations as they were tied to the line managers' 'power over academic careers via probation, tenure, promotion, and performance reviews' (Cheng, 2011, p. 189). Brunetto, in her survey of university managerialism, highlights the control exercised over degrees and courses, to the point of undermining the academic's specific skills. She adds, however, that as these instructions flow down to the departments, the level of compliance will vary between institutions and disciplines (Brunetto, 2002).

In theoretical terms, the regulatory state operates to oversee what Foucault terms the discourse of 'market verification', where activities are measured and verified in terms of the capitalist market (Foucault, 2008). However, Foucault's analysis needs to be augmented with an appreciation of what Harootunian (2015) would see as 'uneven remnant elements' of academic labour regulated differently to the market verification components of academic labour. For instance, regulations can be imposed directly onto academics via managerial course approvals and student satisfaction and employment rates. In contrast, academic autonomy to conduct research (including, for example, working from home) must be brought under a more factory-like framework via requirements of office hours. In other words, Foucault's (2008) notion of bio-power has different effects depending on the relationship to commodification or the aspects of academic labour (non-commodified) left as remnants that are continually being drawn into the logic of capitalist accumulation. The role of the state is to maintain market pressure on universities, which in turn will bring these remnants of professional autonomy into a factory rather than a monastic model.

To illustrate the argument, Australian higher education will be used as a case study. The following section will outline, firstly, the fundamental changes in Australian higher education caused by commodification, through the trend towards the internationalization and massification of student cohorts; secondly, the corporatization of management and its relationship to the regulatory state; and thirdly, the deskilling of Australia's academic labour sector. This will be followed by an analysis of the concept of alienation and resistance to proletarianization.

2.4 Case Study: Australian Higher Education

The 1989 unification of the Australian higher education system was driven by a social-democratic government, which introduced a funding model in which students partly pay for their education via a deferred taxation process (Jayasuriya, 2015). The introduction of this system became both a means for reducing government contributions to higher education and a powerful regulatory tool, opening the way for the transformation of students into commodities and academics into a proletariat (Moodie, 2013; 295–310; Fitzgerald et al., 2012). In 1987, at the beginning of what has been called the neoliberal turn in Australian universities (McCarthy et al., 2017), public funding accounted for 87 per cent of Australian university funds; by 2015 public funding had fallen to 45 per cent, and it is expected to decline further (Marginson and Marshman, 2013; Norton, 2015). Norton (2015, p. 1) calculates that in 2015 universities took A$3.2 billion from student fees as surplus, above what they spent on teaching the students. He also observes that international students generate the greatest surplus, and their contribution to university revenues is critical for university strategies (2015, p. 1). With declining public research funds, universities redirected more than A$2 billion of this surplus into research – that is, one dollar in five of student fees is shifted away from teaching into research (Norton, 2015). Australian universities are thus doubly dependent on student surpluses, and are at especially high risk from any fall in international student enrolments (Fitzgerald et al., 2012).

In broad terms, the total export income generated by international students to the Australian economy ranks third in importance, after iron ore and coal. In 2016 it reached A$20.3 billion, with China accounting for 26 per cent of this income (UA, 2016). The dependence of Australian universities on international student enrolments, and the magnitude of the growth in this sector, can be seen in the following data. In 1996 there were 53,188 international enrolments; in 2016 this figure had jumped to 330,000 (DET, International Student Data, 2016, p. 1; see also Marginson, 2008; Norton and Cherastidtham, 2015). In addition, as universities became dependent on student funds, they also increased their domestic student load: in 1986, 11 per cent of 18- to 24-year-olds went to higher education institutions; by 2015, 36 per cent of this age cohort were enrolled in Australian higher education institutions (Parr, 2015). In 1970, student enrolments in higher education numbered 117,000; in 1998 the figure was 400,000; and by 2016 there were 1.3 million domestic and international students enrolled in Australian higher education institutions (DET, 2016).

Australian universities responded to the rise in student numbers and the need to extract surplus from each student in two ways: an increase in student to staff ratios, and the casualization of the workforce (Marginson, 2000). When the unification of universities began in 1990 and the student fee system was introduced, there were 13 students for every teacher; by 2000 it was 19; and in 2012 it had risen to 24 students per teacher. By 2016, the Australian university student/staff ratio was averaging 30:1, with the lowest at 13.2:1 and the highest at 44:1 (UA, 2017). Furthermore, universities replaced tenured, full-time staff with casual staff. From 1989 to 2013, the percentage of academic staff employed on contingent contracts increased from 40 per cent to 56 per cent, with a corresponding decline in the percentage of academic staff employed in continuing appointments (Andrews et al., 2012).

According to May et al. (2013), by 2011 there were more academic staff working on casual contracts than on continuing contracts of employment, and 90 per cent were employed to conduct teaching. Using superannuation records, May and her colleagues estimate that 60 per cent of Australian academic labour is hired on a casual basis (of which 57 per cent are women) and that they conduct 60 per cent of the teaching (May et al., 2013). According to a report by the Australian Learning and Teaching Council (Percy et al., 2008), the casual academic workforce is basically a 'proletariat' with limited industrial protection and minimal professional standards, such as adequate superannuation or leave entitlements, and with restricted research capacity and constrained academic freedom (see also Kenway et al., 2014; Norton, 2014).

Casualization has thus produced a fundamental shift in the Australian academic labour market, with most teaching now conducted by casual staff, who are highly exploited workers with limited research and course design capacity, and little opportunity to obtain continuing positions (Percy et al., 2008). Where once casual employment was the entry point for a long-term academic career in an Australian university, this is no longer the case. Andrews et al. (2012, p. 7) report that casual staff have limited career prospects and tend to be 'permanent casual staff'. In their analysis of a large-scale survey, May et al. (2013) found that 81 per cent of the casual labour force reported moderate to high levels of financial anxiety. A survey by the National Tertiary Education Union found that, over the last decade, nine out of ten Australian university jobs were casual or part-time, with universities uniformly resisting union efforts to convert casual contracts to full-time positions (Kenna, 2017).

Butler and Athanasiou (2013) regard casual academic labour as meeting the criteria of precarious work, whereby a vulnerable minority are so disadvantaged as to limit their life chances. In Marxist terms, casualization in Australia has reached such a level of exploitation that the casual academic does not even reproduce the level of wage exchange needed to sustain their labour power. In addition, the emergence of such a large pool of casual teachers impacts the working conditions of permanent staff in such forms as teaching-only positions and managerial directives towards standardized teaching. A clear Australian example of this Taylorist managerialism is given by Schapper and Mayson, who demonstrate how the standardization of labour has undermined academic autonomy and deskilled the academic labour force. They outline their efforts to apply their skills in intercultural knowledge to develop a commerce programme, to be taught in Australia, Malaysia, and South Africa. However, their intercultural perspective was rejected when the course was 'standardized' on an Australian–American-centric model to provide 'flexible delivery of [the same] material to large numbers of students' in numerous countries (Schapper and Mayson, 2005, p. 189).

Driving casualization and standardization was the introduction of an overarching regulatory regime to measure and normalize academic labour to serve the burgeoning Australian student market. The rise of internal mechanisms within universities to intensify systems of control over academics in both teaching and research is well recognized in the literature (Deem, 2004; Mingers and Willmott, 2013; Willmott, 2011). Similarly, Roberts and Peters (2008) have observed that the strength of central managerial power within universities has revolved around the assessment and valuing of academic labour based on universal, standard forms of measurement. However, there has been no analysis of how this is linked to the manner of Australian university corporatization and the influence of the regulatory state. These two aspects interlock through the role of corporate leaders, especially vice chancellors, in strategically positioning the university community into the state's market verification system (Marginson and Considine, 2000; Slaughter and Rhoades, 2004) by setting the corporate direction of the enterprise culture (Collini, 2012; Deem, 2004; Hil, 2012).

As the CEO of the enterprise, the vice chancellor is now an important facet of the state's regulatory architecture. The role of the vice chancellor is no longer that of 'first among equals' in the academic community; rather, it is that of a crucial regulatory interlocutor, between local, national, and increasingly global regulatory frameworks. As regulatory interlocutors, vice chancellors are expected to formulate specific institutional missions in a way that demands constant re-engineering and experimentation to respond to regulatory challenges and to create distinctive university brands for the local, national, and international markets. A good example of such experimentation to create a distinctive brand is the implementation of the 'Melbourne model' by Vice Chancellor Davis in first conceptualizing and then gaining Commonwealth government approval for postgraduate entry to professional degrees, which restructured and transformed undergraduate education at the University of Melbourne (James, 2012). The process of implementing such a model required extensive deliberation within the university about the process of organization change. Such forms of institutional re-engineering are an inevitable product of the higher education regulatory state as it becomes implanted into universities.

A further important local consequence of the higher education regulatory state, as noted by O'Brien (2013), is the increased assertion of managerial prerogative over the professional work of academics, in terms of what they do, how they are evaluated, and who they are accountable to. As noted, these issues have become the subject of contention and resistance within Australian universities, but the structural imperatives of the regulatory state have intensified the oversight of professional work through, for example, workload formulas and benchmarks for research intensiveness, which substantially reduce professional autonomy. The issue here is the ability to control professional work – often using the tools of 'regulatory conversations' – rather than the command model of deskilling as analysed by labour process theorists such as Braverman (1974). The interlocutory model now dominant in Australian universities (and in the wider Anglosphere) is subtler but equally effective in the deprofessionalization of academic labour. The point is that the regulatory state transforms the nature and control of academic work and the way it is organized at individual higher education institutions.

As in the United Kingdom and New Zealand, a plethora of regulatory tools has emerged in Australia to regulate academic teaching to the needs of the market. The Course Experience Questionnaire (CEQ) is the first and most prominent instrument in evaluating the 'quality' of academic teaching, which has concentrated on measuring student postdegree employability (Blackmore, 2009, p. 858). According to Henman and Phan (2014), the CEQ plays a critical role in the Australian Graduate Survey, specifically in measuring the part played by academic teaching in directly training students for the demands of the capitalist market, as quantified by after-graduation employment results. For Coates (2005), these capitalist market measurements of teaching come at the expense of knowledge formation in students or effective responses to student diversity. More critically, universities use the CEQ as a performative tool to standardize, compare and regulate academic labour to satisfy the market (Henman and Phan, 2014). Anderson (2006) argues that the measurement of student satisfaction by universities and the regulatory state, as the certified means of attesting to the quality of teaching, is not only crude but is perceived by academics as alienating them from their labour. The regulatory state, using neoliberal verification, asserts that the sole role of teaching is to ensure that students are ready for the labour market; academic claims of knowledge transference are read as self-serving. As such, it is difficult for academics to challenge the imperative of evaluation as it is couched in the discourse of accountability to students vis-à-vis their future employment (Magnusson, 1998). Likewise, Blackmore argues that the student evaluations are a 'pincer movement of managerial and market accountability' over academics, which reflect a lack of trust in academics (Blackmore, 2009, p. 858). If academics do not perform to the regulatory standards of student employability, they are deemed to be the problem within the new commodified system (Connell and Manathunga, 2012; Fitzgerald et al., 2012).

A similar pattern of measuring academic performance in the global market, especially the university ranking system, is also evident in academic research. Mingers and Willmott state that what is measured in research is a science-based 'one size fits all' model, which is akin to a Taylorist 'one best way' approach (Mingers and Willmott, 2013, p. 1053). Following the United Kingdom, Australia adopted this homogenizing approach through the government's Excellence in Research for Australia (ERA) ranking exercise in three tranches: 2010, 2012, and 2015. As a result, Australian universities shape their research data to maximize their rankings. For example, the ERA process in Australia uses the Elsevier-owned Scopus platform to collect citation data for use in discipline rankings. In turn, these products have been promoted within the university sector as a means of measuring and controlling the publication output of academic staff. The point is that these 'technological' platforms have become a crucial part of the armoury of the higher education regulatory state, and a key mechanism for the subsumption of academic labour. It also means that private providers such as Elsevier have become significant regulatory intermediaries that link the state regulatory objectives with more localized reorganization of the academic labour process.

Naturally, this ranking procedure has internal implications for academics, as it has become a system for standardizing research to fit a scientific model (Young et al., 2011). As Gable (2013) notes, the ERA presented Australian universities for the first time with a national comparator, which in turn entered the global ranking system; as such, academic research is weighted in terms of its role in the global positioning of the university. In this process, certain research is recognized as having ranking effects whereas other research is discarded and not entered into ERA submissions. Similarly, Vanclay writes of the paradox between managerial directives and disciplinary knowledge, noting that academics are rewarded for publishing in certain prestigious outlets and punished for publishing in popular but low-ranked outlets (Vanclay, 2012, p. 54). Moreover, as Henman (2015) has extensively shown, universities use their discretionary power to 'game the process', meaning that the published results are an unreliable measure of quality.

As in the United Kingdom, the selection of what outputs to submit to ERA exercises and which individuals are selected by the management to be measured by the university remains opaque and deliberately divisive (Sayer, 2014; Willmott, 2011). Where once research was driven by academics in a purist ('archaic') form of knowledge production (knowledge for knowledge's sake), it has now become an essential part of research ranking, a marker for international student recruitment. As a result, management seeks to coerce academics to conduct research in ways that enhance the university's reputation (Probert, 2013). Connell (2014) notes that research results are used to close departments and terminate staff who are deemed research-inactive in an ad hoc and post-factum manner. Through such regulations within universities, supported by research agencies outside, academic research is now a part of commodification. The quality of research is measured by its citation ratio, and management makes decisions over what counts as good research. In this process, control over academic research is asserted by the institution and verified by the state's research agencies, leading to the deskilling of academic research labour.

2.5 Alienation and Resistance

A substantial amount of research has been published on feelings of alienation among academics in Australian universities (Bexley et al., 2013; Connell and Crawford, 2007). At an applied level, Bexley et al. (2013) note that Australian academics are highly dissatisfied over the continual 'surveillance' of their performances (p. 396) and that they feel so overworked by teaching and administration that their creative research time had been reduced to a minimum (p. 397). Their study suggests that the underlying cause of academic dissatisfaction is how universities are so market driven that they have lost the notion of 'servicing the wider society' (p. 398). Critically, they note that casualization is so deeply entrenched in Australian universities that this is 'undermining the sustainability of the academic profession' (p. 398). Likewise, O'Shea et al. (2016) record that casual staff see themselves as outsiders, and have an overwhelming 'sense of powerlessness' because of their inability to control the sale of their labour or be part of the university processes (p. 332). Bentley et al. (2013) observe that the most satisfied academics are those who have retained their status by adapting to the research performance criteria and being rewarded by promotion. In contrast, the highest level of dissatisfaction is recorded by the wider academic workforce: firstly, over the erosion of the research–teaching nexus in mass 'remedial teaching'; and, secondly, over being directed to publish in accordance with management-determined criteria (Bentley et al., 2013, p. 44).

The concentration on academic feelings of alienation tends to eschew materialist analysis (Connell, 2004) in favour of subject perceptions, where neoliberal subjectivity takes centre stage (Brown, 2015). Connell notes that academic labour has divided subjectivities, where self-interested economic maximizers are oblivious to the class inequalities that surround them, while others look romantically back to the professorial past (Connell, 2004, 2015). Harootunian (2015) regards this bifurcation as offering the seeds of resistance, where the remnants of unevenness offer a space for struggle against combined development – a space to restate and recapture academic professionalism and democratic governance. In contrast, Balibar (2010) argues that struggles over the subsumption of academic labour to the market go beyond (professional) remnants and towards a larger philosophical question regarding the basis for a liberal and equitable social order. In this scenario, the role of academics is to recapture the philosophical sense of universality against the narrow myths of the corporate university and its foundation on 'insider' and 'outsider' staff.

The prevalent sense of alienation inherent in the process of deprofessionalization calls for forms of resistance against such structural change. We believe that academics do seek to resist proletarian identity, but their resistance takes weak forms. In this context, Anderson (2008) argues that while neoliberal subjectivity has been imposed by managerialism, academics use discursive and non-compliant means to retain their identity. Utilizing Scott's (1985) anthropological notion of 'weapons of the weak', Anderson (2008) contends that while these acts may be weak, they can be effective in disarming management. It is for this reason that the strategic direction set by the VCs is important in seeking to lock university staff into the process of serving the university's products and brand. Willmott (2013) makes a similar point when he argues that the pervasive spread of 'corporate culturalism' in universities inculcates compliance (Willmott, 2013). Churchman (2006) asserts that this compliance is deliberately imposed because of the pluralistic nature of the university labour force, and that university managements use homogenizing policies to weaken resistance. Winter (1995, 2009), on the other hand, is less convinced that management can inculcate academics into a unifying view, believing that the divide between academics and academic managers is too great a chasm. Ryan (2012) contends that Australian academics tend to passively resist conformity by withdrawing from university activities as a way of coping with their disempowerment. Lorenz (2012), however, regards academic resistance via subject acts of dissociation and disapproval as ineffectual against the systemic power of the state and university management.

It is worth noting here that there is a dialogue between Marx and Foucault on subjectivity and resistance. For Marx, there is an inseparability between economic practice and the shaping of the subject in responding to the logic of capital. For Foucault, in his earlier works on prisons and mental institutions, power and knowledge relations shaped the technologies of self beyond the production system. When Foucault developed his ideas further in his work on governmentality, he noted that while there is power that creates the conducts of conduct, there are also counter-conducts that push dominant practices against normalization within a more pastoral care frame (see Foucault, 1991, 2008). In Marxist terms, such counter-conducts as forms of resistance have eventually to confront the human need for income to survive; in this way neoliberalism encapsulates its counteracting tendencies by creating insiders and outsiders. This notion of counter-conducts also has resonance with Barnett's (2005) view that insider academics on tenure resist 'being directed' (p. 12), while Sparke (2008) looks to collective resistance across casual and tenured academics in the shape of academic networks, which are an expression of a form of counter-conduct (p. 434). Similar to Balibar's notion of expanding resistance to universal questions, Cook and Jacks (2006) regard the attack on academic freedom as a broad social and political issue, which can unite academics and the broader university community. This is very much the point that

Heath and Burdon (2013) make when they argue that academics faced with increased student loads, job insecurity, and corporate surveillance are looking for new 'prefigurative programs of resistance', a form of 'counter-power within and across institutions' (p. 400). They argue for action that cuts across disciplinary spaces to challenge both neoliberal marketization and university corporatization, especially when these curtail the rights of academics to criticize governments.

These arguments on resistance address the issue of how academics confront cultural, structural, and material processes involved in the appropriation of their skills. Academics have multiple subjectivities but are interpellated (Althusser, 1971) into proletarianization through economic necessity and a will to conformity; yet there remains a counter-conduct sense of professionalism, which seeks to challenge norms. In theoretical terms, Butler (1997) argues against Althusser's interpellation theory as it presumes who would be called into the law of capital rather than seeing how one learns to performs one's subjectivity, separate from a notion of being ideologically hailed into or out of subject conformity. We believe that both sides of this debate have merit. Althusser's (1971) interpellation is akin to Bourdieu's (1980) habitus, inculcating subjects by a disciplinary path into compliance to the logic of capital. Butler (1997), however, alerts us to the fact that authority is not pre-given, and subjects are more free-floating from authority – that is, they perform their roles not as an expression of an authoritative essence.

Balibar's (2015) solution to the paradox of subjectivity is to regard the subject as contested from within by an otherness (of consciousness and affect), and the subject as a citizen interpellated by political power and myth-making that divides citizenry into insiders and outsiders. Therefore, for Balibar (2012), it is impossible to conceive of the subject becoming a citizen without at the same time imagining the citizen becoming an emancipated subject. In practice, academics have a sense of subjectivity (of otherness) but are invoked into proletarian subjectivity by the regulatory state and by university-level engineering. Or, in Butler's terms, they perform their roles as a citation of a norm – now a neoliberal norm. However, their otherness may be the basis of resistance, for example by playing along with corporate power, while retaining their academic subjectivity in research and publications. At issue here is the notion of reflection on the essentializing process that academics face in a marketized academy, where they are situated in a general commodification process.

2.6 Conclusion

This chapter has addressed academic labour from the perspective of uneven and combined development. We noted that globalization has brought international students into universities, in numbers never seen before; at the same time, the reduction in public funding has opened universities to mass enrolment. To manage these fundamental changes, universities, along with the regulatory state, have imposed controls on academic labour, leading to the deprofessionalization of that labour. This deprofessionalization has been effected via the regulatory state and the market-based rules embedded in the universities by 'regulatory intermediaries', and via a discursive practice of regulatory interlocutors, driven from above, with the aim of strategically placing universities within the global ranking system (Jayasuriya, 2015).

This chapter has noted that while there is general recognition of the corporatization of universities, insufficient attention has been paid to the deskilling of academics. It has argued that the pervasive nature of management and the shift from public to private funding, notably through student fees, has segmented the academic workforce. The case study of Australia mirrors what is occurring in other Anglosphere countries, where academics are alienated from their own labour, and where academic work is segmented through casualization and a segregation between teaching and research. This segmentation is facilitated by centralized quantification, verification, and surveillance systems which are used to divide and rule academics. As in other countries, the solidarity of Australia's academics is undermined as individuals compete against each other for students, research funds, and forms of escape into research-only positions, which are akin to the what Harootunian (2015) theorizes as remnants of the past academic life. While there is evidence of academic resistance, it is complex in its responses, contained by the insider/outsider academic separation, and divided across departments and universities. Furthermore, over the last two decades, universities in Australia have concluded enterprise agreements with the academic and professional staff union, the National Tertiary Education Union, which reflect this division. While such agreements were once based on the old professional association principles of academic autonomy, these conditions have gradually been undermined by the universities and employer groups, which seek to impose an industry model that strips away both professionalism and the pastoral care aspects of the agreements. University employer groups aim to sweep away the last vestiges of the professional-based agreements, seeking to erase tenure, academic freedom, and welfare rights such as extended maternity leave, and to reduce employee protection levels to those of the vulnerable casual staff. This shift in university bargaining position reflects the proletarianization of academic labour by the management and university employer groups; union resistance is couched in the remnants of professionalism and reflects the playing out of the contradictions in combined and uneven development. The defence of academic professionalism in the face of proletarianization has some way to go in Australia; nevertheless, the continual state regulations over academic life to meet market demands and the increased efforts of university management to control academic labour and undermine academic unionism infer that academic resistance to commodification is still an active element in the labour process.

References

Althusser, L. (1971) *Lenin and philosophy and other essays* (Trans. A. Blunden). New York: Monthly Review Press.

Anderson, G. (2006) Assuring quality/resisting quality assurance: Academics' responses to 'quality' in some Australian universities. *Quality in Higher Education*, 12(2), 161–173.

Anderson, G. (2008) Mapping academic resistance in the managerial university. *Organization*, 15(2), 251–270.

Andrews, S., Bare, L., Bentley, P., et al. (2012) *Contingent academic employment in Australian universities*. Melbourne: L. H. Martin.

Balibar, E. (2010) At the borders of citizenship: Democracy in transition. *European Journal of Social Theory*, 13(3), 315–322.

Balibar, E. (2012) Civic universalism and its internal exclusions: The issue of anthropological difference. *Boundary 2*, 39(1), 207–229.

Balibar, E. (2015) Foucault's point of heresy: 'Quasi transcendentals' and the transdisciplinary function of the episteme. *Theory, Culture & Society*, 32 (5–6), 45–77.

Barnett, C. (2005) The consolations of 'neoliberalism'. *Geoforum*, 36(1), 7–12. doi:10.1016/j.geoforum.2004.08.006

Barry, J., Chandler, J., and Clark, H. (2001) Between the ivory tower and the academic assembly line. *Journal of Management Studies*, 38(1), 87–101.

Bentley, P. J., Coates, H., Dobson, I., Goedegebuure, L., and Meek, V. L. (Eds). (2013) *Job satisfaction around the academic world*. Dordrecht: Springer.

Bexley, E., Arkoudis, S., and Richard, J. (2013) The motivations, values and future plans of Australian academics. *Higher Education: The International Journal of Higher Education and Educational Planning*, 65(3), 385–400.

Black, J. (2002) Regulatory conversations. *Journal of Law and Society*, 29 (1), 163–196.

Blackmore, J. (2009) Academic pedagogies, quality logics and performative universities: Evaluating teaching and what students want. *Studies in Higher Education*, 34(8), 857–872.

Bourdieu, P. (1980) *The logic of practice*. Stanford: Stanford University Press.

Braverman, H. (1974) *Labor and monopoly capital: The degradation of work in the twentieth century*. New York: Monthly Review Press.

Brown, W. (2015) *Undoing the demos: Neoliberalism's stealth revolution*. Cambridge, MA: The MIT Press.

Brunetto, Y. (2002) The impact of growing managerialism amongst professionals in Australia: A comparative study of university academics and hospital nurses. *Research and Practice in Human Resource Management Journal*, 10(1), 5–21.

Butler, J. (1997) *The psychic life of power*. Stanford: Stanford University Press.

Butler, J., and Athanasiou, A. (2013) *Dispossession: The performative in the political*. Cambridge: Polity.

Chakrabarty, D. (2000) *Provincialising Europe: Postcolonial thought and historical difference*. Princeton: Princeton University Press.

Cheng, M. (2011) The perceived impact of quality audit on the work of academics. *Higher Education Research & Development*, 30(2), 179–191.

Churchman, D. (2006) Institutional commitments, individual compromises: Identity-related responses to compromise in an Australian university. *Journal of Higher Education Policy and Management*, 28(1), 3–15.

Coates, H. (2005) The value of student engagement for higher education quality assurance. *Quality Higher Education*, 11(1), 25–36.

Collini, S. (2012) *What are universities for?* London: Penguin.

Connell, R. (2004) Encounters with structure. *International Journal of Qualitative Studies in Education*, 17(1), 11–28.

Connell, R. (2014) The neoliberal cascade and education: An essay on the market agenda and its consequences. *Critical Studies in Education*, 54(2), 99–112.

Connell, R. (2015) Why Australia needs a new model for universities. *The Conversation.* https://theconversation.com/why-australia-needs-a-new-model-for-universities-43696

Connell, R., and Crawford, J. (2007) Mapping the intellectual labour process. *Journal of Sociology*, 43(1), 187–205.

Connell, R., and Manathunga, C. (2012) On doctoral education: How to supervise a PhD, 1985–2011. *Australian Universities' Review*, 54(1), 5–9.

Cook, H., and Jacks, T. (2006) La Trobe University could face legal action over suspension of Safe Schools co-founder Roz Ward. *The Age.* www .theage.com.au/national/victoria/lawyers-academics-condemn-la-trobe-uni versitys-suspension-of-safe-schools-cofounder-roz-ward-20160602-gp9nmz .html

Deem, R. (2004) The knowledge worker, the manager-academic and the contemporary UK university: New and old forms of public management? *Financial Accountability and Management*, 20(2), 107–128.

DET (2016) Department of Education and Training, ET, International Student Data, 2016. https://internationaleducation.gov.au/research/Inter national-Student-Data/Pages/InternationalStudentData2016.aspx

Fitzgerald, T., Gunter, H., White, J., and Tight, M. (2012) *Hard labour? Academic work and the changing landscape of higher education*. Bingley: Emerald Book Serial.

Forsyth, H. (2014) Disinterested scholars or interested parties: The public investment in self-interested universities. In M. Thornton (Ed.), *Through a glass darkly: The social sciences look at the neoliberal university*, pp. 19–36. Canberra: ANU Express.

Foucault, M. (1991) Governmentality. In G. Burchell, C. Gordon and P. Miller (Eds), *The Foucault effect: Studies in governmentality*, pp. 87–104. Hemel Hempstead: Harvester Wheatsheaf.

Foucault, M. ([1966] 2002) *The order of things: An archaeology of the human sciences*. Oxford: Routledge Classics.

Foucault, M. (2008) *The birth of biopolitics* (Trans G. Burchell). London: Palgrave Macmillan.

Gable, A. (2013) ERA and the performance regime in Australian higher education: A review of policy. (Report No. 6). University of Queensland Social Policy Unit. https://espace.library.uq.edu.au/view/UQ:318772

Harootunian, H. (2015) *Marx after Marx*. New York: Columbia University Press.

Harvey, D. (2010) *The enigma of capital*. Oxford: Oxford University Press.

Harvey, D. (2014) *Seventeen contradictions of capitalism and the end of capitalism*. Oxford: Oxford University Press.

Heath, M., and Burdon, P. (2013) Academic resistance to the neoliberal university. *Legal Education Review*, 23(1/2), 379–401.

Henman, P. (2015) Are Australian universities getting better at research or at gaming the system? *The Conversation.* http://theconversation.com/are-australian-universities-getting-better-at-research-or-at-gaming-the-system -51895

Henman, P., and Phan, N. H. L. (2014) CEQ and the performance regime in Australian higher education: A review of policy content. (Report No. 7). University of Queensland Social Policy Unit. https://espace .library.uq.edu.au/view/UQ:337418/UQ337418_OA.pdf

Hil, R. (2012) *Whackademia: An insider's account of the troubled university.* Sydney: University of New South Wales Press.

James, R. (2012) The whole-of-institution curriculum renewal undertaken by the University of Melbourne, 2005–2011. In P. Blackmore and C. B. Kandiko (Eds) *Strategic curriculum change: Global trends in universities*, pp. 145–159. Abingdon: Routledge.

Jayasuriya, K. (2015) Constituting market citizenship: Regulatory state, market making and higher education. *Higher Education*, 70(6), 973–985.

Kenna, S. (2017) Improving job security through bargaining. NTEU. www .unicasual.org.au/blog/view/post/postId/19485

Kenway, J., Boden, R., and Fahey, J. (2014) Seeking the necessary resources of hope in the neoliberal university. In M. Thornton (Ed.), *Through a glass darkly: The social sciences look at the neoliberal university*, pp. 259–281. Canberra: ANU Press.

Lorenz, C. (2012) 'If you're so smart, why are you under surveillance?' Universities, neoliberalism, and new public management, *Critical Inquiry*, 38(3), 599–629.

Macfarlane, B. (2011) The morphing of academic practice: Unbundling and the rise of the para-academic. *Higher Education Quarterly*, 65(1), 59–73. doi:10.1111/j.1468-2273.2010.00467.x

Magnusson, J. L. (1998) *The evaluation of university teaching: Exploring the question of resistance.* Higher Education Group, Department of Theory and Policy Studies, Ontario Institute of Education, University of Toronto.

Marginson, S. (2008) Universities: Where to now? Conditions for an education revolution. *Dialogue*, 27(1), 3–16. www.assa.edu.au/publica tions/dialogue/2008_Vol27_No1.pdf

Marginson, S., and Considine, M. (2000) *The enterprise university: Power, governance and reinvention in Australia.* Cambridge: Cambridge University Press.

Marginson, S., and Marshman, I. (2013) System and structure. In G. Croucher, S. Marginson, A. Norton, and J. Wells (Eds), *The Dawkins revolution 25 years on*, pp. 56–74. Melbourne: Melbourne University Press.

Marx, K. ([1857] 1993) *Grundrisse: Foundations of the critique of political economy*. London: Penguin.

May, R., Peetz, D., and Strachan, G. (2013) The casual academic workforce and labour market segmentation in Australia. *Labour & Industry: A Journal of the Social and Economic Relations of Work*, 23(3), 258–275.

McCarthy, G., Song, X., and Jayasuriya, K. (2017) The proletarianization of academic labour in Australia. *Higher Education Research & Development*, 36(5), 1017–1030.

Mingers, J., and Willmott, H. (2013) Taylorizing business school research: On the 'one best way' performative effects of journal ranking lists. *Human Relations*, 66(8), 1051–1073.

Moodie, G. (2013) System uniformity. In G. Croucher, S. Marginson, A. Norton and J. Wells (Eds), *The Dawkins revolution 25 years on*, pp. 75–90. Melbourne: Melbourne University Press.

Norton, A. (2014) Mapping Australian higher education 2014–15. Grattan Institute (October). https://grattan.edu.au/report/mapping-australian-higher-education-2014-15/

Norton, A. (2015) The cash nexus: How teaching funds research in Australian universities. Grattan Institute. https://grattan.edu.au/wp-content/uploads/2015/10/831-Cash-nexus-report.pdf

Norton, A., and Cherastidtham, I. (2015) University fees: What students pay in deregulated markets. Grattan Institute (august). http://grattan.edu.au/report/university-fees-what-students-pay-in-deregulated-markets/.

O'Brien, J. (2013) Industrial relations. In G. Croucher, S. Marginson, A. Norton, and J. Wells (Eds), *The Dawkins revolution 25 years on*, pp. 210–229. Melbourne: Melbourne University Press.

O'Shea, S., Lysaght, P., Roberts, J., and Harwood, V. (2016) Shifting the blame in higher education: Social inclusion and deficit discourses. *Higher Education, Research & Development*, 35(2), 322–336.

Parr, N. (2015) Who goes to university? The changing profile of our students. *The Conversation*. 25 May. https://theconversation.com/who-goes-to-university-the-changing-profile-of-our-students-40373

Percy, A., Scoufis, M., Parry, S., et al. (2008) *The RED report, recognition–enhancement–development: The diversity of academic roles to consider appropriate ways forward*. Sydney: Australian Learning and Teaching Council. http://ro.uow.edu.au/cgi/viewcontent.cgi?article=1139&context=asdpapers

Probert, B. (2013) Teaching-focused academic appointments in Australian universities: Recognition, specialization, or stratification? *Australian Policy on Line*, 30 January. http://apo.org.au/research/teaching-focused-academic-appointments-australian-universities-recognition-specialisation

Roberts, P., and Peters, M. A. (2008) *Neoliberalism, higher education, and research*. Rotterdam: Sense Publishers.

Rubin, I. I. (1972) *Essays on Marx's theory of value*. Detroit: Black and Red.

Ryan, S. (2012) Academic zombies: A failure of resistance or a means of survive. *Australian Universities Review*, 54(2), 1–13.

Sayer, D. (2014) *Rank hypocrisies: The insult of the REF*. London: Sage.

Schapper, J., and Mayson, S. (2005) Managerialism, internationalization, Taylorization and the deskilling of academic work: Evidence from an Australian university in internationalizing higher education. In P. Ninnes and M. Hellstén (Eds), *Internationalizing higher education: Critical explorations of pedagogy and policy*, pp. 181–197. CERC Studies in Comparative Education. Dordrecht: Springer Publications.

Scott, J. C. (1985) *Weapons of the weak: Everyday forms of peasant resistance*. New Haven: Yale University Press.

Shore, C. (2008) Audit culture and illiberal governance: Universities and the politics of accountability. *Anthropological Theory*, 8(3), 278–299.

Shore, C., and Wright, S. (2015) Audit culture revisited: Rankings, ratings, and the reassembling of society. *Current Anthropology*, 5(3), 421–444.

Slaughter, S., and Rhoades, G. (2004) *Academic capitalism and the new economy: Markets, state and higher education*. Baltimore: The Johns Hopkins University Press.

Sparke, M. (2008) Political geography – Political geographies of globalization III: Resistance. *Progress in Human Geography*, 32(3), 423–440.

Spivak, J. (1988) Can the subaltern speak? In C. Nelson and L. Grossberg (Eds), *Marxism and the interpretation of culture*, pp. 271–317. Champaign: University of Illinois Press.

Universities Australian [UA] (2017) Universities in Australia in 2016–2017, by student-to-staff ratio. Universities Australia. www.statista.com/statis tics/613204/australia-universities-by-student-to-staff-ratio/

Universities Australian [UA] (2016) International education generates a record $20.3 billion for Australia. www.universitiesaustralia.edu.au/m edia-item/international-education-generates-a-record-20-3-billion-for-australia/

Vanclay, J. K. (2012) What was wrong with Australian journal ranking? *Journal of Informatics*, 6(1), 53–54.

Willmott, H. (2011) Journal list fetishism and the perversion of scholarship: Reactivity and the ABS list. *Organization*, 18(4), 429–442.

Willmott, H. (2013) 'The substitution of one piece of nonsense for another': Reflections on resistance, gaming, and subjugation. *Journal of Management Studies*, 50(3), 429–443.

Winter, R. (1995) The University of Life, plc: The industrialisation of higher education? In J. Smyth (Ed.), *Academic work: The changing labour process in higher education*, pp. 155–178. Milton Keynes: Open University Press.

Winter, R. (2009) Academic manager or managed academic? Academic identity schisms in higher education. *Journal of Higher Education Policy and Management*, 31(2), 121–131.

Young, S., Peetz, D., and Marias, M. (2011) The impact of the journal ranking fetishism in Australian policy-related research: A case study. *Australian University Review*, 5(2), 77–87.

3 Systemic Governance

Convergence or Hybridization?

GILIBERTO CAPANO

3.1 Introduction

Governments try to steer their higher education systems (HESs). One way or another, based on the characteristics of their political systems and their HESs, governments want to have a say in directing their HESs, and their presence in systemic governance arrangements is inescapable.

Systemic governance in higher education – that is, the way in which higher education policy is coordinated through institutionalized arrangements and practices – has received particular attention from scholars over the last four decades, the exact period during which the inherited characteristics of HESs have been significantly changed by the effects of massification, welfare state financial crises, and globalization/internationalization (Huisman, 2009; Paradeise, 2009; van Vught, 1989). Changes in the traditional ways of governing HESs were challenges that governments had to meet. Massification obliged governments to imagine ways in which HESs could afford increasing numbers of students (and, thus, new ways of organizing and funding HEs). Internationalization has implied increasing cooperation and more academic exchange initiatives. In Europe, this kind of cooperation has even led to the Bologna Process (de Wit et al., 2015; Knight, 2006). Globalization has dramatically increased student mobility and led to the creation of higher education hubs, branch campuses and foreign-backed institutions, and a global market for higher education (thus increasing the commodification of higher education) (van der Wende, 2017; Varghese, 2007). Since the 1970s, financial crises have pushed governments to find different ways of funding higher education and increase the efficiency of universities.

These structural changes have been a matter of interest to governments that have increasingly intervened in the field, especially to tackle the aggregate behaviour of HESs to address these changes according to specific political visions and goals. Governments have been obliged to redesign the ways in which they govern HESs, and in doing so they have had to refocus on the main structural problem in higher education: the issue of how to coordinate universities, which are characterized by loose relationships among their internal components and by very different interests.

Thus, governmental reforms have modified not only the organizational characteristics of HESs (e.g., creating vocational tracks in higher education, granting universities more autonomy), but also the way in which these systems are coordinated and steered (e.g., introducing new forms of institutional accountability, evaluation, accreditation, and performance funding).

Overall, a process of convergence has started in which different national and continental traditions have abandoned their historically rooted systemic governance arrangements and have become more similar by steering the governance of HESs from a distance. For example, in continental Europe, the centralized command and control system has been abandoned for a more autonomous design (where governments are apparently more interested in goals than in procedures), whereas in Anglo-Saxon countries, governments have become more interested in leading the system and have become more intrusive. This apparent convergence has also been emphasized in different ways from other perspectives, such as those who have underlined how the introduction of New Public Management (NPM) has radically redesigned the systemic governance of HESs (Braun and Merrien, 1999) and scholars who have emphasized that this convergence is a direct product of neoliberalism (Harvey, 2005; Marginson, 2009).

However, as underlined in the introductory chapter, the analysis of governance shifts in higher education should not take for granted the apparent convergence that observers and scholars too often emphasize. This means that the major top-down processes that have influenced public policy in recent decades – globalization, internationalization, and marketization – have not necessarily driven the same concrete policy solution, at least in the field of governing HESs.

What has really happened in terms of these governance shifts? Is this convergence real or only marginal? How can we theoretically grasp these changes?

In this chapter, I focus on these questions from the sceptic's perspective-by not taking the convergence mantra for granted-to 1) show how scientific research, especially in its theoretical developments, has been obliged to significantly change its assumptions and conceptualizations to address real changes happening in the world of higher education policies and reforms, and 2) assess the existing empirical evidence of a process of national convergence or, even better, of a kind of diversification through hybridization.

The chapter is structured as follows: in Section 3.2, I describe how and why the main problem of systemic governance (coordinating higher education policies) is represented by the loose coupling of HESs. In Section 3.3, the new governance conceptualizations offered by the specialized literature over the last two decades are presented and discussed. In Section 3.4, I characterize the observed waves of reform in the systemic governance of higher education. Section 3.5 is devoted to unpacking systemic governance in HESs from a policy instrument perspective; owing to this theoretical lens, it will be possible to better understand and assess the changes that have occurred and to imagine the future of systemic governance as a world of hybrids and as consequences of either conscious policy design or contingent incrementalism (Section 3.6).

3.2 The Structural Problem of Governing Universities

3.2.1 *Universities as Loosely Coupled Organizations*

The governance problems in higher education are basically twofold: one concerns the institutional dimension (i.e., how an individual university is coordinated and produces its own policies), while the other concerns the systemic dimension (i.e., how national higher education policy is designed and implemented). These two dimensions are strictly connected to each other. In fact, the way in which institutional governance operates is structurally influenced by what governments do or do not do, while systemic governance must take into account the intrinsic characteristics and ways of working of universities as organizations and institutions.

Universities are sui generis institutions whose constitutive nature (the fact that they are federations or confederations of academic subjects and niches) has structural implications for their internal dynamics, as it creates never-ending problems in their institutional governance, and thus has implications for the ways governments design their lines of systemic coordination. Universities bring together groups of individuals performing very different jobs (e.g., the job of a biologist versus that of a historian, or the job of a computer technician versus that of a help desk employee), numerous intertwined decision-making processes, and a great variety of institutional outputs (from basic to applied research and PhD programmes to continuing education courses, etc.). There is a kind of inescapable organizational and functional complexity in universities, and to grasp this complexity, some scholars have proposed terms such as 'multiversity' (Kerr, 1963) and the 'federal or conglomerate form of organization' (Clark, 1995).

Because of such features, universities are considered typical loose-coupling organizations – that is, a form of organized anarchy (Weick, 1976). From this perspective, universities as loose-coupling institutions are characterized (Orton and Weick, 1990) by the following:

a. causal indeterminacy;
b. a fragmented external environment;
c. a fragmented internal environment.

Causal indeterminacy means that the actions of universities are characterized by intrinsic ambiguity and uncertainty regarding means–ends relations and by a variety of contradictory goals. For empirical evidence of this point, one only has to read the statutes of certain universities or the decisions made by their collegial governing bodies to see that linear rationality and causality do not really apply to higher education institutions: universities see themselves as pursuing excellence in research and providing freedom to teach, as well as contributing to the socio-economic development, equity, and accountability of their society. At the same time, they are subdivided into a variety of niches (academic disciplines), each with its own mission, epistemological basis, and professional rules. In such a context, causality is very often the result of chance or serendipity.

A fragmented external environment simply means that a large number of external stakeholders continuously demand several contradictory things from universities (e.g., local economic development, technological applications, and a higher-quality stock of human capital, as well as the selection and education of social and political elites and social mobility). Thus, the expectations of the external environment may be incompatible with those of the universities.

A fragmented internal environment simply refers to the constitutive variety of internal components of universities. Universities are composed of different academic 'tribes', which constantly seek to defend their territories (Becher, 1989); various groups of students who demand very different services; and non-academic staff, who place their own demands on universities. At the same time, there are a variety of institutional levels and structures within universities: collegial governing bodies, faculties, departments, committees, research centres, and institutes. In other words, universities are overcrowded with nested institutional arenas. This internal fragmentation is self-reproducing and self-sustaining, in accordance with self-referential rationality.

Loose coupling complicates the institutional coordination – that is, the internal governance of universities; at the same time, loose coupling explains their ability to adapt and survive. For example, internal fragmentation enables institutions to register a large range of external inputs and demands and to subsequently offer a variety of responses: this ability is an essential resource for institutional adaptation to external challenges. Furthermore, loose coupling provides universities with buffers that mitigate or isolate disturbances from the external world. This buffering capacity also explains an intrinsic feature of the institutional development of universities: they are capable of change, but only by adapting to external changes; their institutional change is based on what Schon (1971) called 'dynamic conservatism'.

All these intrinsic characteristics of universities as organizations represent the object of systemic governance. Overall, their nature as loose-coupling organizations is the real goal of systemic governance arrangements: in fact, due to their nature, higher education institutions are quite difficult to govern at the internal level. If left free to self-govern, they would behave as a confederation (of different disciplines, academic ranks, administrative staff ranks). Thus, the real goal of systemic governance is to steer this fragmented set of institutions and to oblige them to reinforce their internal governance, decreasing the range of loose coupling and pushing them to behave like a corporate organization by assuming a strong institutional mission. So, the real game of systemic governance is determining how to oblige universities and other higher education institutions to behave in a way that is congruent with systemic socio-political goals.

3.2.2 Governance in Higher Education: Inherited Solutions and New Challenges

The governance quandary in higher education is, above all, represented by the intractable problem of how to coordinate a specific institution – the university – which is intrinsically fragmented and composed of a variety of loosely connected groups and interests, and to render it accountable and responsible at both the institutional and systemic levels. Basically, the governance problem consists of inducing universities to behave as institutions and ensuring that the higher education sector as a whole responds effectively to the needs of society.

Overall, systemic governance in higher education perfectly fits the well-accepted assumption that governance is simply a label for grasping how policies are coordinated (problems are identified and defined; solutions are then formulated and implemented) through institutionalized patterns of intertwining behaviours (formal and informal). Thus, systemic governance in higher education can be defined as 'the set of institutionalised arrangements of the modes and practices of policy steering by which all the components of higher education systemic policy making (policy makers, implementers, goals, means, procedures, plans, formal rules, clients and customers) are interrelated and coordinated' (cf. Capano, 2011; Capano et al., 2015). Governance arrangements, therefore, are a set of actors, coordination principles, and policy instruments that together enforce the expected systemic coordination. Clearly, the main target of these governance arrangements in higher education is ensuring that universities behave as expected with respect to the established systemic goals (e.g., increasing the number of citizens with advanced degrees, increasing the average time needed to obtain such a degree, increasing the socio-economic impact of research, increasing the social relevance of the activities of higher education institutions).

This definition of systemic governance obliges us to reason in terms of how the three constitutive elements of any governance arrangement – actors, principles of coordination and policy instruments (such as types of evaluation, types of regulation and types of funding) – are theoretically held together.

Most theoretical efforts to grasp the various ways in which systemic higher education can work have focused primarily on general

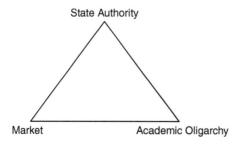

State Authority

Market   Academic Oligarchy

Figure 3.1 Clark's triangle of systemic coordination

principles of coordination that have often taken into account the specific characteristic of HESs and their idiosyncratic character.

The best-known attempt produced Clark's triangle (1983), which consists of the interaction of three mechanisms of systemic and institutional coordination: the state, the market and the academic oligarchy (see Figure 3.1).

Clark proposed three ideal forms of higher education governance: the continental, American, and British types. The constitutive elements of the continental model are systemic, strongly hierarchical coordination through state-centred policies; a lack of institutional autonomy; the powerful, all-pervasive authority of the academic guilds; and faculties and schools constituting confederations of 'chair-holders'. The British model is characterized by substantial institutional autonomy, collegial academic predominance, and a moderate role of the state. Finally, the American model consists of strong procedural autonomy, which is counterbalanced by substantial public monitoring of the quality of performance and results;[1] an important role of external stakeholders (which also means a significant role of political institutions in public universities); and a weaker role of academics in determining the strategic objectives of universities, which is counterbalanced, in accordance with the principle of shared governance, by their more substantial powers in traditional academic matters (e.g., staff recruitment, course content).

This definition of higher education governance has been, and continues to be, the benchmark for any attempt at adjusting theoretical analysis to the radical process of transformation and reform that all HESs have undergone over the last 30 years, albeit at different times and speeds.

This definition is also important since it provides clear examples of how different ways of governing higher education coexist in different geopolitical contexts. However, its characteristics (which substantially commence from the principles of coordination) make this typology slightly static. It also tends to put the three principles of coordination (hierarchy, market and oligarchic power) on the same level: this tendency makes the typology useful from a descriptive perspective, but less fruitful from an explanatory perspective. It appears slightly static because, overall, its ideal-typic nature emphasizes some deep attributes that have characterized a specific historical period (from the 19th century to the 1960s). However, based on the structural trends and changes outlined in the introductory chapter (massification, internationalization, globalization), it is important to be conceptually clear to understand the dynamic evolution of systemic governance. A dynamic perspective needs to focus on the possibility that the three general principles of coordination can combine to create hybrid shapes of systemic governance.

3.3 New Systemic Governance Modes in Higher Education

The historically rooted models of governance in Western countries, masterfully represented by Clark's ideal types, have shown their limitations when faced with contemporary challenges. Each inherited governance equilibrium has been obliged to change. In the past, universities were never subjected to similar pressure to dramatically change their hundred-year-old governance practices and equilibria: after different waves of reform, the landscape is now almost unrecognizable.

We know perfectly well what happened: societies and governments started to take great interest in higher education because of a global context of strong competition in which the quality of human capital must be continuously improved and new technological solutions found to support economic development. Society (and governments) began to demand increasingly more from higher education. For example:

- a rapid increase in participation rates to transform an elite system into a mass system and universal education, as Martin Trow theorized more than 30 years ago (Trow, 1974);

- increased diversification of educational demands (general education, specialized education, life-long learning courses, distance learning courses, internationalization of courses, research training);
- greater knowledge generation;
- development of training and technology for local communities;
- education designed to spur economic development.

These new demands have arisen, almost paradoxically, as public funding has been cut in response to state fiscal crises. Public funding is of fundamental importance for all HESs (with the partial exception of that of the United States). Thus, HESs have been required to do more than they had to in the past and, if possible, to do it faster, continued reductions in public funding notwithstanding. Moreover, universities have suddenly been asked to be transparent and accountable. Unlike in the past, universities are being asked to report on their use of resources (both public and private) and on the results of their utilization. They are held accountable for financial and physical resources, teaching quality, student recruitment, faculty appointments, research resources, productivity, knowledge transfer, rigour in management and quality assurance, and the well-being of students and staff.

This tremendous external pressure has definitively torn down the walls of the ivory tower. One inevitable consequence of this trend has been the structural pressure to change inherited and historically rooted governance arrangements. Thus, Clark's triangle no longer captures what is taking place in higher education because, overall, his triangle is focused on the distribution of authority in a specific system, and because it allows us to understand which of the three principles of coordination is prevalent or what mix of authority is at work; it is less capable of explaining ongoing changes or governance dynamics. Overall, Clark's theorization captures three possible principles of coordination in higher education; in doing so, he adds the academic oligarchy to the two most commonly adopted theoretical principles of social coordination (hierarchy and the market). However, the massification of society and, consequently, of higher education has not only drastically reduced the national influence of the academic oligarchy (whose power, for example, has been clearly diminished in continental Europe owing to the autonomist policies adopted by governments), but has also forced governments to play a different role in higher education. On the basis of the empirical evidence, the role of government in higher education and, above all, in addressing its systemic governance is inescapable.

This theoretical shift has been captured by the dichotomization proposed by van Vught (1989), who outlines two possible governance models: the *state control model* and the *state supervising model*. In the first, which is characteristic of the continental European tradition, the state regulates the procedural aspects and often the content of student access, the recruitment and selection of academic staff, the examination system, the degree requirements, and the content of curricula. At the same time, academics maintain considerable power over the internal life of universities. In this model, universities are weak institutions because the important power relationships are those connecting local academic guilds to central bureaucracies. The state supervising model is characteristic of the English-speaking world, where universities are stronger (and are usually governed based on academics and internal management sharing) and the state plays a subtler role by *steering from a distance*. Other types, designed to encapsulate the features of other forms of higher education governance, have also been proposed (see, for example, Becher and Kogan, 1992, and Braun and Merrien, 1999). In all of the aforementioned cases, the state plays an important role, whether positive or negative.

The focus on state/government proposed by van Vught was a watershed in the analysis of systemic governance in higher education because it emphasizes that the role of government is the real point of reference for any theorization with respect to systemic governance in higher education.

Capano (2011) has proposed an extension of this theoretical framing of the centrality of public authority by assuming that governments design systemic modes for the governance of higher education by exercising their power in determining the goals of the system (and, thus, of the institutions) and the means that can be adopted in pursuit of these goals. This dichotomization produces a typology of systemic governance modes within higher education (see Figure 3.2). It must be emphasized that this typology assigns to each of the four types of governance arrangements specific policy instruments that are considered internally consistent with each of them.

Hierarchical governance and procedural governance represent the two traditional governance modes in which the state plays a pivotal role in command and control. With hierarchical governance, governance directly decides the goals and means through detailed directives. The government is a hegemonic actor, and it therefore directly coordinates all aspects of

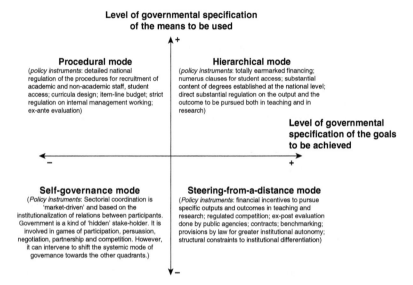

**Level of governmental specification
of the means to be used**

Procedural mode
(*policy instruments*: detailed national
regulation of the procedures for recruitment of
academic and non-academic staff, student
access; curricula design; item-line budget; strict
regulation on internal management working;
ex-ante evaluation)

Hierarchical mode
(*policy instruments*: totally earmarked financing;
numerus clauses for student access; substantial
content of degrees established at the national level;
direct substantial regulation on the output and the
outcome to be pursued both in teaching and in
research)

**Level of governmental
specification of the goals
to be achieved**

Self-governance mode
(*Policy instruments*: Sectorial coordination is
'market-driven' and based on the
institutionalization of relations between participants.
Government is a kind of 'hidden' stake-holder. It is
involved in games of participation, persuasion,
negotiation, partnership and competition. However,
it can intervene to shift the systemic mode of
governance towards the other quadrants.)

Steering-from-a-distance mode
(*Policy instruments*: financial incentives to pursue
specific outputs and outcomes in teaching and
research; regulated competition; ex-post evaluation
done by public agencies; contracts; benchmarking;
provisions by law for greater institutional autonomy;
structural constraints to institutional differentiation)

Figure 3.2 Types of systemic governance modes in higher education policy

policy making. The hierarchical governance of higher education is typified
by situations in which the state imposes its goals and methods on universities (which means that universities have limited procedural or substantial autonomy, the assigned funding is completely targeted by the
state, and there is little or no quality assessment). This is the case with
earmarked funding (for technological research, for example) or where
a set number of students are allowed to enrol in a specific subject.

In procedural governance, the actors involved (regardless of whether
they are public or private) are sufficiently free to choose their goals, but
to pursue those goals they are obliged to follow the procedural regulations decided by public institutions. In such cases, the prevailing actor is
the central bureaucracy, frequently leading to privileged relationships
with the most important sectoral interest groups (which, in the field of
higher education, are the academic guilds and academic subjects themselves). For example, in many continental European countries, the state
obliges universities to follow rules governing academic staff recruitment and promotion, tuition, and curricula. The procedural quadrant
perfectly fits Burton Clark's defined continental model of systemic
university governance. Here, it must be noted that the procedural and
hierarchical modes may overlap. In fact, the hierarchical mode absorbs

the policy instruments of the procedural mode, although there is a substantial difference in the working logic of these two forms of direct government intervention: the procedural mode is characterized by room for substantial decisions to be made from the bottom up. In fact, the procedural mode gives the academic oligarchies of universities the freedom to choose the content of academic business. This freedom of choice is considerably limited under the hierarchical mode simply because this mode imposes substantial constraints on the content of decisions. Furthermore, in both governance mode types, the direct role of the government profoundly constrains the capacity of universities to act as corporate bodies.

The steering-from-a-distance and self-governance modes represent two models in which governmental influence is apparently of an indirect nature. In the steering-from-a-distance mode, the government is strongly committed to the pursuit of collective targets but nevertheless leaves policy actors enough freedom to choose the means by which they will reach those targets. In doing so, the government adopts certain specific policy strategies designed to encourage policy actors to comply with governmental objectives (e.g., increasing student numbers, investing in applied research). In this mode of systemic governance, systemic policy coordination is guaranteed by a complex set of regulations and, very often, by the presence of a public institution (agency or authority) acting as a broker. The government tries to influence institutional behaviour not by issuing direct commands but by applying soft rules, providing financial incentives and evaluating performance. In this governance arrangement, the government may directly intervene to redesign the internal institutional governance of public higher education institutions, depending on the nature of national trajectories and traditions. This situation has occurred in many continental European countries, where since the beginning of the 1990s, governments have changed the rules of the internal governance of universities by assuming that they must behave as corporate actors to be effective in following the strategy of steering from a distance. The steering-from-a-distance mode assumes that both sides of systemic governance – the government and the individual universities – act in a responsible and accountable manner. Governments are supposed to clearly indicate their systemic goals and the nature of the incentives and constraints that universities are to take into account when planning their actions. Universities are supposed to establish their own institutional strategies in a rational manner – that is, by trying to identify the equilibrium among governmental input, their own internal resources, and the socio-economic context in which they operate.

In the self-governance mode, on the other hand, the government leaves the policy arena almost completely free. It is assumed that the fundamental criterion of sectoral coordination is based on the institutionalization of relations between participants. However, the government reserves the right to intervene when necessary, thus changing the governance mode and policy tools. Simply put, in the self-governance model of higher education, institutions are free to choose what they want to do and how to do it. In contrast to what one may imagine, the self-governance model is not a marginal model; indeed, the British and American forms of systemic governance, as proposed by Clark, fit (or, rather, fitted) perfectly within this quadrant.

This typology can be quite useful not only in reconceptualizing governance in a specific way that continues to give a pivotal role to governments in the 'age of governance', but also in understanding the direction of governance shifts in higher education. However, real problems emerge when the governance of all countries converges on one of the quadrants, as is certainly the case with higher education policy. In fact, there is a shared opinion that most countries have been shifting towards the model of steering from a distance. At the same time, studies have begun to underline that this convergence is only presumed and that although all countries have followed a common template, they are redesigning the governance of their HESs by following specific national interpretations of that template. Overall, this typology helps clarify the move towards a common template, but apparent convergence towards the same quadrant does not necessarily mean that differences in national systemic governance approaches are decreasing. In this sense, the spatial representation of the four quadrants clearly indicates that what can make the difference is the precise location of each country in the four spaces and, in the case of convergence towards the steering-at-a-distance quadrant, the exact place and time inside and eventually outside this quadrant.

3.4 Governance in Higher Education: Waves of Reform

Governments have changed their higher education governance policies to address new challenges that have called for a radical rethinking of governance models at the institutional and systemic levels.

In general, the basic levers of reform can be summarized as follows: institutional autonomy, funding mechanisms, quality assessment of research and teaching, internal institutional governance, and changing state roles (see Amaral et al., 2002; Capano et al., 2016; CHEPS, 2006; Enders and Fulton, 2002; Gornitzka et al., 2005; Huisman, 2009; Jarvis and Mok, 2019; Lazzaretti and Tavoletti, 2006; Maassen and Olsen, 2007; Paradeise et al., 2009; Shattock, 2014; Trakman, 2008).

It should be noted that governments had, and continue to have, a predominant role in the reform of governance in higher education. This is also the case with public universities in the United States, where state governments have been very active (Capano and Woo, Chapter 11 in this volume; El-Khawas, 2005; Leslie and Novak, 2003; McLendon, 2003a, 2003b).

The basic levers mentioned above have been moulded differently at the national level, although some common features have emerged:

– In European countries, governments have abandoned the state control model in favour of steering universities from a distance (by granting more autonomy to institutions). In countries in Europe, such as the Netherlands (De Boer, Enders, and Leisyte, 2007), Sweden (Bladh, 2007), Denmark (Carney, 2006), and Austria (Lanzendorf, 2006), and outside Europe, such as Japan (Oba, 2010), China (Yang et al., 2007), and South Korea (Rhee, 2010), governments have radically changed the institutional arrangements of universities by abandoning the traditional democratic mechanisms for electing institutional leaders and governing bodies and replacing them with an appointment system. The supervisory role of the state (Neave and van Vught, 1991) is implemented by steering founded on new methods of coordination that are no longer based on 'hard' rules but on 'soft' contracts, targets, benchmarks, indicators, and continual assessments.

– In the English-speaking world, governments have increased their intervention and regulation, despite a tradition of institutional autonomy. In the United Kingdom, Australia, and New Zealand, governments have substantially restructured their governance frameworks by creating national agencies for the assessment of research and teaching and through a strong commitment to realigning the behaviour of universities with socio-economic requirements. At the same time, public universities in the United States have been strongly

encouraged to adopt a more competitive stance to obtain more funding from private sources in a substantial process of marketization
(Altbach et al., 2011; Geiger, 2004).

- In Asia and Latin America, more complex dynamics exist due to
different academic traditions, political contexts, and financial situations. Here, it is necessary to underline structural differences in terms
of the ratios of public to private institutions between Europe and the
USA, Latin America, and Asia. Above all, it must be underlined that
in India and East Asia, as well in many Latin American countries,
there is a high number of private institutions and that, in many cases,
the number of such institutions, which are favoured by governmental policies, has increased in recent decades (Brunner and Villalobos,
2014; Varghese, 2015). In some cases, the expansion of private
higher education is due to the lack of public funding (and thus
governments have pushed for this expansion to include more citizens
in higher education) or to the specific goal of perpetuating the elitist
nature of their public systems. However, in these different structural
contexts, governments have also been very active in introducing
different forms of institutional accountability, research evaluation,
contractualization, and performance funding. Furthermore, in East
Asia, governments have extensively redesigned higher education governance to push institutions towards differentiation and competition
(Jarvis and Mok, 2019; Shin, 2018).

In this context of substantial redesign of the borders and general
frameworks of systemic coordination in higher education, certain other
features are present in all of the most important countries:

- Institutional autonomy does not mean independence, nor does
it mean academic freedom. Rather, it means the capability and the
right of a higher education institution to determine its own course of
action without undue interference from the state, but in a context
that is strongly influenced by the state. In this sense, the common
interpretation of institutional autonomy is that of a policy instrument designed to increase the effectiveness of higher education policies. Thus, in countries operating under the continental mode (which
includes most East Asian systems), where institutional autonomy
was either weak or non-existent, governments have started to
grant greater institutional autonomy; on the other hand, in systems

where university institutions have traditionally been highly autonomous (not only in the English-speaking world but also in Latin
American public universities), governments have started to interfere
in institutional behaviour by, for example, introducing new regulations, assigning targets, and increasing pressure for inter-institutional
competition. In Asia, for example, especially in the Eastern part, the
interpretation of the autonomist policy has led to the 'incorporation'
of universities in a context where the role of the state has increased
(Shin, 2018).

– Funding traditionally earmarked for the functioning of universities
  has been abandoned in favour of lump-sum grants; additionally,
  different types of targets and performance funding mechanisms
  have been introduced.
– The amount of the public funds assigned to universities is often
  based on output-oriented criteria and performance-based contracting systems.
– There is strong pressure to increase private funding (by increasing
  tuition fees and selling services and research to private actors).
– National agencies or committees for the evaluation and assessment
  of the quality and performance of teaching and research in higher
  education institutions have been established in most countries in
  Europe, Asia, and Latin America.
– Increasing the rate of privatization of a system can be a tool used by
  governments to pursue specific systemic goals.
– In recent years, many governments have pushed their HEs to diversify their institutional missions.
– Competition for funding (not only in research but also in teaching)
  has increased.
– Evaluation has been introduced in different ways and is often linked
  to funding.

From the comparative picture sketched here, the forms of systemic
governance within higher education policy are radically changing. The
question remains, how are they changing? If we examine the plethora
of comparative studies of governance shifts in higher education
that have been produced over the last 20 years, clearly, at the systemic
level, governance arrangements have shifted towards steering from
a distance.

First, it is interesting to observe that the bureaucratic arrangement (the traditional method of the controlling state) has been abandoned (or at least significantly reduced) by European countries and by countries such as China, Japan, and South Korea.

Second, the principal shift in the governance mode is clearly in the direction of steering from a distance (albeit via different trajectories and at differing speeds), indicating that the prevailing governance arrangement is characterized by the main steering role of the government, which corresponds to increased autonomization and corporatization of universities. Clearly, this trend is influenced by the specific nature of national contexts and policy legacies since it is a process whereby each governance arrangement is redesigned and remoulded by remixing the components of the previous arrangement.

Third, the governance shift towards steering from a distance underlines the actual need for governments to control policy performance by stating targets and the means by which they are to be pursued. In the sphere of higher education, this governmental commitment means that universities are considered instruments for the implementation of governmental policy (and in this sense, institutional autonomy is considered functional – that is, for producing systemic results, rather than an intrinsic characteristic of universities). Furthermore, this shift means that governments are dissatisfied with the traditional bureaucratic arrangement: procedural power and control (the bureaucratic arrangement) are no longer considered either efficient or effective.

A point of contact emerges between the type of analysis that I am proposing and the scholars who characterize all reforms in higher education policy as 'neoliberal' and, thus, based on privatization, deregulation, managerialization and limitation of academic freedom (Marginson, 2009; Olssen and Peters, 2005). The shift towards the steering-from-a-distance governance mode represents a peculiar watershed in the historical evolution of higher education in which universities, probably for the first time, are being asked to prove their social value and are less free to pursue their research and teaching goals.

However, from my perspective, which is focused on governance shifts in higher education, this watershed is not necessarily negative. Increasing pressure on the academic world from external elements (asking for more social relevance from higher education), the use of managerial techniques in higher education institutions, the reduction of regulation (more institutional autonomy), and the introduction of evaluation have redesigned higher education systemic governance to ensure it is still functional and relevant in its social context. Can we really imagine that HESs could be left alone to respond to the challenges of massification, globalization, and internationalization? From a governance perspective, what is included under the definitional umbrella of neoliberalism in higher education means, from the empirical point of view, something different: more state and not less state; more governmental presence and not privatization (although some forms of privatization are used, they are always tools to reach systemic goals).

Finally, the corporatization and autonomization of universities are also ways by which academic guilds are deprived of power, which could be positive for accountability and fit purposes (because academic power is very often self-interested). From this perspective, then, the increasing institutional autonomy of universities and the related increase in accountability requested by governments should be not confused with decreasing academic freedom. Here, there is a risk of overlap in individual rights (the freedom to teach and to research), institutional property (autonomy), and related accountability. Often, it seems that the weakening of academic power in ruling universities is confused with decreasing academic freedom, yet they are two different phenomena.

3.5 Unpacking Governance Modes: Towards Hybrid Modes of Systemic Governance

3.5.1 *The Governance Equalizer: Five Dimensions of Governance Modes in Higher Education*

If there is a general trend towards designing and implementing the steering-from-a-distance mode in higher education, does this mean that there is finally a clear process of convergence worldwide? This could be the case, although there are signals of different national interpretations and of different ways in which the elements of the common template have been followed.

This issue was dealt with for the first time by de Boer, Enders, and Schimank (2007, 2008), who proposed analysing governance shifts not through a typological approach but by focusing on changes in the main components of governance arrangements (which compose the 'governance equalizer'). They hold that the following five dimensions are the most relevant for composing every systemic governance arrangement:

1) *State regulation*, which refers to the authority of governments and state bureaucracies and the degree to which these actors prescribe and regulate institutional behaviours;
2) *Stakeholder guidance*, which refers to the degree to which actors external to higher education institutions are capable of addressing them;
3) *Academic self-governance*, which refers to the degree to which academic communities, disciplines, and guilds have a real role in and impact on decision making with respect to other actors/ stakeholders;
4) *Managerial self-governance*, which refers to the role of university leadership in steering institutions and in affecting the systemic level; and
5) *Competition*, which refers to the degree to which coordination based on resource scarcity influences institutional behaviours and thus addresses systemic governance arrangements and dynamics.

According to the authors, these five constitutive dimensions are independent of each other and do not follow a zero-sum logic. For example, less state regulation does not mean more competition or more academic self-governance, and more competition does not mean less state regulation or less academic self-governance. These five dimensions can be combined in different ways, creating various possible configurations and, thus, various national hybrid modes of systemic governance. In this book, De Boer and Huisman (Chapter 12) demonstrate that this way of thinking can be fruitful in describing the characteristics and many variants of systemic governance in the European context. Certainly, this way of thinking and analysing governance allows us to better comprehend the phenomenon itself and, above all, to go further with respect to some traditional views, such as the intrinsic antinomy between state regulation and marketization and between academic self-governance and the influence of external stakeholders. The truth is that combinations of these dimensions can vary greatly and take unexpected shapes, contradicting certain theoretical assumptions.

Thus, the governance equalizer helps us go further and analyse governance arrangements in higher education in terms of hybrids.

This framework should be considered an absolute watershed. In fact, in the literature on higher education governance, and in the more extensive literature on governance, there is a tendency to expect that the actual modes of governance are intrinsically coherent, which means that the policy instruments adopted are coherent (ideationally) with the prevailing general principle of coordination. Thus, strong regulations are expected when hierarchy prevails, and incentives and competition are expected when market logic prevails. In reality, things are more complex, and it appears that these kinds of categorizations work only up to a certain point, in the sense that they are capable of grasping the trend but are too generic to grasp the substance. Thus, the governance equalizer represents a first effort to overcome genericity and to open the world of intrinsic hybridity of governance arrangements in higher education.

3.5.2 Going Deeper: The Policy Mix and Hybridity in Higher Education Systemic Governance

This theoretical assumption matches perfectly with the rising awareness of the idea that any coherence between policy instruments and a given ideational framework or goal has been superseded (Bressers and O'Toole, 2005; Capano et al., 2012; Howlett, 2005; Gunningham and Sinclair, 1999) for the simple reason that it is empirically fallacious and inconsistent with the facts.

This is very often justified as an outcome of the ambiguous preferences of policy makers. However, it could also be assumed that incoherence between the general principles of coordination and the instruments adopted is intrinsic to any governance arrangement. In fact, any selection of policy instruments is characterized by an intrinsic policy-mix trend (Bressers and O'Toole, 2005; Howlett, 2004) and should therefore be considered the result of miscellaneous ideas, interests, and technologies and deemed institutionalized in certain specific, recurrent contingencies. Thus, in keeping with the literature, a policy mix is a combination of policy instruments belonging to different instrument categories or pertaining to different policy paradigms/belief systems/ideologies (Ring and Schröter-Schlack, 2012; Del Rio and Howlett, 2013).

The policy-mix concept originated in the economics literature during the 1960s and was largely restricted to the field of economics until the early 1990s (Flanagan, Uyarra and Laranja, 2011). It has since been adopted in other policy fields, such as childcare policy (Gunningham and Young, 1997; Stroick and Jenson, 1999), environmental policy (Sorrel and Sijm, 2003) and innovation policy (Borràs and Edquist, 2013). Furthermore, all studies of good governance promoted by the OECD and by other international organizations tend to focus on the best mix of policy instruments adopted in pursuit of certain specific policy goals (OECD, 2007, 2010). By focusing on the base elements of governance arrangements, this literature on policy instruments substantially underlines that hybridity is more common than expected and that finding strictly coherent governance modes is empirically improbable. Additionally, the potential hybrid nature of systemic governance in higher education has been clearly hypothesized in the specialized literature. In fact, almost 20 years ago, based on a comparative study of Europeans HESs, Gornitzka and Maassen (2000) clearly stated that although they had identified a 'general move towards the supermarket steering model', 'in practice this model will not be found in its pure form' (p. 284). They thus proposed the empirically evident hybrid nature of the steering-from-a-distance model, at least in the European case. However, this evidence can certainly push for a more general assumption regarding the intrinsic nature of hybrid governance in HESs in the contemporary world. In fact, as I have tried to show, a brief look at the content of various waves of reform of governance in HESs that have been pursued worldwide gives the impression that there is much in common, but also much that is different. In fact, while governance arrangements everywhere try to mix state steering with institutional autonomy, the shapes of these mixes are very different in terms of the real content of the design adopted.

Explaining these differences is very important, and Jungblut and Vukasovic (2013) show what kind of theoretical interpretation could be proposed for this purpose. However, from an analytical perspective, a more fine-grained categorization or an analytical framework for grasping the content of hybrids in systemic governance in higher education is, for me, more urgent. To that end, the emerging literature on policy mixes is a source of inspiration. Overall, if governance modes are hybrids that mix together different things and encompass 'different steering instruments, institutional structures and steering relationships'

(Gornitzka and Maassen, 2000, 283), why not start from policy instruments?

3.5.3 Focusing on Policy Instruments to Unpack the Governance Conundrum

An analytical grid is needed to determine what really happened in the governance shifts in higher education in recent decades. This fine-grained grid is necessary not only to better describe the characteristics and composition of the actual governance arrangements (the different varieties of steering-from-a-distance modes), but also because without a reliable classification, it will be impossible to really connect these governance shifts with policy performance (considering that, overall, governments have continuously changed systemic governance arrangements precisely to improve systemic policy performance).

Basing this analytical grid on policy instruments means focusing on what governments really do when they design policies and on the real components of policy reforms (that are composed of policy instruments). It is by bringing together policy instruments and making them work that governments steer systemic governance (Howlett, 2000; Salamon, 2002; Vedung, 1998). But how can policy instruments be used to distinguish the different hybrids in higher education systemic governance? This question is not a simple one, because there could be different points of departure. Better operationalizing the concept of evaluation, for example, would be important. Very often, evaluation is conceived in the literature as a new strategic tool of recent reforms. How can we operationalize it and identify its various potential impacts? Additionally, precisely because at least one evaluative practice has been introduced in every country, how can we distinguish among these practices?

To address these questions, a specific research design has been proposed to analyse governance shifts and their effects on HESs in Western European countries (Capano and Pritoni, 2019a; 2019b; Capano et al., 2019). This research design is based on a specific conceptualization that draws from the classification tradition of policy instruments (Ingram and Schneider, 1990; Phidd and Doern, 1983; Vedung, 1998; Howlett, 2011) and combines the Vedung and Salaman proposals. Following this perspective, four specific families of substantial policy instruments are established: *expenditure*, *regulation*, *information*, and *taxation* (which is considered the bearer of a different political economy with respect to expenditure and thus must be taken into account separately). Each family of policy instruments is conceptualized as inducing specific behaviours. Expenditure drives remuneration, regulation drives behavioural control, information is the bearer of persuasion, while taxation – depending on the way in which it is designed – can induce both behavioural control and remuneration. It must be observed that all four families of substantial tools can drive higher or lower degrees of coercion based on how much they leave individuals free to choose among alternatives. For example, taxation can be highly coercive when a general tax increase is established, but at the same time it can have a low degree of coercion when many targeted tax exemptions exist. Regulation can be really strong or very soft based on the type of behavioural prescription. Expenditure can be non-coercive in the case of subsidies but very demanding when targeted funding is delivered. Information can be very coercive when compulsory disclosure is imposed or really soft when monitoring is applied. This specification regarding coercion is very important when the analytical focus is on governance modes in higher education because it sheds light on why the steering-from-a-distance model has too often been assessed as very coercive or, in some cases, as a kind of reregulation (Donina et al., 2015; Enders et al., 2013): the real point is that, as shown by the conceptualization of policy instruments proposed earlier, governments can also be quite regulatory when steering from a distance if they adopt highly coercive types of regulation, taxation or information. Less regulation does not mean less steering; thus, coercion can also be applied from a distance and in different ways.

This distinction becomes even clearer when, by following the lessons of Salamon (2002), for each family of policy instruments the specific forms through which they can be delivered are extracted and designed. Thus, for each type of substantial policy instrument, there are different ways of delivery in which regulation, expenditure, taxation, and information can affect reality. For example, what matters when governments use expenditure to steer the system is not only the amount of money on the table but also the various forms through which it can be delivered, such as grants, subsidies, loans, lump-sum transfers, and targeted transfers. According to the same logic, regulation can be designed by imposing specifying behaviours (such as a national procedure for staff recruitment), enlarging the range of opportunities (such as granting more autonomy to the internal organization of universities), or establishing specific public organizations (such as national agencies for accreditation or evaluation). Information can take the shape of neutral administrative disclosure, annual monitoring, diffusion, etc. Taxation can be delivered through tuition fees, user charges, exemptions, etc.

Thus, different recruiting systems, mechanisms for gaining access to higher education, or quality assurance systems have different effects even though they can all be classified as regulatory tools; however, based on how they are designed, they can be more or less coercive. Grants are less coercive than loans and can be bearers of different effects; even though they are both classified as expenditures, lump-sum transfers and performance-based funding are profoundly different ways through which higher education institutions can obtain funding: the former leave more autonomy for universities, while the latter is more coercive and thus consistently limits behaviour. Nationally driven tuition systems, very decentralized systems, and income/merit/service-based fees systems induce different behaviours (in both institutions and students) because they are different forms of delivering taxation. Finally, ranking systems, national monitoring, quality assurance, and research assessments are all delivery vehicles belonging to the information family; however, they induce quite different effects on behaviours.

Developing this argument, Capano and Pritoni (2019b) and Capano, Pritoni and Vicentini (2019) proposed two specific classifications of the shapes of policy instruments in higher education. The simpler of the two classifications is presented in Table 3.1.[2]

Unpacking governance modes through the shapes of these 24 instruments opens the analysis to many different research opportunities:

1. It increases the analytical and descriptive capacity to grasp how governments change the instrumental side of governance arrangements over time and, thus, to detect the real content of the governance arrangement that governments have been pursuing over time. Then, by focusing on the different shapes of policy instruments, a more detailed reconstruction of governance shifts can be provided with respect to the usual description in terms of a greater or lesser market or more or less hierarchy or by putting every country in only one basket (currently, the steering-from-a-distance mode).
2. It offers an analytical tool to better define the characteristics of the governance hybrids possible.

Table 3.1 *Classification of policy instruments and their shapes*

Family of Policy Instruments		Shapes
Regulation	R1	Assessment, evaluation and accreditation (procedural rules)
	R2	Agency for assessment, evaluation, and accreditation
	R3	Content of curricula: more constraints
	R4	Content of curricula: more opportunities
	R5	Academic career and recruitment: more constraints
	R6	Academic career and recruitment: more opportunities
	R7	Regulation on students (admission and taxation): more constraints
	R8	Regulation on students (admission and taxation): more opportunities
	R9	Institutional and administrative governance: more constraints
	R10	Institutional and administrative governance: more opportunities
	R11	Contracts
	R12	Rules on goals in teaching
Expenditure	E1	Grants
	E2	Subsidies and lump-sum funding
	E3	Targeted funding
	E4	Loans
	E5	Performance-based institutional funding
	E6	Standard cost per student
Taxation	T1	Tax exemption
	T2	Tax reduction for particular categories of students
	T3	Service-based student fees
Information	I1	Transparency
	I2	Certifications
	I3	Monitoring and reporting

Source: Capano et al. (2019)

3. It could offer a theoretical framework for assessing the results obtained by reforming systemic governance.

3.5.4 Discovering Varieties of Hybrid Governance in Higher Education

By following this logic, it is possible to disentangle the problem of the hybridity of systemic governance and, at the same time, to better understand how policy mixes have been selected and composed from a comparative perspective. Furthermore, this way of working should allow a more fine-grained description of how the same policy template has actually been adopted in different countries in recent decades, thus making it possible to abandon the steering-from-a-distance label for something that better describes reality.

Here, I can only show the considerable potential of this way of reasoning and operationalizing governance arrangements. The point of departure is the three varieties of steering from a distance that Capano and Pritoni (2019a) drew from their analysis of changes in the instrumental composition of the systemic governance modes in 12 European countries (by also considering the level of public funding and the level of tuition fees). Table 3.2 presents these three types of hybrid steering-from-a-distance modes.

The three hybrids show that the mode of steering from a distance can be implemented in at least three ways. First, the performance-oriented mode focuses on performance, which means that a significant part of public funding is based on the assessment of teaching and research. Some might expect this mode to be the most diffused hybrid (due to the rhetoric that characterizes the public discourse on evaluation worldwide), but this expectation does not correspond to the empirical evidence. In fact, among the 12 cases that the authors investigated, only England (and, in part, Italy) fits this hybrid. The peculiarity of this hybrid probably explains why it is limited to these few cases and systems. The Americas (except, perhaps, Brazil) and Asia have emphasized performance as the pillar criterion for governing their HESs (with the exception of New Zealand, which has pioneered the performance-oriented hybrid since the 1980s).

The reregulated mode is characterized by strong proceduralization imposed by governments, a relevant presence of target/performance

Table 3.2 *Types of hybrid systemic governance modes in higher education*

Types of steering from a distance	Main/leading instruments different mixes of R, Ex, Tax, and Info + public funding + tuition fees
Performance-oriented mode	– Significant percentage of public funding; based on the results of research assessment – Use of information tools – Many regulations for administrative procedures – Significant percentage of public funding based on evaluation of teaching performance – Student support based on loans – Relatively high tuition fees
Reregulated mode	– Many procedural constraints on the main activities (recruitment, promotion, postdoc, teaching content and organization of degrees, student admissions) – Proceduralization of quality assurance – Target funding/performance funding – Average/low public funding – Low tuition fees
Goal-oriented mode	– Clear systemic goals stated by governments – Many opportunities in admissions, curricula, and institutional autonomy – High public funding – Information instruments (monitoring, reporting) – Strategic use of target/performance funding – Student support based mostly on grants – High performance and target funding – No/low tuition fees

funding, and the tendency to not increase tuition fees. In this hybrid, evaluative practices are proceduralized and push for compliance over performance. This hybrid is adopted by governments that cannot invest too much in higher education and that try to steer their HEs by mixing common procedural rules and different types of evaluation and quality assurance. This hybrid appears to have the most potential for diffusion worldwide (especially in countries with legacies of bureaucratic systemic governance in higher education).

The goal-oriented hybrid is characterized primarily by the presence of clear goals stated by governments that then design their systemic steering by mixing high public funding, strategic use of evaluation, and enormous student support. This hybrid is likely to be another European peculiarity since it is present in the Nordic countries, which maintain broad welfare states. However, what makes the difference here is the strong capacity of the government to design clear systemic goals to which the institutions are asked to contribute.

These three types of hybrid governance provide a useful point of departure for further research and for analysing systemic governance from a comparative perspective. For example, many Asian governments (China, Japan, Malaysia) seem to steer their HESs through a reregulatory approach, while others (Singapore, Hong Kong) do so through a goal-oriented approach. It would also be interesting to apply this framework to Latin America and to the states and provinces of the United States and Canada where, for example, Quebec has clearly adopted a reregulative mode, while most other provinces have adopted the goal-oriented hybrid, although with the substantial difference that many of them have increased tuition fees.

These three hybrid types of governance show that it is possible to conceptually reduce the variety of national interpretations of the steering-from-a-distance mode that have been implemented in Europe. At the same time, this way of theoretically and empirically analysing systemic governance appears to be quite promising because it allows us to shed light on the characteristics of the policy mixes in a very detailed manner. Clearly, these three hybrids could be biased because they are continental specific and thus cannot be considered exhaustive, especially because in European HESs the private sector is marginal, whereas in other national systems the private sector can be large in size. However, this missing dimension could certainly be included in a revised framework of systemic governance in higher education.

3.6 The Age of Hybridity

Governing HESs is not an easy task. Societies are very demanding, while HESs are fragile and intrinsically fragmented. One way or another, governments are in charge of addressing their HESs. To address new socio-economic challenges, governments have partially (although, in some cases, substantially) inherited their ways of governing HESs. Consequently, they have ostensibly followed a common template (the steering-from-a-distance mode), but there is clear empirical evidence that the results are very different. In every country, evaluation, quality assurance, performance/target funding, and contractualization have been mixed in different ways. Thus, we need a better theorization to grasp what has happened and to understand what could happen. I propose taking the public policy literature on policy instruments seriously and focusing any analytical framework for systemic governance on the operationalization of policy instruments. Therefore, this instrumental framework can be accompanied by other dimensions, such as the percentage of public funding, the structure of tuition fees, and the public/private divide in the organization of higher education itself. With this toolbox, it will be possible to describe and, most likely, to gauge the many differences and to finally transcend the generic meaning of steering from a distance. We have entered the age of hybridity, and in this age we must stay. This hybridization of governance in higher education raises a relevant issue with respect to more general themes related to the characteristics of governance and their relationships with issues of political and social relevance.

First, the hybridization of governance makes it more complex to reason about the effects of marketization in higher education. Marketization does not necessarily mean privatization, nor does it mean more competition between institutions. On the contrary, it seems that what is hidden by the hybrid forms of governance is that, in some countries, families and students face higher financial costs.

Second, globalization and internationalization have not been conducive to a common way of steering higher education governance. The hybridization I have shown demonstrates that national paths and social values are resilient, and the need to change higher education governance has been dealt with through national interpretation.

Third, governments can steer their HESs from a distance in different ways and through different policy mixes. They can also strongly reregulate the system through specific procedures regarding accreditation, evaluation, and funding that do not appear to be but are in fact very constraining.

Finally, governance shifts in higher education reflect a complex process through which governments respond to external challenges and structural environmental changes by drastically redesigning their systemic governance arrangements to make their HESs responsive and accountable. In doing so, governments have not followed specific ideological lines, but have mixed coordination principles and policy instruments according their needs, legacy, and contexts.

Notes

1. The important influence exercised by US governments (both federal and state) on the institutional behaviour of universities is often underestimated. The federal government plays a crucial role in the earmarking of enormous amounts of funds for research and student aid programmes, using its financial weight to profoundly influence both public and private universities (especially those that are particularly committed to high-quality research). State governments play a crucial role since they are both the 'owners' and the 'regulators' of public universities (Berdahl, 1999).
2. In this format, 24 instrumental shapes are proposed. In Capano and Pritoni (2019a), the instrumental specification is even more detailed and proposes 43 instrumental shapes.

References

Altbach, P. G., Gumport, P. J., and Berdahl, R. O. (Eds) (2011) *American higher education in the twenty-first century: Social, political, and economic challenges*. Baltimore: John Hopkins.

Amaral, A., Jones, G., and Karseth, B. (Eds) (2002) *Governing higher education: National perspectives on institutional governance*. Dordrecht: Kluwer Academic Publishers.

Becher, T. (1989) *Academic tribes and territories*. Buckingham: Open University Press.

Becher, T., and Kogan, M. (1992) *Process and structure in higher education*, 2nd ed. London: Routledge.

Berdahl, R. (1999) Universities and governments in the 21st century: The US experience. In Dietmar Braun and Francoise-Xavier Merrien (Eds), *Towards a new model of governance for universities? A comparative view*, pp. 59–77. London: Jessica Kingsley.

Bladh, A. (2007) Institutional autonomy with increasing dependency on outside actors. *Higher Education Policy*, 20(3), 243–259.

Borràs, S., and Edquist, C. (2013) *The choice of innovation policy instruments*. CIRCLE Papers, University of Lund, n.4.

Braun, D., and Merrien, F.-X. (1999) Governance of universities and modernisation of the state: Analytical aspects. In D. Braun and F.-

X. Merrien (Eds), *Towards a new model of governance for universities? A comparative view*, pp. 9–33. London: Jessica Kingsley.

Bressers, H. T. A., and O'Toole, L. J. (2005) Instrument selection and implementation in a networked context. In P. Eliades, M. M. Hill and M. Howlett (Eds), *Designing government: From instruments to governance*, pp. 132–153. Montreal and Kingston: McGill-Queen's University Press.

Brunner, J. J., and Villalobos, C. (Eds) (2014) *Politica de Educacìon Superior en Iberoamérica*. Santiago: Ediciones Universidad Diego Portales.

Capano, G. (2011) Government continues to do its job. A comparative study of governance shifts in the higher education sector. *Public Administration*, 89(4), 1622–1642.

Capano, G., Howlett, M., and Ramesh, M. (Eds) (2015) *Varieties of governance*. London: Palgrave MacMillan.

Capano, G., Regini, M., and Turri, M. (2016) *Changing governance in universities: Italian higher education in comparative perspective*. London: Palgrave MacMillan.

Capano, G., and Pritoni, A. (2019a) Varieties of hybrid systemic governance in European higher education. *Higher Education Quarterly*, 73(1), 10–28.

Capano, G., and Pritoni, A. (2019b). Exploring the determinants of higher education performance in Western Europe: A qualitative comparative analysis. *Regulation & Governance*, online first, March.

Capano, G., Pritoni, A., and Vicentini, G. (2019) Do policy instruments matter? Governments' choice of policy mix and higher education performance in Western Europe. *Journal of Public Policy*, online first, March.

Capano, G., Reyner, J., and Zito, A. (2012) Governance from the bottom up: Complexity and divergence in comparative perspective. *Public Administration*, 90(1), 56–73.

Carney, S. (2006) University governance in Denmark: From democracy to accountability? *European Educational Research Journal*, 5(3 & 4), 221–233.

CHEPS (2006) *The extent and impact of higher education governance reform across Europe*. Final Report to the Directorate General for Education and Culture of European Commission. http://ec.europa.eu/education/.

Clark, B. (1983) *The higher education system: Academic organization in cross national perspective*. Berkeley: University of California Press.

Clark, B. (1995) Complexity and differentiation: The deepening problem of university integration. In D. Dill and B. Sporn (Eds), *Emerging patterns of social demand and university reform: Through a glass darkly*, pp. 159–169. Oxford: Pergamon Press.

De Boer, H., Enders, J., and Leisyte, L. (2007) Public sector reform in Dutch higher education: The organizational transformation of the University. *Public Administration*, 85(1), 27–46.

De Boer, H., Enders, J., and Schimank, U. (2007) On the way towards new public management? The governance of university systems in England, the Netherlands, Austria, and Germany. In D. Jansen (Ed.), *New forms of governance in research organizations: Disciplinary approaches, interfaces and integration*, pp. 137–152. Dordrecht: Springer.

De Boer, H., Enders, J., and Schimank, U. (2008) Comparing higher education governance systems in four European countries. In N. C. Soguel and P. Jaccard (Eds), *Governance and performance of education systems*, pp. 35–54. Dordrecht: Springer.

Del Rio, P., and Howlett, M. (2013) Beyond the 'Tinbergen Rule' in policy design: Matching tools and goals in policy portfolios. Working Paper no. LKYSPP13-01. Lee Kuan Yew School of Public Policy WP Series.

de Wit, H., Deca, L., and Hunter, F. (2015) Internationalization of higher education – What can research add to the policy debate? In A. Curaj, L. Matei, R. Pricopie, J. Salmi, and P. Scott (Eds), *The European Higher Education Area*, pp. 3–12, Dordrecht: Springer.

Donina, D., Meoli, M., and Paleari, S. (2015) Higher education reform in Italy: Tightening regulation instead of steering at a distance. *Higher Education Policy*, 28(2), 215–234.

El-Khawas, E. (2005) The push for accountability: Policy influences and actors in American higher education. In A. Gornitzka, M. Kogan, and A. Amaral (Eds), *Reform and change in higher education*, pp. 287–303. Dordrecht: Springer.

Enders, J., and Oliver Fulton, O. (Eds) (2002) *Higher education in a globalising world*. Dordrecht: Kluwer.

Enders, J., De Boer, H., and Weyer, E. (2013) Regulatory autonomy and performance: The reform of higher education revisited. *Higher Education*, 65(1), 5–23.

Flanagan, K., Uyarra, E., and Laranja, M. (2011) Reconceptualising the 'policy mix' for innovation. *Research Policy*, 40(5), 702–713.

Geiger, R. (2004) *Knowledge and money: Research universities and the paradox of the marketplace*. Palo Alto: Stanford University Press.

Gornitzka, A., Kogan, M., and Amaral, A. (Eds) (2005) *Reform and change in higher education*. Dordrecht: Springer.

Gornitzka, Å., and Maassen, P. (2000) Hybrid steering approaches with respect to European higher education. *Higher Education Policy*, 13(3), 267–285.

Gunningham, N., and Sinclair, D. (1999) Regulatory pluralism: Designing policy mixes for environmental protection. *Law and Policy*, 21(1), 49–76.

Gunningham, N., and Young, M. D. (1997) Toward optimal environmental policy: The case of biodiversity conservation. *Ecology Law Quarterly*, 24, 243–298.

Harvey, D. (2005) *A brief history of neoliberalism*. Oxford: Oxford University Press.

Howlett, M. (2000) Managing the 'hollow state': Procedural policy instruments and modern governance. *Canadian Public Administration*, 43(4), 412–431.

Howlett, M. (2004) Beyond good and evil in policy implementation: Instrument mixes, implementation styles and second generation theories of policy instrument choice. *Policy and Society*, 23(2), 1–17.

Howlett, M. (2005) What is a policy instrument? Policy tools, policy mixes and policy-implementation styles. In P. Eliadis, M. M. Hill, and M. Howlett (Eds), *Designing government: From instruments to governance*, pp. 311–350. Montreal and Kingston: McGill-Queen's University Press.

Howlett, M. (2011) *Designing public policies: Principles and instruments*. London: Routledge.

Huisman, J. (Eds) (2009) *International perspectives on the governance of higher education*. London: Routledge.

Ingram, H., and Schneider, A. I. (1990) The behavioral assumptions of policy tools. *The Journal of Politics*, 52(2), 510–529.

Jarvis, D.S.L and Joshua Ka Ho Mok (Eds) (2019) *Transformations In Higher Education Governance in Asia: Policy, Politics and Progress*. Singapore: Springer.

Jungblut, J., and Vukasovic, M. (2013) And now for something completely different? Re-examining hybrid steering approaches in higher education. *Higher Education Policy*, 26(4), 447–461.

Kerr, C. (1963) *The uses of university*. Cambridge: Harvard University Press.

Knight, J. (2006) *Higher education crossing borders: A guide to the implications of the GATS for cross-border education*. Paris: UNESCO/ Commonwealth of Learning.

Lanzendorf, U. (2006) Austria – From hesitation to rapid breakthrough. In B. Kehm and U. Lanzendorf (Eds), *Reforming university governance – Changing conditions for research in four European countries*, pp. 99–134. Bonn: Lemmens.

Lazzaretti, L., and Tavoletti, E. (2006) Governance shifts in higher education: A cross national comparison. *European Educational Research Journal*, 5(1), 18–37.

Leslie, D. W., and Novak, R. J. (2003) Substance versus politics: Through the dark mirror of governance reform. *Educational Policy*, 17(1), 98–120.

Maassen, P., and Olsen, J. P. (Eds) (2007) *University dynamics and European integration*. Dordrecht: Springer.

Marginson, S. (2009) Hayekian neo-liberalism and academic freedom. *Contemporary Readings in Law and Justice*, 1(1), 86–114.

McLendon, M. (2003a) Setting the governmental agenda for state decentralization of higher education. *Journal of Higher Education*, 74(5), 479–515.

McLendon, M. (2003b) State governance reform of higher education: Patterns, trends, and theories of the public policy process. *Higher Education Handbook of Theory and Research*, 27(4), 57–143.

Neave, G., and van Vught, F. (1991) *Prometheus bound*. London: Pergamon Press.

Oba, J. (2010) Governance of the incorporated Japanese national universities. In K. Mok (Ed.), *The search for new governance of higher education in Asia*, pp. 85–102. London: Palgrave.

OECD (2007) *Instruments mixes for environmental policy*. Paris: OECD.

OECD (2010) *OECD science, technology and industry outlook 2010*. Paris: OECD.

Olssen, M., and Peters, A. (2005) Neoliberalism, higher education and the knowledge economy: From the free market to knowledge capitalism. *Journal of Education Policy*, 20(3), 313–345.

Orton, D., and Weick, K. E. (1990) Loosely coupled system: A reconceptualization. *Academy of Management Review*, 15(2), 203–223.

Paradeise, C., Reale, E., Bleiklie, I., and Ferlie, E. (Eds) (2009) *University governance: Western European comparative perspectives*. Dordrecht: Springer.

Phidd, R., and Doern, G. B. (Eds) (1983) *Canadian public policy: Ideas, structure, process*. Toronto: Methuen.

Rhee, B.-S. (2010) Incorporation of national universities of Korea: Dynamic forces, key features, and challenges. In K. Mok (Ed.), *The search for new governance of higher education in Asia*, pp. 67–84. London: Palgrave.

Ring, I., and Schröter-Schlack, C. (Eds) (2012) Instrument mixes for biodiversity policies. *POLICYMIX Report*, Issue No. 2/2011.

Salamon, L. M. (2002) *The tools of government: A guide to the new governance*. New York: Oxford University Press.

Schon, D. A. (1971) *Beyond the stable state*. New York: Random House.

Shattock, M. L. (Ed.) (2014) *International trends in university governance*. London: Routledge.

Shin, J. C. (Ed.) (2018) *Higher education governance in Asia*. Dordrecht: Springer.

Sorrel, S., and Sijm, J. (2003) Carbon trading in the policy mix. *Oxford Review of Economic Policy*, 19(3), 420–437.

Stroick, S., and Jenson, J. (1999) *What is the best policy mix for Canada's young children?* Study no. F-09. Ottawa: Canadian Policy Research Network.

Trakman, L. (2008) Modelling university governance. *Higher Education Quarterly*, 62 (1–2), 63–83.

Trow, M. (1974) *Problems in the transition from elite to mass higher education.* Paris: OECD.

Van Vught, F. (Ed.) (1989) *Governmental strategies and innovation in higher education.* London: Jessica Kingsley.

Varghese, N. V. (2007) *GATS and higher education: The need for regulatory policies.* Paris: International Institute of Educational Planning.

Varghese, N. (2015) *Reshaping higher education in Asia: The role of private sector.* Singapore: The Head Foundation.

Vedung, E. (1998) Policy instruments: Typologies and theories. In M. L. Bemelmans-Videc, R. C. Rist, and E. Vedung (Eds), *Carrots, sticks, and sermons: Policy instruments and their evaluation*, pp. 21–58. New Brunswick: Transaction.

Weick, K. E. (1976) Educational organizations as loosely coupled systems. *Administrative Science Quarterly*, 21(1), 1–19.

Wende, van der, M. (2017) Opening up: higher education systems in global perspective. London: Centre for Global Higher Education, UCL Institute of Education. Working paper no. 22.

Yang, R., Vidovich, L., and Currie, J. (2007) Dancing in a cage: Changing autonomy in Chinese higher education. *Higher Education*, 54(4), 575–592.

4 Institutional Governance

Factors, Actors, and Consequences of Attempting to Converge on the Anglo–American Model

MARINO REGINI

In this chapter I will analyse the factors, actors, and consequences of the changes in institutional governance that have taken place in European universities in the last 30 years. These changes are often described as an incremental process of convergence, with higher education (HE) institutions in continental Europe increasingly assuming characteristics associated with the Anglo–American model of university governance. Although national reforms of HE governance have been conducted independently, they have nevertheless been based on similar assumptions and have largely shared the same goals. This is why, in a very general sense, the governance reforms undertaken in continental Europe may be seen as repeated attempts to converge towards what is generally regarded as the most successful HE model – namely, the Anglo–American one.

The view that the European HE systems are becoming increasingly uniform is supported by various versions of the 'theory of convergence' of social institutions within the advanced economies (Kerr, 1983). Yet a convergence of goals does not necessarily imply convergent trajectories to achieve those goals. And a convergence of attempts does not necessarily mean converging results. What recent reforms of the governance of European HE systems have tried to achieve is an increased convergence of different universities' institutional features and behaviour. In a general context of policy convergence, governments have tried to force their universities to adopt similar institutional and organizational forms. However, although inspired by the same common template – the Anglo–American university governance model, actively promoted by the EU (European Commission, 2006) – national strategies have clearly interpreted this template according to their inherited legacies. This has made the convergence process more problematic. National reforms have been elaborated and implemented by the universities' internal actors – with their power resources, culture, learning abilities – which have acted as 'filters' vis-à-vis the planned reforms (Capano and Regini, 2014). Even more importantly, this has meant that the consequences of national reforms of university governance have largely differed from the expected results (Regini, 2015).

This chapter is organized as follows. First, I will address a few preliminary questions. Is there anything like an 'Anglo–American model' of HE governance? If so, to what extent can we speak of attempts at 'convergence' on such a model by continental European universities, and to what extent do the actual trajectories of change differ in the various European HE systems? Also, what are the main objectives and directions of change? I will then turn to the different factors of change of institutional governance, assessing their respective explanatory power. This will be followed by a brief discussion of the role of the main internal and external actors in changing institutional governance. Finally, I will analyse the unintended consequences of university governance reforms and will propose a few factors that can account for such unexpected outcomes.

The focus of the analysis will be on changes in institutional (or internal) governance, although these changes can often be understood only in relation to specific aspects of systemic (or external) governance,[1] such as university autonomy, competition, and assessment. In fact, it is on changes in systemic governance that most HE scholars tend to focus. In the words of Ferlie et al. (2009, p. 6), 'most publications analysing how HE systems work and are transformed pay exclusive attention to the state–universities relationships'. Yet, these authors continue, 'the content of recent public policies most likely consist in reconfiguring the status, internal structures, governing bodies, field of responsibilities, decision-making processes, and scope of action of HE institutions'.

4.1 Attempts to Converge: On What and to What Extent?

4.1.1 The Anglo–American Model

The United Kingdom and the United States have two very different HE systems in terms of the role of the state, public/private composition, type of internal differentiation, etc. Yet, in terms of institutional governance, changes that have taken place in the United States are not too dissimilar from the 'liberalization plus managerialism' that has characterized the British HE system over the last 30 years. Schulze-Cleven and Olson (2017) see the American 'trajectory of corporatization' as a combination of three main trends: a decline in the public funding of universities based on number of students enrolled, the increased participation in the HE sector of for-profit providers supported by public authorities, and the adoption by public universities of governance and management styles similar to those of for-profit providers.

The first two trends – and especially the shrinking of resources provided by the state – fostered a transformation of the American HE system that, in the widely used typology of institutional change provided by Streeck and Thelen (2005), would be termed 'institutional drift and conversion'. This has paved the way for the third trend. The for-profit providers' practices – from the organization of education delivery to human resource management – have become a benchmark for all American HE institutions. Similarly, growth in the number of managers has occurred at a much faster pace than faculty positions across all types of public institutions (Schulze-Cleven and Olson, 2017).

In the United Kingdom, the HE system was traditionally based on a large degree of autonomy of individual universities that were not regulated by general laws except for common frameworks on a few matters such as salaries. Universities were financed by a funding agency that, until 1986, planned distributive block grants in a highly conservative manner. Internally, the universities drew on a large administrative apparatus, but did not conceive of themselves as organizations with their own strategies. Internal distribution of power was based on the pre-eminent role of professors and on collegial decisions. This changed in 1985, when the Jarrett Report repudiated academic collegiality and election of vice-chancellors as the governing rules of universities: the United Kingdom thus became the first European country to offer individual universities the possibility to appoint a CEO type of leader (Paradeise et al., 2009a).

More generally, the United Kingdom has been the frontrunner in the reform of both systemic and institutional governance, moving towards a vision of universities as 'corporate enterprises' and towards new models of verticalized governance. This means that HE in the United

Kingdom is now strictly managed and market driven (Ferlie et al., 2009). A continuous process of reform characterized by a series of official reports that followed the 1985 Jarrett Report (e.g. the Dearing Report in 1997 and the Lambert Report in 2003), focusing in particular on the question of governance, led to the redesigning of the overall framework of the United Kingdom's HE policy. Although universities have preserved their formal status as self-governing bodies (with the exception of the former polytechnics, whose institutional governance was established by a law passed in 1992), increasing governmental pressure has led to the substantial verticalization of the internal decision-making process, and thus to a weakening of the self-governing academic bodies' collegial power (Capano and Regini, 2014). Governmental pressure has encouraged universities to strengthen their 'steering core' through the internal verticalization of power (Middlehurst, 2004) and a process of substantial reorganization. As a result, internal governance has undergone significant changes, through the reinforcement of a managerial mode of governance and the shift from a private to a state-driven approach (Shattock, 2008).

4.1.2 Objectives and Directions of Change in the Governance of European Universities

In the last 20 years or so, most continental European countries have attempted to converge on these Anglo–American trends by reforming both the systemic and the institutional governance of their universities. This has involved a major process of transformation, as the traditional model rooted in these countries was at odds with the principles and objectives that informed the governance of American and British universities. In continental Europe, HE systems were regulated by a number of laws defining detailed substantive rules implemented by the relevant ministries. Both resource allocation and organizational decisions were made by central bureaus in the ministry, without taking the individual universities' specific circumstances into account. As to the universities themselves, they were not asked to make strategic decisions but were seen as administrative bodies, although professors usually enjoyed a high degree of individual autonomy. Degrees and curricula were nationally defined, and universities were usually not responsible for most financial and human resource decisions.

The key features of institutional governance in this traditional model were collegiality, consensual (often collusive) decision making, and distributive outcomes. The internal structure of university governance reflected its organizational weakness: at each organizational level (university, faculty, department), appointed administrative staff shared the floor with elected academic leaders. Neither party had much strategic capacity, with both lacking the tools of strategic decision makers. Consequently, leadership functions were usually restricted to representation and internal consensus building across disciplinary fields. Rather than a CEO heading a big organization, the rector was a sort of 'institutional integrator' among colleagues, a primus inter pares using status resources rather than a functional position to lend academic legitimacy to university decisions (Paradeise et al., 2009a). These decisions were taken by the academic oligarchy, often in direct interaction with the ministry, and ratified by an executive board.

In the 1970s other groups, such as non-permanent teaching and research staff, students, and non-academic personnel, gained some formal rights of participation, but the dominant position of the professors was not shaken. This 'democratization' of the universities – namely, the involvement of all internal actors in university governance – had the effect of adding more bureaucracy and never-ending meetings at which no decisions were taken at all. Partly for this reason, this 'democratic revolution' gave way in the following decades to a 'corporate enterprise model' of university governance.

This process of change has been described by various authors, who highlight different aspects of the transformation of both systemic and institutional governance. Some of them focus on major policy changes that have taken place over recent decades in areas such as the rise of quality assessment and accreditation (Musselin and Teixeira, 2014; Schwarz and Westerheijden, 2004) or on transformations in the structure and modes of funding (Amaral et al., 2002; Meek et al., 2010). Others highlight different types of policies: the facilitation and freeing of market forces by the adoption of competitive mechanisms for the allocation of government support for universities; empowering users by mandating the provision of academic quality information to students as well as by increasing utilization of tuition fees for university funding; and specifying contractual relations between government and the universities by tying research funding to clearly defined indicators of university output (Dill, 2014). Finally, a further group of authors point to the fact that, starting in 1997 in the Netherlands, university leaders have increasingly become accountable no longer to an elected university council but to a board of trustees. In countries such as France and Italy the elective model remained unquestioned, yet even there, presidential power has been gradually strengthened (Paradeise et al., 2009a). In Germany, too, the formal strengthening of managerial governance started in the 1990s, with an increase in the decision-making competencies of rectors and deans in all states. Thus, academic self-governance has indeed been formally weakened (Schimank and Lange, 2009).

This turn towards a 'corporate enterprise model' of institutional governance has several objectives, which in continental Europe have been carried out by the state. We highlight four main components of this model (Regini, 2015):

a) Verticalization of decision-making processes. The objective is to enhance the efficiency of universities through a strong leadership, insulated from veto powers and spoils-system practices. This objective explains why all the national reforms have attributed crucial functions of strategic management to the rector/president/vice chancellor. Some of these reforms go so far as to assume that the rector is chosen on the basis of managerial capacity and not on the basis of the consensus that s/he enjoys; and the same assumption applies to the heads of the intermediate structures (deans or department chairs), increasingly seen as the rector's partners in the university's governance.

b) Openness to the external world. The goal here is not only to promote greater transparency in the management of universities and to make them better tuned to the needs of the economy and society, but also to draw on abilities that have been developed in corporate organizational contexts, which are presumed to be more efficient. This entails the allocation of decision-making functions concerning the budget, and, more generally, supervision/control of the work of the rector's office, to a relatively small body (board of governors) in which members external to the university have a significant weight and role, and counterbalance the greater executive powers of the rector.

c) Disempowerment of the self-governing bodies. The collegial body traditionally representative of the academic community (e.g. the

academic senate) is increasingly assigned only consultative functions, mostly limited to the management of teaching and research.
This process often extends to the collective bodies representing the
intermediate structures (faculty councils).

d) Rationalization of the university's structures or organizational
units. This implies a more precise allocation of responsibilities to
faculties, departments, and schools in order to introduce a simple
and consistent organizational model by embedding them more
closely in the overall organization. A further purpose of rationalization is to achieve economies of scale and a well-defined chain of
responsibility.

If we take these four components together, we might say that they
aim at modifying the nature of universities as loosely coupled systems through the tightening of the internal decision-making process,
not by means of bureaucratic rules and procedures, but by redistri-
buting power, roles, and competencies, and by moving towards
a more managerial organizational model based on a functional hierarchy. Universities are asked to become 'organizational actors'
(Krücken and Meier, 2006) capable of behaving strategically
(Whitley, 2008).

4.1.3 Differences in the Design and the Implementation of Reforms

European governments' HE policies have tried to converge towards
a common template of systemic governance – that is, the 'steering from
a distance' model (Kickert, 1997; Neave and van Vught, 1991; van
Vught, 1989). To pursue this strategy, as noted, European governments
have adapted the institutional governance arrangements of their universities, which according to Clark's (1983) typology belong to the
Continental governance model,[2] to the model of the English-speaking
countries. They have fostered more institutional leadership, more managerial steering, and fewer collegial decisions. This process, strongly
supported by the European Union, has entailed a significant break with
tradition. Although national reforms of HE governance have been conducted independently, they have been based on similar assumptions and
have largely shared the same goals, leading to the perception that the
governance reforms undertaken in continental Europe represent an

attempt to converge towards the Anglo–American model (Capano and Regini, 2014).

However, Paradeise et al. (2009a, p. 218) argue that 'it is tempting but probably wrong to infer from similar trends towards autonomy, rational management, and control that reform outcomes result from implementation of identical ideas, the theoretical and operational model of which would have been provided by the UK'. In fact, they maintain, communication between national university systems was quite poor as recently as the beginning of the 1980s. Each system tended to see the problems it faced as specific problems, rather than as manifestations of more general trends. Foreign experiences were either ignored or rejected as inadequate. So, while the repertoire of reform instruments might appear to be shared between all European governments, 'this does not mean that they spread by benchmarking or diffusion of good practices. It is only ex post that we can evoke a "repertoire", since it did not necessarily exist as such before being called up to face local issues' (2009a, p. 218).

Be this as it may, there is no doubt that all European HE systems have been exposed to largely similar pressures for change. But have the responses to these pressures been equally uniform? Or have Europe's universities responded to the common challenges in different ways? This is of course a key question addressed by several contributions to this volume (see, for example, Chapters 3, 5, 8, and 10). As already noted, the view that the responses of national HE systems have grown more uniform – through mechanisms of isomorphism, explicit imitation of best practices, or organizational learning via trial and error – is supported by the various versions of a 'theory of convergence' of social institutions within the advanced economies. This theory, which periodically reappears in the social sciences, holds that external challenges and pressures for change are so powerful that they drastically reduce the likelihood of any alternative responses. All convergence theories are underpinned by the idea that the modernization of institutions must follow established paths, essentially dictated by exogenous factors (Kerr, 1983). Although pre-existing institutional arrangements, as well as 'loser' groups, may offer some resistance, all they really manage to do is to delay the course of history.

As far as HE is concerned, however, convergence theories run the risk of reductionism when assuming that a general policy strategy, or a national law reforming universities' institutional governance, can directly determine the meso-/micro-level outcomes in a homogeneous way. If we focus on individual institutions and not just on national systems, we can get a better understanding of the interaction between external pressures and internal institutional features, and we can better evaluate the actual ways in which universities respond to external pressures for change. The expected changes are interpreted, elaborated, and implemented by the internal governance arrangements, which 'filter' the planned reforms. Hence, despite a series of common national policy goals and reform strategies, important differences persist, grounded not only in the national interpretation of the common policy template that governments wanted to pursue, but also in the different institutional trajectories and internal dynamics. The eventual outcome in terms of institutional governance and organization is influenced by pre-existing internal governance styles and by the behaviour of the internal actors in question. More precisely, the differences in the design of reforms may be due to path dependency or to the role played by different actors in different national contexts. On the other hand, the differences in implementation are usually due to policy legacies, to the various degrees of resistance that the actors concerned may raise, or to the unintended consequences of reforms that, for contingent reasons, appear more clearly in some contexts than in others.

These observations can be accommodated within a neo-institutionalist framework. Neo-institutionalism comes in numerous guises (DiMaggio and Powell, 1983; Hall and Taylor, 1996; Mahoney and Thelen, 2010; North, 1990; Williamson, 1985). The basic idea, however, is that pre-existing institutions play a key role in shaping responses to exogenous factors by acting as a filter or intervening variable between external pressures and the responses to them. The pre-existing institutional context, in fact, provides actors with a set of resources and constraints which they must necessarily take into account when choosing among different alternatives, and which consequently shape their actions. The strong influence of legacies is precisely what makes institutional change necessarily adaptive. Change can take a variety of forms, such as 'displacement, layering, drift, conversion, or exhaustion' (Streeck and Thelen, 2005, pp. 19–30 [qt. p. 24]). Since the institutional context varies from one country to the next, rooted as it is in their diverse histories, the neo-institutionalist perspective has no difficulty in recognizing, and accounting for, the divergent responses to common challenges: different options are pursued because the pre-existing institutions, and their role in mediating the impact and direction of change, are different.

So, what appears at first sight as a striking convergence between European countries actually covers a great variety of implementation processes, in terms of the rate and pace of change as well as in terms of path dependence of national patterns (Paradeise et al., 2009a). Whether or not they were inspired by the same common template – the English-speaking HE systems' governance model – European national reforms have clearly interpreted the 'common policy strategy' according to their inherited legacies. Although all countries have opted for similar policy instruments (greater institutional autonomy, stronger institutional governance, increased competition for funding and students, greater reliance on assessment and evaluation), the national policy strategies have combined these common policy tools in different policy mixes, according to their past legacies and traditions. These variations are expected to affect the governmental design of the reform of institutional governance in universities, and to significantly influence the set of constraints upon the institutional behaviour of the universities.

Furthermore, national reforms have to be implemented, and thus their outcome is in the hands of the very target of the reforms – that is, the universities themselves. Despite the fact that they share the same traditions, differences can emerge even between universities within the same country, and thus their interpretation of the 'common policy strategy' may well differ. Not only may universities within the same country belong to different types, their traditional internal dynamics, specific institutional cultures, and legacies may significantly influence the process of change itself. The provision of reform laws, or the features of governmental policies, influence but do not determine the nature of the relationship between external pressures, institutional type, and internal political-cultural factors. Hence, we may expect to find significant differences in the organizational effects of national reforms and of external pressure for change, not only at the national level but also at the level of individual universities (Capano and Regini, 2014).

Finally, even the new traits of institutional governance that we find in all European universities and that differ most markedly from the traditional arrangements of 20 or 30 years ago do not appear stable, as 'reforms continue everywhere' (Paradeise et al., 2009b, p. 227). Or, in the words of Schimank and Lange (2009, p. 66), 'the university system was forced out of its old equilibrium without having found a stable new one. As a result, the picture drawn here might be a snapshot that does not cover events and developments that may happen tomorrow.'

4.2 Factors of Change of Institutional Governance

The literature that discusses the factors behind change of institutional governance tends to focus on two broad types of factors: on the one hand, the role of ideas, paradigms, narratives, and, more specifically, of the set of assumptions and prescriptions that are known as New Public Management (NPM); and on the other, the role of interests and of power relations among the actors, stakeholders, and interest groups concerned.

While these are undoubtedly key factors of change, I maintain that the specific directions that change has taken in the last 20 years or so can be better understood if a further factor is taken into account. This is what we may call the failure or unsustainability of the previous institutional arrangements. This failure can help to explain the lack, or at least the weakness, of alternative ideas to challenge the hegemony of NPM recipes even when it becomes clear that these recipes have major shortcomings or unintended consequences. This failure may also account for the dramatic shifts in power relations and for the relatively weak opposition by the 'losers' of the process – that is, the individual and collective actors whose roles are diminished in the new configuration of institutional governance.

4.2.1 The Role of Ideas: The Diffusion and the Limits of NPM

The rationales underlying changes in European HE systems have been the subject of significant debate, with many authors pointing to the influence of NPM recipes to explain the reforms in higher education and research. For Musselin and Teixeira (2014), however, these interpretations are convincing at an aggregated level but are not backed up by empirical data and more precise analysis.

Some authors have suggested that the rationales which were mobilized to push for changes, and the rhetoric used to make sense of these changes, can be linked to two main narratives of public service reform: New Public Management, and Network Governance (Ferlie et al., 2009). However, only the first one is fully spelled out to show how it could influence HE reforms. In this view, the NPM relies on three things: (1) markets (or quasi markets) rather than planning; (2) strong performance measurement, monitoring, and management systems, with a growth of audit systems rather than tacit or self-regulation; and (3) empowered and entrepreneurial management rather than collegial public sector professionals and administrators.

It has been noted that the post-war European welfare states, especially those characterized as 'universalistic' (Esping-Andersen, 1990), did not develop the notion of evaluating public investments by measuring their returns. The idea of linking investments and returns in education and research was a new phenomenon that emerged during the 1980s, together with the idea of correlating education supply with the needs of the economic system: 'Indeed, the increasing influence of rational choice theories, translated in the public sector as New Public Management, led analysts to consider continental European universities of the 1980s as loosely coupled professional bureaucracies (Weick, 1976) lacking major properties of formal organizations such as strong principal–agent relationships' (Paradeise et al., 2009a, p. 203).

A number of more general assumptions have also been identified that formed a background to the reforms carried out in the last 20 years and that were widely shared even by scholars and policy makers who were not sympathetic to the NPM prescriptions. First, and most widespread, is the assumption that competition among independent organizations is superior to state monopolies as a means of achieving the social benefits of increased innovation and efficiency. But, as Dill (2014) suggests, two further assumptions are also relevant: the public choice assumption that rational user choice is more efficient than government bureaucracy as a means of controlling the rent-seeking behaviour of government-supported organizations; and the principal–agent assumption that transaction costs, including monitoring the self-interested behaviour of professionals, can be minimized through better specified contracts.

4.2.2 The Role of Actors' Interests and Power Relations

The second factor that is commonly referred to in explaining recent changes in university governance is the transformation of power relations among the main HE actors with their different interests. A major problem with this explanation, however, is that the various actors of

HE systems have not just different, but often also internally contra-dictory, interests.

- Governments have a 'structural' interest to improve the performance of their HE systems in order to increase both the competitive advantage of their economies and the employability of their citizens. But they must, at the same time, contain the enormous growth of public expenditure entailed by mass university systems and the cost of basic research.
- Universities and other HE institutions, when designing curricula, must take into account the demands for skills coming from the economic system and especially from the local context. But they must, at the same time, consider the types of scientific specialization of their faculty, so as to exploit their strengths in the competition with other HE institutions.
- Academic oligarchies may resist institutional change, seeing it as an attack on their prerogatives and routines, or on traditional values of the scientific community, or even on the need for high-quality education independent from external demands. But they may also appreciate the modernization of educational methods and the closer links with the labour market that go with it; and some faculty members can even welcome the chance to pursue their own interests as 'academic capitalists' (Amaral et al., 2003) outside their institutions.
- Students and their families could potentially benefit from a modernization and rationalization of the educational supply which is geared towards improving employability in the labour market for graduates. But this potential benefit may not materialize, as the 'democratization' of access to tertiary education also increases competition for highly qualified jobs, leading to an 'inflation of credentials' (Collins, 1979). Also, families often try to contain the costs of enrolling their children in higher education institutions, an attempt which contradicts their demand for better quality from such institutions.
- Finally, firms usually demand a type of training and research strictly related to their specific needs. But they may also recognize the desirability of a wider repertoire of knowledge beyond what is needed immediately, as this may be a condition for helping innovation.

In short, the role played by each of these actors and stakeholders in the transformation of institutional governance cannot be simply deduced from their own interests, as these are not unambiguous and are susceptible to modification by external factors or through interaction (Regini, 2011).

That said, the most urgent need to change university governance and the most powerful pressures to undertake such reform have come from the interest of governments of any colour who face the rising costs – financial and organizational – of the massification of their HE systems. As a consequence of these costs, spending per student has decreased. The problem was exacerbated in the 1990s with the emergence in Europe of the notion of knowledge-based economies, putting higher education at the very core of engines of economic dynamism:

The tension between the increasing perceived role of higher education as a source of competitive strength for knowledge-based societies and the ineluctable decrease of per capita public investment in higher education was to be solved by reorganizing the national system of higher education and research to do things better, quicker and at lower costs, and to differentiate missions between HE institutions. (Paradeise et al., 2009a, pp. 199–200)

In terms of power relations between the relevant HE actors, the main trends during this period were the collapse of the academic communities' power, as the growth in their numbers undermined their role as oligarchies, and the increase in the influence of external stakeholders. Again, the advent of a knowledge-based economy, and the rhetoric surrounding the 'Lisbon strategy' launched by the European Council in March 2000, reinforced these trends. They highlighted an interest by external actors in the utilization of HE products (human capital and research results) to an extent previously unknown. For university administrations and academic communities, a new trade-off thus emerged between the chance to increase the employability of their graduates and to partly compensate for reduced state funding, on the one hand, and the risk of losing control over processes of knowledge creation, use, and transmission on the other. A less oligarchic and less cohesive academic community felt forced to somehow redefine its values and objectives, as well as to integrate its traditional teaching and research duties with a plethora of new organizational and service-provision roles. More generally, the traditional values of academic communities, university administrations, and states were often superseded by managerial–entrepreneurial considerations that infiltrated these actors' behaviour to varying degrees. A divergence between traditional models of governance of HE institutions and the new needs of the sector became apparent everywhere (Regini, 2011).

4.2.3 The Failure/Unsustainability of the Previous Governance Arrangements

Ideas, interests, and power relations are undoubtedly key factors of change. However, we may assume that the NPM ideas on changing institutional governance could have become less hegemonic, and the academic communities could have exercised a far greater influence in effecting this change, if the traditional governance arrangements had not repeatedly shown their severe limitations. In what follows I will try to briefly substantiate this assumption.

In all continental European countries, HE had traditionally developed as a sector of public administration ruled by laws and central norms but actually governed by academic oligarchies. The traditional distribution of power in academic systems was termed 'collegial', but the reality has often been described as a sort of 'co-optation oligarchy'. The well-known problems of such collegial governance were conflicts of interests, amateurism, unclear attribution of responsibilities, and decisional inefficiency. 'Even though external pressures to some extent succeed imposing managerialism, the traditional assets of power within the oligarchies are simply reshuffled and reconstructed in order to minimize the changes' (Marini and Reale, 2016, p. 112). Collegialism, it has been argued, developed as a sort of zero-sum game, where power was exercised by influential senior chairs and other dominant individuals in an oligarchy of guilds and fiefdoms (Trowler, 2010). As a consequence, institutional governance in continental European universities has continued to be largely based on a spoils system, often leading to collusive decisions rather than selective ones and to situations of stalemate when external challenges required more radical change.

On the other hand, attempts to ensure the 'democratic revitalization' of pathological and over-bureaucratized forms of public administration within the university context suggested strong stakeholder participation in the governance of the institution. This took different forms. Some countries (Germany, the Netherlands) passed new laws and created university boards consisting partly or exclusively of non-university members, expected to play the role of the American board of trustees and to set priorities, approve the budget, etc. Other countries, such as the United Kingdom, introduced non-academic members in their national research councils (Ferlie et al., 2009). Again, the problem was exacerbated in the 1990s with the emergence in Europe of the notion of a knowledge-based economy. This new vision of the social and economic role of higher education in society coincided with the perception that it was unable to answer the labour market's needs. This led to the emerging idea that the HE institutions might be used more effectively as policy instruments in this connection (Paradeise et al., 2009a).

Overall, the sense of the failure of university governance to stand up to old problems and new challenges became so widespread that an alternative type of institutional arrangement was generally regarded as necessary by political élites that often were not even aware of NPM recipes. Quite simply, the previous arrangements seemed no longer sustainable and the obvious alternative was to look at forms of institutional governance that seemed appropriate to the new situation.

4.3 Relevant Actors and Types of Action

4.3.1 The Traditional Actors

In the traditional type of university governance that characterized continental European countries up to the 1980s, the only two relevant actors were the state on the one hand and the academic communities on the other.[3] Universities were just 'loosely coupled organizations' unable to pursue institutional strategies beyond those of their professors, and key stakeholders such as students or firms were seen as merely passive users. The concept of a 'market' for HE had no actual room for application, because the market can only operate where the supply of goods or services is oriented towards a demand, and exchanges are based on prices determined by the interaction of such supply and demand. This was not the case in the traditional European university. In that institution, the 'goods supplied' were the production of culture and knowledge through research, and the transmission of this culture – and the values and lifestyles which accompanied it – to the national élites who could access it and who had been socialized to it. The almost exclusive 'producers' of this particular type of goods were (academic) communities which acted on the basis of norms and values shared among themselves. They were regulated by the state, which set the rules and standards for their recognition but delegated the definition of their objectives to the institutions. The organization of the supply of such goods was thus left to the self-regulation of the academic communities, within limits and at 'prices' fixed by the state.

Furthermore, not only was the supply not organized in relation to a demand, but no real demand existed – or at least, it would be difficult to identify the bearers of such a demand, capable of orienting the supply and influencing the terms of trade. First, a diffuse demand for higher education in the sense that is understood today did not exist. The very limited segment of the youth population who enrolled in the universities (usually less than 10–15 per cent of the relevant age cohort) wanted to acquire the credentials to access the professions or the technical and managerial positions which required that level of education, and had little reason to worry about the correspondence between the content of their studies and their future occupational roles. Their families, like the enterprises, the public administrations, and the professional associations, focused on the credentials and thus on the status which could be acquired within the social stratification system, rather than on the content and methods of education, set by the academic communities within a general regulatory framework provided by the state.

Second, the demand for 'social appropriation' of the results of research carried out in the universities was very weak and dispersed. A Fordist production system such as that prevailing in Europe based its competitiveness on the mass production of standard goods and on low labour costs, rather than on constant product and process innovation that depended in a crucial way on research. The laboratories of the large enterprises were mostly sufficient for their own needs, while university research did not respond, except in particular cases, to specific demands advanced by the production system.

To summarize, in the traditional HE systems, education and research were conceived of not so much as specific goods 'supplied' by an organization (the university) in response to an articulated demand, but rather as public goods whose production was financed and regulated by the state but entirely delegated to academic communities, which were the sole depositories of the know-how necessary to decide how to organize this production. From this also derived the traditional governance models of the universities of continental Europe, often described as sets of lecturers organized into faculties headed by a minister.

4.3.2 'New' Actors Enter the Scene

Such a traditional HE structure was destabilized only when other parties besides the state and the academic community were recognized as legitimate actors by the latter and hence acquired some degree of power or influence. The first such 'new' actor is the individual university, as an organization endowed with its own interests, distinct from those of the academic communities within it, and with enough autonomy from the state to pursue these interests, even in competition with each other. The existence of autonomous universities, which appears to be taken for granted today, was what differentiated the HE systems of the Anglo–American world from those of continental Europe until relatively recently. In the latter, it was only in the 1980s and 1990s that the granting by the state of some managerial autonomy – though often limited and partial – to the universities enabled them to become subjects with interests distinct from the academic communities and from the state. This process has been described as 'turning the university into an organizational actor' (Krücken and Meier, 2006. See also De Boer et al., 2007; Musselin, 2006; Whitley, 2008).

The shift from administrative bodies to strategic actors requires the strengthening of individual universities' internal steering capabilities. A common feature in all countries is the promotion of strategic planning at the level of individual universities, most often as a basis for negotiating the allocation of resources. By making plans compulsory before budgetary negotiations, ministries have stimulated identity assertion by universities (Paradeise et al., 2009a).

Patterns of decision making within universities have thus clearly evolved. They reflect the emergence of universities as collective actors and their increasing institutional autonomy (Berdahl, 1990). Of course, this autonomy is criticized: strategic plans are easier to write than to implement, and although more decisions are made, they are generally more incremental than radical (Musselin and Paradeise, 2009). Nevertheless, all this has made possible (though not necessarily effective) the adoption by university administrations of a logic of action different from the previous one, which was limited to making agreements between the academic communities, and to the bureaucratic management of the funds provided and the rules dictated by the state.

Hence, the first 'new' actor was the individual university acquiring an identity and the ability to pursue its organizational interests autonomously. But in the same time period, two other key groups acquired awareness of their collective identity as legitimate actors in the HE system, or were recognized as performing such a role by the state: the potential students and their families on the one hand, and enterprises on the other. Obviously, these actors have always existed, but it is only when they start being conceived as bearers of interests (stakeholders) in the HE system, or when they are invited to elaborate and articulate a coherent 'demand' for the products and the functioning of such HE systems, that universities are induced to enter an exchange relationship with them. It is in these situations that a market logic can, at least theoretically, become relevant in both the reorganization of the traditional functions of universities (teaching and research) and their modes of operation and management (provision of services to students and enterprises, management of their funds, assessment mechanisms, governance structures, etc.) (Regini, 2011).

4.4 The Unintended Consequences of Institutional Governance Reforms

According to Musselin and Teixeira (2014), there are three different but complementary ways of looking at reforms. The first is to be attentive to their evolution, to identify their internal contradictions, the redefinitions and the reorientations they experience. The second is to look at their implementation in a comparative way. The third and final way is described thus:

[A]nother major issue when analyzing policy reforms in higher education refers to the frequent contrast between expected and actual results. Higher education is particularly well known for being a traditionally complex field to be reformed, and higher education institutions have a reputation for resistance to change and subversion of policy initiatives, mainly due to the strong devolution of power to lower levels of the institution. (Musselin and Teixeira, 2014, p. 12)

I believe that this last way of looking at reforms – namely, the 'contrast between expected and actual results' – is by far the most fruitful for understanding actual change in institutional governance. I will, therefore, focus on the unintended consequences of recent reforms of university governance in Europe, and will then try to understand why the production of such unintended consequences tends to be the rule in all European HE systems.[4]

Various strands of literature in the social sciences have highlighted how top-down change processes, such as the reforms of university governance in Europe, inevitably produce effects somewhat different from those expected. Those who are subject to the change but have not been involved in the reform design tend to put up resistance and to deploy their power or cognitive resources in order to blunt the most disruptive effects of the change. Cerych and Sabatier (1986), for instance, examine a series of university reforms conducted in Europe in the 1970s to understand the factors behind policy success or policy failure. On the basis of these findings they conclude that higher education reforms may succeed, but they highlight the forces that work against reforms: the most powerful of these forces is the capacity of various groups to mobilize resistance against the introduction of a reform.

However, I maintain that it is more interesting – besides being more original – to focus on the unintended consequences of governance reforms in the Mertonian meaning of outcomes that are not the ones anticipated by the actors. In his seminal article on the 'unanticipated consequences of purposive social action', Merton (1936) was not dealing with the obvious and often widespread resistance and obstacles to 'purposive social action', but with how this action is designed by actors who do not fully anticipate its consequences for one of the following reasons: ignorance stemming from the existing state of knowledge; error; immediacy of interests, namely exclusive concern with short-term effects of action; or basic values that lead to an action irrespective of its long-term results. In Merton's analytical framework, therefore, it is cognitive limits, value orientations, and the shortcomings of rationality that account for the unintended outcomes of reforms, even in the absence of significant resistance to them. Moreover, these unforeseen consequences are not necessarily undesirable: in fact, they may be unexpected benefits as much as unexpected drawbacks.

Reforms of HE governance are no exception to the type of 'purposive social action' that produces important unanticipated consequences, but to date little attention has been paid to this aspect. In what follows I will, therefore, focus my analysis on this. If set in relation to the four main components of the corporate enterprise model described earlier, we may highlight the following unintended consequences:

- The resilience of self-government. Undermining the self-government of collegial bodies does not remove the need for the expertise of academics when decisions are to be taken and strategies devised. Nor does it affect the 'resilience' of a culture and practice of self-government typical of the academic community. This need and this resilience produce unintended consequences that can be summarized as the emergence of new forums for discussion (or the strengthening of old ones) between the university executive and representatives of the academic staff, which work as functional substitutes for the self-governing bodies that have been dramatically weakened. In some countries, these forums consist of institutionalized meetings between rector and deans or department directors. In other countries they more often take the form of a number of advisory or preparatory committees (specified in the university statutes or established ad hoc), which draw on the expertise of academics. Finally, informal relational and consultative networks come to the fore. Of course, networks of this kind have always existed, but they assume new importance precisely where the old collegiate bodies (senate, faculty council) have been most disempowered.
- The weakness of governing boards with lay members. At best, the obvious lack of internal knowledge by the external members of the boards of governors tends to cause difficulties in the effective functioning of those bodies. But at many universities this has an even more damaging unintended consequence: the bodies comprising external members – to whom the reformers assigned the role of supervising and counterbalancing the executive (the rectorate) by leveraging their economic and social role – are often 'captured' by the very same executive bodies over which they are supposed to exercise supervision and control.
- The emergence of a collective leadership. If a 'rector leader' is to fulfil the crucial strategic management functions deriving from the verticalization of decision-making processes, s/he needs a team more stable and better able to work as a group compared with the collaborators of the former 'primus inter pares rector', who were usually assigned only specific tasks. All the reforms conceive the rector as an individual leader in charge of a formally monocratic role, but they design a set of key functions that in practice require a collective

leadership. The role assumed by the rector's team has the unintended and 'beneficial' consequence of attenuating the problem of the dependence of the university's governance on the personal characteristics of an individual leader, so that the decisions taken by the executive are more shared and less random.

- The fluctuations between centralization and decentralization. Finally, rationalization of organizational structures has had temporary positive effects, but at the same time it has revived unresolved organizational dilemmas which the old model of governance had remedied with compromises. To what extent can the university executive decentralize functions and responsibilities to the internal units in order to involve them in the overall organization, and to what extent should it instead centralize them so as to obtain standard performances? The resurgence of these dilemmas has the unforeseen consequence of a frequent oscillation between decentralization and centralization, which seems to contradict the pursuit by universities of a coherent pattern of reorganization.

These unexpected outcomes are evidenced, to varying extents and in different ways, by many universities in different European countries. I shall now illustrate them in some detail.

4.4.1 The Resilience of Self-government

All European reforms of institutional governance have drastically disempowered the traditional collegial bodies. But, as the empirical evidence drawn from several case studies of European universities shows, this has generally produced an unexpected outcome: the emergence of new, less institutionalized forms of self-government by the academic community.

As far as formal decision-making processes are concerned, a probably unsurprising finding is the widespread use of advisory and preparatory committees, or of similar forms of assembly composed mainly of academics. These committees and assemblies apparently play a more crucial role than in the past not only in the university's management, but also in decisions on strategy. As concerns outcomes, on the other hand, top-level decisions taken without broad consensus seem to be extremely rare at all the universities for which we have empirical information. The reason is that an extensive informal network of relationships and consultation is activated before any such decisions are reached. Taken together, these two findings indicate that the disempowerment of the traditional collegial governing bodies of the university has produced an unexpected outcome: self-government by the academic community still continues, in different, less institutional forms, by means of what we may refer to as 'functional substitutes' (Regini, 2015). In the words of Paradeise et al. (2009a, p. 224), 'decision-making competencies of rectors and deans have been extended in many countries, for instance in the 1990s in Germany, and in 2007 in France. Yet academic self-governance remains very strong in most countries, because daily operations are based on informal, long-lasting, and non-hierarchical peer relationships, and academic contributions remain largely based on personal commitment.' Or, to quote Schimank and Lange (2009, pp. 65–66):

[A]cademic self-governance [in Germany] ... has indeed been weakened formally. It, however, continues to more-or-less stay alive in a more informal manner. At the moment, most measures to build managerial self-governance remain incomplete. The prevailing consensus-oriented culture of the academic profession compels many, in leadership positions, to act as if they had no new powers. Thus, formal competencies remain unused, and consensus, among professors at least, is still sought by rectors and deans ... But the most important reason for 'cooperativeness' is that many persons in leadership positions have internalized the traditional organizational culture of consensus during their long academic socialization.

This unexpected outcome, of course, can partly be explained by the 'resilience' at all levels of a self-government culture typical of the academic community. But it probably also indicates the limitations – highlighted in the next section – of a managerial approach to university governance and the need to make the most of the expertise of academic staff, albeit in more informal, less institutional terms.

4.4.2 The Weakness of Governing Boards with Lay Members

Almost everywhere, university governance reforms inspired by a corporate enterprise model have assigned crucial governing functions to relatively small non-elective bodies (boards of governors or equivalent) which include stakeholders or external members expected to represent general interests, particularly those of the socio-economic system in which the university is embedded. An assumption of these reforms has been that because external members are used to dealing with strategic alternatives in their own work environment, they can do so more effectively than members working within the university. But the everyday practice of universities raises several doubts about this assumption. Even in countries where the reforms have been most radical, the boards of governors seem to be rather weak bodies.

The empirical evidence, drawn from case studies of universities in several European countries, clearly shows the shortcomings of boards of governors in assuming the role of effective counterweights to the power of the rector in the highly verticalized decision-making system established by the reforms. In fact, in a governance structure where the rector and his/her team perform strategic functions, and not just executive and managerial ones, it becomes difficult for the board of governors to contribute actively to those functions or to exercise effective supervision. The more the realm of decisions extends from such issues as housing or student fees to research strategies or choice of the products to be evaluated, the less the external members of the board of governors are able to contribute, as they obviously lack these skills or sufficient knowledge of the scientific environment.

Hence, for various reasons, governing boards with lay members prove largely ineffective in their intended role of acting as counterweights to the rector and the senior management team by virtue of their economic and social backgrounds. These difficulties are particularly evident at the universities of countries which most radically gave key governing functions to these small, non-elected bodies with a considerable presence of lay members.

4.4.3 From Individual to Collective Leadership: The Growing Importance of the Rector's Team

One major objective of all institutional governance reforms in Europe, as we saw earlier, has been the verticalization of decision-making processes in order to enhance the efficiency of universities through a strong leadership, shielded against veto powers and spoils-system practices. This objective has largely been achieved in all countries, but the empirical evidence shows that the team flanking the rector has become increasingly important as an effective management body. The verticalization of the decision-making process is therefore to some extent counterbalanced by the institutionalization of a collegiate structure of governance. Consequently, decisions are the result of collective work, and less dependent on the rector's individual traits. As Ferlie et al. (2009, p. 17) put it, 'in terms of senior management style, there is an emphasis on softer leadership skills, visioning and networking based approaches; there is an emphasis on distributed leadership and team based approaches rather than the highly individualized management typical of NPM'.

At British universities the number of pro-vice chancellors has increased substantially in recent years, and the senior management team has extended its range of action in response to the need to strengthen the 'strategic capacity' of universities to undertake their more extensive functions (Middlehurst, 2013; Shattock, 2013). Besides the vice-rectors, the presence of senior professionals in the collegial governing body resolves the historical duality between academic decision-making bodies and administrative ones. Usually the rector's team works as a strong executive able to take decisions and implement them. More generally, the idea that university leadership can only be collective now appears well established. Hence, the rector's individual traits are somewhat tempered by the collective nature of the decision-making process.

4.4.4 The Fluctuations between Centralization and Decentralization

Two studies by Hogan, carried out in 2005 and 2012, respectively, and reported by Shattock (2013), show that between 1993 and 2002, of 81 British universities examined, 74 per cent reorganized their intermediate structures (usually by reducing the number of faculties, but sometimes by abolishing them altogether or by converting them into colleges) and their departments (sometimes by merging them into schools which may or may not pertain to the faculty); and that between 2002 and 2007 this process accelerated further. Hence, British universities began to reorganize their academic structures well before their continental counterparts, primarily in order to create a few, generally large, units. This reorganization brought with it a decentralization of financial management, which in many universities has extended to decisions concerning human resources allocation. This decentralization of functions and powers has been justified by the argument that increased numbers due to the explosion of the 'mass university' caused a decision-making overload for the university's centre, forcing it to delegate numerous decisions to the lower levels. However, Shattock (2013) argues that the recent economic crisis, with the widespread perception of the volatility of the financial situation and the risks connected therewith, has led to recentralization. The prospect of downsizing due to austerity policies has persuaded senior university leaders to retrieve decision-making powers regarding resources previously delegated to the periphery. The same effect is produced by national research assessment exercises, which raise expectations of rewards and incentives to be managed by the centre.

The empirical evidence drawn from case studies of universities in different European countries shows that these uncertainties – or this oscillation between decentralization to the university's periphery and centralization to its senior leadership – concern not only British universities but also those of other countries. Overall, these fluctuations between decentralization and recentralization appear to be the unexpected outcome of rationalization policies that seek uniform, simplified answers to complex organizational dilemmas for which there is no one-size-fits-all solution. What is the optimal size of a university's organizational units? Should they be large enough to allow for economies of scale and for a strong voice in negotiations with the executive, or small enough to foster identity and a sense of membership? To what extent can the university executive decentralize functions and responsibilities to these units in order to involve them in the overall organization, and to what extent should it centralize instead so as to obtain standard performances? The rationalization policies have led to the resurfacing of these and other organizational problems which the old governance model had attempted to resolve through compromise solutions (Capano and Regini, 2014).

4.5 How Can We Account for the Unexpected Outcomes of Institutional Governance Reforms?

Why did these unintended consequences of the reforms of university governance, which entail a partial failure of the objective to converge on the Anglo–American model, occur, to a greater or lesser extent, in most European higher education systems? In the HE literature we find different answers to this question.

A first answer has already been mentioned when discussing the seminal work by Cerych and Sabatier (1986), namely the ability of academic communities to mobilize against reforms that tend to shift power from them to the institutional leadership. This type of explanation is still the most widespread in the HE literature. It is well synthesized, for instance, by Paradeise et al. (2009a, p. 225): 'The most radical reform programs may turn out to be counter-productive each time they crash with the harsh realities of power distributions.' More recently, Musselin and Teixeira (2014, p. 12) have written along the same lines: 'Higher education is particularly well known for being a traditionally complex field to be reformed, and higher education institutions have a reputation for resistance to change and subversion of policy initiatives, mainly due to the strong devolution of power to lower levels of the institution.'

A second explanation is what, in game theory, we could call a failure by states and universities to build a cooperative game between them, as mutual distrust leads to a vicious circle. This is the account that Schimank and Lange (2009, p. 63) offer of the German case:

Ministries have fallen back to regulation because they began to distrust the universities' willingness to continue in the direction of the agreed-upon targets. This distrust is not totally unjustified because the ability of the university leadership, with whom the ministry negotiates to implement general goals one level below in faculties and institutes, is still rather limited ... However, the ministry's behaviour has generated, on the university side, distrust in the commitment of the political side to the proclaimed shift from regulation to external guidance. Thus, mutual distrust has reinforced itself. But as long as nobody believes that the other side believes in mission-based contracts, they remain a facade behind which the old game is continued.

These and other explanations implicitly assume that these trends are not to be found only in the HE system, but exemplify a dynamics typical of all public sectors based on highly professionalized communities: a dynamics of mutual suspicion and power confrontation between the communities holding onto their traditional values, and States that try to make them more accountable by streamlining and 'rationalizing' the decision-making system. This assumption is clearly spelled out by Ferlie et al. (2009, pp. 2, 7):

The organizational similarities with other professionalized public sector settings such as health care are more important than the differences: European universities are largely dependent on the state for financing; the state is concerned to regulate their behaviour as they influence citizens' life chances significantly; they contain a mix of professional and bureaucratic elements and they operate within strongly structured institutionalized fields ... We can thus develop the argument that European nation-states are increasingly seeking to steer their HE systems, along with other key public services, in directions which are consistent with national policies.

There is, however, an alternative type of explanation. I will argue that the reasons for the production of unintended consequences of institutional governance reforms reside in a generalized and systematic underestimation by the reformers of the specific nature of universities and their functioning, which makes it difficult to import models developed in other contexts such as businesses or public administrations. In addition, we often find a generalized and systematic underestimation of two other characteristics of university institutions everywhere: the organizational complexity due to the plurality of functions entrusted to universities, which makes rationalization aimed at simplification problematic and sometimes counterproductive; and the marked diversity of higher education institutions, which makes the adoption of homogeneous and standardizing models difficult and often ineffective.

4.5.1 *The Specific Nature of Universities*

An underestimation of the specific nature of universities seems to be largely responsible for the first two types of unintended consequences mentioned herein – that is, the difficult functioning of governing bodies comprising members from outside the university, and the emergence of new forms of self-government that appear to be functional substitutes for the disempowerment of the traditional collegial bodies. The corporate enterprise model of governance, which has inspired national reforms to varying extents, assumes that decisions should be taken not by the representatives of those who benefit or suffer from such decisions (the academic staff), but by persons representing the broader interests of society; society finances the universities and therefore wants to ensure that it optimizes the available benefits.

This governance model is undoubtedly legitimized by the vices of self-government, which Adam Smith (1776) identified more than two centuries ago as opportunism and collusive or self-referential choices. In fact, the problems of the collegial self-government of universities are even broader: they include inefficient decision making, an opaque chain of responsibility, spoils-system practices, and amateurism. The corporate enterprise model finds legitimacy in these vices of self-government and proves superior in terms of efficiency, rapidity, and the ability to make selective choices. However, the unresolved problem of this model when applied to institutions such as universities is that scientific communities are the only ones in a position to assess the problems and prospects within their own areas. The public goods produced by universities (highly qualified human capital and research results) are very specialized goods, the features of which can only be determined by their producers, and not by the bureaucracy or the market. The most promising directions for research, which researchers are most likely to achieve which results, the most appropriate knowledge to be conveyed – these are all choices which only the scientific communities can make, and university bureaucracies are obliged to leave such choices to those communities (Whitley, 2000).

The main organizational dilemma thus becomes the following: should preference be given to solutions that prevent collusive and self-referential choices, or to inside knowledge of the situations requiring action to be taken? The absence of collusive and self-referential choices implies that the bodies which propose or decide the allocation of resources cannot consist of those that use such resources. On the other hand, as indicated, only scientific communities are in a position to evaluate problems and prospects in their own areas. It is not easy to find balanced solutions to this dilemma. However, policy makers often lack even an awareness of the very terms of the dilemma. The reasons for this, in Mertonian terms, are a mix of errors of analysis (concerning the university's specificities), the prevalence of short-term interests in productive and efficient universities over a long-term interest in the effective production of public goods, and the predominance of a value system that tends to neglect the very idea of public goods.

4.5.2 The Plurality of University Functions and Organizational Complexity

The verticalization of decision making that has led to a strengthening of rectors' powers everywhere has also been inspired to a large extent by a corporate model of governance. To make rapid, effective, and non-collusive decisions possible, it appeared necessary to protect the rector from veto powers and to define his/her role no longer in the traditional terms of primus inter pares, but in terms similar to those of the managing director of a large company.

However, rectors (at least at European universities) are not managers by profession, but academics. As such, they are directly aware of the enormous complexity of universities as organizations called upon to perform several different functions – teaching, research, knowledge transfer, social engagement, support to local development – usually by reconciling the needs and habits of very different subject areas. These are complex organizations that, for this very reason, require an executive possessing a range of widely varied characteristics and abilities. As argued by Middlehurst (2013, p. 283):

[V]ice-chancellors' own perceptions of their roles and the characteristics associated with them suggest four sets of necessary competences: academic-related characteristics associated with gaining credibility and influence; business-related characteristics to deal with diversified funding streams and 'branding' of institutions; managerial and leadership characteristics associated with two key responsibilities: an external representative profile (locally, nationally and internationally) and working with and through a senior management team, an Academic Board or Senate and a governing body; and fourth, personal characteristics including physical and intellectual resilience (emotional resilience is increasingly important too).

All this requires a collective leadership that can only be exercised by a team more stable and better able to work as a group compared with the collaborators of the former rector primus inter pares, who were usually assigned only specific tasks.

4.5.3 *The Heterogeneity of HE Institutions*

Finally, the uncertain and contradictory effects of rationalization can be accounted for by an underestimation not only of the organizational complexity, but also of the heterogeneity of universities, which makes adoption of homogeneous and standardizing models difficult and often ineffective.

A good example of this is the Italian reform of universities introduced in 2010, which was designed to simplify the internal structure of universities by abolishing faculties and transferring all functions to departments, without considering the very different effects that this 'simplification' would produce in large universities compared to small ones. In general, the goal of simplification proved much easier to achieve in small and medium-sized universities than in large and very large ones. In fact, at small and medium-sized universities, the pre-reform departments have been replaced by larger departments roughly equal in number to the old faculties. At these universities, therefore, the reform has achieved the goal of unifying, in one single organization, competences that were previously shared between the faculties and the old departments. Consequently, the new organizational structure enables the university executive to frequently and directly interact with the organizational units (still few in number), and simultaneously enables the organizational units to maintain their right to representation in the governing bodies (in particular, the academic senate).

At the larger universities, however, the reform has led to the creation of new departments, often surpassing – sometimes considerably – the number of the old faculties. At these universities, therefore, the competences previously assigned to the faculties and departments have indeed been unified, but to the detriment of the organization's compactness. Hence, while at the small and medium-sized universities the net effect of the reform on internal organizational structures has been actual simplification – that is, the concentration of decisions into organizational units of the same size as the old faculties – at the large and very large universities the concentration of decisions has been accompanied by a fragmentation of organizational units.

To conclude, one reason for the occurrence of unintended consequences of institutional governance reforms may be identified as the generalized, systematic underestimation by reformers of certain specific characteristics of universities. Some authors argue that 'paradoxes' (Hood, 2000) or unintended consequences of reforms have occurred in many other public sectors as well, following their subjection to NPM. However, while the strict implementation of this ideology may contribute to the emergence of the unintended consequences discussed herein, it is the specificity of university institutions that seems to play a key role. Evidence suggests that this specificity is very poorly understood, leading to it being underestimated or totally overlooked by policy makers (Regini, 2015). In other words, some outcomes of university reforms were not anticipated and could not have been anticipated even by a very careful policy design, not just because the reforms were value-driven, but because of the clear cognitive limits of policy makers, unable to grasp the specificity of higher education institutions.

Notes

1. By 'governance' in the HE field, we mean the 'process' and the 'structure' by which decisions are formulated and implemented as a result of the interaction of all those involved (Capano, 2011; Klijn, 2008). This definition can be applied at both the institutional and the systemic levels. The latter refers to the relationships between universities and the state as regulator. Institutional governance – which is the object of the current analysis – relates to the way individual universities are internally governed, namely by authority relations at the organizational level.
2. According to Burton Clark (1983), the Continental model is characterized by systemic, strongly hierarchical coordination through state-centred policies; no institutional autonomy; the powerful, all-pervasive authority of the academic guilds; and faculties and schools constituting confederations of chair-holders.
3. This section and the following one draw heavily on Regini (2011).
4. This section and the following one draw on Regini (2015) and on Capano et al. (2016).

References

Amaral, A., Fulton, O., and Larsen, I. M. (2003) A managerial revolution? In A. Amaral, V. L Meek, and I. M. Larsen (Eds), *The higher education managerial revolution?*, pp. 275–296. Dordrecht: Kluwer.

Amaral, A., Jones, G., and Karseth, B. (Eds) (2002) *Governing higher education: National perspectives on institutional governance.* Dordrecht: Kluwer.

Berdahl, R. (1990) Academic freedom, autonomy and accountability in British universities. *Studies in Higher Education*, 15(2), 169–180.

Capano, G. (2011) Government continues to do its job. A comparative study of governance shifts in the higher education sector. *Public Administration*, 89(4), 1622–1642.

Capano, G., and Regini, M. (2014) Governance reforms and organizational dilemmas in European universities. *Comparative Education Review*, 58 (1), 73–103.

Capano, G., Regini, M., and Turri, M. (2016) *Changing governance in universities: Italian higher education in comparative perspective.* London and New York: Palgrave Macmillan.

Cerych, L., and Sabatier, P. (1986) *Great expectations and mixed performance: The implementation of higher education reforms in Europe.* Stoke-on-Trent: Trentham Books.

Clark, B. R. (1983) *The higher education system: Academic organization in cross-national perspective.* Berkeley: University of California Press.

Collins, R. (1979) *The credential society: An historical sociology of education and stratification.* New York: Academic Press.

De Boer, H., Enders, J., and Leisyte, L. (2007) Public sector reform in Dutch higher education: The organizational transformation of the university. *Public Administration*, 85(1), 27–46.

Dill, D. (2014) Public policy design and university reform: Insights into academic change. In C. Musselin and P. N. Teixeira (Eds), *Reforming higher education: Public policy design and implementation*, pp. 21–37. Dordrecht: Springer.

DiMaggio, P. J., and Powell, W. (1983) The iron cage revisited: Institutional isomorphism and collective rationality in organizational fields. *American Sociological Review*, 48(1), 147–160.

Esping-Andersen, G. (1990) *The three worlds of welfare capitalism.* Princeton: Princeton University Press

European Commission (2006) *Delivering on the modernisation agenda for universities: Education, research and innovation.* http://ec.europa.eu/invest-in-research/pdf/comuniv2006_en.pdf

Ferlie, E., Musselin, C., and Andresani, G. (2009) The governance of higher education systems: A public management perspective. In C. Paradeise, E. Reale, I. Bleiklie, and E. Ferlie (Eds), *University governance: Western European comparative perspectives*, pp. 1–19. Dordrecht: Springer.

Hall, P., and Taylor, R. (1996) Political science and the three new institutionalisms. *Political Studies*, 44(5), 936–957.

Hood, C. (2000) Paradoxes of public-sector managerialism, old public management and public service bargains. *International Public Management Journal*, 3(1), 1–22.

Kerr, C. (1983) *The future of industrial societies: Convergence or continuing diversity.* Cambridge, MA: Harvard University Press.

Kickert, W. (1997) Public governance in the Netherlands: An alternative to Anglo-American managerialism. *Public Administration*, 75(4), 731–752.

Klijn, E. (2008) Governance and governance networks in Europe. *Public Management Review*, 10(4), 505–525.

Krücken, G., and Meier, J. (2006) Turning the university into an organizational actor. In G. S. Drori, J. W. Meyer, and H. Hwang (Eds), *Globalization and organization: World society and organizational change*, pp. 241–257. Oxford: Oxford University Press.

Mahoney, J., and Thelen, K. (Eds) (2010) *Explaining institutional change: Ambiguity, agency, and power.* New York: Cambridge University Press

Marini, G., and Reale, E. (2016) How does collegiality survive managerially led universities? Evidence from a European survey. *European Journal of Higher Education* 6(2), 111–127.

Meek, V. L., Goedegebuure, L., Santiago, R., and Carvalho, T. (Eds) (2010) *The changing dynamics of higher education middle management.* Dordrecht: Springer.

Merton, R. (1936) The Unanticipated consequences of purposive social action. *American Sociological Review*, 1(6), 894–904.

Middlehurst, R. (2004) Changing internal governance: A discussion of leadership roles and management structures in UK universities. *Higher Education Quarterly*, 58(4), 258–279.

Middlehurst, R. (2013) Changing internal governance: Are leadership roles and management structures in United Kingdom universities fit for the future? *Higher Education Quarterly*, 67(3), 275–294.

Musselin, C. (2006) Are universities specific organizations? In G. Krücken, A. Kosmützky, and M. Torka (Eds), *Towards a multiversity? Universities between global trends and national traditions*, pp. 63–84. Bielefeld: Transcript Verlag.

Musselin, C., and Paradeise, C. (2009) France: From incremental transitions to institutional change. In C. Paradeise, E. Reale, I. Bleiklie, and E. Ferlie (Eds), *University governance: Western European comparative perspectives*, pp. 21–49. Dordrecht: Springer

Musselin, C., and Teixeira, P. (2014) Introduction. In C. Musselin and P. N. Teixeira (Eds), *Reforming higher education: Public policy design and implementation*, pp. 1–17. Dordrecht: Springer

Neave, G. R., and van Vught, F. (1991) *Prometheus bound: The changing relationship between government and higher education in Western Europe.* Oxford: Pergamon Press.

North, D. C. (1990) *Institutions, institutional change and economic performance.* Cambridge: Cambridge University Press.

Paradeise, C., Reale, E., and Goastellec, G. (2009a) A comparative approach to higher education reforms in Western European countries. In C. Paradeise, E. Reale, I. Bleiklie, and E. Ferlie (Eds), *University governance: Western European comparative perspectives*, pp. 197–225. Dordrecht: Springer.

Paradeise, C., Reale, E., Goastellec, G., and Bleiklie, I. (2009b) Universities steering between stories and history. In C. Paradeise, E. Reale, I. Bleiklie, and E. Ferlie (Eds), *University governance: Western European comparative perspectives*, pp. 227–246. Dordrecht: Springer.

Regini, M. (2011) *European universities and the challenge of the market.* Cheltenham: Edward Elgar.

Regini, M. (2015) Conseguenze non previste delle riforme: i mutamenti della governance universitaria in Europa. *Stato e Mercato*, 104(2), 159–188.

Schimank, U., and Lange, S. (2009) Germany: A latecomer to New Public Management. In C. Paradeise, E. Reale, I. Bleiklie, and E. Ferlie (Eds), *University governance: Western European comparative perspectives*, pp. 51–75. Dordrecht: Springer.

Schulze-Cleven, T., and Olson, T. (2017) Worlds of higher education transformed: Toward varieties of academic capitalism. *Higher Education*, 73(6), 813–831.

Schwarz, S., and Westerheijden, D. (2004) *Accreditation and evaluation in the European higher education area.* Dordrecht: Kluwer

Shattock, M. (2008) The change from private to public governance of British higher education: Its consequences for higher education policy making, 1980–2006. *Higher Education Quarterly*, 62(3), 181–203.

Shattock, M. (2013) University governance, leadership and management in a decade of diversification and uncertainty. *Higher Education Quarterly*, 67(3), 217–233.

Smith, A. (1776) *An inquiry into the nature and causes of the wealth of nations.* London: Strahan and Cadell.

Streeck, W., and Thelen, K. (Eds) (2005) *Beyond continuity: Institutional change in advanced political economies.* Oxford: Oxford University Press.

Trowler, P. R. (2010) UK higher education: Captured by new managerialist ideology? In V. Meek, L. Goedegebuure, R. Santiago, and T. Carvalho (Eds), *The changing dynamics of higher education middle management*, pp. 197–211. Dordrecht: Springer

van Vught, F. (1989) *Governmental strategies and innovation in higher education.* London: Jessica Kinsley.

Weick, K. F. (1976) Educational organizations as loosely coupled systems. *Administrative Science Quarterly*, 21(1), 1–19.

Whitley, R. (2000) *The intellectual and social organization of the sciences.* Oxford: Oxford University Press.

Whitley, R. (2008) Universities as strategic actors: Limitations and variations. In L. Engwall and D. Weaire (Eds), *The university in the market*, pp. 23–37. London: Portland Press.

Williamson, O. E. (1985) *The economic institutions of capitalism.* New York: Free Press.

5 | Capture and Drift in Emerging International Governance Arrangements

The Role of Meta-organizations in Higher Education Quality Assurance

ÅSE GORNITZKA, PETER MAASSEN, AND BJØRN
STENSAKER

5.1 Introduction

In a number of countries and in a number of policy areas throughout
the world, the last two decades have witnessed the emergence of new
agencies in public sector governance (Trondal, 2014). Such agencies
are normally established through public law, take on distinct functions specifically delegated from national governments, and are
granted some autonomy in their operations (Christensen and
Lægreid, 2006). The governance of higher education has reflected
this development, and new national agencies – not least within the
area of external quality assurance – have been created in a range of
countries in Europe, Asia, Africa, and South America (Stensaker,
2011; Westerheijden et al., 2007). As such, trends in the governance
of higher education can be said to converge with trends in public
sector governance in general.

However, as part of a more connected world, driven by growing
internationalization and globalization, it is also possible to identify the
emergence of new types of regulatory organizations at the supra-
national level (Ahrne and Brunsson, 2008). These organizations may
be involved in the creation of new voluntary standards in areas that are
internationally unregulated (Brunsson et al., 2000); they may be an
international extension of existing national agencies (Levi-Faur, 2011);
or they may, as in the case of Europe, be created through legislative
delegation from the European Union (Thatcher and Coen, 2008). The
agencification that has taken place at the national level has been

conducive to the transformation of the emerging European administrative order (Curtin and Egeberg, 2008, p. 640). Agencies with relative autonomy from ministerial departments at the national level are able to connect to 'sister' agencies in other European countries and to executive bodies at the European level. New executive capacity has been amassed through the establishment of supra-national agencies with pan-European responsibilities, representing a parallel agencification at the European level (Levi-Faur, 2011; Thatcher and Coen, 2008; Trondal, 2014). In the literature on governance, this development is often associated with increased regulatory complexity, which some characterize as multilevel and multi-actor governance networks (Danielsen and Yesilkagit, 2014; Maggetti, 2014).

While much attention has been given to agencification within the European Union (EU) in governance studies in general (Trondal and Peters, 2013), the field of higher education has not reflected this development due to the EU's lack of formal competence in this specific policy area (Maassen and Olsen, 2007). However, the fact that formal European agencies cannot be established in the field of higher education does not imply that there is a total absence of regulatory initiatives in this area (Gornitzka and Stensaker, 2014). For example, new organizational forms in higher education quality assurance have emerged in Europe during the last decade, hinting at new ways in which governance beyond the level of the nation state may develop. We believe that higher education and the recent developments within quality assurance in Europe are interesting examples of emerging attempts to regulate higher education at the supra-national level, and may also be of relevance to other regions in the world where processes of internationalization and globalization are unfolding in policy spaces with limited formal competence.

This chapter therefore examines the establishment and functioning of two European meta-organizations in the area of higher education quality assurance, and how these organizations have contributed to changing the governance of European quality assurance. We do this by: 1) describing these meta-organizations and their development; 2) analysing how these meta-organizations have worked to establish new rules and standards in the quality assurance area; and 3) analysing their role in the emerging governance space of higher education in Europe.

5.2 Reforming European Higher Education: A Short Description of the Empirical Context

European higher education has experienced two decades of reform and change following the introduction of the Bologna Process in the early 2000s (Kehm et al., 2009). Through the Bologna Process a number of European countries agreed to harmonize their higher education systems through changes in degree structures, credit systems, and, not least, in building up external quality assurance as a way to ensure transparency while also upholding academic standards (Westerheijden et al., 2007). Following the Bologna Process, external quality assurance has become one of the most visible activities driving European integration in this sector. While external quality assurance might have many purposes, this chapter focuses on how it can be linked to governance of higher education (Stensaker and Harvey, 2011), and specifically to the increasingly multilevel and multi-actor dynamics emerging in the sector, where issues relating to governance go beyond national borders.

At the national level, external quality assurance has played an important role as a regulatory instrument ensuring quality in countries aiming for more university autonomy, in deregulated and in more market-driven systems (Dill and Beerkens, 2010; Olsson and Peters, 2005; Westerheijden, 2001). As part of this process, governments have set up new national systems of external quality assurance, and new national agencies have emerged with special responsibilities for conducting and overseeing the quality assurance systems (Brennan and Shah, 2000; Schwarz and Westerheijden, 2004). Such agencification is a rather familiar development at the national level in many European countries that have initiated reforms in the public sector (Christensen and Lægreid, 2006; Fisher, 2004).

As part of the Bologna Process in Europe, new so-called meta-organizations – organizations whose membership consists of other organizations (Ahrne and Brunsson, 2008) – have been established at the pan-European level in the quality assurance area. These organizations belong to the increasing number of new organizations, networks, and agencies occupying and developing the EU administrative space (Egeberg and Trondal, 2009; Levi-Faur, 2011; Trondal and Peters, 2013). Two such meta-organizations are particularly interesting. ENQA (European Association for Quality Assurance in Higher Education) is an umbrella organization which represents quality assurance agencies from the member states of the European Higher Education Area. ENQA was, for example, given responsibility for developing European standards and guidelines in the area of quality assurance – standards that countries signing onto the Bologna declaration at a later date have adopted nationally (Stensaker et al., 2010). EQAR (European Quality Assurance Register for Higher Education) is a register listing all agencies that comply with standards and guidelines for quality assurance in Europe; listing on EQAR allows quality assurance agencies to operate within the European Higher Education Area. These meta-organizations can be said to play a range of different roles and to have many different functions. However, an overlapping purpose is their ambition to develop, implement, and oversee standards for how external quality assurance should be conducted at the European, national, and institutional levels. As such, one could claim that these meta-organizations are key instruments for achieving greater convergence within the European Higher Education Area and represent a significant development of transnational governance initiatives in higher education.

5.3 Meta-organizations, Multilevel, and Multi-actor Governance: Theoretical Considerations

Quality assurance in higher education has many links to governance, including but not limited to governmental reform initiatives aiming at institutional decentralization, autonomy, and accountability (Dill and Beerkens, 2010; Stensaker, 2003; Stensaker and Harvey, 2011; Westerheijden, 1999; Westerheijden et al., 2007). In Europe, quality assurance has been a vital part of the Bologna Process, and several policy initiatives have been taken to strengthen the European dimension in this area, creating new regulatory standards and guidelines with considerable impact (Gornitzka and Stensaker, 2014). These developments are of interest to those studying public administration, globalization, and European studies, implying the possibility of linking these areas which tend to be treated independently in the scholarly debate (Trondal, 2014).

In principle, the creation of agencies is about transferring governmental activities vertically to more specialized organizations (Trondal, 2014, p. 545). Public sector reforms in general, and regulatory reforms in particular, have seen both vertical specialization, where tasks are hived off from ministries and transferred to relatively independent agencies positioned at arm's length from direct political and ministerial steer, and horizontal specialization, where agencies are differentiated according to the government's tasks as administrator, regulator, or purchaser versus service provider (Christensen and Lægreid, 2006). Normally, such developments take place within national borders.

In Europe, interesting developments have arisen when these national agencies travel abroad and form networks which, over time, tend to create new meta-organizations (Ahrne and Brunsson, 2008). Thatcher and Coen (2008) have suggested that many European networks have gradually developed stronger organizational structures. The European Commission may be a key driver behind the transformations of such organizations (Levi-Faur, 2011); alternatively, the Commission may develop its own agencies, often building on established transnational networks of national agencies (Trondal, 2014).

Due to the limited formal competence of the EU in matters concerning higher education, it has not been possible for the EU to establish its own agencies, and some of the tasks usually taken on by European agencies have instead been given to other types of organizations, such as ENQA and EQAR. The development of new meta-organizations in the quality assurance arena gives rise to some theoretically interesting puzzles. While the creation of new supranational agencies is often related to strengthening political capacity, coordination, and convergence (Maggetti, 2014, p. 482), it also signifies new multi-actor and multilevel governance processes in Europe, which could potentially increase what some have labelled organizational uncertainty (Power, 2007) and others, institutional complexity (Greenwood et al., 2011). This is because national agencies gain some autonomy from their ministries by engaging in EU networks and meta-organizations (Bach and Ruffing, 2013). New meta-organizations and transnational regulatory networks tend to gain bureaucratic autonomy and become increasingly independent of their founders (Danielsen and Yesilkagit, 2014) while at the same time becoming more open to influences from individual experts, organized expertise, and other interest organizations (Neshkova, 2014). This dynamic can be described from different perspectives; based on existing research on European governance arrangements and their development, we distinguish between what we will label a *capture* perspective and a *drift* perspective.

The basic assumption of the capture perspective is that new meta-organizations are created either as an external 'takeover' of existing informal networks or as an extension of the responsibilities of existing national agencies (Levi-Faur, 2011; Maggetti, 2014). The European Commission is normally a key driver behind such developments, and there are currently more than 30 EU agencies (Trondal, 2014, p. 546) that have become integral components of the Commission's policy-making and implementation processes. Although neither ENQA nor EQAR are meta-organizations under European Commission jurisdiction, they can still be exposed to capture – for example, if they are assigned important tasks by the EU, or if projects they carry out are funded by the EU. This could be seen as a case of supra-national capture. However, these meta-organizations can also theoretically be captured by various expert and interest organizations, not least due to the (democratic) legitimacy provided by the latter (Neshkova, 2014, p. 72). Elken (2015) has recently shown how the development of the European Qualification Framework can be explained by the latter perspective. A potential implication is that what was created as an autonomous meta-organization may become dependent on and co-opted by other external actors (Trondal, 2014, p. 546) – that is, subject to expert or stakeholder capture.

The basic assumption of the drift perspective, on the other hand, is that new meta-organizations are able to maintain a relatively high level of autonomy vis-à-vis other actors, and that they might even try to strengthen their autonomy and influence in the governance of a specific area (Maggetti, 2014). There are a number of possible variations within this broader perspective. One is that these meta-organizations gain a 'life of their own' and over time find their place in an institutional order. Bureaucratic autonomy of such meta-organizations can be seen as a precondition for developing competent governance capacity in a policy area. Yet, new meta-organizations may have a 'dark' side, as Maggetti (2014, p. 481) has suggested, leading them to become selective, opaque, and more inward looking in their activities (see also Ahrne and Brunsson, 2008). In principle, the work that ENQA and EQAR do, could – deliberately or by chance – serve to extend their regulatory powers, for example through the development or adoption of specific regulatory procedures or activities that are taken up as templates for reform within the governance domain. In European higher education quality assurance, the growth and expansion of accreditation as a specific and dominant form of external quality assurance may be seen as an example of such creeping influence on regulatory practices (Stensaker, 2011). Two implications of such 'drift' may be weakened democratic accountability and the rise of more technocratic governance arrangements.

These two perspectives are not mutually exclusive: combinations of capture and drift are indeed imaginable. However, in the analysis that follows, these two perspectives will be treated independently to aid our understanding of the directions of change in this governance area. In our discussions of the findings, we will come back to the possible links between capture and drift, and their possible implications for the governance of the sector.

5.4 Data and Methods

In analysing the development and roles of ENQA and EQAR, we draw on two different data sources. First, we have collected, systematized, and analysed publicly available reports, policy initiatives, and policy briefs on and by these two meta-organizations from the time of their establishment onwards. This written material includes historical reflective accounts by individuals central to the development of the two organizations, but also external evaluation reports of the agencies, and their strategic plans. These documents have been thematically analysed with respect to how the agencies describe their role, how they position themselves as interest organizations, and the internal dynamics between ENQA and EQAR. Second, this has been complemented by a review of the existing literature on European quality assurance in higher education, focusing particularly on descriptions and analyses of the development of ENQA and EQAR with respect to governance and regulation in the field. This allows for a more reliable way of establishing knowledge of key events and processes in the development of the agencies.

When systematizing the data, we looked especially for examples of capture and agency drift in line with our initial expectations. In the reporting of our findings, we will first describe the historical development of the European agencies in quality assurance, before going into the indications of capture and drift respectively.

5.5 The Establishment and Functions of New Meta-organizations in European Higher Education Quality Assurance

5.5.1 National Developments Leading to the Establishment of ENQA and EQAR

A number of contributions have described the build-up of European quality assurance in higher education (see, for example, ENQA, 2008, 2012, 2015; Gornitzka and Stensaker, 2014; Rozsnyai, 2003; Schwarz and Westerheijden, 2004; Westerheijden, 1999; Westerheijden et al., 2007). Hence, these developments will not be described in detail here. Nevertheless, national developments, not least the creation of national agencies in quality assurance, provide an important historical backdrop for later European developments in this area and are worthy of some introductory attention.

The first governmental agencies in Europe were established in the United Kingdom, France, the Netherlands, and Denmark in the mid- to late 1980s, with other countries quickly following suit. It did not take long for national agencies to expand their activities to the European level (Westerheijden, 1999; Westerheijden et al., 1994). The formal argument driving this expansion was the stimulation of policy learning between countries, not least concerning methodologies and their application across geographical borders. When the Bologna Process was initiated a few years later (Schwarz and Westerheijden, 2004), activities in the quality assurance area were seen as a way of addressing the need to build trust in the mobility and mutual recognition schemes for students and academic staff that were central to the Bologna Declaration.

Quality assurance was high on the political agenda in Europe, as evidenced by numerous ministerial meetings, and in 2000 a new network consisting of national quality assurance agencies (ENQA) was established. Together with the other members of the so-called E4 group – the European University Association (EUA), the European Student Union (ESU), and EURASHE (the association for non-university higher education institutions in Europe) – the ENQA network, which in 2004 was formalized into a new association with its own staff and office, was given responsibility for developing the first European Standards and Guidelines for Quality Assurance (ESG) which was launched in 2005 (Thune, 2010).

As part of this process, ENQA had also committed itself to developing a European register for quality assurance agencies (Thune, 2010, p. 12), although the initial development of this register gave rise to what Williams (2010, p. 16) described as 'long and protracted discussions among the E4 group about the precise structure and function of such a register'. A key point of discussion was whether the register should be developed as part of ENQA, or as a separate entity scrutinizing potential members in an independent procedure (Williams, 2010, p. 17). While ENQA argued for the former option, the rest of the E4 – EUA, ESU, and EURASHE – argued for the latter position.

After lengthy discussion, the register, named EQAR, came into operation in 2008 as an independent stakeholder-driven meta-organization. ENQA had to relinquish its ambition to host the register as part of the ENQA structure, although it did reach a compromise with the rest of the E4 group that ENQA members should not have to submit two independent evaluations to become members of the two respective agencies (Williams, 2010, p. 17). The background to the disagreement among the E4 members was mainly related to the possibility that EQAR creates for universities and colleges to 'select' their own evaluators in a more deregulated market for quality assurance (Gornitzka and Stensaker, 2014). This option depends on the opening up of domestic quality assurance to foreign providers, which a number of European countries currently allow (EQAR, 2013, p. 2). In short, the formalization of quality assurance in Europe has created the opportunity for a transfer of regulatory power from the domestic to the European level.

Interpreting this shift in regulatory responsibility is a challenging task as it is not clear who is actually in control of this development, and because national governments are still quite influential with respect to the design and function of quality assurance domestically (Westerheijden et al., 2014). For domestic quality assurance agencies in Europe, registration in EQAR is on a voluntary basis. However, becoming a member is not a straightforward process. In EQAR, all important decisions about whether agencies should be included or not are taken by the so-called Register Committee, consisting of 11 members; the E4 group together have control through their combined eight members (two members each). This means that the two key meta-organizations in this field are tightly interwoven in their internal governance, but also that interest organizations such as ESU, EUA, and

EURASHE, through their combined six votes, have the majority of votes in this important decision-making body.

5.5.2 Indications of Capture

ENQA and EQAR are thus two different meta-organizations with two different purposes. While ENQA started out as a member and interest organization for domestic quality assurance agencies, with a history stretching back before the Bologna Process, EQAR can be seen more as a child of that process, with various interested parties wanting to have a say in how it should be designed and how it would work.

Given its focus on quality assurance, it is perhaps not surprising that ENQA wanted to be in control of the new Register that was to be developed. In the early days of the Bologna Process, ENQA argued strongly that the new Register should be under the wings of ENQA, and that EQAR should be no more than 'a small database', as one of the previous presidents of ENQA formulated it (Williams, 2010, p. 17). This attempt by ENQA to capture EQAR failed (Curvale, 2010, p. 22), mainly because the other members of the E4 group resisted the idea of ENQA having control of the new Register. For example, when the E4 group was mandated to develop the first version of the European Standards and Guidelines for Quality Assurance (ESG) – which forms the regulatory basis for both ENQA and EQAR – ENQA tried to take control by coordinating the various working groups involved in the process. The other group members did not cooperate, as the then president of ENQA has stated: 'I invited EUA, EURASHE, and ESIB [now ESU] to appoint members for the ENQA working groups … However, the three other organisations preferred to set up their own background groups' (Thune, 2010, p. 13).

Hence, it seems that the different interest groups involved in the development of the standards and guidelines did not want to be too closely associated with ENQA in this crucial phase. As described, the process ended with EQAR being established as an independent agency, and the E4 group sharing their influence over the key regulatory decision-making body within EQAR, the Register Committee. The fact that the E4 group has 8 out of 11 members of this body, and that the ESU, EUA, and EURASHE together control six out of the 11 members, is an indication that EQAR may indeed have been captured by interest groups.

For ENQA, this situation was seen as unfortunate, not only because the other E4 members had a vital say in the decision making of EQAR, but also because it created the potential for an EQAR 'takeover' of ENQA members, making the latter meta-organization seem less important: 'Given that expertise in quality assurance is in general short supply, it would be sad if a listing in the Register were to be preferred to access to the developmental opportunity of ENQA membership' (Williams, 2010, p. 18).

Although the European Commission can be said to have played only a modest part in the establishment of the Register – this formally being a decision taken by the signatory countries of the Bologna Declaration – the role of the Commission is still significant. As one of the former presidents of ENQA has stressed, 'there may come a point where the Register is seen as more politically important than ENQA. Its relationship to the European Commission has always been close, not least because of the Commission's financial support and its evident desire to loosen the links between national agencies and national higher education systems' (Williams, 2010, p. 18). The worries hinted at in this statement suggest that the European Commission also has considerable interest in EQAR and that it sees the Register as a tool for strengthening its influence on European higher education – fuelled by the ability of the Commission to fund EQAR's operations.

What, then, is EQAR's view of this development? An external evaluation of EQAR in 2011 stressed that EQAR saw the relationship with ENQA as critical to the future (Daniel et al., 2011, p. 13). Being a very small organization, it seems that the legitimacy of EQAR is partly dependent on ENQA members applying for membership of the Register. In the early days of the Register, some ENQA agencies did not apply for EQAR membership, as they waited to see what value-added would be provided by the new organization (Daniel et al., 2011, p. 12). However, over time membership of ENQA agencies in EQAR has steadily increased (EQAR, 2013). Whether this means that ENQA is in the process of being captured by EQAR is an open question.

5.5.3 *Indications of Drift*

While our data provide evidence of possible capture, there are also ample indications of drift with respect to both ENQA and EQAR. The fact that the E4 group was given the mandate to develop regulatory measures in the quality assurance area seems not only to have caused some tensions within the E4 group, but also led on certain occasions to the group joining forces. For example, in the early days of the Bologna Process, when some governments were not convinced about the advantages of increasing the regulatory machinery in this area, and when ENQA was still quite optimistic about its ability to control the new Register, a former president of ENQA described his actions in the following way: 'I succeeded, with the support of the EUA, EURASHE, and ESIB [now ESU], in convincing several ministerial sceptics that the proposed Register was not an unduly bureaucratic prospect' (Thune, 2010, p. 14).

This statement can be read as an example of agency drift, not least since the president of a sample of governmental agencies had to engage in activities to persuade their founders about the need to allocate more regulatory power to quality assurance agencies. The statement also suggests that ENQA had, in the early days, the ambition to be more than a network for exchange of expertise, seeing itself as a key actor in building the European Higher Education Area (see also Curvale, 2010, p. 21). Over time, the meta-organization became a consultative member of the Bologna Follow-Up Group (BFUG), which strengthened its role in the political decision-making process in Europe. Later presidents of ENQA have underlined this and pointed to the need for ENQA to strengthen its role as a key political actor with material influence on European higher education developments (Hopbach, 2010, p. 24). In this context, it is interesting to read the self-reflections of one of the former presidents of ENQA: '[an] important lesson we had learned is that the main cornerstone of all the ENQA activities must be to serve its member agencies, and work on European quality assurance issues on the basis of the secured mandates from its members' (Thune, 2010, p. 14).

The question one can ask here is, of course, whether serving the interest of national member agencies is the same as serving the interest of the national founders of the agencies? One might also speculate whether EQAR has started to drift. Several voices have expressed concerns about whether the initial voluntary registration of agencies in EQAR may shift over time. In the words of one of the former presidents of ENQA: 'Will the current voluntary status of inclusion in the Register eventually become the norm, then an expectation and finally a requirement?' (Williams, 2010, p. 18).

According to the external panel evaluating EQAR in 2011, the Register should indeed develop its strategic capacity (Daniel et al., 2011, p. 8), although the panel acknowledged that many of those to whom it spoke during the evaluation process argued that EQAR's role was regulatory, and not strategic, and that focusing more on strategic aspects would lead to 'mission drift' (Daniel et al., 2011, p. 7). After the external evaluation, EQAR decided to strengthen its strategic capacity, and in the subsequent strategic plan developed in 2013, EQAR emphasized its more autonomous role, downplaying the stakeholder interests and highlighting its ability to take proportionate, consistent, fair, and objectives decisions (EQAR, 2013, p. 1). Whether such autonomy will be given to EQAR by those stakeholders already tightly involved in its decision making remains to be seen.

5.6 Discussion and Conclusion

Based on the data available, the development of quality assurance in higher education in Europe shows indications of both capture and drift in the two key meta-organizations established. When returning to our initial assumptions, the case of EQAR can be more easily linked to the capture perspective, while the case of ENQA fits more closely with assumptions related to the drift perspective. If we compare higher education to other governance areas, the results demonstrate both convergence and divergence. The historical establishment of European meta-organizations in the quality assurance area are quite similar to developments in other policy areas. The fact that ENQA started out as a more informal network before establishing itself as a formal association is in line with a number of similar transformations of networks into new meta-organizations (Levi-Faur, 2011). Over time, ENQA has developed its capacity to take on more developmental projects related to quality assurance, and although the organization has not built up a large administrative staff in Brussels, it still runs a number of projects, drawing on the sizeable capacity found in its member agencies. It is also possible to identify a stronger formalization of rules and regulations associated with membership activities, which could be interpreted as a sign of emerging drift. The development of EQAR followed a very different trajectory, and the agency has far fewer capabilities to draw upon compared with ENQA. The lack of such capabilities is also an argument for the potential capture of EQAR from various stakeholders. In this perspective, it is quite easy to see the significance and role of the European Commission driving the development of the administrative space in the region (Trondal, 2014) – although the Commission plays a more behind-the-scenes role in higher education than in other policy arenas.

Our case study also highlights some unusual aspects that may stimulate renewed reflection with respect to multilevel and multi-actor governance arrangements in Europe, and may also have relevance for other regions in the world. As the field of higher education continues to be exposed to growing internationalization and globalization processes, issues of how such developments should be governed have been on the agenda for quite some time (Stensaker and Harvey, 2011; Westerheijden, 1999). What makes European higher education quality assurance an interesting case in regulatory matters is that it provides an example of how governance arrangements may develop in previously unregulated international policy spaces. It allows us a glimpse into the ways future global governance arrangements might emerge, even when national governments attempt to maintain control over their higher education systems.

While the creation of EU agencies in other policy areas is normally associated with the aims of convergence and harmonization (Maggetti, 2014), the field of higher education quality assurance is somewhat ambivalent about this aim. As one former president of ENQA stated some years ago: 'ENQA does not promote the creation of a unified, pan-European quality assurance regime' (Hopbach, 2010, p. 24). The interesting twist here is, of course, that ENQA has been a key driver behind the development of the current European Standards and Guidelines (ESG) in the field of quality assurance, suggesting that it is not quite clear what these standards and guidelines should mean in practice. Moreover, empirical studies have demonstrated the diverse ways in which standards and guidelines have been applied when domestic agencies have been evaluated in the past (Stensaker et al., 2010). This flexible practice suggests that international meta-organizations might function as buffers mediating between the global trends towards convergence, standards, and accountability, and the needs for national autonomy and control.

The fact that there are two agencies operating in the European area of quality assurance also hints at the potential competition that may arise when unregulated policy spaces develop new governance arrangements. When these two meta-organizations entered into the policy discussion about the future of higher education quality assurance, they became involved in considerable political rivalry. Over the course of time, the relationship between ENQA and EQAR has been quite turbulent, characterized by both inflexibility and considerable tensions (Curvale, 2010, p. 20), although there are also periods where ENQA and EQAR seem to function and collaborate in a consensual and constructive manner (Hopbach, 2010, p. 24). From an outside perspective, the two agencies appear to be tied together and quite dependent on each other. EQAR provides ENQA with the legitimacy of being an 'objective' and 'neutral' verifier of expertise in the quality assurance area. ENQA provides EQAR with its core membership, signifying the importance of EQAR as a regulatory gatekeeper. ENQA could also be seen as one of the core actors behind the founding of EQAR, having committed to the establishment of this organization in the early 2000s. While one could argue that ENQA had its own plans for capturing EQAR in the beginning, other interest organizations also entered the game, creating a policy dynamic in which national governments and even the European Commission were left on the sidelines. This may indicate that new international multilevel governance arrangements – and the political rivalry that can develop as a consequence of them – may give more power to and increase the influence of interest and stakeholder organizations.

The establishment of EQAR, and the ambition to create a 'market' for quality assurance where universities and colleges can choose their evaluators inside and outside national borders, is another example of the potential global relevance of the European case reported here. These types of meta-organizations could, on the one hand, become the basis for establishing regional regulatory networks of a similar nature outside Europe, matching developments in regulation of other sectors (see Berg and Horrall, 2008). Or the ENQA and EQAR could extend their activities to give them a global reach. While exporting quality assurance services is an aspiration for many governments in different corners of the world, it is not yet a common form of internationalization of quality assurance, or a strong focus for many national agencies (ENQA, 2015, p. 5). Some national agencies that are a member of both ENQA and EQAR are nevertheless quite active in such cross-border activities. Recent evidence suggests that when these agencies operate abroad, only half of them inform the local agencies of the jurisdictions within which they operate (ENQA, 2015, p. 24). Whether this development – from a governance perspective – stimulates more transparency and accountability is another question.

References

Ahrne, G., and Brunsson, N. (2008) *Meta-organizations*. London: Edward Elgar Publishing.

Bach, T., and Ruffing, E. (2013) Networking for autonomy? National agencies in European networks. *Public Administration*, 91(3), 712–726.

Berg, S. V., and Horrall, J. (2008) Networks of regulatory agencies as regional public goods: Improving infrastructure performance. *Review of International Organizations* 3(2), 179–200. doi:10.1007/s11558-007-9028-8

Brennan, J., and Shah, T. (2000) *Managing quality in higher education: An international perspective on institutional assessment and change*. Buckingham: Open University Press.

Brunsson, N., and Jacobsson, B. (2000) *A world of standards*. Oxford: Oxford University Press.

Christensen, T., and Lægreid, P. (2006) Agencification and regulatory reform. In T. Christensen and P. Lægreid (Eds), *Autonomy and regulation: Coping with agencies in the modern state*, pp. 8–49. Cheltenham: Edward Elgar.

Curtin, D., and Egeberg, M. (2008) Tradition and innovation: Europe's accumulated executive order. *West European Politics*, 31(4), 639–661.

Curvale, B. (2010) Toward the European quality assurance dimension: Fostering the participation of ENQA members. In F. Crozier, N. Costes, P. Ranne, and M. Stalter (Eds), *ENQA: 10 Years (2000–2010): A decade of European co-operation in quality assurance in higher education*, pp. 20–22. Brussels: ENQA.

Daniel, J., Brittingham, B., Burns, L., et al. (2011) *Review of the European Quality Assurance Register for Higher Education*. Brussels: EQAR.

Danielsen, O. A., and Yesilkagit, K. (2014) The effects of European regulatory networks on the bureaucratic autonomy of national regulatory authorities. *Public Organization Review*, 14(3), 353–371.

Dill, D. D., and Beerkens, M. (2010) *Public policy for academic quality*. Dordrecht: Springer.

Egeberg, M., and Trondal, J. (2009) National agencies in the European administrative space: Government driven, commission driven or networked? *Public Administration*, 87(4), 779–790.

Elken, M. (2015) Developing policy instruments for education in the EU: The European Qualifications Framework for lifelong learning. *International Journal of Life-Long Education*. 34(6), 310–326.

ENQA (2008) *Quality procedures in the European Higher Education Area and beyond: Second ENQA survey*. Helsinki: ENQA.

ENQA (2012) *Quality procedures in the European Higher Education Area and beyond: Third ENQA survey*. Brussels: ENQA.

ENQA (2015) *Quality procedures in the European Higher Education Area and beyond: Internationalisation of quality assurance agencies.* Brussels: ENQA.

EQAR (2013) *Strategic plan 2013–2017.* Brussels: EQAR.

Fisher, E. (2004) The European Union in the age of accountability. *Oxford Journal of Legal Studies,* 24(4), 495–515.

Gornitzka, Å., and Stensaker, B. (2014) The development of a European regulatory space. *Policy & Society,* 33(3), 177–188.

Greenwood, R., Raynard, M., Kodeih, F., Micelotta, E. R., and Lounsbury, M. (2011) Institutional complexity and organizational responses. *Academy of Management Annals,* 5(1): 317–371.

Hopbach, A. (2010) Conclusions. In F. Crozier, N. Costes, P. Ranne, and M. Stalter (Eds), *ENQA: 10 Years (2000–2010): A decade of European cooperation in quality assurance in higher education,* pp. 23–24. Brussels: ENQA.

Kehm, B., Huisman, J., and Stensaker, B. (Eds) (2009) *The European Higher Education Area: Perspectives on a moving target.* Rotterdam: Sense Publishers.

Levi-Faur, D. (2011) Regulatory networks and regulatory agencification: Towards a single European regulatory space. *Journal of European Public Policy,* 18(6), 810–829.

Maassen, P., and Olsen, J. P. (Eds) (2007) *University dynamics and European integration.* Dordrecht: Springer.

Maggetti, M. (2014) The rewards of cooperation: The effects of membership in European regulatory networks. *European Journal of Political Research,* 53(3), 480–499.

Neshkova, M. I. (2014) Does agency autonomy foster public participation? *Public Administration Review,* 74(1), 64–74.

Olsson, M., and Peters, M. A. (2005) Neoliberalism, higher education and the knowledge economy: From the free market to knowledge capitalism. *Journal of Educational Policy* 20(3), 313–345.

Power, M. (2007) *Organized uncertainty: Designing a world of risk management.* Oxford: Oxford University Press.

Rozsnyai, C. (2003) Quality assurance before and after Bologna in the Central and Eastern Region of the European Higher Education Area with a focus on Hungary, the Czech Republic and Poland. *European Journal of Education,* 38(3), 271–284.

Schwarz, S., and Westerheijden, D. F. (Eds) (2004) *Accreditation and evaluation in the European Higher Education Area.* Dordrecht: Kluwer Academic Publishers.

Stensaker, B. (2003) Trance, transparency and transformation. The impact of external quality monitoring in higher education. *Quality in Higher Education,* 9(2), 151–159.

Stensaker, B. (2011) Accreditation of higher education in Europe: Moving towards the US model? *Journal of Educational Policy*, 26(4), 757–769.

Stensaker, B., and Harvey, L. (2011) *Accountability in higher education*. New York: Routledge.

Stensaker, B., Harvey, L., Huisman, J., Langfeldt, L., and Westerheijden, D. (2010) The impact of the European standards and guidelines in agency evaluations. *European Journal of Education*, 45(4), 577–587.

Thatcher, M., and Coen, D. (2008) Reshaping the European regulatory space: An evolutionary analysis. *West European Politics*, 31(4), 806–836.

Thune, C. (2010) ENQA 2000–2005: From the launch of a professional network to the success in the Bologna of a new association. In F. Crozier, N. Costes, P. Ranne, and M. Stalter (Eds), *ENQA: 10 Years (2000–2010): A decade of European co-operation in quality assurance in higher education*, pp. 9–15. Brussels: ENQA.

Trondal, J. (2014) Agencification. *Public Administration Review*, 74(4), 545–549.

Trondal, J., and Peters, B. G. (2013) The rise of European administrative space: Lessons learned, *Journal of European Public Policy*, 20(2), 295–307.

Westerheijden, D. F. (1999) Where are the quantum jumps in quality assurance? Developments of a decade of research on a heavy particle. *Higher Education*, 38(2), 233–254.

Westerheijden, D. F. (2001) Ex oriente lux? National and multiple accreditation in Europe after the fall of the wall and after Bologna. *Quality in Higher Education*, 7(1), 65–76.

Westerheijden, D. F., Brennan, J., and Maassen, P. A. M. (Eds) (1994) *Changing contexts of quality assessment*. Utrecht: Lemma/CHEPS.

Westerheijden, D. F. Stensaker, B., and Rosa, M. J. (Eds) (2007) *Quality assurance in higher education*. Dordrecht: Springer.

Westerheijden, D. F., Stensaker, B., Rosa, M. J., and Corbett, A. (2014) Next generations, catwalks, random walks and arms races: Conceptualising the development of quality assurance schemes. *European Journal of Education*.

Williams, P. (2010) From Bergen to the register: A long and winding road. In F. Crozier, N. Costes, P. Ranne, and M. Stalter (Eds), *ENQA: 10 Years (2000–2010): A decade of European co-operation in quality assurance in higher education*, pp. 16–19. Brussels: ENQA.

6 Understanding Convergence and Divergence in the Internationalization of Higher Education from a World Society Perspective

RENZE KOLSTER AND
DON F. WESTERHEIJDEN[*]

6.1 Introduction

Changing discourses frequently put new demands on higher education systems,[1] giving rise to new objectives, responsibilities, and expectations (Meyer et al., 1997). At the macro level, the forces which change discourses include globalization, demographic fluctuations, and shifts in economic hegemony (Maassen et al., 2012; de Wit et al., 2015). Put in more practical terms, higher education systems and institutions are, inter alia, expected to:

- Compete with other higher education systems/institutions around the world for funding and students;
- Collaborate with other higher education systems/institutions around the world on research, education, and valorization to solve the grand challenges facing the world;
- Contribute to a country's competiveness (e.g. innovation capacity) and diplomatic strength (i.e. soft power);
- Prepare students for the twenty-first century by teaching the skills that will enable them to be engaged global citizens and to find sustainable employment in a globalized world.

The way governments around the world have reacted to these new demands and pressures has been surprisingly similar. Governments

[*] The authors would like to thank Jelena Brankovic (Bielefeld University) and participants of the 2016 HKU-USC-Conference of Public Policy for their valuable comments on earlier versions of this chapter.

156

ranging from Estonia and Kazakhstan to Australia and Malaysia want their higher education systems to internationalize. This means that the purpose, function, identity, mission, strategy, and delivery of higher education at the national, sectoral, and organizational levels must all have an international, intercultural, or global dimension (Knight, 2015). Even where higher education systems and local conditions could hardly be more different in terms of, for example, history, status, connectedness, student backgrounds, and the number and type of institutions, the rationales, strategies, and policies that governments use to promote internationalization are strikingly similar – focusing on the economic benefits of incoming international students, attracted through national promotion strategies, based on the higher education system's reputation and quality. It is as if there was some kind of overarching authority obliging countries to internationalize their higher education systems.

This chapter will argue that, while the similarities in approaches to internationalization lead to convergence across higher education systems, actual practices and governance arrangements also show continued divergence. By adopting a cultural/phenomenological approach as part of the world society theory perspective (Meyer et al., 1997), this chapter aims to provide a cultural rather than a functional explanation for the remarkable degree of convergence, while not losing sight of divergence. Taking this cultural perspective to both frame and explain the proliferation of the internationalization discourse in higher education – and the resulting convergence and divergence – has, to the best of our knowledge, not been done before in the academic literature.

To further our understanding of the internationalization discourse and the implications for the governance of higher education, we ask the following research question: how can the rationales and practices underpinning the internationalization of higher education be understood from a world society perspective? To answer this question, we first outline the world society theory (Section 6.2). We then highlight patterns of convergence (Section 6.3), followed by signs of divergence, in rationales and practices (Section 6.4). The chapter closes with a discussion and conclusion (Section 6.5).

6.2 World Society Theory and Internationalization

Overall, convergent and divergent rationales and practices are little explored in the academic research on internationalization (Buckner,

2017). A number of theoretical insights can be helpful in such an exploration. First, convergent and divergent rationales and practices may be indications of the 'garbage can model' in higher education (Cohen et al., 1972), explaining the decoupling between policy intentions and outcomes (Hasse and Krücken, 2014). Decoupling could explain how the convergence of internationalization rationales and strategies can coexist with divergence from these rationales in policies, and thus in outcomes.

Second, convergence and divergence may be explained from the perspective of the Europeanization of higher education policies (Maassen and Stensaker, 2011), in which European directives increasingly influence the logics, and thus the policies, at national and institutional levels. For European higher education, the Bologna Process is the visible policy force that influences national higher education policy arenas. However, countries have implemented the Bologna action lines (convergence) with various interpretations and at differing rates of adoption (divergence) (Westerheijden et al., 2010). Most relevant for our argument are the Bologna actions lines that focus on the mobility of students and staff, the overall internationalization of higher education systems and institutions, and the international visibility of the European Higher Education Area. Convergence is visible, for example, in the growing number of agencies tasked with internationalization of higher education systems, while divergence is shown in the intensity of national marketing efforts directed towards prospective international students (BFUG, 2009).

The Europeanization perspective might explain some of the converging rationales and practices among and within European countries. However, given that converging internationalization rationales and practices are also apparent in many non-European countries, other underlying forces must be at play. This leads us to the third theoretical perspective: world society theory, which sees the world as an integrated social system driven by a shared world culture, on which rationalized scripts for progress are based. The world culture and the related scripts (in terms of rationales, strategies, and policies) lead to convergence and divergence – with convergence being easier to see. From this world society perspective, we contend that convergence results from isomorphism – that is, actors across the world following the same models, norms, or scripts to a much higher degree than their very different positions, interests, and resources would lead one to expect if actions were purely (economically) rational. World society theory maintains that many national socio-economic developments are influenced by global scripts for progress (Meyer, 2000; Ramirez and Tiplic, 2014). Scripts emerge in a global environment; they shape the identities, rationales, and activities used and undertaken by nation states, organizations, and individuals (Ramirez and Tiplic, 2014). The driving force is the so-called world culture, comprising a preferred set of activities, behaviours, principles, and objectives (ideals). It has been argued that today's world culture is 'characterized by a belief in individual and collective progress, justice and equality, which are pursued through science and rational action' (Buckner, 2017, p. 475). More specifically, science has become the leading rationale in contemporary world culture, and its implications can be seen in every global discourse, including higher education (Drori et al., 2003; Meyer, 2010). Science provides the 'causal and normative arguments on how different actors all around the world – from nation-states to individuals – should behave and organize their affairs to be recognized as legitimate, modern actors' (Krücken and Drori, 2009, p. 17).

A number of actors are involved in the diffusion of world culture, including international organizations (e.g. OECD, EU, UNESCO), public and private organizations (e.g. consultants and NGOs), and individuals. These actors can promote scripts of progress to nation states, thus introducing scripts that have rationality and legitimacy on the world stage. This process can explain the isomorphism found in many aspects of nation states' governance arrangements (e.g. in terms of followed rationales, policies, and involvement of actors; Meyer et al., 1997). An important aspect of this perspective is the 'Otherhood status' of certain actors, which allows them to – in an apparently disinterested way – promote scripts with authority, so that they 'instruct and advise actors on how to be better actors in light of general principles' (Meyer, 2010, p. 7). The Otherhood status of, for example, supra-national organizations, scientists, and consultancy firms (i.e. 'therapeutic authorities'; Meyer, 2000, p. 239) is seen as important for the diffusion of world culture.

Particularly for higher education strategies and policies, the emergence of – or an increase in the authority ascribed to – international and supranational organizations is relevant (Hasse and Krücken, 2014; Martens and Wolf, 2009). These actors undertake standard-setting activities; they provide and incentivize global scripts. Illustrating the role of such actors, the OECD and UNESCO collect data on international mobility flows and benchmark the performance of different countries. Through their efforts, we know that higher education worldwide comprises an increasing number of students who study outside their country of citizenship: numbers have jumped from 0.8 million in 1975 to 4.5 million in 2012 (OECD, 2015). By 2025, it is predicted that up to 8 million students will study abroad (Helms, 2014). These statistics lead to country-specific insights. One example is the OECD's comparison of the internationalization of doctoral and master's studies, which shows that 'The United States hosts 38% of international students enrolled in a programme at the doctoral level in OECD countries. Luxembourg and Switzerland host the largest proportion of international students, who make up more than half of their total doctoral students' (OECD, 2016, p. 1). The OECD's role in advising governments on how to approach internationalization is also relevant here (see Hénard et al., 2012). In the world society perspective, such examples demonstrate the Otherhood status of these actors, and thus their role in the diffusion of the internationalization script.

In Europe, the European Union (EU) is the prime example of a supranational organization promoting standardization, harmonization, and alignment of European higher education systems (Tight, 2007). Internationalization of higher education has become a preferred means to this end. Consequently, the EU has introduced policies that facilitate mobility of staff and students, such as the Erasmus programme, as well as international cooperation between higher education institutions (HEIs), such as the Erasmus Mundus programme, encouraging HEIs to start joint programmes. Inspired by the activities and scripts emerging from the EU's example, the Association of Southeast Asian Nations (ASEAN) and other regional groupings of countries began to introduce similar policies – for example, the ASEAN International Mobility for Students programme.

It should be noted that actors promoting the internationalization of higher education script have not only materialized on the international level, but also at the level of national government entities. Examples of such national agencies are CampusFrance, the British Council, DAAD (Germany), and Nuffic (Netherlands). These 'national government entities are increasingly sharing the policy-making space with regional government entities and a broad community of quasi-governmental and independent non-profit organizations – as well as with higher education institutions themselves' (Helms et al., 2015, p. 51; also see Dodds, 2009).

Explaining the diffusion and legitimization of global developments through the lens of world culture is a key insight of world society theory. For instance, proponents of world society theory argue that the diffusion and legitimization of the nation state model is a key example of the existence of a world culture (Meyer, 2000; Meyer et al., 1997). Without there being a dictating central authority, the nation state model has become the standard script for newly established countries. It is further argued that nation states act on other globally accepted and promoted scripts, such as human rights, democracy, and economic development (Meyer, 2010). Similarly, through the diffusion of world culture, education came to be seen as a highly rationalized script for the development of nation states (Krücken et al., 2007). As part of this, scientifically rationalized models for the governance, functioning, and goals of higher education spread across the globe as part of the shared world culture, despite the lack of any central authority. Buzzwords circling around higher education strategies and policies can be attached to this shared culture – for example, excellence, world-class, accountability, third mission, employability, and indeed, as argued in this chapter, internationalization (Buckner, 2017; Horta, 2009). All can be seen as transnational principles of progress that are part of the world culture shared by a wide range of actors (Frank and Gabler, 2006, cited in Ramirez and Tiplic, 2014).

Yet, world culture may also lead to divergence. Inherent within world culture are inconsistencies and conflicts; activities, behaviours, principles, and objectives (ideals) may be at odds with each other (Meyer et al., 1997). For example, objectives of economic development often contradict objectives of equality (Buckner, 2017). Likewise, internationalization of higher education may contradict other objectives, such as equal access to higher education or the importance of higher education systems to national knowledge economies. Objectives themselves might even create conflicts (Meyer et al., 1997) – for example, by increasing competition between actors for resources, such as higher education institutions competing for international students. It should also be noted that objectives of world culture are translated differently in local contexts. For example, most countries claim to adhere to the objectives of democracy, yet democratic practices and their institutional embodiments vary widely. It is probable that this also applies to internationalization: while adhering to the same ideal, HEIs' practices within and between countries may vary. Taking mobility as an obvious example, some focus on outgoing mobility, others focus on incoming mobility. Similarly, countries may claim to be internationalized, while most of the international students are from one particular, neighbouring country (e.g. mainly German students in the Netherlands). Furthermore, the dominant model for progress may claim expected outcomes, 'regardless of whether the expected outcomes are actually attained' (Ramirez and Tiplic, 2014, p. 440), thus suggesting a disconnection between objectives and outcomes. Divergent practices suggest symbolic ceremonial action or conformity, meaning divergence between objectives, rationales, and practices – that is, a loose coupling or decoupling (Buckner, 2017; Hasse and Krücken, 2014; Meyer, 2000; Meyer et al., 1997).

To sum up our argument, it appears that internationalization of higher education is, by and large, a globally favoured and chosen script for the further development of higher education systems. This implies that internationalization of higher education has become part of world culture, with actors of Otherhood status promoting the internationalization script, and agentic actors (nation states, HEIs, and students) acting upon it (Meyer, 2010). The implication is that every higher education system must internationalize if it is to be taken seriously in the wider world (Ramirez and Tiplic, 2014, p. 453).

Having outlined the world society theory and its connection to the internationalization of higher education, we can highlight several theoretical expectations, which we will explore in the following sections. First, we expect to see convergence in scripted rationales, suggesting that increasingly similar rationales are used to justify the internationalization of higher education. Second, we expect these scripts to lead to convergence in internationalization strategies and policies. Third, world culture is not without inconsistencies, hence we expect to see some divergent practices. After a reflection on the limitations of this chapter, the next sections will discuss these aspects.

With the goal of furthering the theoretical understanding of the internationalization of higher education, this chapter takes a macro perspective. Such a perspective contains the inherent risk of over-generalization. The evidence presented in the chapter is inevitably based on limited, and at points anecdotal, examples, which can be deceptive: in the words of Goldfinch and Wallis (2010, p. 1102), 'structures that seem similar at a distance may vary widely in practice'. The chapter should be read and interpreted with this limitation in mind. Indeed, the same applies to the interpretation of world culture; it is not static, it can and does change over time (Meyer et al., 1997). Hence, recent trends towards greater nationalism – embodied, for instance, by the Brexit vote in the United Kingdom and the 2016 presidential election outcomes in the United States – may signal a tension in the norms and values of the contemporary world culture (Buckner, 2017). Will this change the discourse of internationalization? The world society theory offers some comfort to the proponents of internationalization; all signs indicate that internationalization is embedded within both Otherhood and agentic actors, such as UNESCO, the OECD, HEIs, and students, making it far more difficult for any nation state to alter the discourse fundamentally (Meyer et al., 1997). This argument, in combination with the eternal quest for resources, means that internationalization is unlikely to be just a temporary fashion (Alasuutari, 2015).

6.3 Signs of Convergence

6.3.1 Convergence in Scripted Rationales

If internationalization of higher education has indeed become part of the world culture, and through that a scripted activity of higher education, we would expect to see HEIs and national governments across the world undertake similar activities based on similar rationales. This process of isomorphism would decrease national distinctiveness in the organization of higher education and its goals (Meyer et al., 1997; Ramirez and Tiplic, 2014). Yet, there is legitimacy and claims of relevance in conformity. Uniqueness in socio-economic development can be seen as a sign of divergence from the global script, and thus from the global world culture, and may be seen as both less legitimate and less relevant (Meyer, 2000; Ramirez and Tiplic, 2014). Framed in the context of converging pressures on higher education systems worldwide, for example through international benchmarks, this section describes the rationales behind the internationalization of higher education.

6.3.1.1 Performance of Higher Education Systems

It appears to have become a common understanding in the internationalization discourse that to be excellent in teaching and research, an institution has to be international (Marginson, 2016; Ramirez and Tiplic, 2014). The key contributors to this discourse are the international benchmarks of higher education performance. For example, transnational standards for internationalization are diffused through the indicators included in university rankings. In fact, with the exception of the Shanghai Academic Ranking of World Universities, all the major global university rankings include at least a few indicators for internationalization, mainly the number or ratio of international students and staff (Federkeil et al., 2012), as well as a heavy focus on internationally published and cited articles. The proliferation of global rankings as such is a sign of – and impetus for – increased global competiveness (Alasuutari, 2015; Teichler, 2009; van Vught and Ziegele, 2012) and has been criticized for promoting a script – namely, the world-class research university as the only viable model for successful universities (Marginson, 2009; Salmi, 2009).

The importance of research being of international standard is also highlighted in research performance assessments, such as the United Kingdom's Research Excellence Framework or Hong Kong's Research Assessment Exercise. The former assesses research output on a scale ranging from nationally recognized to world-leading.[2] The latter uses the number of refereed articles in prestigious international journals as a proxy for research productivity (de Boer et al., 2015). It is not only the global university rankings and national research assessments that contribute to benchmarking of higher education systems: the new international and supra-national actors are also active in this area. As discussed, the OECD and UNESCO both publish data on international mobility flows, and in that way provide benchmarks for the performance of countries.

6.3.1.2 The Rationales

The overarching objectives of internationalization of higher education can be categorized in four, partially overlapping, rationales: academic, social/cultural, economic, and political (de Wit, 1999, 2009, also see Seeber et al., 2016).

- The academic rationale is related to the idea that internationalization can improve the quality of higher education in the host country (e.g. internationalization of curricula and improved didactical/pedagogical approaches). Key here is mobility, which facilitates collaboration among previously separated groups of students and academics. Related to this may also be the rationale of prestige and reputation, which links to the visibility of the higher education system and its HEIs.
- The social/cultural rationale encompasses internationalization with the aim of meeting global challenges, increasing mutual understanding, and enhancing students' sense of global citizenship; it thus stresses the responsibility of students, and higher education, to address and solve these global challenges.
- Economic rationales for internationalization relate to workforce development, and short-term as well as long-term economic gains. The workforce rationale recognizes, first, that graduates are vital for knowledge economies. In order to become or remain economically competitive, graduates should have international competences that allow them to operate in globalized work environments. Second, it recognizes that countries may benefit. Host countries benefit from brain-gain: incoming students may contribute to the economy as graduates contributing their skills to the host country. Home countries benefit from brain-circulation: students educated abroad bring new and increased competencies to the economy when they return as graduates. The economic gains rationale focuses on long-term national economic development (with a clear link to the workforce rationale), as well as on the short-term revenue accrued through tuition fees and students' expenditure on living costs.
- The political rationale focuses on gains in public diplomacy and soft power. Related to this are the establishment of relationships abroad between individuals and between organizations (i.e. brain-circulation). The image or brand recognition abroad of the country and its higher education system are also relevant here. The political rationale may entail links to national interests, for instance by allowing students to gain linguistic and intercultural competences; strengthening bonds between historically or geographically connected countries may also be seen as political arguments for internationalization.

A number of publications indicate that the political and economic rationales have gained in importance in global internationalization trends (Seeber et al., 2016; van Vught et al., 2002; de Wit et al., 2015). This is apparent in 'the increased importance of reputation (often symbolized by rankings), visibility and competitiveness; the competition for talented students and scholars; short-term and/or long-term economic gains; demographic considerations; and the focus on employability and social engagement' (de Wit et al., 2015, p. 27). The focus on employability is a strong component of the political and economic rationales for internationalization. Ilieva and Peak (2016, p. 4) found that 'While the majority of the countries have introduced student-friendly and welcoming visa policies, a much smaller number (Australia, Germany and more recently Russia) have widened access to their labour market for international students'. However, in a footnote they indicate that they have seen other countries also giving greater access to their labour markets to international students: these include, inter alia, the Netherlands, Sweden, Canada, and New Zealand (Ilieva and Peak, 2016, p. 4; see also Helms et al., 2015). This development is in line with the increased focus on privatization of international higher education through revenue generation (de Wit et al., 2015). In other words, the economic rationale of internationalization triumphs over, for example, the academic (improved quality of higher education) rationale of internationalization (Luo and Jamieson-Drake, 2013; Seeber et al., 2016; van Vught et al., 2002).

6.3.1.3 How Rational Are the Rationales?

The convergence on rationales described above can be linked to scientific evidence. As indicated, the economic rationale of internationalization has been most prominent, and has been promoted since at least the beginning of this century (van Vught et al., 2002). An increasing number of countries justify their focus on internationalization (particularly mobility) by showing its economic benefits. Examples can be drawn from Australia, Germany, the Netherlands, the USA, and the United Kingdom, where studies often focus on measuring the impact of international students on monetary gains to the local economy or to higher education, in terms of consumer expenditure and tuition fees, respectively (e.g. EP-Nuffic, 2016; Munch and Hoch, 2013). Australia provides perhaps the most telling example (Rizvi, 2011). Its international education sector contributes A$20 billion (around US$15 billion) to the national economy; it is the country's leading services export, and overall has been the third-biggest export sector for more than a decade (Ross and Hare, 2016; van Vught et al., 2002). At the individual level, studies on international experiences commonly focus on students' increased employability (see, e.g., Brandenburg et al., 2014; Crossman and Clarke, 2010; Jones, 2013; King and Ruiz-Gelices, 2003).

However, scientific evidence is also available for the academic benefits of internationalization. Studies linked to this rationale mainly focus on the academic benefits to students. As the overview paper by Malicki and Potts (2013) shows, students whose higher education experience has included a component of studying abroad do better academically upon return to their regular study programme. They achieve improved academic performance and higher graduation rates. This might be related to findings that suggest that an international experience increased students' independence, self-confidence, and openness to new ideas. Those that had a longer international experience (more than one year) were more likely to obtain a PhD. Intergenerational effects were also found: students whose parents had had an international study experience were more likely to study abroad. Although improved academic quality of classrooms hosting international students, or being taught an international curriculum by international faculty (i.e. the international classroom), are often claimed (Delgado-Márquez et al., 2013; Jones, 2013), empirical evidence to support these claims appears to be largely absent (Luo and Jamieson-Drake, 2013). Nevertheless, internationalization has been linked to the prestige and reputation of HEIs (Delgado-Márquez et al., 2013).

Studies on the social/cultural benefits of internationalization also largely focus on the benefits to students. Evidence has been found for students gaining international competences, such as intercultural awareness, global perspectives, and cultural understanding through an international experience or through interacting with students from diverse backgrounds, making them better equipped as global citizens (Chieffo and Griffiths, 2004; Luo and Jamieson-Drake, 2013; Malicki and Potts, 2013; Trede et al., 2013). In the specific case of Europe, a European identity (King and Ruiz-Gelices, 2003) is often claimed as an outcome of internationalization of higher education. Yet, the evidence is not consistent, with some studies claiming a relationship, while others find weak or no correlation.[3] Moreover, while Europe's Bologna

Process was originally connected to a 'cultural rationale linked to European citizenship and identity, Bologna evolved towards an economic programme' (Sin and Neave, 2016, p. 1448), suggesting once again that social and cultural benefits may be becoming less important than economic ones.

One weakness of studies looking into the benefits of internationalization to students is that they rely heavily on self-reported gains. In other words, gains in international competences and skills are rarely measured objectively.[4] Nevertheless, self-reported gains might have an important signalling function to employers. This function is important, as studies indicate that employers value graduates with international competences, especially foreign language proficiency, knowledge and understanding of differences in culture and society, and the ability to work with people from different cultural backgrounds (see Crossman and Clarke, 2010; Malicki and Potts, 2013).

The political rationale – that is, gains in public diplomacy and soft power – appears to be the least researched of the four rationales. Yet, there are claims that international education in general, and specific policies such as the USA's Fulbright Scholarship programmes, can be linked to a country's soft power (Altbach and Peterson, 2008; Nye, 2004; Rizvi, 2011). Although scarce, the available evidence does indeed suggest a positive relationship between internationalization (through exchange, scholarships, and education hubs) and public diplomacy (Ferreia de Lima, 2007; Lee, 2015). Political and economic issues related to brain-drain – with its negative consequences for the sending countries – and brain-gain, for host countries, are rationalized using the concept of brain-circulation. Brain-circulation stresses the mutual benefits of international mobility: knowledge and practices are shared between sending and host countries. Some evidence suggests that this is indeed taking place (Appelt et al., 2015). Interestingly, this implies that world culture is not only *taught* through higher education, but also *spreads* through higher education (Meyer, 2000, 2010).

Although this discussion of academic evidence on the effects of internationalization is by no means exhaustive, it does suggest that there is research-based evidence for many of the claimed effects of internationalization, while others may be collectively claimed – or, rather, presumed (Meyer, 2010; Meyer et al., 1997). We can therefore state that internationalization of higher education is a largely, though not fully, rational activity, based on institutionalized rationales, as maintained by the world society perspective. As such, internationalization is a scripted activity that is legitimized not necessarily because of its 'real' benefits, but primarily because it is part of world culture – the collectively believed benefits that are institutionalized among actors mimetically (Meyer, 2010). Consequently, we expect to find diffusion of the 'internationalization script' echoed in internationalization practices, resulting in convergence (Meyer et al., 1997).

6.3.2 Signs of Convergence through the Internationalization Script

Following world society theory, to be taken seriously in the wider world a higher education system needs to be open to international students. Internationalization has become a method through which national governments signal the relevance of their higher education system. One way to do this is to copy 'best practices' (Meyer, 2000; Ramirez and Tiplic, 2014), which is a term to rationalize the mimicking of scripts that seem to be part of the world culture, even if they have not been proven to be 'best' in the national context.

'Best practice' scripts are more likely to be copied from nation states that are perceived to be successful in terms of their economy, military, politics, or other social aspects (Meyer et al., 1997); in short, policy emulation is a consequence of the political rationale. Nation states that are seen as successful 'occupy a higher stratum in the world system and exert greater influence on other nation-states by providing global models and examples' (Jang, 2000, p. 253). Consequently, we would expect to see countries that are performing well in terms of internationalization providing models that are adopted by other nation states. The best performing countries in terms of incoming mobility are the USA, the United Kingdom, and Australia.

Following scripts implies convergence of governance arrangements. For instance, many countries introduce national scholarship programmes for international mobility, increase their international marketing efforts abroad, launch study programmes taught in the language of the successful countries (i.e. English), join international university networks to facilitate student exchange, introduce more lenient policies to allow international students to find employment in their host country, and add indicators of internationalization to their performance funding models (Becker and Kolster, 2012; European Commission et al., 2015). Related to such 'best practices', and largely based on recent studies (Helms et al., 2015; Ilieva and Peak, 2016), we discuss in more detail below the convergence in national internationalization strategies, the focus on mobility, and promotion strategies.

6.3.2.1 Internationalization Strategies

Reinforcing the role of states as enablers of internationalization (Horta, 2009), a wide range of higher education authorities have introduced strategies with that aim (de Wit et al., 2015). Among these are Belgium (Flemish community), Canada, Denmark, Estonia, Finland, Germany, Ireland, Japan, Kazakhstan, Malaysia, the Netherlands, Norway, Poland, Spain, and Switzerland.[5] The introduction of internationalization strategies in countries that are not widely known for academic excellence is noteworthy. Consequently, even small or upcoming higher education systems are actively converging towards the internationalization script (e.g. Latvia, Estonia, Turkey, Egypt, and Vietnam; see Ilieva and Peak, 2016). Reflecting on the internationalization efforts of 26 countries, Ilieva and Peak (2016, p. 4) conclude: 'There is a rise in the number of countries with commitment towards international higher education at the national level, which is evidenced through their IHE [international higher education] strategies, some of which are reflected in reformed higher education legislations. These are strong signals of readiness to engage internationally and to support their higher education systems' global positioning.'

6.3.2.2 Focus on Mobility

The political and especially economic rationales are evident in the strategies mentioned earlier. Taking a closer look, many internationalization strategies focus on mobility. In fact, mobility is often the only national internationalization goal (Ilieva and Peak, 2016). This is also observed by Helms et al. (2015, p. 52): 'Finally, when it comes to the myriad approaches to internationalization articulated by policies around the world, there is one dimension seen across the vast majority: mobility.' Ilieva and Peak (2016, p. 4) add: 'Student mobility is one of the best developed areas of national-level policies on IHE. This is evidenced by the strong performance of 23 out of the 26 countries studied here.' Many countries have set recruitment targets for incoming as well as for outgoing mobility to encourage higher education institutions to internationalize their learning environments (Ilieva and Peak, 2016). This suggests that countries are mainly interested in short-term economic output (Helms et al., 2015) rather than in the academic or social/cultural rationales of internationalization (Helms et al., 2015; Seeber et al., 2016; de Wit et al., 2015).

6.3.2.3 Promotion Strategies

An important part of the strategy for internationalization introduced in many countries is marketing and promotion, aiming to attract international students (Dodds, 2009). Again, many countries have adopted converging approaches. First, the governments' internationalization agencies have adopted similar online promotion strategies, as indicated by the proliferation of 'study in . . . [country]' websites (Helms et al., 2015). Second, the larger host countries, particularly, have established overseas offices, often linked to their embassies, where services are provided to prospective students, country-focused promotion is disseminated, and international academic collaboration is smoothed (Ilieva and Peak, 2016). Third, promotion strategies are largely based on similarity rather than on unique selling points: all claim reputation and quality for their higher education systems (Ramirez and Tiplic, 2014).[6] As a proxy for reputation or quality, the countries' performances in global rankings have been widely adopted in marketing efforts. Countries – and their higher education institutions – strive to move up the ladder, for example by attracting international students and staff, but even more by undertaking international research, which on average leads to more publications in international journals and has a higher impact. Consequently, international research collaboration has increasingly become part of the national-level research assessments which determine the levels of funding for HEIs (see Section 6.3.1.1 on 'Performance of Higher Education Systems', and Ilieva and Peak, 2016).

Convergence may also be observed in the aspects that make countries attractive to international students (Cremonini and Antonowicz, 2009; Kolster, 2014). We have already mentioned the national scholarship schemes to support inbound and outbound student mobility (see also Ilieva and Peak, 2016). Such scholarship schemes – like the marketing efforts – may be targeted specifically at certain countries that are deemed to be of particular interest. Indeed, there is also a degree of convergence in the choice of target countries (Dodds, 2009), with China, India, Brazil, Mexico, and Indonesia featuring quite frequently.

6.4 Signs of Divergence

Notwithstanding the many signs of convergence, and partly indicated by recent studies (Helms et al., 2015; Ilieva and Peak, 2016), the rationales and practices associated with internationalization also show signs of divergence to other scripts, rationales, and practices. This divergence can to some extent be attributed 'to the eclectic adoption of conflicting principles' (Meyer et al., 1997, p. 154). In other words, divergence can be explained by internationalization contradicting and being contradicted by other scripts and rationales of the same or different actors, which in turn leads to conflicting practices. Divergent practices might occur where 'it is easier to alter policy talk than to promote substantial organizational change' (Ramirez and Tiplic, 2014, p. 443). To illustrate this divergence, the next section discusses divergent, decoupled practices in the internationalization of higher education related to conflicts between national and international interests, migration regulations, mobility, employment, and tuition fees.

6.4.1 *Higher Education to Serve International or National Interests?*

Helms et al. (2015, p. 63) state: 'Without question, approaches to internationalization of higher education should be firmly rooted in the needs of each country's particular higher education system and squarely focused on advancing our own specific institutional and national objectives.' Yet, as indicated by their focus on mobility, countries' needs and interests appear to boil down to obtaining resources, rather than the nobler academic, social, and cultural rationales (see Seeber et al., 2016). The internationalization objective is partly founded on the hypothesized necessity of higher education systems to be international in order to compete on the same level (European Commission, 2013). However, the connection to the national agenda highlights the economic rationale for education and research to serve the national knowledge economy (Maassen, 2014;

Nybom, 2007). Similarly, as a result of internationalization, the work and the population of HEIs are becoming more international and diverse, while national governments simultaneously regard the same HEIs as belonging to and serving the nation (Buckner, 2017; Kolster, 2014; Maassen, 2014). In other words, governments are more likely to view the knowledge and the graduates produced within their higher education system as vital for their national economy, while the academics producing the knowledge and the graduates absorbing it might frame their work more in terms of global interests, such as addressing global challenges. As Sutton and Deardorff (2012) suggest, overcoming the divergence between collective and individual interests would need a reconceptualization of the ideas behind comprehensive internationalization, thus 'requiring a more internationalized form of internationalization, one that positions global engagement, collaboration, goals, and responsibilities at its core' (cited in Helms et al., 2015, p. 64). Arguably, this should happen not only at the organizational level, but also at the national level.

6.4.2 Migration Regulations and Mobility

Strict immigration regulations frequently affect HEIs' capacity to achieve international mobility goals (Becker and Kolster, 2012). Visa restrictions clearly highlight divergence in national policies; while internationalization strategies are generally accepted in the higher education community, opening borders and removing barriers remains a sensitive issue more widely. In other words: 'The prospect of losing the economic returns from international students and the income provided by fee-paying students does not seem to dissuade some governments from imposing stricter regulations on international students' (Van Damme, 2016). The United Kingdom might be the prime example of this: with its highly successful internationalization strategy, it has nevertheless – perhaps responding to popular demand – restricted access through visa restrictions over recent years (Ilieva and Peak, 2016; also see King and Ruiz-Gelices, 2003). In contrast, Australia's efforts to streamline student visa applications are thought to have positively affected international demand for its higher education system (Helms et al., 2015).

As outlined in in Sections 6.3.1 and 6.3.2 on convergence in internationalization strategies and policies, countries' internationalization goals stress student mobility. However, the long-term effect of mobility on the internationalization of higher education might be limited, as connections are largely lost once students have returned to their home countries. International connections are also lost under the slowly emerging trend for many host countries to retain international students for their own labour market. Moreover, international students appear to have little interaction with domestic students unless induced to do so by deliberate interventions (see, e.g., Leask, 2009; Luo and Jamieson-Drake, 2013). Longer-lasting effects on the internationalization of higher education could be achieved by focusing on the mobility of teachers and academics rather than students. Connections created through academic mobility are thought to have greater permanence, yet staff mobility appears to have a much lower priority in the internationalization strategies of all countries (Helms et al., 2015).

The focus on mobility may also have a shadow side. The inflow of international students can put pressure on the accessibility of higher education for domestic students: 'Some Singaporeans now wonder whether such a warm embrace of globalization has restricted opportunities for them and their children ... There appears to be a prevailing sense of frustration with the government's perceived efforts to attract international students while not providing sufficient places for local students' (Waring, 2014, p. 880, cited in Helms et al., 2015, p. 58).[7]

6.4.3 Employment and Tuition Fees

Making higher education more international will undoubtedly lead to students seeking and obtaining employment abroad: studies have found that mobile students are more likely to live abroad after obtaining their degree (European Commission, 2014; Helms et al., 2015; King and Ruiz-Gelices, 2003). This provokes questions about the costs and benefits of public financial support to students (Kolster, 2014): why would either the host or the sending country invest in the education of mobile students if there is uncertainty about their contributing to the country's economy afterwards? The increased efforts of host countries to keep foreign students in their labour market can be seen in the light of this contradiction (de Wit et al., 2015).[8] Likewise, the focus on stimulating outgoing mobility by some countries (e.g. China and Germany) may have a negative effect on the domestic return to higher education as skilled graduates might well remain abroad to find (better) employment opportunities. Knowing that mobile students are likely to become mobile professionals, combined with the increasing importance attached to the economic rationale for internationalization, may ultimately affect the paradigms governing public/private funding rationales (Kolster, 2014).

A practice which follows the economic rationale for internationalization but at the same time exemplifies divergence is the trend for many European higher education systems to charge higher tuition fees to students from outside the European Economic Area (EEA). This acceptance and even promotion of inequality, with students from different backgrounds paying different prices for the same 'product', makes foreign students in Europe more like 'consumers' than their privileged EEA counterparts (Neave and Maassen, 2007). Short-term gains from tuition fees apparently override longer-term gains for the labour market (as emphasized in the preceding paragraph). With respect to tuition fees and funding for higher education, Finland is an interesting case. Finland offers free tuition for EEA students, but plans to introduce tuition fees for non-EEA students, which would make Finnish HEIs less attractive to international students. At the same time, internationalization indicators rewarding mobility figure in the Finnish performance funding model (de Boer et al., 2015).[9]

6.5 Discussion and Conclusion

The world society theory suggests that there is a world culture that provides nation states and other actors with scripts for progress. These scripts are promoted through Otherhood actors, rationalized through scientific research, and provide legitimacy to those enacting them. This chapter has framed the emergence of internationalization of higher education in this perspective, viewing internationalization as a global script for progress, where cultural enactment is more important than the actual realization. This provides a valuable insight into why and how countries – from a cultural perspective – strive for internationalization of higher education. It may also explain why the rationales and practices of the internationalization of higher education show a high degree of convergence, but also some divergence, as there are conflicts with other scripts.

In terms of convergence, many countries started to internationalize their higher education systems on the basis of converging economic and political rationales. This made attracting international students, academics, and funding a top priority. The ways in which countries try to realize this priority are largely similar: marketing, scholarships, in-country offices or agents, branch campuses, strategic alignments in (international) networks, and by highlighting their quality and reputation. In other words, countries are using similar internationalization practices, and base them on similar rationales (Kolster, 2014; van Vught et al., 2002; de Wit et al., 2015). Consequently, we observe convergence of ideas and aspirations; convergence of external pressures; convergence in legislation, organizational structures, and policy design around 'policy rhetoric' and around policy practice and implementation (de Wit et al., 2015). The high degree of convergence can be explained by nation states enacting global scripts for progress.

Yet, enactment of these scripts may not actually lead to making higher education systems more international. Following the world society perspective, legitimacy derives from claiming to be internationalized. This phenomenological perspective may explain the divergence associated with the internationalization of higher education. To be more specific, despite countries' visible and formal commitment to the internationalization of higher education (e.g. active promotion and internationalization strategies), several diverging practices, such as migration policies and tuition fee regulations, suggest the prevalence of symbolic or ceremonial conformity and the decoupled nature of countries' internationalization policies. As Helms et al. (2015, p. 45) state in relation to the notion of internationalization as a comprehensive, cross-cutting phenomenon: 'there are a small number of policies visible on the global landscape that take a more expansive position on what can and should be undertaken and achieved in this arena'. In other words, the internationalization rationales and practices of countries appear to pay lip-service to the inherent implications of internationalization, but – as illustrated by the divergent practices discussed here – do not fully follow these objectives. From a world society perspective, these are indications that there is a degree of decoupling between the implications of internationalization and policies, as well between practices and implementation (Buckner, 2017; Hasse and Krücken, 2014; Meyer et al., 1997).

Regarding these divergences, we focused in this chapter on inherent contradictions and decouplings, but we did not highlight the correlations with governance arrangements in governments, other system-level actors, or higher education institutions. It is apparent, though, that in systems which have more powerful international and supranational actors (such as the EU in the context of the Bologna Process) there are stronger pressures towards convergence than in higher education systems without (e.g. New Zealand or South Africa).

Moreover, the conflicts among objectives allow some room for agency: when world culture scripts contradict one another, authorities may use other arguments to legitimize their policy choices. This does not mean, however, that policy choice in the absence of clear guidance from world culture is completely free or random. Path dependencies, local power balances, and economic and other contexts may push towards certain choices and arrangements. For instance, the economic rationale for the internationalization of higher education is much less controversial in the USA, the United Kingdom, and Australia as compared to Scandinavian countries, while countries in the Global South with growing populations hold different views on student mobility and brain-circulation than those in the global North with ageing populations.

That said, the overview of convergent and divergent rationales and practices presented in this chapter suggests that the calls by Helms et al. (2015) and Ilieva and Peak (2016) for greater synergies in countries' internationalization practices are justified. Further research is needed to explore the convergence and divergence of the internationalization of higher education and its implications for the governance of higher education through more empirically grounded studies.

Notes

1. In our conceptualization, a higher education system is the collection of higher education institutions under the jurisdiction of a governmental authority, which sets rules and provides conditions under which the higher education institutions operate.
2. For more information, see www.ref.ac.uk/.
3. For an overview of the European identity literature, see Bergmann (2015).
4. Admittedly, this is difficult to do given the vagueness surrounding the concepts and their learning outcomes (Trede et al., 2013).
5. See www.iau-aiu.net/content/national-policies.
6. This might be the rational thing to do, as 'nation-states do not want to appear too different from each other' (Alasuutari, 2015, p. 167)

7. Similar pressures on the accessibility of higher education to domestic students appear to exist in Hong Kong (international students taking up scarce places) and in China (lower admission standards for international students). See Leung and Sharma (2017); Sharma (2017).
8. Note that for host countries, this also contradicts the brain-circulation argument: it is an effort to increase brain-gain (hence brain-drain for the sending country), but not brain-circulation.
9. Similar arrangements in performance funding models have been made in Croatia and Poland (European Commission et al., 2015).

References

Alasuutari, P. (2015) The discursive side of new institutionalism. *Cultural Sociology*, 9(2), 162–184.

Altbach, P. G., and Peterson, P. M. (2008) Higher education as a projection of America's soft power. In W. Yasushi and D. L. McConnell (Eds), *Soft power superpowers: Cultural and national assets of Japan and the United States*, pp. 37–53. Abingdon and New York: Routledge.

Appelt, S., van Beuzekom, B., Galindo-Rueda, F., and de Pinho, R. (2015) Which factors influence the international mobility of research scientists? In A. Geuna (Ed.), *Global mobility of research scientists: The economics of who goes where and why*, pp. 177–213. London: Academic Press.

Becker, R., and Kolster, R. (2012) *International student recruitment: Policies and developments in selected countries*. The Hague: Nuffic.

Bergmann, L. (2015) *The Erasmus program and European identity: Does studying abroad foster a feeling of European identity?* Bachelor's thesis. Enschede: University of Twente.

BFUG (2009) The European Higher Education Area (EHEA) in a global context: Report on overall developments at the European, national and institutional levels. Approved by BFUG at its meeting in Prague, 12–13 February 2009.

de Boer, H., Jongbloed, B., Benneworth, P., et al. (2015) *Performance-based funding and performance agreements in fourteen higher education systems*. Enschede: Center for Higher Education Policy Studies.

Brandenburg, U., Berghoff, S., Taboadela, O., et al. (2014) *The ERASMUS impact study: Effects of mobility on the skills and employability of students and the internationalisation of higher education institutions*. Luxembourg: Publications Office of the European Union.

Buckner, E. S. (2017) The changing discourse on higher education and the nation-state, 1960–2010. *Higher Education*, 74(3), 473–489.

Chieffo, L., and Griffiths, L. (2004) Large-scale assessment of student attitudes after a short-term study abroad program. *Frontiers: The interdisciplinary journal of study abroad*, 10, 165–177.

Cohen, M. D., March, J. G., and Olsen, J. P. (1972) A garbage can model of organizational choice. *Administrative Science Quarterly*, 17(1), 1–25.

Cremonini, L., and Antonowicz, D. (2009) In the eye of the beholder? Conceptualizing academic attraction in the global higher education market. *European Education*, 41(2), 52–74.

Crossman, J. E., and Clarke, M. (2010) International experience and graduate employability: Stakeholder perceptions on the connection. *Higher Education*, 59(5), 599–613.

Delgado-Márquez, B. L., Escudero-Torres, M. A., and Hurtado-Torres, N. E. (2013) Being highly internationalised strengthens your reputation: An empirical investigation of top higher education institutions. *Higher Education*, 66(5), 619–633.

Dodds, A. (2009) Liberalization and the public sector: The pre-eminent role of governments in the 'sale' of higher education abroad. *Public Administration*, 87(2), 397–411.

Drori, G. S., Meyer, J. W., Ramirez, F. O., and Schofer, E. (2003) *Science in the modern world polity: Institutionalization and globalization*. Stanford: Stanford University Press.

EP-Nuffic (2016) *Report of a study to measure how many students stayed in the Netherlands after graduating in 2008–09*. The Hague: EP-Nuffic.

European Commission (2013) European higher education in the world. Communication from the Commission to the European Parliament, the Council, the European Economic and Social Committee and the Committee of the Regions, Brussels, 11 July.

European Commission (2014) *Effects of mobility on the skills and employability of students and the internationalisation of higher education institutions*. Luxembourg: Publications Office of the European Union.

European Commission, EACEA, and Eurydice (2015) *The European Higher Education Area in 2015: Bologna Process implementation report*. Luxembourg: Publications Office of the European Union.

Federkeil, G., van Vught, F. A., and Westerheijden, D. F. (2012) An evaluation and critique of current rankings. In F. A. van Vught, and F. Ziegele (Eds) *Multidimensional ranking: The design and development of U-Multirank*, pp. 39–70. Dordrecht: Springer.

Ferreia de Lima Jr, A. (2007) The role of international educational exchanges in public diplomacy. *Place Branding and Public Diplomacy*, 3(3), 234–251.

Frank, D. J., and Gabler, J. (2006) *Reconstructing the university: Worldwide shifts in academia in the 20th century.* Stanford: Stanford University Press.

Goldfinch, S., and Wallis, J. (2010) Two myths of convergence in public management reform. *Public Administration,* 88(4), 1099–1115.

Hasse, R., and Krücken, G. (2014) Coupling and decoupling in education. In B. Holzer, F. Kastner, and T. Werron (Eds) *From globalization to world society,* pp. 197–214. New York: Routledge.

Helms, R. M. (2014) *Campus internationalization: Going international.* Washington, DC: American Council on Education. www.acenet.edu/the-presidency/columns-and-features/Pages/Going-International.aspx.

Helms, R. M., Rumbley, L. E., Brajkovic, L., and Mihut, G. (2015) *Internationalizing higher education worldwide: National policies and programs.* Washington, DC: American Council on Education.

Hénard, F., Diamond, L., and Roseveare, D. (2012) *Approaches to internationalisation and their implications for strategic management and institutional practice.* Paris: OECD, Institutional Management in Higher Education.

Horta, H. (2009) Global and national prominent universities: internationalization, competitiveness and the role of the State. *Higher Education,* 58 (3), 387–405.

Ilieva, J., and Peak, M. (2016) *The shape of global higher education: National policies framework for international engagement, emerging themes.* London: The British Council.

Jang, Y. S. (2000) The worldwide founding of ministries of science and technology, 1950–1990. *Sociological Perspectives,* 43(2), 247–270.

Jones, E. (2013) Internationalization and employability: The role of intercultural experiences in the development of transferable skills. *Public Money & Management,* 33(2), 95–104.

King, R., and Ruiz-Gelices, E. (2003) International student migration and the European 'year abroad': Effects on European identity and subsequent migration behaviour. *International Journal of Population Geography,* 9 (3), 229–252.

Knight, J. (2015) Updated definition of internationalization. *International Higher Education,* 33. doi:10.6017/ihe.2003.33.7391

Kolster, R. (2014) Academic attractiveness of countries: A possible benchmark strategy applied to the Netherlands. *European Journal of Higher Education,* 4(2), 118–134.

Krücken, G., and Drori, G. S. (Eds) (2009) *World society: The writings of John W. Meyer.* Oxford: Oxford University Press.

Krücken, G. A., Kosmutzky, A., and Torka, M. (Eds) (2007) *Towards a multiversity? Universities between global trends and national traditions.* Bielefeld: Transcript Verlag.

Leask, B. (2009) Using formal and informal curricula to improve interactions between home and international students. *Journal of Studies in International Education*, 13(2), 205–221.

Lee, J. T. (2015) Soft power and cultural diplomacy: Emerging education hubs in Asia. *Comparative Education* 51(3), 353–374.

Leung, M., and Sharma, Y. (2017) Row over funds for mainland Chinese overseas students. *University World News*, Issue No. 447, 16 February.

Luo, J., and Jamieson-Drake, D. (2013) Examining the educational benefits of interacting with international students. *Journal of International Students*, 3(2), 85–101.

Maassen, P. (2014) A new social contract for higher education? In G. Goastellec and F. Picard (Eds) *Higher education in societies: A multi scale perspective*, pp. 33–50. Rotterdam: Sense Publishers.

Maassen, P., and Stensaker, B. (2011) The knowledge triangle, European higher education policy logics and policy implications. *Higher Education*, 61(6), 757–769.

Maassen, P., Nerland, M., Pinheiro, R., et al. (2012) Change dynamics and higher education reforms. In M. Vukasović, P. Maassen, M. Nerland, B. Stensaker, and A. Vabo (Eds) *Effects of higher education reforms: Change dynamics*, pp. 1–17. Rotterdam: Sense Publishers.

Malicki, R., and Potts, D. (2013) The outcomes of outbound student mobility: A summary of academic literature. Frenchs Forest, NSW: AIM Overseas. http://aimoverseas.com.au/wp-content/uploads/2013/08/UAAs iaBoundOutcomesResearch-Final.pdf

Marginson, S. (2009) University rankings, government and social order: Managing the field of higher education according to the logic of the performative present-as-future. In M. Simons, M. Olssen, and M. Peters (Eds) *Re-reading education policies: Studying the policy agenda of the 21st century*, pp. 584–604. Rotterdam: Sense Publishers.

Marginson, S. (2016) The role of the state in university science: Russia and China compared. Working paper No. 9. London: Centre for Global Higher Education.

Martens, K., and Wolf, K. D. (2009) Boomerangs and Trojan horses: The unintended consequences of internationalising education policy through the EU and the OECD. In A. Amaral, G. Neave, C. Musselin, and P. Maassen (Eds) *European integration and the governance of higher education and research*, pp. 81–107. Dordrecht: Springer Netherlands.

Meyer, J. W. (2000) Globalization sources and effects on national states and societies. *International Sociology*, 15(2), 233–248.

Meyer, J. W. (2010) World society, institutional theories, and the actor. *Annual Review of Sociology*, 36, 1–20.

Meyer, J. W., Boli, J., Thomas, G. M., and Ramirez, F. O. (1997) World society and the nation-state. *American Journal of Sociology*, 103(1), 144–181.

Munch, C., and Hoch, M. (2013) *The financial impact of cross-border student mobility on the economy of the host country.* Berlin: German Academic Exchange Service.

Neave, G., and Maassen, P. (2007) The Bologna Process: An intergovernmental policy perspective. In P. Maassen and J. P. Olsen (Eds) *University dynamics and European integration*, pp. 135–154. Dordrecht: Springer Netherlands.

Nybom, T. (2007) A rule-governed community of scholars: The Humboldt vision in the history of the European university. In P. Maassen, and J. P. Olsen (Eds) *University dynamics and European integration*, pp. 55–80. Dordrecht: Springer Netherlands.

Nye Jr, J. S. (2004) *Soft power: The means to success in world politics.* New York: PublicAffairs.

OECD (2015) *Education at a glance 2015: OECD indicators.* Paris: OECD Publishing.

OECD (2016) The internationalisation of doctoral and master's studies. *Education Indicators in Focus*, 39. Paris: OECD Publishing.

Ramirez, F. O., and Tiplic, D. (2014) In pursuit of excellence? Discursive patterns in European higher education research. *Higher Education*, 67(4), 439–455.

Rizvi, F. (2011) Theorizing student mobility in an era of globalization. *Teachers and Teaching*, 17(6), 693–701.

Ross, J., and Hare, J. (2016) Foreign students reap $20bn. *The Australian*, 20 November. www.theaustralian.com.au/national-affairs/education/interna tional-education-reaps-record-20bn/news-story/d850079eec0e4bb688c7b22 e60591c5f

Salmi, J. (2009) *The challenge of establishing world-class universities.* Washington, DC: World Bank.

Seeber, M., Cattaneo, M., Huisman, J., and Paleari, S. (2016) Why do higher education institutions internationalize? An investigation of the multilevel determinants of internationalization rationales. *Higher Education*, 72(5), 685–702.

Sharma, Y. (2017) Row over 'easy' admission for international students. *University World News*, Issue No. 448, 22 February.

Sin, C., and Neave, G. (2016) Employability deconstructed: Perceptions of Bologna stakeholders. *Studies in Higher Education*, 41(8), 1447–1462.

Sutton, S., and Deardorff, D. K. (2012) Internationalizing internationalization: The global context. *IAU's Horizons*, 17(3)/18(1), 16–17.

Teichler, U. (2009) Internationalisation of higher education: European experiences. *Asia Pacific Education Review*, 10(1), 93–106.

Tight, M. (2007) Bridging the divide: A comparative analysis of articles in higher education journals published inside and outside North America. *Higher Education*, 53(2), 235–253.

Trede, F., Bowles, W., and Bridges, D. (2013) Developing intercultural competence and global citizenship through international experiences: Academics' perceptions. *Intercultural Education*, 24(5), 442–455.

Van Damme, D. (2016) Is international academic migration stimulating scientific research and innovation? OECD *Education and Skills Today blog*, 9 March. http://oecdeducationtoday.blogspot.co.uk/2016/03/is-international-academic-migration_9.html

van Vught, F. A., and Ziegele, F. (Eds) (2012) *Multidimensional ranking: The design and development of U-Multirank*. Dordrecht: Springer.

van Vught, F. A., van der Wende, M. C., and Westerheijden, D. F. (2002) Globalization and internationalization: Policy agendas compared. In O. Fulton, and J. Enders (Eds), *Higher education in a globalizing world: International trends and mutual observations*, pp. 103–120. Dordrecht: Kluwer.

Waring, P. (2014) Singapore's global schoolhouse strategy: Retreat or recalibration? *Studies in Higher Education*, 39(5), 874–884.

Westerheijden, D. F., Beerkens, E., Cremonini, L., et al. (2010) *The first decade of working on the European Higher Education Area: The Bologna Process independent assessment – Executive summary, overview and conclusions*. Vienna: European Commission, Directorate-General for Education and Culture.

de Wit, H. (1999) Changing rationales for the internationalisation of higher education. *International Higher Education*, Spring, 2–3.

de Wit, H. (2009) *Internationalization of higher education in the United States of America and Europe*. Charlotte: IAP.

de Wit, H., Hunter, F., Howard, L., and Egron-Polak, E. (2015) *Internationalisation of higher education*. Brussels: European Parliament.

7 Convergence through Research Performance Measurement?
Comparing Talk and Practices in Australia, Canada, and the United Kingdom

JENNY M. LEWIS*

7.1 Introduction

At any given moment in the world today, individuals, small groups of people, and organizations of any size, as well as sub-national and national governments and world regions, are busy comparing their performance with that of others. With an ongoing attachment to the idea that governments (or, at least, Western liberal democracies) should be held accountable, and a continuing adherence to what is loosely called New Public Management (NPM), publicly funded services have, accordingly, been subjected to ever-greater levels of scrutiny through the lens of performance measurement.

Higher education has been at the forefront of this emphasis in measurement, particularly with regard to research. Many governments have used national research performance assessment regimes as a means to pursue their strategic goals for the higher education sector. Such systems evaluate and sort universities into tiers that are (more or less) visible to the public gaze. The impact of these performance measurement exercises is in some cases reputational, and in others more financially consequential, with substantial effects on the funding allocated to universities. Internationally, the mushrooming of world rankings of universities is testament to the fact that in higher education there is a strong emphasis on 'measuring up' to some world standard. University executives pay close attention to the Times Higher Education, Shanghai Jiao Tong, Quacquarelli Symonds, and other

* This work was supported by an Australian Research Council Future Fellowship (FT110100110). Many thanks to Isabel Jackson for her second coding of the interview transcripts.

184

world rankings of universities to see how their reputation in this global market is holding up.

National measurement systems can be seen to serve an important function with regard to governance, and a desire to control (Radin, 2006; Smith, 1995) and to steer policy sectors in particular directions. Performance measures became increasingly fashionable with the rise of NPM because they provide the opportunity for government to retain firm control over departments using a hands-off strategy (Carter, 1989), and to incentivize the behaviour of subordinate governments (Bertelli and John, 2010). This dynamic is in operation in the higher education sector of many nations. Performance measurement is closely linked to a governance strategy of steering universities in terms of what type of research is done, how it is conducted, and what kind of research is most highly valued (Lewis, 2013).

This chapter begins from an assumption that research performance measurement is an important instrument of governance (Bjørnholt and Larsen, 2014), designed to steer the higher education sector in a specific direction. Performance measurement is always a political decision, and it is about both accountability and control (Lewis, 2015a). It is directed at many different entities – policy making processes, organizations, individuals (see Talbot, 2005); it serves multiple purposes (Behn, 2008); and it represents a variety of goals and values. In order to focus on the level of convergence between nations, this chapter examines the range of stated purposes that sit behind the decision to measure performance.

The empirical examination that follows looks at Australia, Canada, and the United Kingdom, and is focused on assessing convergence in 'talk' about performance measurement by senior administrators, rather than convergence in content and practices (Pollitt, 2001). It seeks to uncover how performance measurement is labelled and represented in these countries, and to examine the level of similarity across the three nations. Hence, performance measurement is a specific example of a governance instrument which is utilized to shed light on how the higher education sector is being steered in various locations. Australia, Canada, and the United Kingdom were chosen because of the broad similarities in their global position in higher education. But there is also an important difference: Canada, unlike the other two countries, has no national research assessment framework. Hence, this chapter provides a comparison of divergence in practices, given that two of the cases have implemented such systems while the third has not.

7.2 Higher Education Policy

Much has been written about an apparent similarity in the transformation of higher education in numerous nations, related to a common set of exogenous processes, political and economic logics, and governance trajectories (see the Introduction to this volume). The literature generally concludes that this uniform set of pressures results in convergence in the application of particular tools and governance outcomes. We will return to this assumption of convergence shortly. For the moment, it is important to briefly summarize these international trends.

Over the last three decades, Western governments have substantially altered their strategies for governing higher education and research policy. Nation states have become more proactive in defining what is valued as research 'outputs' and in identifying research priority areas. States have taken up new modes of governance to address concerns about value for money, and to direct attention and funds towards research in a way that brings it closer to national economic policy. This has redefined the relationships between governments, individual universities and groups of universities (such as the Russell Group of research-intensive universities in the United Kingdom), and academic discipline-based societies and associations. Governments and funding agencies have become far more influential in setting directions and priorities for research (Whitley, 2010).

To achieve this, governments have used both NPM and Network Governance-based instruments. These have different sets of drivers associated with them, but they have both been used in many countries (Lewis, 2015b). The rise of performance measurement is closely related to the spread of NPM, which has flourished as a policy paradigm and control technology in higher education in the United Kingdom (Deem et al., 2007), but also in other nations. One of its most important tools has been the measurement of academic productivity and the increasing specification of which kinds of research outputs are most highly valued. The spread of a performative and evaluative culture has been implemented through research performance evaluation systems in many countries (Scott, 2009). The United Kingdom exported performance-based research assessment systems to Australia and New Zealand. These systems have also had impacts in European countries and beyond (Whitley and Gläser, 2007; Whitley et al., 2010).

However, as King (2010) has argued, even in states where liberalization, deregulation, and NPM ideas have dominated the reform of higher education in recent decades, there is remarkable variation in how these ideas and policy instruments have been adapted to local conditions, and they have been utilized in quite different ways. The insights of institutionalism should lead us to not be surprised by this finding – after all, governance in any nation is surely shaped by the particular institutional arrangements that are in place, which continue to have an important effect on any new ideas and reform directions. The growing corporatization of universities and increased reliance on managerial and market rationalities to allocate resources are both widespread, but also uneven in application and effects.

Convergence is a fuzzy analytical concept, unable to capture the complexity of reform when it is put into motion in different contexts (Pollitt, 2001). While the pressures on higher education governance are similar in many countries, and the effects of isomorphic pressures are certainly apparent both within and across nations, change is also influenced by local ideas, interests, and institutions. As Pollitt (2001) argues, we should think about convergence in terms of talk, practices, and labels, which rarely line up with decisions, actions, and results. Talk often converges across nations around a set of ideas that ought to be applied. Practices sometimes become more similar, but not always. Labels often converge, but this does not carry through to actual content. And in the final analysis, even when talk and labels converge, decisions, actions, and results often do not.

In summary, a rising interest in universities as tools of the knowledge economy, a desire to evaluate the productivity of universities, and the more general shift to allocating funds based on activity and outputs have all contributed to the introduction of performance measurement systems in many nations. They are tools used very deliberately by governments to steer universities (at arm's length) in line with their strategic interests. However, we should not leap to the conclusion that these systems are naturally or necessarily convergent with regard to decisions, actions, and results.

7.3 Performance Measurement as a Tool for Governing

The escalation of performance measurement in the public sector, beginning in the 1970s, is often associated with economic decline, increased international competition, and a new set of objectives related to cutting budgets and increasing the efficiency and effectiveness of public bureaucracies. NPM came to be seen as the solution to the budgetary challenges facing all sectors and all levels of government in many different countries. Christopher Hood's (1991) classic statement of NPM describes it as containing a number of doctrinal components, including hands-on professional management, explicit standards and measures of performance, and greater emphasis on output controls. Performance measurement is clearly central to NPM, which supported a new belief that previous problems could be avoided if there was more measurement and more management.

On paper, the explicit purpose behind performance measurement is to improve performance. Beyond this, there are many different reasons why it might be introduced. It may be for the purposes of evaluation, to discover if a programme is doing what it is supposed to do. It might be used to control the performance of those working in a programme or service of interest. It might be simply a means of controlling the budget for a particular area, or determining how much money is being spent to achieve some desired output. It might even be a means of driving centrally determined goals and priorities. Sometimes performance measurement is undertaken in order to eliminate a programme, sometimes it is used to support a new direction, and sometimes it is about maximizing returns on taxes and accountability to the public (Radin, 2006). Among the many different reasons why public managers measure performance, Behn (2008) has listed eight: to evaluate, control, budget, motivate, promote, celebrate, learn, and improve.

The institutional approach to the topic of performance measurement by Brignall and Modell (2000) shows the need to go beyond the assumptions underpinning much of the literature on performance measurement. Their analysis demonstrates the different interests and values represented by funding bodies, professional service providers, and purchasers of public services. Some significant questions about performance measurement include who decides on the measures and how they are linked to an organization's structure and functioning. Multiple stakeholders inside and outside compete to set performance measures that will advance their own interests (Kanter and Summers, 1987). Despite the explicit purpose of improvement, it is clear that the implicit purpose of performance measurement can be any number of things, and that it is ultimately about some form of control (Lewis, 2015a).

Further to this, political institutions are the structural means by which those in power pursue their interests (Moe, 1990). Hence, public bureaucracies, whether the performance measurement criteria are externally or internally devised, are institutions of coercion and redistribution: the structural choices made in their creation are implicitly linked to the need of governments to control them, while providing them with some autonomy. If these organizations are also the creators of (their own or others') performance measures, their control is explicitly observable in the decisions they make about goals, targets, and which data to collect.

Talbot (2005) lists a number of the possible functions of performance measurement. It may be used for accountability and transparency; for generating information to inform user choice; for reporting on success against stated aims; for improving efficiency; for increasing the focus on outcomes and effectiveness; for assisting decision making about resource allocation; and for adding value through issues such as equity, probity, and building social capital. This list points to some of the different audiences for performance information (governments, managers, service users). It also indicates some different purposes for it (meeting targets, making the best use of resources, improving outcomes), and some possible values that might underlie it other than the purely economic (equity, justice, inclusion).

Clearly, performance measurement has multiple concerns. As noted earlier, these include what is done and how (processes as the key concern), as well as the results of what is done (outputs or outcomes as the key concern). In addition, it might serve merely as a presentational device to assure the intended audience that all is well (ceremonial) (Collier, 2008). Some claim that performance measurement has become an end in itself, its main purpose being to generate measures (Schick, 2001). But the mere existence of performance measures certainly has an impact on the functioning of individuals and organizations.

A question that logically follows the decision to measure performance is the question of what should be measured. A good place to begin in answering this question is to distinguish between policy performance, organizational performance, and individual performance (Talbot, 2005). A policy focus is the most complete, because it is not confined to a single organization or tier of government. But it is diffuse and difficult to pin down, and attributing performance to a particular policy is problematic. Focusing on organizations is easier because it allows for performance to be related to resourcing and accountability and for models from the private sector to be imported and used. Individual performance is more closely related to human resource management. So performance measurement might occur at the policy or system level (nations), at the organizational level (universities), or at the individual level (academics).

Performance measurement is a specific policy instrument, aligned with NPM as an overall governance mode. It has been increasingly applied to higher education and numerous other policy sectors in many countries since the 1980s, and so provides a useful focal point for examining convergence in the sector. Higher education has witnessed its widespread application as reforms have focused on competition as a means to direct the behaviour of universities. An emphasis on demonstrating that expenditure is not 'wasteful', and that public funds are being used in an efficient and effective manner, ensures that the sector is scrutinized carefully. A more detailed examination of the research performance systems in each of the three nations considered in this chapter follows in the next section.

7.4 Comparing Three Nations

Australia, Canada, and the United Kingdom have much shared history and similar political institutions. In relation to the concerns of this book about convergence and diversity, all three compete in the global higher education market. This, plus other institutional factors, lead these three nations to be considered as quite similar cases, and therefore likely to be strongly convergent in rhetoric but also in actions. However, some important institutional differences are worth surveying before the examination of convergence begins.

Each of these countries has a Westminster model of parliamentary government in place. The United Kingdom is a unitary state – although devolution has seen some instances where Scotland and Wales have begun to assert a degree of local autonomy against the UK government. It is institutionally the most centralized of the three nations under

Table 7.1 *Three nations in comparison*

	United Kingdom	Australia	Canada
State structure	Unitary centralized coordinated	Federal, strongly coordinated	Federal, loosely coordinated
Dominant governance mode[1]	Core NPM	Core NPM	NPM limited
National performance framework for higher education (research)[2]	Research Excellence Framework Linked to substantial amount of funding (25%)	Excellence in Research for Australia (ERA) Linked to small amount of funding (6%)	None Linked to funding (related to a range of indicators, not solely research) in Alberta and Ontario

Notes and sources
1. Based on Pollitt and Bouckaert's (2011) classification of main public management reform type in these nations.
2. From Hicks (2012); OCUFA (2006).

consideration in this chapter. Australia and Canada are both federations of states/territories/provinces, but they have disparate versions of federalism. Australia represents a strongly coordinated version of federalism, while coordination in Canada is weaker (see Table 7.1). In effect there is not one higher education system in Canada, but 13 systems (one for each province and territory).

In Australia, the constitution enumerates the powers of the Commonwealth (federal) level, leaving the residual powers with the states. The Commonwealth has very few exclusive areas of power, and the concurrent powers of legislation suggest a system focused on intergovernmental cooperation (Emy and Hughes, 1988). However, the Commonwealth's largely exclusive power over direct taxation makes the Commonwealth a powerful policy actor (Painter, 2000). State/territory governments depend to a large extent on Commonwealth grants, but they retain varying levels of control over a range of important policy areas. They have a relatively small amount of control in higher education.

Canada has a highly competitive and decentralized political structure and, as a result, quite uncoordinated public policies (Tomblin, 2000). Braun et al. (2002) label the Canadian system as a 'power separation model', in which a separation of jurisdictional authority and bipolarity predominates, in addition to competition. Indeed, the system was designed to protect cultural and economic diversity and to make it correspondingly difficult to impose/coordinate policies. With respect to fiscal federalism, the Canadian federal government has considerable scope to take unilateral action in terms of developing and using fiscal instruments, raising revenues, and restricting the transfer of revenue. The federal level and the provinces have some autonomy from each other in terms of elements such as sales taxation and in expenditures where each level has exclusive responsibilities (Braun et al., 2002). However, an element of fiscal interdependence has entered into several core policy sectors where provinces have had traditional jurisdiction, including higher education.

These different government arrangements are reflected in the different approaches to (national) performance measurement of these nations. The United Kingdom was an early adopter of NPM reforms, and has applied a raft of managerial reforms followed by market-based reforms. Australia was not far behind on these trajectories. In Pollitt and Bouckaert's (2011) classification, these are both core NPM states, meaning that they most fully embraced the principles of both managerialism and competition (Considine and Lewis, 1999). Performance measurement at the national level is widespread in both Australia and the United Kingdom.

While Canada shared much of the rhetoric of NPM in the early days, it did not go as far as other nations in implementing NPM. It embraced the marketization idea, but it also held on to the tradition of a fairly stable and neutral civil service, which moderated the pace and scope of change (Pollitt and Bouckaert, 2011). Higher education exemplifies this difference. There is no national framework or set of performance measures. There is, however, substantial funding for research activities and infrastructures that support research collaboration and specific research priorities. A national Performance Measurement Framework applies to all programmes and all government departments and is aligned with setting strategic objectives for these. The decentralized governmental regime of Canada, along with its different governance approach (more limited managerialism and competition and greater institutional autonomy) and its greater emphasis on research grants to direct priorities, make it distinctive (Capano, 2015).

As noted earlier, since the 1980s, many nation states have become proactive in defining and measuring research 'outputs'. The United Kingdom was the first mover in 1986, and Australia followed in 1995. A total of 14 countries had some kind of system by 2010 (Hicks, 2012). These systems account for relatively small amounts of funding compared to grants and teaching funding: they amount to around 6 per cent of total revenue in Australia, but a more substantial 25 per cent in the United Kingdom (Hicks, 2012). In addition, they have important reputational effects, and universities are keenly aware of this.[1] Research status and standing are significant because of the influence of world rankings of universities. These are substantially based on measures of research quantity and quality.

The research assessment systems of Australia and the United Kingdom are broadly comparable, and have influenced each other's attempts to measure research performance. They rest on assessments that include publication quantity and quality as important components. Unlike other countries (Whitley and Gläser, 2007), there are funding allocations tied to these research performance measures. As such, these two national systems are among the most interventionist variants of research assessment. The central steering by these national governments, backed up by the rewards for increased research productivity, can only be ignored by individual universities if they are willing to accept significant losses of funding (Lewis, 2013).

Canada, on the other hand, has not introduced a national-level system of measurement for research performance. Several provinces (Alberta, Ontario, British Columbia, Saskatchewan, and the Maritime provinces) have introduced indicators: performance indicators related to enrolments and graduations in Alberta and Ontario; a range of indicators in British Columbia; institution-specific indicators in Saskatchewan; and student outcomes, resources, and labour market analysis in the Maritimes. Only two provinces (Alberta and Ontario) have tied these to funding (OCUFA, 2006). Some summary information on the three case nations is provided in Table 7.1.

This comparison highlights the similarities and differences of the three nations' dominant governance modes, and their research performance practices (specifically related to national research assessment systems). An in-depth empirical examination of 'talk' was undertaken through the use of interviews. These were conducted with senior administrators in departments, funding agencies, and performance measurement agencies related to higher education in each of the three countries during 2014–2015. In government departments, these people were generally at director level, with some line responsibility for performance measurement. In other agencies, the individuals were generally the CEO or equivalent. A total of 16 people were interviewed, and these were split fairly evenly across the three nations (see the Appendix for more details).

The number of different organizations involved in measuring performance is large, and a small number of interviews cannot possibly hope to cover the entire gamut of perspectives. Hence, the analysis that follows should be considered as representing the views of just a few of the many individuals and organizations involved, which might potentially be a small subset of the range of responses that would be uncovered by interviewing more people in different agencies. Nevertheless, these interviews provide an insight into these senior administrators' understandings of the purpose of performance measurement in higher education, at the policy and strategy-setting level.

The interviews were recorded and transcribed. In answering a set of broad questions, the interviewees responded in different orders and in varied combinations, not closely following a tightly ordered, question-and-answer script. The transcripts were then read with two different aims: first, to uncover the multiple stated purposes of performance measurement; and second, to identify common and unique themes. The first reading was centred on creating lists of answers under the headings shown in Tables 7.2 to 7.4, regardless of where the responses occurred within the interview. The second reading was used in combination with the lists shown in the tables, to identify themes that were common across the nations for a particular policy sector and themes that were unique.

To increase the reliability of this process, the author (and interviewer) and a second coder individually extracted the first lists for each case, and then searched for commonalities and differences across the nations and the policy sectors. There was substantial overlap between the two different coders, but additional detail was also picked up by the second coder. Where differences in interpretation occurred, the second coder's version was rechecked against the transcript by the first coder (author and interviewer). In cases where there were

Table 7.2 *Performance measurement talk in Australia*

Who is involved?	*National government and departments/agencies:* The Government. The Minister. Politicians. Cabinet. Opposition. Prime Minister and Cabinet. Treasury. Department of Education. Carrick Institute (now Australian Learning and Teaching Institute, Department of Education). Department of Finance. Department of Industrial Relations. Department of Health. Department of Foreign Affairs and Trade. Office of the Chief Scientist. National Health and Medical Research Council. Australian Research Council. *Accreditation and standards:* Accreditation bodies. Tertiary Education Quality Standards Association. Council of Private Higher Education. TAFE Directors. Higher Education Standards Panel. *The university peak bodies:* Group of 8. Universities Australia. Innovative Research Universities. Regional Universities Network (2). Deputy Vice Chancellors Research Networks. *Learned societies:* Australian Academy of Technological Sciences and Engineering (3). The four learned academies. Australian Council of Learned Academies. *Others:* Business Council of Australia.
Why measure?	National and global competitiveness (2). Diversification. Knowledge economy. Alignment with industry desires. Compliance. Money, spending, wastage. Training. Quality assurance. Risk. Transparency. Integrity. Influence the behaviour of universities (3)
Measure what?	Research quality. Publications. Impact factors. Citations. Metrics. Research income. Impact, industry collaboration. Patents. Teaching quality. International student attrition. Student satisfaction and outcomes (retention, completion, graduate outcomes). Research Higher Degree completions. Threshold standards. Governance.

Table 7.2 *(cont.)*

Measure how?	Excellence in Research for Australia (ERA). Block grants to universities (SRE). Higher Education Research Data Collection. Peer assessment. Teaching awards. Regulation and standard-setting agencies (AQF, HESP, TEQSA). Statutory accounts to parliament. Financial analysis. Reviews by universities, experts, consulting firms, overseas experts.
Who resists?	Academics. The Group of 8. Universities Australia. Vice Chancellors. Deputy Vice Chancellors Research.
Why?	Workload of collating data (e.g. ERA). Lack of clarity of processes. System not capturing what it should. Not comparable across disciplines.

conflicting interpretations, the author's version was used. When the same response was recorded from different interviewees – this was mostly with regard to the 'who is involved?' question – the number of mentions is shown in brackets in Tables 7.2 to 7.4.

7.5 Performance Measurement in Three Nations

The responses from interviewees for the three countries are shown in Tables 7.2, 7.3, and 7.4. In answering the question 'who is involved?', interviewees named a series of national political positions and organizations (e.g. government, ministers, Cabinet), government departments and authorities, and research funding agencies as being involved in measuring performance. In Canada, provincial ministers and ministries and agencies (where this work occurs) were nominated. Regulation, accreditation, and standards bodies were mentioned in Australia and the United Kingdom, but not in Canada. Peak groups for universities (e.g. The Group of 8 in Australia, the Russell Group in the United Kingdom) and Vice Chancellors were mentioned in Australia and the United Kingdom, but not in Canada. Learned societies were nominated in Australia and Canada, but not in the United Kingdom. Individual

Table 7.3 *Performance measurement talk in Canada*

Who is involved?	*National government and departments/agencies:* Federal Government. Science and Technology Innovation Council. Statistics Canada. Canada Foundation for Innovation (CFI). Social Sciences and Humanities Research Council (SSHRC). Canadian Institutes for Health Research (CIHR). National Science and Engineering Research Council (NSERC). *Provinces:* Provincial Ministers. Provincial Ministries. Provincial Directors General. Premiers. (Ontario) Ministry of Training, Colleges and Universities. Higher Education Quality Council, Ontario (HEQCO). *Learned Societies:* Council of Canadian Academics. *Others:* Individual Institutions (universities, colleges). Association of Universities and Colleges of Canada (AUCC). Students.
Why measure?	Global competitiveness. Research priorities and funding. Access. Quality. Accountability. Funding (value for money). Match learning outcomes with labour market needs (2). Training the next generation. Data used for provincial policy direction. Institutional planning. Celebrating success.
Measure what?	Costs (funding ratios). Value per dollar. Enrolments. Rates of graduation (2). Graduate employment (3). Student attrition. Satisfaction (students, graduates, employers). Outputs not outcomes. Conferences. Papers published. Bibliometrics. Innovation. Commercialization. *No targets, not research impact.*
Measure how?	Financial audit, Performance Measurement Framework. Surveying graduates and employers. Survey of student engagement. Strategic research plans. Knowledge mobilization plan. Achievement report. Maclean's ranking, international rankings.

Table 7.3 (*cont.*)

Who resists?	Individual institutions (universities, colleges), academics.
Why?	Causes problems via increased expectations and workload. Institutional autonomy. It's 'un-Canadian'.

Table 7.4 *Performance measurement talk in the United Kingdom*

Who is involved?	*National government and departments/agencies:* The Government. No. 10 Downing Street policy unit. Treasury. Department of Business, Innovation and Skills. The Home Office. Office of Fair Access. Higher Education Funding Council of England (HEFCE). Research councils. Higher Education Statistics Agency. *Regulation and standards:* Competing regulators. Quality Assurance Agency for Higher Education. *The university peak bodies:* The sector. Universities UK. Russell Group. University Alliance. *Others:* Individual universities. Oxford and Cambridge. Imperial, University College London. Vice Chancellors. Charities that fund research. The market.
Why measure?	Economic policy – the knowledge economy. International competitiveness. Innovation. 'Something for something'. To 'cut the costs'. Efficiency. Accountability. Quality. Social mobility (access) (2).
Measure what?	Income. Impact of research. Business–industry links. Research excellence. Bibliometrics. Reputation. Financial position. Return on investment. Teaching quality. Numbers into higher education, retention and graduation rates. Graduate earnings. Student experience and satisfaction.
Measure how?	Research Excellence Framework (REF). Research block grants. International league tables. Universities' own indicators. Graduate surveys. National Student Survey (2). Memorandum of Assurance and Accountability.
Who resists?	Institutions. Individuals. *Nobody ('resistance is difficult')*
Why?	Distorts academic practice (2). Focuses on the wrong things. Burden of data collection. *Will cost people's jobs.*

universities were mentioned in Canada and the United Kingdom, including powerful individual universities (e.g. Oxford and Cambridge) in the United Kingdom. These lists reflect the different national arrangements and contexts, but also are likely to reflect the slightly different mixes of people interviewed in each case.

In all three nations, common responses regarding the purpose of measurement ('why measure?') were a desired shift to the knowledge economy and global competitiveness, and a set of issues related to costs, value for money, accountability, quality, and efficiency. Training and workforce requirements were mentioned in Australia and Canada. Policy and planning were mentioned in Canada, social mobility was mentioned in the United Kingdom, and driving the behaviour of universities was mentioned in Australia. Celebrating success was nominated in Canada, but not the other two nations.

For interviewees in all three nations, the response to 'measure what?' was based around the three general areas of teaching and learning, research, and impact/engagement. Funding and costs were also nominated and industry collaboration was emphasized in all three cases. Measures of student retention, completion, satisfaction, and graduate outcomes were also seen as important in all three nations. The most notable discrepancy is that in Canada there are no targets set and no evaluation of research impact.

For Australia and the United Kingdom, not surprisingly, their respective research assessment frameworks were mentioned (the ERA and the REF) in answering the 'measure how?' question, as were several other national data collections, funding allocations, and regulators/standard-setting agencies. Statutory accounts and financial audits were nominated in Australia and Canada, and teaching awards and reviews by a range of organizations were mentioned in Australia. International rankings were reported as important for Canada and the United Kingdom. Canada's general Performance Measurement Framework (for public sector departments), the learned academies' work on bibliometrics, and Maclean's newspaper rankings were nominated in the absence of a national research assessment system.

Finally, the 'who resists?' question came down to individual institutions and academics in all three nations, as well as peak university groups, Vice Chancellors, and Deputy Vice Chancellors Research in Australia. In the United Kingdom, 'nobody' was the reply from one interviewee. Reasons for any resistance to performance measurement were cited as concerns about the distortion of priorities and practices, increased workload (all three nations), and focusing on the wrong things (Australia and the United Kingdom). One Canadian interviewee described resistance as occurring because such assessment was seen to be 'un-Canadian', while the interviewee in the United Kingdom who stated that nobody resisted said that this was because it would cost people's jobs.

Based on this analysis, there seems to be a high level of convergence in talk about performance measurement between the three nations. First, there is a good deal of agreement that the main purposes are to support the knowledge economy, innovation, and links to business. An example that captures this is:

To foster world class research through our investments; to make sure that we attract and retain top talent; to ensure that the investments we make allow for the training of the next generation – i.e. the, what we call, highly qualified personnel in Canada; and the most challenging one to measure is that we foster innovation and commercialization through our investments. (Canada)

Some of the main divergences were, for Australia, the discussion of measurement as a means to influence the behaviour of universities ('That's what the metrics are about doing; changing behaviour'), while in the United Kingdom the social mobility agenda was mentioned by two different interviewees, one in relation to the knowledge economy – 'Social mobility is, well first of all, widening participation, which is more people going to university, . . . it's about the fact that we need to have a high skills economy' – and one pointing out the differing views on what this means:

Social mobility is an interesting example . . . Do you care about opportunities for the few so that everyone has the opportunity of going to Oxford or Cambridge if they want to? Or do you say 'That's absurd, that's only going to benefit a small number even though the opportunity is open to everyone' and in practice, what matters is the hundreds of thousands of students who go to universities.

The Canadian example (with no direct link between measurement and funding at the national level) describes a different view of measurement:

Performance measurement and reporting, you know, shouldn't – it shouldn't be a burden, it should be a celebration [laughs], and that the more we can do in a way that recognizes things that are already valued by the research community, the more organic it will be ... The less it's about accountability, and the more it's about celebrating the results of, you know, the hard work that people have done, and the importance of it, the better ... there are no explicit performance targets set, and they're – I think, unlike the UK and Australia, we haven't gone so far at the federal research level in terms of allocating funding on such a – quite a controlled basis.

For the 'measuring what?' question, interviewees in all three nations identified the common themes that appear in this quote:

There's teaching and learning, there's research and there's impact or knowledge exchange ... there's a general acceptance that these are the core business of universities, significant spend is made by government in support of those core businesses and it's appropriate that they should be really on the receiving end of some scrutiny around the acquittal of those funds. (Australia)

This was either combined with notions of accountability for funds – as in the above quote – or this was mentioned separately, but it was common to all nations.

The narratives that highlight some distinctive approaches to the purposes of performance measurement for each of the three nations are disclosed in the following quotes. The Australian example emphasizes costs, and perceptions of wastage and lack of relevance of the higher education sector:

So every time budget process comes around, Finance and to an extent, PM and C will say, 'Well there's all this wastage. We need to clean up the wastage. We'll take a cut and we'll, you know, administer you a dose of medicine and then we'll also require you to better target ... Just don't spend as much on all those basket-weavers'. (Australia)

Accountability and regulation driven by measurement was apparent in all three cases, but strongest in the United Kingdom:

This is actually to do with notions of accountability, and accountability running into governance ... how do they know how things are going? They don't unless they've got a measure. And so we are driven towards measurements. (United Kingdom)
    Essentially we regulate on the basis that, 'if you want our money you have to do this'. (United Kingdom)

7.6 Conclusion

The analysis contained in this chapter about the convergence and diversity of higher education governance across nations, represented in the talk of senior administrators about performance measurement, suggests several conclusions. The first is related to the impact of systems of measuring performance, which sit within different national structures of government. As could be expected, the United Kingdom has the strongest and clearest line of measurement of higher education across the country, from the Higher Education Funding Council of England to the universities. In the Australian case, the performance measurement of universities is centrally driven without having to negotiate with states/territories. This effectively bypasses the subnational level of government. A number of umbrella groups of universities appear to be particularly important actors in the Australian context.

For Canada, a national newspaper and international rankings provide performance information at the national level and in relation to the rest of the world. Of course, the provinces/territories are active in creating performance measures for the policy sector themselves. Some provinces/territories have developed their own performance measurement systems, and two have tied funding to these, although student enrolments and outcomes feature more prominently than research in these areas. In summary, who is involved, and who resists, is substantially shaped by higher education governance arrangements in the specific country context.

An examination of government documents and websites, combined with an analysis of these interviews, supports a fairly strong convergence on what is measured across nations – at least in broad terms (research excellence and impact, teaching quality and student outcomes for higher education). Not surprisingly, given the original reason that performance measurement became popular as a tool of NPM reformers, value for money seems to be paramount as a purpose. The purposes are also surprisingly convergent in general. Overarching goals can be discerned, such as supporting the knowledge economy and increasing competitiveness for higher education in all nations – even for Canada, which stands apart given its lack of a national research performance framework. What is measured also shares a good deal of commonality across these three nations.

On the other hand, the means of collection and reporting (the 'how') varies in line with different national governance arrangements. Clearly, the combination of national structures and the broad direction of governance trends in these three countries combine so that policy instruments (such as research performance measurement) are centralized and consequential for the higher education sector in some cases, and absent in others. However, the stated purposes attributed to performance measurement have a good deal in common, although local contexts and current policy agendas and directions help to frame the purposes of measurement, or reframe measurement to fit the new policy direction.

Canada's lack of a research performance measurement framework suggests the persistence of governance drivers for higher education in that nation that are different to those in operation in the United Kingdom and Australia. Given this, perhaps it is surprising that the level of convergence in talk about its purpose and what is measured is so high across all three nations. However, this fits with Pollitt's (2001) point that convergence is ill-defined and needs to be interrogated as convergence of rhetoric, decisions, actions, and results. In this case, convergence of rhetoric seems to be in place, despite the lack of convergence in specific actions.

Treating performance measurement as an important instrument for governing higher education, and analysing performance measurement talk in different nations, points to a high level of convergence, despite local differences in the tools applied to steer national systems. This finding also serves to highlight the effects of globalization on higher education: countries without national research performance measurement systems appear to be articulating the same goals and measuring similar things. Global mechanisms for defining high performance, such as world university rankings, no doubt play a substantial role in this standard-setting and diffusion of ideas about what is important and how it should be measured. Such mechanisms of governance, established by actors other than national governments, and copied around the world, may turn out to be exerting greater convergence pressures on the governance of higher education than the application of policy tools which are translated and adjusted to the national context. But that is a line of inquiry for a different research project.

Appendix: List of Agencies (and Numbers of People) Interviewed

Australia

- Department of Employment and Training, Higher Education Division (1)
- Department of Employment and Training, Research Funding and Policy Division (1)
- Tertiary Education Quality and Standards Agency (1)
- Group of 8, current Chair (1)
- Universities Australia, current President (1)

Canada

- Association of Universities and Colleges Canada (1)
- Higher Education Quality Council of Ontario (1)
- Social Sciences and Humanities Research Council of Canada (2)
- Canada Foundation for Innovation (1)
- Ontario Ministry of Training, Colleges and Universities (2)

United Kingdom

- Higher Education Funding Council of England (2)
- The Russell Group, current Chair (1)
- Universities UK, CEO (1)
- REF expert panellist (1)

Notes

1. The American system of research evaluation run by the National Research Council is private and not linked directly to funding at all, but it still generates a significant response from institutions (Hicks, 2009).

References

Behn, R. D. (2008) Why measure performance? Different purposes require different measures. *Public Administration Review*, 63(5), 586–606.
Bertelli, A. M., and John, P. (2010) Performance measurement as a political discipline mechanism. University of Southern California Law School, Law

and Economics Working Paper Series No 112. Berkeley Electronic Press. http://law.bepress.com/usclwps-lewps/art112

Bjørnholt, B., and Larsen, F. (2014) The politics of performance measurement: 'Evaluation as mediator for politics'. *Evaluation*, 20(4), 400–411.

Braun, D., Bullinger, A., and Wälti, S. (2002) The influence of federalism on fiscal policy making. *European Journal of Political Research*, 41(1), 115–145.

Brignall, S., and Modell, S. (2000) An institutional perspective on performance measurement and management in the 'new public sector'. *Management Accounting Review*, 11, 281–306.

Capano, G. (2015) Federal strategies for changing the governance of higher education: Australia, Canada and Germany compared. In G. Capano, M. Howlett, and M. Ramesh (Eds), *Varieties of governance: Dynamics, strategies, capacities*, pp. 103–130. Basingstoke: Palgrave Macmillan.

Carter, N. (1989) Performance indicators: 'Backseat driving' or 'hands off' control? *Policy and Politics*, 17(2), 131–138.

Collier, P. M. (2008) Performativity, management and governance. In J. Hartley, C. Donaldson, C. Skelcher, and M. Wallace (Eds), *Managing to improve public services*, pp. 46–64. Cambridge: Cambridge University Press.

Considine, M., and Lewis, J. M. (1999) Governance at ground level: The front-line bureaucrat in the age of markets and networks. *Public Administration Review*, 59(6), 467–480.

Deem, R., Hillyard, S., and Reed, M. (2007) *Knowledge, higher education, and the new managerialism*. Oxford: Oxford University Press.

Emy, H., and Hughes, O. (1988) *Australian politics: Realities in conflict*. Melbourne: Macmillan.

Hicks, D. (2009) Evolving regimes of multi-university research evaluation. *Higher Education*, 57(4), 393–404.

Hicks, D. (2012) Performance-based university research funding systems. *Research Policy*, 41(2), 251–261.

Hood, C. (1991) A public management for all seasons. *Public Administration*, 69(1), 3–19.

Kanter, R. M., and Summers, D. V. (1987) 'Doing well while doing good': Dilemmas of performance measurement in non-profit organizations and the need for a multiple-constituency approach. In W. W. Powell (Ed.) *The non-profit sector: A research handbook*, pp. 98–110. New Haven: Yale University Press.

King, R. (2010) Policy internationalization, national variety and governance: Global models and network power in higher education states. *Higher Education*, 60(6), 583–594.

Lewis, J. M. (2013) *Academic governance: Disciplines and policy*. New York: Routledge.

Lewis, J. M. (2015a) The politics and consequences of performance measurement. *Policy and Society*, 34(1), 1–12.

Lewis, J. M. (2015b) Research policy as 'carrots and sticks': Governance strategies in Australia, the United Kingdom and New Zealand. In G. Capano, M. Howlett, and M. Ramesh (Eds), *Varieties of governance: Dynamics, strategies, capacities*, pp. 131–150. Basingstoke: Palgrave Macmillan.

Moe, T. M. (1990) Political institutions: The neglected side of the story. *Journal of Law, Economics, and Organization*, 6 (Special Issue), 213–253.

OCUFA (Ontario Federation of University Faculty Associations) (2006) *Performance indicator use in Canada, the US and abroad*. Ottawa: OCUFA.

Painter, M. (2000) When adversaries collaborate: Conditional co-operation in Australia's arm's length federal polity. In U. Wachendorfer-Schmidt (Ed.), *Federalism and political performance*, pp. 130–145. London and New York: Routledge.

Pollitt, C. (2001) Convergence: The useful myth? *Public Administration*, 79 (4), 933–947.

Pollitt, C., and Bouckaert, G. (2011) *Public management reform: A comparative analysis* (3rd ed.). Oxford: Oxford University Press.

Radin, B. A. (2006) *Challenging the performance movement: Accountability, complexity and democratic values*. Washington, DC: Georgetown University Press.

Schick, A. (2001) Getting performance measures to measure up. In D. W. Forsythe (Ed.), *Quicker, better, cheaper: Managing performance in American Government*, pp. 39–60. Albany: Rockefeller Institute Press.

Scott, P. (2009) Foreword. In A. Brew and L. Lucas (Eds), *Academic research and researchers*, pp. xiii–xviii. London: Society for Research into Higher Education and Open University Press.

Smith, P. (1995) On the unintended consequences of publishing performance data in the public sector. *International Journal of Public Administration*, 18(2–3), 277–310.

Talbot, C. (2005) Performance management. In E. Ferlie, L. Lynn, and C. Pollitt (Eds), *The Oxford handbook of public management*, pp. 491–517. Oxford: Oxford University Press.

Tomblin, S. (2000) Federal constraints and regional integration in Canada. In U. Wachendorfer-Schmidt (Ed.), *Federalism and political performance*, pp. 146–174. London and New York: Routledge.

Whitley, R. (2010) Reconfiguring the public sciences: The impact of governance changes on authority and innovation in public science systems. In R. Whitley, J. Gläser, and L. Engwall (Eds), *Reconfiguring knowledge production: Changing authority relationships in the sciences and their consequences for intellectual innovation*, pp. 3–47. Oxford: Oxford University Press.

Whitley, R., and Gläser, J. (Eds) (2007) *The changing governance of the sciences: The advent of research evaluation systems.* Dordrecht: Springer.

Whitley, R., Gläser, J., and Engwall, L. (Eds) (2010) *Reconfiguring knowledge production: Changing authority relationships in the sciences and their consequences for intellectual innovation.* Oxford: Oxford University Press.

8 Accountability and Governance in European Higher Education

MICHAEL DOBBINS AND JENS JUNGBLUT

8.1 Introduction

Varying notions of societal, political, scientific, and socio-economic accountability have always been inherent in the missions of universities. However, in the past two or three decades, accountability has surged to become a guiding concept and primary justification for a multitude of higher education (HE) reforms in Europe and beyond. Leveille goes as far as to define accountability as the 'lingua franca of higher education' (2006, p. 8), which prompts action from policy makers, educational leaders, students, employers, and various other stakeholders.

Although accountability is at least touched on in nearly every account of current HE developments, only a few HE scholars have attempted to further theorize accountability and its forms, implications, and practical significance. In this chapter, we attempt to advance the debate by focusing on European HE in the age of Bologna, international rankings, massification, and underfunding. We begin our analysis by addressing the manifold socio-economic forces which have put accountability centre stage in contemporary HE discourse and reforms. We then outline numerous state-of-the-art conceptualizations of accountability in general and in HE specifically. Following the lead of Huisman and Currie (2004), we wish to move beyond normative statements and generalized descriptions by analysing the emergence of 'accountability regimes' in four large European countries – Germany (North Rhine-Westphalia), France, Poland, and Romania – with distinctly different paths of development in HE. This will enable us to identify cases of convergence and divergence in different settings.

8.2 The Growing Relevance of Accountability in Higher Education Governance

Universities in Europe have traditionally enjoyed a large degree of public trust, which came with extensive rights to self-government. The ideal of professional autonomy and academic freedom were justified by a widespread view of universities as distinct societal institutions that required a special status (Enders et al., 2013). This high degree of freedom was based on a pact between HE, the state, and society, which was grounded in the belief that the independence of universities from political or corporate influence was a necessary precondition for them to function properly (Gornitzka et al., 2007). Therefore, the state often acted as a guardian of the university, providing it with public funding and the legal guarantee of self-governance and protection of academic freedom (Enders et al., 2013). Van Vught (1997) referred to this form of governance as 'state control', as the government directly interfered in procedural decisions in HE.

This general description of the relationship between the state and universities holds true for both models of HE governance that have most significantly shaped HE in continental Europe: the state-centred model and the Humboldtian model of academic self-rule. In the *state-centred model*, universities were perceived as appendages of the state bureaucracy and subordinate institutions to the ministries responsible for HE. They were often regulated through uniform national laws, and were directly accountable to the state (Clark, 1983). This mode of governance relied mainly on hierarchical forms of accountability, with state bureaucrats in ministries as key decision makers. On the other hand, the *Humboldtian model*, which put great emphasis on the professional autonomy of university professors, guaranteed a considerable amount of substantive freedom, for example, in curricula or areas of research. However, the state tightly regulated procedural matters, while laws prescribed in great detail the tasks and duties of universities in order to justify the public funding invested in them (Berdahl, 1990; Clark, 1983). Academics operating in a Humboldtian tradition have generally perceived themselves as primarily or solely accountable to their scientific community (Dobbins et al., 2011).

These different modes of governance, which relied mainly on hierarchical forms of accountability through direct control, have undergone significant changes in recent decades. First, HE massification has made it an increasingly important political issue (Jungblut, 2016). As a growing percentage of the electorate is directly affected by HE and increasing shares of public budgets are spent on it, politicians sense a greater need to control the quality and delivery of universities' services to society. This trend is intensified by shrinking public funds and growing demands for efficiency and effectiveness in the public sector (Huisman and Currie, 2004; Pierson, 1998; Trow, 1996). For HE systems characterized by high public spending, governments must justify the expenditure of tax money to electorates, while universities in systems with high private spending (i.e. tuition fees) must prove that they are delivering what their 'consumers' (i.e. students and parents) are paying for (Leveille, 2006, p. 6).

Second, relationships between the state and HE providers have also undergone significant changes in the 'knowledge society' (Gornitzka et al., 2007). Most notably, the decision-making autonomy of universities and HE providers regarding procedural, financial, personnel, and substantive matters has been significantly enhanced (Estermann et al., 2011). Governments have retreated from direct control of the inner workings of universities and moved towards 'arms-length steering', or what van Vught (1997) defines as 'state supervision'. As a result, ex ante control through legislation and bureaucratic procedures has been replaced by demands for providers to justify their operations ex post through diverse accountability measures (Neave, 2009, 2012).

A third important rationale behind the move towards more autonomy and accountability was the realization that HE, with its increased complexity of tasks, is becoming harder, if not impossible, to steer through direct ministerial intervention. This coincided with a burgeoning discourse on the weakening capacity of governments to regulate various social spheres (Rose, 2000) and to coordinate local stakeholder interactions (Pressman and Wildavsky, 1984). Therefore, governments have increasingly relied on principal–agent relationships, which enable universities to use their expertise and proximity to the primary activities of the sector (teaching and research) to ensure the quality of provision, while governments employ accountability measures to monitor the performance of the agents (Clark, 1998; Enders et al., 2013).

These trends are by no means exclusive to HE, but are also affecting the broader public sector. Following the rise and popularity of New Public Management (NPM) since the 1980s, many countries have revisited the governance of public organizations (Pollitt and

Bouckaert, 2011). With a focus on institutional autonomy, learning from the private sector, and creating a leaner state, NPM reforms were geared towards improving efficiency, enhancing the responsiveness of public agencies, and improving managerial accountability (Christensen and Lægreid, 2015). The key promise was that better public sector performance would follow from effective vertical managerial accountability. This was often accompanied by a growing reliance on market mechanisms (Gingrich, 2011); in HE, this included the strengthening of executive leadership, professionalization of management structures, development of strategic capacities, and increased university competition (Dobbins et al., 2011; Enders et al., 2013).

These changes in governance arrangements were further expedited by the increasing international coordination through transnational platforms for policy learning, such as the Bologna Process. Internationalization was reinforced by growing global markets for HE services, global university rankings, and activities of international organizations such as the OECD (Gornitzka, 2007; Martens and Jakobi, 2010; Martens et al., 2010; Vögtle et al., 2011). One specific idea promoted in the context of the Bologna Process was the inclusion of stakeholder groups in HE governance (Vukasovic et al., 2017). The incorporation of representatives of diverse organized interests in newly created governance structures such as university boards has shifted the thrust of accountability, as universities now often have to justify their performance not only to the state but also to societal representatives directly involved in their steering. This also accords with a post-materialist understanding of participatory models of governance and a more democratic form of public sector steering (Olsen, 1988, 2007), through which increasingly critical and sophisticated citizens not only assess the performance of public service providers, but also wish to shape decision-making processes within them (Inglehart, 1997).

Overall, increased institutional autonomy and accountability can be seen as two sides of the same coin. It is thus not surprising that after the wave of reforms aimed at increasing institutional autonomy, there are a growing number of scholars claiming that these reforms did not fulfil their purpose or even decreased the level of 'real' autonomy. In other words, the expansion of accountability-oriented mechanisms has imposed greater restraints on the ability of HE providers to act autonomously (Christensen, 2011; Enders et al., 2013). Regardless, HE governance can increasingly be seen as a balancing act in a multi-actor, multilevel, and multi-issue environment, in which universities are under pressure to justify and legitimize academic processes and outputs (Huisman and Currie, 2004; Marginson and Rhoades, 2002). Thus, many HE systems are still in a phase of experimentation to identify the levels of autonomy and accountability-promoting measures most appropriate for them (Estermann et al., 2011).

8.3 Forms and Conceptualizations of Accountability

The overview of the multitude of catalysts for increasing accountability in HE has shown that accountability can take different shapes and forms. It has been described as a 'complex and chameleon-like term' (Mulgan, 2000, p. 555). One key question is whether accountability is seen as a virtue or a normative concept, or whether it is regarded as a mechanism or an institutional relationship in which an actor can be held to account by others (Bovens, 2010). We focus on the latter understanding in this chapter.

Despite covering a broad set of understandings, different accountability concepts have a common core as they pertain to some form of answerability for performance (Romzek, 2000) or an 'obligation to explain and justify conduct' (Bovens, 2007, p. 450). This means that universities are expected to report to others, and explain, justify, and answer questions about how resources have been used and with what kind of results (Trow, 1996). According to Burke (2004, p. 2) one has to ask: 'Who is accountable to whom, for what purposes, for whose benefit, by which means, and with which consequences?'

Given the broad variation in definitions of accountability it is not surprising that there are many different typologies with varying levels of detail. Bovens et al. (2008) offer a tool to assess public accountability structured along three perspectives. First, the *democratic perspective* follows the central idea that accountability helps to control and legitimize government actions by connecting them with the democratic mandate provided through the chain of delegation from the electorate. Second, the *constitutional perspective* sees accountability as a way to prevent or uncover abuses of public authority. Third, the *learning perspective* sees accountability as a way to generate feedback so that governments and public agencies can increase their effectiveness and efficiency. Christensen and Lægreid (2015) also distinguish three different forms of accountability. However, their approach follows a different logic and differentiates between actors' relations. Their first category, *political accountability*, is similar to the first perspective of Bovens et al. (2008), and is based on principal–agent relationships that describe the delegation of authority from voters through politicians to public agencies. Their second category is related to the position of an actor within a public sector hierarchy, where superiors hold subordinates accountable for performance, which they term *administrative accountability*. The final category is based on the idea of monitoring outputs and results and making actors who are responsible carry out accountability tasks if the output is not in line with agreed performance criteria. This form is called *managerial accountability*.

In yet another conceptualization, Romzek (2000) differentiates four types of accountability. These types are structured along two dimensions. The first dimension measures the degree of autonomy of actors, which can be either low or high, while the second dimension addresses whether the source of control is internal or external. In situations of low autonomy and internal control, *hierarchical accountability* describes relationships based on close supervision of individuals who have low work autonomy and minimal discretion. In situations of low autonomy and external control, principal–agent relationships based on legislative and constitutional structures establish an external oversight of performance and compliance with mandates. This *legal accountability* differs from hierarchical accountability as it describes relationships between two actors who are not interlinked through hierarchy, but rather controlled through outside rules and regulations. In situations where the actors have significantly more discretion to pursue relevant tasks, meaning there is a high degree of autonomy, Romzek differentiates between *professional* and *political accountability*. The difference between these types is based on the source of the standard against which their actions are measured. While in professional accountability the standards are derived from internalized norms and appropriate practices, political accountability is based on the ideal of responsiveness to concerns from key stakeholders, where actors have the discretion to decide whether and how to respond to key stakeholder concerns.[1] Table 8.1 provides an overview of these four types of accountability.

Table 8.1 *Overview of Romzek's four types of accountability*

	Low autonomy	High autonomy
Internal control	Hierarchical accountability	Professional accountability
External control	Legal accountability	Political accountability

These conceptualizations share common components that focus on procedural or managerial accountability, meaning how things are done, and components that assess substantive accountability, meaning what is done. These foci reflect the basic dichotomy that Berdahl (1990) proposed regarding different forms of university autonomy, in which procedural autonomy encompasses issues related to the management of the institution, while substantive autonomy refers to issues relating to main areas of scholarly work – teaching and research. Based on Romzek's (2000) conceptualization, we now present different groups of accountability instruments used in HE and link them to the values and behavioural expectations inherent in the four types of accountability. In general, the instruments of accountability can have varying characteristics. They can be soft mechanisms based on monitoring or explanation, or hard mechanisms based on justification (Huisman and Currie, 2004). Further, they can be tied to real consequences or to the act of reporting and making performance transparent, instruments which may otherwise be perceived to exert sufficient pressure to ensure compliance (Christensen and Lægreid, 2015). Finally, the different types of instruments can be used in arrangements between diverse sets of actors. In HE this can include, for example, the state and its ministries, public sector agencies such as quality assurance agencies or funding councils, HE institutions and their management, representative bodies of academics and students, trade unions, employers or business representatives, and umbrella organizations such as rectors' conferences.

For the purposes of our study we structure accountability instruments in HE into three groups. The first group includes *performance indicators* and *performance-based funding mechanisms*. This encompasses public funding distribution based on output-oriented formulas as well as performance contracts between ministries and universities (de Boer et al., 2015; Jongbloed and Vossensteyn, 2001). These measures have become more popular in light of massification and increasing tuition fees and are often used by governments as forms of softer steering in situations of increased institutional autonomy. This type of instrument emphasizes efficiency as a core value and, depending whether the performance agreement used is within a university or between a ministry and a university, it can be seen as either a hierarchical or a legal form of accountability in Romzek's (2000) terms.

The second group of accountability instruments involves various forms of *quality assurance* and *quality control*. These instruments have become increasingly widespread, in part due to their prominence in the Bologna Process. Public authorities often play a key role in quality assurance (QA) systems as they provide the necessary legitimacy and, even in highly decentralized HE arrangements such as the United States, the state remains a key actor (Gornitzka and Stensaker, 2014). QA systems can entail differing components, such as accreditation, student evaluations, or peer review (Dill and Beerkens, 2010), and are typically based on the values of expertise, but also responsiveness. Depending on whether the instrument is based on internal values and norms or the perceptions of different stakeholder groups, it can be seen as either a professional or a political form of accountability.

The third group of accountability instruments addresses the idea of directly *including* stakeholders in HE governance. This may involve internal stakeholders, such as academics and students, and thus reflect a democratic vision of the university (Olsen, 2007), as well as external stakeholders, such as trade unions and employer federations, which indicates greater responsiveness to the university's relationship with civil society (Jongbloed et al., 2008). These different groups can be incorporated into either existing or new structures, such as university boards or quality assurance bodies. While instruments focusing on internal stakeholder groups can be viewed as *professional accountability* measures, instruments focusing on external stakeholders are a form of *political accountability*. Table 8.2 provides an overview of the different accountability instruments and how they relate to Romzek's types of accountability.

Table 8.2 *Overview of the different accountability instruments*

Accountability instrument	Type of accountability
Performance indicators & performance-based funding	- If used within university: <u>hierarchical accountability</u> - If used between ministry and university: <u>legal accountability</u>
Quality assurance	- If based on internal values: <u>professional accountability</u> - If based on external values: <u>political accountability</u>
Stakeholder involvement in higher education governance	- If focus is on internal stakeholders: <u>professional accountability</u> - If focus is on external stakeholders: <u>political accountability</u>

8.4 Accountability in Contemporary Higher Education Governance

Following these classifications, we now focus on the emergence of accountability-oriented policies in the university systems of France, Germany (North Rhine-Westphalia), Poland, and Romania. Originally entrenched in a highly state-centred governance tradition, French universities have undergone a striking transition towards academic entrepreneurialism and a stronger emphasis on research since the mid-2000s (Dobbins, 2017; Musselin, 2009). Facing tremendous pressures to remain internationally competitive, German HE has recently shifted towards a marketized paradigm, while upholding crucial elements of its Humboldtian tradition. Polish HE offers a particularly fascinating case. After quickly eradicating most traces of its communist, centralized-bureaucratic governance model and reinvigorating its Humboldtian tradition after 1989, Polish public HE has proven relatively reform-resistant until recently, despite the parallel expansion of one of the world's largest private HE systems (Duczmal, 2006). Historically embedded in an extremely bureaucratic, state-centred model, Romania was quicker to embrace market-oriented steering practices in the mid-1990s and, as will be shown, devised a multitude of new mechanisms and instruments to institutionalize the concept of accountability in HE governance (Dobbins, 2011).

8.4.1 France

The original French tradition of academic freedom and autonomy (Gieysztor, 1992, p. 108) was uprooted during a phase of all-embracing nationalization in the sixteenth and seventeenth centuries. Under Napoléon, universities essentially became teaching institutions entrusted with the realization of national political and ideological objectives (Neave, 2001, p. 37), while specialized elitist institutions (*grandes écoles*) were created. Until the 1960s, universities did not exist autonomously due to the devolution of decision making to the faculties. In 1984, universities were declared autonomous institutions, but remained under the supervision of the Education Ministry (Chevaillier, 2007) and were thus primarily subject to hierarchical accountability to the state. The gradual increase in autonomy of French universities in the past 25 years entailed the emergence of an extensive multilateral accountability regime, which manifests across three interlinked dimensions: performance indicators and performance funding, quality assurance, and stakeholder participation.

8.4.1.1 Performance Indicators and Performance-based Funding

Foundations for a greater performance orientation were laid in the early 1990s with the introduction of the so-called *contractualisation* procedure. Universities were called on to present strategic development plans, on the basis of which they concluded four-year contracts with the state. The *politique contractuelle* subsequently not only prompted university management to more systematically reflect on accountability issues, but also led to the introduction of state-defined performance criteria in the mid-1990s. The state then began to allocate funding in a more selective manner, a trend reinforced by the 2001 funding law for public institutions ('Loi organique relative aux lois de finance' – LOLF). As of 2006, state funding for all public institutions – including nearly all HE institutions – was to be increasingly distributed on a performance basis (*logique de performance*). Universities were required to draw up expenditure reports for parliament (*projets annuels de performance*), on the basis of which parliament set priorities and objectives for universities, which were operationalized in the four-year contracts (Kaiser, 2007). Upon successful performance, universities were granted extra *crédits* which they could expend at will. Thus, this form of accountability enabled universities to acquire additional autonomy over teaching.

Due to the still comparatively low degree of university autonomy, *contractualisation* essentially still functioned as a hierarchical accountability measure until the mid-2000s, whereby the performance component remained relatively limited. However, rattled by its very poor standing in international HE rankings (Dalsheimer and Despréaux, 2008) and a burgeoning discourse on France's declining innovative and competitive potential (Aghion and Cohen, 2004), French HE was increasingly affected by the 'governance by comparison' (Martens et al., 2007) wave in the late 2000s. This led to a sustained push for university autonomy, while the state aimed to reinforce the performance-oriented accountability dimensions. Specifically, the ministry broke with the tradition of state control of content (e.g. study programmes and curricula) and again drew on the *politique contractuelle* as a vehicle to grant universities greater substantive and procedural autonomy. The 2007 law, 'Loi relative aux libertés et responsabilités des universités' (also known as LRU 2007 or 'Loi Pécresse') massively enhanced university autonomy and the powers of university management, thus turning *contractualisation* into a more legal accountability measure based on a principal–agent relationship (Comité de Suivi/LRU, 2011). Unlike the previous line-item budgeting process, universities now effectively receive global budgets (LRU 2007: Art. L. 712–9). In addition to a series of new stakeholder-oriented and QA-related accountability instruments (see below), university management (*conseil d'administration*) became both the beneficiary of newly granted autonomy and the 'enforcer' of a new managerial accountability regime. Although some employment and promotion procedures are still state-defined (Estermann et al., 2011), university presidents now employ staff on a terminable or indefinite basis and even pay performance bonuses to staff members (LRU 2007: Art. 19). University researchers and academics are therefore increasingly subject to managerial oversight. University teachers and researchers now must cope with expanded managerial accountability measures towards the increasingly powerful administrative councils (*conseils d'administration*) and university presidents, who still find themselves accountable to the state via the formal legal *contractualisation* procedure and other QA measures (see below).

8.4.1.2 Quality Assurance

Even before the massive Bologna-related push for QA in the 2000s, France had operated a state-centred QA system for HE. The so-called

Bayrou Reform of 1997 introduced the obligatory evaluation of universities by the state Comité National d'Evaluation (CNE), in order to increase their public accountability (Musselin, 2001). However, the evaluations generally had a soft character without any significant sanctions for any quantifiable weak performance of individual institutions or academics. The Bologna Process and repeated poor French performance in international rankings, however, triggered profound institutional changes aimed at enhancing the political and hierarchical accountability of universities. In 2007, the pre-existing evaluation bodies responsible for different types of HE[2] were merged into the Agence de l'évaluation de la recherche et de l'enseignement supérieur (AERES), which now externally evaluates study programmes, entire HE institutions, and research institutions. The agency is unique due to its diverse membership: AERES not only consists of French and international academics and researchers, but also student and university management representatives and members of the Centre national de la recherche scientifique (CNRS).

These procedures reflect a shift away from the traditional model of control-oriented ministerial evaluation and towards evaluation of academic 'products'. The output-based indicators range from research and teaching performance, study offers, student satisfaction, and quality of student life to relationships with external research institutes and management of human resources. Importantly, the agency is one of the first in Europe to rely on bibliometric criteria (i.e. journal impact factors) to assess the research performance of individual academics and pass on the results to university management.[3] The ex post focus on research output and the inclusion of CNRS representatives are indicative of an increasing research orientation in French universities and thus the re-embracing of traditional Humboldtian notions of professional accountability towards the research community. As shown, however, the new accountability regime is multipolar and aims to safeguard both internal accountability (i.e. university management and internal stakeholders) and external accountability (i.e. towards the state) in the provision of services to students, the research community, and civil society stakeholders (see below). In fact, to bolster its legitimacy, the AERES regularly subjects itself to an evaluation of its own operations by European experts.

8.4.1.3 Stakeholder Governance
As an additional form of political accountability, French HE began to embrace the notion of stakeholder governance at an early stage. In the

early 1990s, for example, policy makers started to focus on university modernization and mobilization in terms of addressing the economic needs of the French economy. The *contractualisation* procedure increasingly focused on the development of HE steering strategies in line with local socio-economic interests (INRP, 2005, p. 41). For example, the programme 'Université du troisième millénaire' was geared towards fostering more systematic coordination with local and regional public authorities and businesses, especially regarding the funding of HE research projects (Quinio, 1998). With these new 'alliances', existing forms of vertical state steering and hierarchical accountability were juxtaposed with new forms of accountability towards external stakeholders, resulting in novel polycentric governance patterns (INRP, 2005, p. 41; Musselin and Paradeise, 2009).

While the *politique contractuelle* was initially applied to align academic outputs with national socio-economic interests, the government has more recently recalibrated its stakeholder accountability strategy. One core component of the LRU 2007 law is the state-imposed reform of the main university government body, the *conseil d'administration*, whose membership structure is now prescribed by the state. It must consist of 20 to 30 members (instead of the previous 60), approximately 40 per cent of whom are supposed to be lecturing researchers (*enseignants-chercheurs*). A significant change is the co-agenda-setting power for external stakeholders, of which at least one is to be head of a leading enterprise, while regional representatives (two or three), students (approx. one-fifth of the membership) and administrative staff (approx. one-tenth of the membership) are also included (LRU 2007: Art. 7). Thus, France has taken a different path to Germany (see below) by merging academic and administrative management into one body and by refraining from governing bodies exclusively under academic control (i.e. academic senates).

8.4.2 Germany (North Rhine-Westphalia)

Due to Germany's federal structure and the responsibility of the *Bundesländer* for HE policy and governance, this chapter will focus on one of the *Länder* in order to explore accountability-related developments. We have selected North Rhine-Westphalia, which has the largest population, a large number of HE institutions, and has recently been subject to several reform initiatives that increased institutional autonomy and accountability. Historically, German HE followed the Humboldtian model and was characterized by the strong role of the professoriate, especially regarding substantive matters, and the direct influence of the state on procedural issues (Dobbins and Knill, 2014; van Vught, 1997). This is also one reason why there was no quality assurance or monitoring of HE activities before Bologna (Dobbins and Knill, 2014). The situation in Germany is thus similar to that of France in the sense that hierarchical governance prevailed with regard to procedural matters. Contrary to the French example, however, and due to stronger professorial control over substantive matters and internal university decision-making structures, Germany historically relied on professional accountability. Since the end of the 1990s there has been a decisive shift towards institutional autonomy, state supervision, and accountability measures instead of the classical forms of direct control (Dobbins and Knill, 2014; Schimank and Lange, 2009). As we show in the following sections, performance agreements, performance-based funding, quality assurance, and stakeholder governance have been crucial components of this development.

8.4.2.1 Performance Indicators and Performance-based Funding
Contrary to many other *Länder*, performance has long been a part of the HE funding model in North Rhine-Westphalia, even before the most recent wave of governance reforms (Keller and Dobbins, 2015). However, these reforms put a greater emphasis on using performance agreements to move from hierarchical decrees to a form of HE funding that is negotiated between the ministry and the universities, thus loosening the hierarchical form of accountability. In 2004, the Ministry for Science and Research started to negotiate performance agreements (*Zielvereinbarungen*) with single HE institutions with the aim of granting them more autonomy. In these agreements the ministry used production goals to incentivize universities to move towards a form of management by objectives and thus pay greater attention to their organizational output. However, the agreements generally lacked serious sanctions for universities that did not perform, as they only entailed fiscal rewards for fulfilment of the agreement and no means of sanctioning those institutions that failed to perform (Dobbins and Knill, 2014). They can therefore be seen as soft instruments of accountability.

The large-scale governance reforms of the Christian-democratic and Liberal coalition government in 2006 led to a greater focus on output-oriented steering by increasing the share of performance-based funding to 20 per cent of overall budgets (Keller and Dobbins, 2015). Moreover, decisions on student numbers admitted to each university were now based on performance agreements. By turning universities into bodies under public law, the reform also made HE institutions in North Rhine-Westphalia almost completely autonomous regarding procedural matters (de Boer et al., 2015). The legal changes can thus be described as a shift from hierarchical accountability towards legal accountability. The performance agreements run over a period of two years and have specified areas that are covered and are subject to output measurements.[4] These include, for example, research, teaching, gender issues, internationalization, and institutional profiling (de Boer et al., 2015).

With these new performance agreements, the state also shifted towards an indicators-based funding scheme in which the number of graduates, the number of completed PhDs, and the amount of third-party research funding would constitute part of the HE budget. Nevertheless, at 20 per cent, the share of this performance-based component remained rather low and the largest part of university funding still came from the lump-sum basic grant (Dobbins and Knill, 2014). In 2013, the new Social-democratic and Green governing coalition changed the indicators of the performance-based component, replacing the number of PhD graduates with the share of female professors, while at the same time increasing the overall share of the performance-related portion of the HE budget to approximately 23 per cent. Thus, 77 per cent of funding is still distributed through the basic block grants (de Boer et al., 2015).

In reaction to the perceived excessive university autonomy, the coalition of Social-democrats and Greens again increased the role of the state in the strategic development of HE by giving parliament and the ministry more power (Jungblut, 2016). In addition, the 2014 HE law also required universities to report in greater detail on how they spent their basic funding (de Boer et al., 2015) and compiled a new state-wide plan for university personnel, developmental, and budgetary affairs. Finally, the government introduced a clause allowing the ministry to penalize universities that did not fulfil their performance agreements (de Boer et al., 2015). This last decision in particular turned the performance agreements into hard tools of accountability, placing universities under more pressure to justify their performance and aligning this with financial consequences. These changes in the governance arrangements reflect a move away from a focus on internalized norms and thus a shift from legal accountability to hierarchical accountability with a greater role for the parliament and the ministry. At the same time, the shift in the performance indicators suggests a stronger focus on political rather than professional accountability.

8.4.2.2 Quality Assurance

As mentioned previously, Germany did not have a formalized QA system prior to the Bologna Process. While teaching and research quality was assured through forms of professional accountability and the internalized norms of the academic community, the quality of procedural decisions was assured through hierarchical accountability and ministerial control. However, Bologna heralded the introduction of a sophisticated QA system in Germany. This process began with the creation of the Accreditation Council (*Akkreditierungsrat*) in 1998, whose task is to certify QA agencies that are then allowed to perform accreditations of study programmes and HE institutions. These accreditations are performed both ex ante and ex post in the form of regular re-accreditations. In particular, the 2006 decision to transfer the power to approve new study programmes from the ministry to the accreditation agencies (Keller and Dobbins, 2015) brought about a shift from hierarchical accountability to professional but also political accountability. The QA agencies had to include in their assessment panels both professors and students – that is, internal expertise that follows the internalized norms of HE – but also work-life representatives who introduced external expertise from key stakeholders. However, the majority of the panel members were always from within HE, thus reinforcing professional accountability.

The system evolved further in the following years, but the central role of QA agencies and the dominance of internal actors in their auditing panels did not change significantly. One of the key developments was a general move towards institutional evaluations of internal QA procedures instead of detailed accreditations of single study programmes. If the QA system of a university is deemed acceptable in these institutional evaluations, then the institution is allowed to evaluate its own study programmes using the same principles that are applied by QA agencies. These institutional accreditations are also subject to re-accreditation after a number of years. Additionally, HE institutions in North Rhine-Westphalia have the responsibility to evaluate teaching activities and, if determined necessary by the ministry, they can be required to hold a peer review audit of the institution's QA system at any given time (Hochschulfreiheitsgesetz 2006 §7: para. 2). These recent developments have strengthened the focus on professional accountability as more trust is placed in universities to organize their own QA based on the general principle of inclusion of both internal and external expertise. As successful accreditation is a pre-requisite for a university to be able to run a study programme, the QA system can be seen as a hard mechanism of accountability, which is tied to real consequences.

8.4.2.3 Stakeholder Governance

The internal governance of German universities has traditionally been based on the central role of professors, who hold the majority of seats in senates and all other internal governance bodies. Students, academic, and non-academic staff are also represented. As a result, the traditional governance structure emphasized internal norms and values, and thus professional accountability. As part of the large-scale university reforms of the late 1990s and early 2000s, nearly all *Bundesländer* started to introduce university boards (*Hochschulräte*) (Mayntz, 2002). These new governance bodies aimed to enhance university autonomy by transferring some of the decision-making power from the ministries to the university boards. The boards include representatives from diverse stakeholder groups, both from within the universities and from outside, and the *Bundesländer* have different procedures for naming or selecting members of these boards (Hüther, 2010).[5] North Rhine-Westphalia introduced university boards in 2006 and transferred a large part of the supervisory power of the ministry to these boards (Keller and Dobbins, 2015). This represents a shift from hierarchical accountability of the university to a ministry and towards more professional and political accountability to internal and external groups of stakeholders.

Compared to the other *Länder*, the university boards in North Rhine-Westphalia have a particularly high level of personnel and procedural competencies (Hüther, 2010). At the same time, they are based on the principle that representatives of external stakeholders form the majority in the board and thus put a greater emphasis on political accountability. Following the shift in the governing coalition from the Christian-democrats and Liberals to the Social-democrats and Greens in 2010, the role of the university boards was re-evaluated and some of their powers transferred to other internal governance bodies (Jungblut, 2016). In particular, following the 2014 HE law, university boards lost responsibilities to the university senates and the newly introduced student commissions on examination regulations (de Boer et al., 2015). This represents a shift away from political accountability and towards professional accountability.

Overall, North Rhine-Westphalia has seen a significant reduction in the level of hierarchical accountability and direct state control of HE since the early 2000s through increases in the autonomy of universities. This came with a parallel increase in other forms of accountability. Using Romzek's (2000) conceptualization one can say that North Rhine-Westphalia started from a high level of hierarchical accountability and moved towards a mixture of other forms of accountability. While the use of performance agreements can be seen as a form of legal accountability, the quality-assurance system relies mainly on professional accountability. Stakeholder governance initially focused on political accountability and moved, after the change in the governing coalition, towards professional accountability.

8.4.3 Poland

We turn now to explore the emergence of HE accountability regimes in two post-communist countries. As noted, Poland quickly reverted to its pre-war Humboldtian governance model, while granting public universities extensive autonomy over their organizational structures as well as personnel and funding matters (Kwiek, 2014). The transfer of decision making to high-ranking academics, who governed universities through academic senates, left few possibilities for university management, the state, or other external stakeholders to counterbalance autonomy with a comprehensive accountability regime (World Bank, 2004, p. viii). Simultaneously, though, liberal state regulations fostered the expansion of non-research-oriented private universities (Duczmal, 2006), which structurally aligned themselves with Anglo–American management methods and frequently employed public university academics seeking extra pay. This led to a dualism of two distinctly different governance regimes, with public universities sticking to the re-institutionalized model of academic self-rule (Dobbins, 2014). Despite the shocks inherent in the introduction of the market economy, and the burgeoning market-oriented private HE sector, public HE remained insulated from socio-economic stakeholders, as the professoriate was quick to create institutions to assert academic interests vis-à vis the state. This included the General Council for Higher Education (Rada Główna Szkolnictwa Wyższego) and Polish Rectors Conference (KRASP), which vigorously promoted the principle of academic self-governance as a vehicle for democratizing Poland.

8.4.3.1 Quality Assurance

To the detriment of an all-embracing accountability regime, Polish HE policy makers spent much of the 1990s coping with the democratization of universities, the enormous expansion of HE, and the severe underfunding of public HE. The Bologna Process and concerns over the quality of programmes delivered by private providers gave a crucial impetus to the institutionalization of a new quality assurance regime. In 2001, the State Accreditation Commission (Państwowa Komisja Akredytacyjna; since 2011 Polska Komisja Akredytacyjna) began evaluating the quality of programmes in public and private universities, while authority to close ineffective programmes was returned to the state. The Commission members are appointed by the Ministry of Higher Education and Science upon nomination by academic senates and the General Council for HE, but also professional and employers' associations. The relatively strict minimal standards aim to ensure strong external stakeholder participation and influence over the orientation of programmes. However, in its early stages state accreditation focused primarily on teaching quality and services to students, with research output subject – at best – to weakly institutionalized peer review mechanisms. In other words, Polish academics – unlike their French counterparts – were still largely unburdened by hierarchical accountability towards the state, at least with respect to the QA regime.

The ministry thus used the Bologna process as a lever to reinforce the hierarchical accountability of universities. While many Polish public universities still design their own structures and programmes autonomously, they now require consent from the Accreditation Committee for all structural and substantive matters (Polish HE Law 2004: Art. 8).

The Bologna process thus served to balance academic self-rule with quality assurance and broader socio-economic pressures. The members of the committee are appointed by the minister responsible for HE after nomination by university senates, KRASP, the General Council, and national scientific associations, whereby employers' organizations and student and parliamentary representatives are also formally included.[6] However, the heavy presence of the academic profession still gives primacy to professional accountability over hierarchical accountability towards the state. The recent Polish HE Act of 2011 does place greater emphasis on managerial accountability within universities. Similar to France, the act enables university management to employ lecturers temporarily, and to subject them to performance evaluations of research and teaching activities. While non-professorial teaching and research staff are evaluated every two years, academics with a professorial title are evaluated at least every four years (Polish HE Act 2011: Art. 132; see also Dakowska, 2015). Thus, the new managerial accountability regime constitutes a shift away from the idea of 'almighty professors'.

8.4.3.2 Performance Indicators and Performance-based Funding

The funding system has also recently undergone substantial changes. Poland initially maintained its system of incremental, input-based funding from the communist and early post-communist phase. The funding algorithm was based on the number of students and the ratio of students to highly qualified teaching staff (Jongbloed, 2003; World Bank, 2004), and funds were distributed proportionately to the previous year's expenditure after adjustment for inflation. At the university level, highly autonomous faculties and professorial chairs hindered the emergence of proactive university management structures and hence the strategic intra-university allocation of funds. The parallel existence of a large private university sector, in which public university professors often earned a side income, left little space for introducing new performance-based funding incentives at public universities (see Dobbins, 2011).

Yet the 2011 HE Act injected new dynamics into the HE funding policy. While the lion's share of funding still remains input-based, several performance-oriented mechanisms were introduced. Specifically, the government now awards extra funding to a select group of 25 leading faculties designated as 'National Scientific Leading-Edge Centres' (Krajowe Naukowe Ośrodki Wiodące – KNOW). To this end, the state conducts an evaluation of qualitative scientific output indicators every five years (Dakowska, 2015). Moreover, the government is currently attempting to include HE institutions in its research funding system, which has been strongly output-driven since the early transformation phase. Similar to the previous British Research Assessment Exercise (replaced by the Research Excellence Framework in 2014), HE institutions are increasingly subject to evaluations focusing on publications, patents, registered contacts with industrial partners, and awarded degrees. These are conducted by a national institution for the evaluation of scientific units (Komitet Ewaluacji Jednostek Naukowych – KEJN) and two institutions dedicated to applied research (Narodowe Centrum Badań i Rozwoju – NCBR) and fundamental research (Narodowe Centrum Nauki – NCN), which fund projects on a competitive basis. Nevertheless, it is important to note that research-generated revenues account for less than 20 per cent of public university budgets.

8.4.3.3 Stakeholder Governance

Recently, there have been noticeable attempts to juxtapose professional accountability (i.e. to the scientific community) and hierarchical accountability (i.e. to the state) with external socio-economic accountability and internal accountability through stakeholder-oriented policies. Despite the formal inclusion of employer representatives in the General Council in the 1990s, notions of an isolated scientific community and academic self-rule prevailed until recently. Due to frequent simultaneous commitments to public and private institutions, high-ranking academics have shown little interest in allowing external economic stakeholders to participate in institutional governance. Hence, few linkages to promote contracted or joint research, personnel exchanges, sharing of equipment, and joint patenting activities have been established (World Bank, 2004).

In addition to formally stipulating external stakeholder participation in the Accreditation Commission (approximately 10 per cent) (Art. 46.1), the 2011 HE Act also introduces various additional modifications to align HE services with stakeholder preferences. For example, it requires universities to create systems to follow up on the professional

development of alumni and mandates the inclusion of employer stakeholders in the General Council (Art. 46.1). Analogous to the French
approach, the ministry is also pushing to incorporate employer representatives into curriculum design at the university management level,
but has refrained from legally prescribing their obligatory participation
(Shaw, 2014). Nevertheless, the ministry has heavily invested in the
organization of joint activities with business and HE representatives,
not least through the targeted allocation of EU cohesion funds to
technology transfer centres (so-called incubators). This strategy has
also coincided with efforts to forge closer ties between the Polish
regions (*województwa*) and self-governing territorial districts
(*samorząd*) (OECD 2006).

  Besides these new external accountability measures, the Bologna
Process has resulted in a stronger focus on internal political accountability, somewhat at the expense of professional accountability. One
notable Bologna side effect is the greater incorporation of students into
decision-making matters.[7] This entails the direct representation of
students in academic senates, which has increased pressure on faculties
to design curricula in line with student and labour market demands and
to pursue improvements in teaching quality.

8.4.4 Romania

Similar to Poland, Romania experienced an impressive educational
expansion during the phase of democratization, resulting in
a 250 per cent increase in student numbers and a nearly three-fold
increase in the number of institutions, from 42 to 111, between 1990
and 1999 (OECD, 2000, pp. 125, 129). Yet the path towards university autonomy was much more sluggish than in Poland, as remnants of the previous state-centred bureaucratic system persisted well
into the 1990s. While some groups of academics mobilized to protect
academic freedom and greater university autonomy, the state was
reluctant to grant HE institutions greater procedural self-
management capacities (Reisz, 2004). Thus, a mixture of extensive
state planning and restricted academic autonomy prevailed, while –
aside from the removal of its ideological component – the bureau-
cratic-hierarchical accountability regime inherited from communism
remained largely intact. However, the Romanian accountability trajectory differed significantly from that of Poland. While Poland

pursued policies of 'economic shock therapy', which only marginally manifested themselves in public HE, Romania applied a policy of 'higher education shock therapy', with significant ramifications for the accountability regime.

Long before their Polish counterparts, Romanian policy makers drew on the rhetoric of the entrepreneurial university, NPM, and performance-based governance. This resulted in a large-scale strategy pursued by education minister Andrei Marga to 'remove the last vestiges of communist heritage' (Marga, 2002, p. 123) and bring the HE system into line with the socio-economic needs of Romania and Western models of HE governance (Marga, 2002, p. 122). The sweeping 1997 reform resulted in an all-encompassing overhaul of the system of governance and a massive increase in university autonomy, reshaping the role of the Ministry of Education, university management, and university–society relations. As shown in the following, accountability-enhancing instruments were rapidly introduced in all three of our core dimensions.

8.4.4.1 Performance Indicators and Performance-based Funding

In the late 1990s, the Romanian government aimed to align its HE funding model with the market-oriented governance ideal-type (Dobbins et al., 2011). In significant contrast to Poland, the 1997 reform package introduced lump-sum funding, while also forcing universities to diversify their funding base through tuition fees and non-state sources (Ministerul Educației Naționale, 2002). The increase in procedural autonomy and subsequent strengthening of university management enabled university managers to strategically distribute both state and non-state funding on the basis of competitive negotiations with individual faculties, taking account of their performance (Consiliul Național pentru Finanțarea Învățământului Superior, 2005). This policy of accountability towards university management was aimed at promoting educational innovations at the faculty level and was mirrored by the policy pursued in France 10 years later.

The Bologna Process gave a further impetus to performance-based funding on two levels. While the lump-sum funding granted to universities after the 1997 reforms was mainly input based, the ministry increased the performance-based component in the 2000s (CNpFÎS, 2005). A new system of competitive grants, which prioritized research relevant to contemporary socio-economic developments in Romania, was established. Along these lines, several pilot projects for doctoral studies were introduced, enabling the state and universities to quantitatively evaluate the progress of dissertation projects (Curaj et al., 2015). And, again similar to the French case, the Romanian government expanded the use of bibliometric data and domestic university ranking systems to all HE institutions, departments, and individual researchers (Vîiu et al., 2012).

8.4.4.2 Quality Assurance

The early paradigmatic shift towards managerialism, product control, and marketization was also reflected in the QA system developed in the context of the Bologna Process and introduced in 2006. The Romanian Agency for Quality Assurance in Higher Education (Agenția Română de Asigurare a Calității în Învățământul Superior – ARACIS), for example, authorized academic curricula and programmes developed by faculties and approved by academic senates. Largely modelled on British practice (see Dobbins 2011), the new Romanian accreditation procedure constitutes a shift towards 'product control' and focuses on an elaborate catalogue of accountability- and quality-promoting measures for institutions and university programmes. The process, which is followed up by re-accreditation every five years, involves evaluation of an extensive range of performance indicators, including a combination of self-evaluation, external assessment, peer review, and student evaluations. The initial self-evaluation report provides the basis for external evaluation by ARACIS through a three-dimensional process focusing on *institutional capacity*, *quality management* (including student evaluations), and *educational efficiency*. In additional to professional accountability to the research community, the evaluation attaches priority to the relevance of academic programmes for the labour market and financial efficiency (ARACIS, 2006). The procedure thus moves beyond mere peer review mechanisms. However, it is important to note that while external stakeholders (i.e. members of professional organizations, non-academic business professionals, and international assessors) were heavily involved in the process in the 2000s (ARACIS, 2006), senior academics have since then regained control over the agency, thus tilting the balance towards professional accountability.[8]

8.4.4.3 Stakeholder Governance

Interestingly, Romanian universities draw on a much longer tradition of university–industry synergies than is true of the other three case studies. In the communist era, Ceauşescu attempted to turn universities into industrial breeding grounds by forcing universities and industrial firms to cooperate closely, as the state attempted to synchronize the demands of the planned economy with university programmes (Dobbins, 2011).

In the late 1990s, Romania sought to revive this historical practice. Specifically, a crucial aim of the government's push for decentralized decision making and university autonomy was to encourage partnerships between the academic and business spheres, thus creating incentives for universities to match the skills of graduates with labour market demands (Nicolescu et al., 2000, p. 5). Thus, somewhat contrary to the Humboldtian ideal, universities were supposed to become vehicles for problem solving and regional economic growth (Ministerul Educaţiei Naţionale, 2002). The push for external, socioeconomic accountability was also reflected comparatively early in the systematic integration of external stakeholders into university management structures. The impetus here was essentially a mixture of domestic policy emulation and transnational pressures for the marketization of universities. Two rather successful post-communist Romanian universities, Babeş-Bolyai University of Cluj-Napoca and the University of Iaşi, have each involved employers' representatives in the design of the strategic university plans since the 1990s,[9] an approach which was quickly emulated by other institutions. This trend was reinforced by tax incentives granted to firms for collaborating with HE institutions, thus bringing Romania into line with Anglo-Saxon market-oriented approaches.

With the aim of greater political accountability, the state is now also pushing for multiple HE institutions to form university consortia as a means to boost their research capabilities and cater to the needs of regional businesses (Curaj et al., 2015). The state is also providing new funds for universities and university consortia to create business start-ups. Driven by the new discourse centred on notions of knowledge transfer and the capitalization of knowledge, these reforms aim to enhance scientific production per se and explicitly push for a stronger orientation towards the economic utility of research outputs.

8.5 Comparative Conclusions

In the past 15 years we have witnessed a diverse array of efforts to further institutionalize the notion of accountability in the academic heartlands of the four countries examined in this chapter. As a result, governance arrangements have become more multilateral and multi-faceted. The preceding analysis has admittedly painted a simplified picture of a much more complex set of underlying realities, each comprising nuanced national accountability arrangements subject to wide-ranging perceptions concerning how these have impacted different actors. Our overview is an attempt to contribute to disentangling rhetoric from reality by providing a systematic framework to assess cross-national experiences in HE reform in terms of the evolution of governance regimes and the focus on accountability. Table 8.3 presents our overall findings for these four large HE systems. The results reveal that all four systems have implemented accountability-oriented changes across all three of our analysed dimensions, often in the context of decreasing direct control of the state and increasing institutional autonomy of universities.

The question that now arises is: what role have pre-existing HE legacies and governance/institutional arrangements played in explaining the direction and degree of policy change? In other words, did countries rooted in the Humboldtian tradition (Germany and Poland) pursue different reform trajectories than those rooted in the state-centred tradition (France and Romania)? Historical institutionalists might be inclined to argue that state-centred systems are more likely to favour hierarchical and political accountability mechanisms due to the pre-eminent role of the state in coordinating HE, whereas Humboldtian-oriented systems may tend to double-down on their stronger tradition of professional accountability due to the dominant position of the professoriate. The empirical evidence, however, seems to suggest the contrary. For example, we can observe efforts to apply performance-based funding and accountability to university management, establish far-reaching quality assurance systems, and promote external stakeholdership in all four countries. Thus, despite extremely heterogeneous starting points, all four systems have embraced and visibly implemented new forms of accountability in all analysed dimensions. While the two countries with a stronger hierarchical accountability tradition (France and Romania) have expanded professional

Table 8.3 *Overview of accountability mechanisms in four European higher education systems*

Country	Traditional form of accountability	Overall trend	Performance indicators	Quality assurance	Stakeholder governance
France	Hierarchical accountability	Strong shift towards administrative accountability, shift to legal accountability through *contractualisation*; increased political accountability (via external stakeholders); increased professional accountability	- Performance-based criteria applied in *contractualisation* procedure (hierarchical accountability) - More performance-based funding allocation within universities (administrative accountability)	- New QA body and bibliometric data (hierarchical accountability) - Strong inclusion of researchers (professional accountability) - Focus on student outcomes/satisfaction (political accountability)	- Heavy presence in *conseil d'administration* (political accountability)
Germany (North Rhine-Westphalia)	Hierarchical accountability + professional accountability	Reduction in hierarchical accountability and shift towards more political accountability through a growing	- *Zielvereinbarungen* (state–university agreements) with strong performance component (hierarchical accountability)	- New QA procedures of accreditation and re-accreditation - Strong inclusion of academics (professional	- Introduction of powerful university boards with strong representation of diverse stakeholder groups (until

		involvement of stakeholder groups; persisting importance of professional accountability in the context of quality assurance and recent shifts in the role of university boards	- Universities are transformed into bodies under public law (more legal accountability) - More performance-based funding by state and growing influence of parliament and ministry after 2014 (more hierarchical accountability)	accountability) and students/ practitioners (political accountability)	2014) (political accountability) - Recent loss of power of university councils (more professional accountability)
Poland	Non-existent account-ability regime (1990–2000)	Increased efforts to balance hierarchical accountability with professional accountability; creeping managerial accountability	- Performance-based rewards from state to leading faculties (hierarchical accountability) - Performance-oriented research evaluation (hierarchical accountability)	- Accreditation system (primarily professional accountability)	- Presence in General Council, Accreditation Commission (political accountability) - State-promoted joint activities with external stakeholders (political accountability)

Table 8.3 (*cont.*)

Country	Traditional form of accountability	Overall trend	Performance indicators	Quality assurance	Stakeholder governance
Romania	Hierarchical accountability	Strong shift towards administrative accountability, increased political accountability (via external stakeholders); increased professional accountability	- Performance evaluations of individual researchers/teachers (administrative accountability) - Performance-based funding allocation within universities (administrative accountability) - State-administered competitive research grants (hierarchical accountability)	- Multidimensional QA procedures - Shift towards professorial dominance (professional accountability)	- Involvement in design of university strategic plans (political accountability)

(i.e. the academic profession) and political (i.e. external stakeholders) accountability, the Humboldtian-oriented countries have complemented pre-existing forms of professional accountability with new instruments of hierarchical and political accountability. Thus, it is legitimate to speak of a broad convergence of national HE accountability regimes at least with regard to the scope and depth of accountability, although not necessarily with regard to the type of instruments used. For example, we could identify stronger efforts to institutionalize managerial accountability (i.e. university management) in the two countries embedded in the state-centred tradition (France and Romania). This process has been more sluggish in both countries with stronger structural remnants of the chair system: Germany and Poland.

Similar to developments in other parts of the public sector, the HE systems also moved away from uniform modes of governance towards a more pluralist mix of accountability measures. While this overarching trend is clearly visible in all four cases presented in this chapter, the differences that persist between the countries are also a key finding. This applies, for example, to the absence of target agreements (*contractualisation* in France, *Zielvereinbarungen* in Germany) in the two post-communist countries analysed here, as well as in most other Central and Eastern European countries. This may reflect the absence of historical continuity of public administration bodies in Central and Eastern European countries and an ongoing mistrust between academics and the state.

These general findings of overall convergence upon preservation of peculiar national policy instruments are in line with previous studies which found that the Bologna Process – while triggering a certain degree of convergence – still has not led to completely similar HE systems throughout Europe (Estermann et al., 2011; Vögtle et al., 2011). Thus, with regard to the rearranged relationship between the state and HE, European reform agendas interact with national traditions (or institutional path dependences) when shaping policy developments (Gornitzka and Maassen, 2014). Yet despite national idiosyncrasies, our findings give credence to the far-reaching impact of processes of Europeanization and globalization in HE, which in some cases have transformed pre-existing policies and structures and in others have, at the very least, led to the accommodation of new accountability instruments within historical configurations.

Our analysis opens up several avenues for future research. Above all, scholars should consider taking a more actor-centred approach to HE accountability. For example, future studies should further scrutinize our finding of converging accountability regimes, at least regarding the scope of instruments applied. As we have largely focused on legislative amendments and innovations, it would be useful to assess how the new accountability mechanisms function in practice 'on the ground' and to what extent various actors have mobilized in order to water down their actual impact and effectiveness. Moreover, it would be interesting to discern whether, and to what extent, partisan preferences have shaped the accountability regimes over time. Here one might consider exploring not only the classical right–left divide, but also the impact of liberal or green parties on forms of accountability. One might be inclined to assume that liberal parties will pursue a tougher, more comprehensive QA regime in the name of university competition and performance and force the incorporation of economic stakeholders, while green parties may prefer stronger (non-economic) stakeholder regimes in the name of university democratization. In this context, another avenue for research would be to assess the role of academic interest groups (e.g. student unions, professorial interest groups) in shaping the accountability regimes, while also focusing on issues of executive capacity in education policy. Here, public policy theories that highlight the interaction of diverse sets of actors in shaping policy processes might be helpful tools to unpack the increasingly complex interactions in this multi-actor policy field. Finally, we hope that our conceptual and empirical analysis will stimulate research on the impact of accountability and governance structures on crucial dimensions of institutional performance in HE, such as research output, student satisfaction, graduate employability, and university–industrial collaboration.

Notes

1. One of the most detailed conceptualizations of accountability is presented by Bovens (2007). He differentiates a total of 15 types of accountability, which are grouped in 4 bigger clusters.
2. Comité national d'évaluation (CNE), Comité national d'évaluation de la recherche (CNER), and Mission scientifique, technique et pédagogique (MSTP).

3. Numerous university presidents have expressed their displeasure with the purportedly overbearing state quality assurance and evaluation activities (Le Monde, 2008).
4. The average length of these agreements is 40 pages, and they are published by the ministry.
5. Only Bremen does not have any form of a university board, while Brandenburg has one board for all universities in the state.
6. See the website of the Polska Komisja Akredytacyjna: http://www .pka.edu.pl/
7. Interview with the Director, Center for Higher Education Policy Studies (CBPNiSzW), University of Warsaw (November 2008)
8. See the ARACIS website – Consiliul ARACIS: www.aracis.ro/consiliul/
9. Interview with Pro-rector of the University of Iaşi, December 2008; see also Marga (2002).

References

Aghion, P., and Cohen, É. (2004) *Education et croissance*. Paris: La documentation française.

ARACIS (2006) Methodology for External Evaluation, Standards, Standards of Reference, and List of Performance Indicators of the Romanian Agency for Quality Assurance in Higher Education.

Berdahl, R. (1990) Academic freedom, autonomy and accountability in British universities. *Studies in Higher Education*, 15(2), 169–180. doi:10.1080/03075079012331377491

de Boer, H., Jongbloed, B., Benneworth, P., et al. (2015) *Performance-based funding and performance agreements in fourteen higher education systems*. Enschede: University of Twente, Center for Higher Education Policy Studies. www.utwente.nl/bms/cheps/publications/Publications%2 02011/C11HV018%20Final%20Report%20Quality-related%20fund ing,%20performance%20agreements%20and%20profiling%20in%20 HE.pdf

Bovens, M. (2007) Analysing and assessing accountability: A conceptual framework. *European Law Journal*, 13(4), 447–468. doi:10.1111/ j.1468-0386.2007.00378.x

Bovens, M. (2010) Two concepts of accountability: Accountability as a virtue and as a mechanism. *West European Politics*, 33(5), 946–967. doi:10.1080/01402382.2010.486119

Bovens, M., Schillemans, T., and 't Hart, P. (2008) Does public accountability work? An assessment tool. *Public Administration*, 86(1), 225–242. doi:10.1111/j.1467-9299.2008.00716.x

Burke, J. C. (Ed.) (2004) *Achieving accountability in higher education: Balancing public, academic, and market demands.* San Francisco: Jossey-Bass.

Chevaillier, T. (2007) The changing role of the state in French higher education. In D. Westerheijden and S. Schwarz (Eds), *Accreditation and evaluation in the European Higher Education Area*, pp. 159–174. Dordrecht: Springer.

Christensen, T. (2011) University governance reforms: Potential problems of more autonomy? *Higher Education*, 62(4), 503–517. doi:10.1007/s10734-010-9401-z

Christensen, T., and Lægreid, P. (2015) Performance and accountability: A theoretical discussion and an empirical assessment. *Public Organization Review*, 15(2), 207–225. doi:10.1007/s11115-013-0267-2

Clark, B. R. (1983) *The higher education system: Academic organization in cross-national perspective.* Berkeley: University of California Press.

Clark, B. R. (1998) *Creating entrepreneurial universities: Organizational pathways of transformation.* New York: Pergamon.

Comité de Suivi/LRU (2011) 'De nouvelles relations avec l'État'. http://media.enseignementsup-recherche.gouv.fr/file/Autonomie_universites/30/6/LRU_part3_168306.pdf

Consiliul Naţional pentru Finanţarea Învăţământului Superior (2005) 'Optiuni pentru viitor. 10 ani de activitate'. Ministerul Educaţiei şi Cercetării.

Curaj, A., Deca, L., Egron-Polak, E., and Salmi, J. (Eds) (2015) *Higher education reforms in Romania: Between the Bologna Process and national challenges.* Dordrecht: Springer.

Dakowska, D. (2015) Between competition imperative and Europeanisation: The case of higher education reform in Poland. *Higher Education*, 69(1), 129–141.

Dalsheimer, N., and Despréaux, D. (2008) Les classements internationaux des établissements d'enseignement supérieur. *Éducation et Formation*, 78, 151–173.

Dill, D. D., and Beerkens, M. (Eds) (2010) *Public policy for academic quality: Analyses of innovative policy instruments.* Dordrecht: Springer.

Dobbins, M. (2011) Explaining different pathways in higher education policy in Central and Eastern Europe: The cases of Romania and the Czech Republic. *Comparative Education*, 47(2), 223–245.

Dobbins, M. (2014) Exploring the governance of Polish public higher education: Balancing restored historical legacies with Europeanization and market pressures. *European Journal of Higher Education*, 5(1), 18–33.

Dobbins, M. (2017) Convergent or divergent Europeanization? An analysis of higher education governance reforms in France and Italy. *International Review of Administrative Sciences*, 83(1), 177–199.

Dobbins, M., and Knill, C. (2014) *Higher education governance and policy change in Western Europe: International challenges to historical institutions*. Basingstoke: Palgrave Macmillan.

Dobbins, M., Knill, C., and Vögtle, E. M (2011) An analytical model for the cross-country comparison of higher education governance. *Higher Education*, 62(5), 665–683.

Duczmal, W. (2006) The rise of private higher education in Poland: Policies, markets and strategies. PhD Thesis. Enschede: University of Twente, Center for Higher Education Policy Studies.

Enders, J., de Boer, H., and Weyer, E. (2013) Regulatory autonomy and performance: The reform of higher education re-visited. *Higher Education*, 65(1), 5–23. doi:10.1007/s10734-012-9578-4

Estermann, T., Nokkala, T., and Steinel, M. (2011) *University autonomy in Europe II: The scorecard*. Brussels. European University Association.

Gieysztor, A. (1992) Management and resources. In H. de Ridder-Symoens (Ed.), *A history of the university in Europe, Volume 1: Universities in the Middle Ages*, pp. 108–143. Cambridge: Cambridge University Press.

Gingrich, J. R. (2011) *Making markets in the welfare state: The politics of varying market reforms*. Cambridge: Cambridge University Press.

Gornitzka, Å. (2007) The Lisbon Process: A supranational policy perspective. In P. Maassen and P. J. Olsen (Eds), *University dynamics and European integration*, pp. 155–178. Dordrecht: Springer Netherlands.

Gornitzka, Å., and Maassen, P. (2014) Dynamics of convergence and divergence. Exploring accounts of higher education policy change. In P. Mattei (Ed.), *University adaptation in difficult economic times*, pp. 13–29. Oxford: Oxford University Press.

Gornitzka, Å., Maassen, P., Olsen, J. P., and Stensaker, B. (2007) Europe of knowledge: Search for a new pact. In P. Maassen and J. P. Olsen (Eds), *University dynamics and European integration*, pp. 181–214. Dordrecht: Springer Netherlands.

Gornitzka, Å., and Stensaker, B. (2014) The dynamics of European regulatory regimes in higher education: Challenged prerogatives and evolutionary change. *Policy and Society*, 33(3), 177–188. doi:10.1016/j.polsoc.2014.08.002

Huisman, J., and Currie, J. (2004) Accountability in higher education: Bridge over troubled water? *Higher Education*, 48(4), 529–551. doi:10.1023/B:HIGH.0000046725.16936.4c

Hüther, O. (2010) *Von der Kollegialität zur Hierarchie? Eine Analyse des New Managerialism in den Landeshochschulgesetzen.* Wiesbaden: VS Verlag für Sozialwissenschaften.

Inglehart, R. (1997) *Modernization and postmodernization: Cultural, economic, and political change in 43 societies.* Princeton: Princeton University Press.

INRP (2005) L'Enseignement supérieur sous le regard des chercheurs. Les dossiers de la vielle. Lyon: Institut Nationale de la Recherche Pégagogique, Cellule de Veille Scientifique et Technologique. https://ife.ens-lyon.fr/vst/DS-Veille/Dossier_enseignement_superieur.pdf

Jongbloed, B. (2003) Institutional funding and institutional change. In J. File and L. Goedegebuure (Eds), *Real-time systems: Reflections on higher education in the Czech Republic, Hungary, Poland, and Slovenia*, pp. 115–146. Enschede: University of Twente, Center for Higher Education Policy Studies.

Jongbloed, B., Enders, J., and Salerno, C. (2008) Higher education and its communities: Interconnections, interdependencies and a research agenda. *Higher Education*, 56(3), 303–324. doi:10.1007/s10734-008-9128-2

Jongbloed, B., and Vossensteyn, H. (2001) Keeping up performances: An international survey of performance-based funding in higher education. *Journal of Higher Education Policy and Management*, 23(2), 127–145. doi:10.1080/13600800120088625

Jungblut, J. (2016) Re-distribution and public governance: The politics of higher education in Western Europe. *European Politics and Society*, 17(3), 331–352. doi:10.1080/23745118.2016.1140395

Kaiser, Frans (2007) Higher education in France: Country report. *International higher education monitor*. Twente: CHEPS.

Keller, A., and Dobbins, M. (2015) Das Ringen um autonome und wettbewerbsfähige Hochschulen: Der Einfluss von Parteipolitik, fiskalpolitischem Problemdruck und historischen Vermächtnissen auf die Hochschulpolitik der Bundesländer. *Beiträge zur Hochschulforschung*, 37 (2), 28–55.

Kwiek, M. (2014) Structural changes in the Polish higher education system (1990–2010): A synthetic view. *European Journal of Higher Education*, 4 (3), 266–280.

Le Monde (2008) *La loi sur l'autonomie des universités mise en œuvre progressivement*, 25 July.

Leveille, D. (2006) *Accountability in higher education: A public agenda for trust and cultural change.* Berkeley: Center for Studies in Higher Education.

Marga, A. (2002) Reform of education in Romania in the 1990s: A retrospective. *Higher Education in Europe*, XXVII(1–2), 123–135.

Marginson, S., and Rhoades, G. (2002) Beyond national states, markets, and systems of higher education: A glonacal agency heuristic. *Higher Education*, 43(3), 281–309. doi:10.1023/a:1014699605875

Martens, K., and Jakobi, A. P. (Eds) (2010) *Mechanisms of OECD governance: International incentives for national policy-making?* Oxford: Oxford University Press.

Martens, K., Rusconi, A., and Leuze, K. (Eds) (2007) *New arenas of education governance: The impact of international organisations and markets on educational policy making*. Basingstoke: Palgrave Macmillan.

Martens, K., Nagel, A.-K., Windzio, M., and Weymann, A. (Eds) (2010) *Transformation of education policy*. Basingstoke: Palgrave Macmillan.

Mayntz, R. (2002) University councils: An institutional innovation in German universities. *European Journal of Education*, 37(1), 21–28.

Ministerul Educaţiei Naţionale (2002) *Reforma învăţământului In Anul 2000 (Acţiuni Majore)*. Bucharest: Ministerul Educaţiei Naţionale

Mulgan, R. (2000) Accountability: An ever-expanding concept? *Public Administration*, 78(3), 555–573. doi:10.1111/1467-9299.00218

Musselin, C. (2001) *La longue marche des universités françaises*. Paris: PUF.

Musselin, C. (2009) The side effects of the Bologna Process on national institutional settings: The case of France. In A. Amaral, G. Neave, and C. Musselin (Eds), *European integration and the governance of higher education and research*, pp. 181–205. Dordrecht: Springer.

Musselin, C., and Paradeise, C. (2009) France: From incremental transitions to institutional change. In C. Paradeise, E. Reale, I. Bleiklie, and E. Ferlie (Eds), *University governance: Western European comparative perspectives*, pp. 21–49. Dordrecht: Springer.

Neave, G. (2001) The European dimension of higher education. In J. Huisman, P. Maassen, and G. Neave (Eds). *Higher education and the nation state: The international dimension of higher education*, pp. 13–73. Amsterdam: Pergamon.

Neave, G. (2009) The evaluative state as policy in transition: A historical and anatomical study. In R. Cowen and A. Kazamias (Eds), *International handbook of comparative education*, pp. 551–568. Dordrecht: Springer Netherlands.

Neave, G. (2012) *The evaluative state, institutional autonomy and re-engineering higher education in Western Europe: The prince and his pleasure*. Basingstoke: Palgrave Macmillan.

Nicolescu, L., Sapatoru, D., and Paun, L. (2000) Public and private initiatives in higher education: The case of Romania. Polonie Hongrie Aide à la Réconstruction ÉconomiqueAction for Cooperation in Economics (PHARE-ACE) Report.

OECD (2000) *Reviews of national policies for education: Romania*. Paris: OECD.

OECD (2006) *OECD thematic review of tertiary education: Country background report for Poland*. OECD: Warsaw.

Olsen, J. P. (1988) Administrative reform and theories of organization. In C. Campbell and B. G. Peters (Eds), *Organizing governance, governing organizations*, pp. 233–254. Pittsburgh: University of Pittsburgh Press.

Olsen, J. P. (2007) The institutional dynamics of the European university. In P. Maassen and J. P. Olsen (Eds), *University dynamics and European integration*, pp. 25–54. Dordrecht: Springer Netherlands.

Pierson, P. (1998) Irresistible forces, immovable objects: Post-industrial welfare states confront permanent austerity. *Journal of European Public Policy*, 5(4), 539–560. doi:10.1080/13501769880000011

Pollitt, C., and Bouckaert, G. (2011) *Public management reform: A comparative analysis* (3rd ed.). Oxford: Oxford University Press.

Pressman, J., and Wildavsky, A. (1984) *Implementation: How great expectations in Washington are dashed in Oakland; Or, why it's amazing that federal programs work at all*. Oakland: University of California Press.

Quinio, P. (1998) 'Pour financer le plan Université du troisième millénaire. Allègre compte sur les régions. Libération, 3 December: www.liberation.fr/s ociete/0101264216-pour-financer-le-plan-universite-du-troisieme-millenaire -allegre-compte-sur-les-regions.

Reisz, R. (2004) Hochschulautonomie in Rumänien zwischen 1990 und 2000. *Die Hochschule*, 1/2004, 185–202.

Romzek, B. S. (2000) Dynamics of public sector accountability in an era of reform. *International Review of Administrative Sciences*, 66(1), 21–44. doi:10.1177/0020852300661004

Rose, N. (2000) Government and control. *British Journal of Criminology*, 40 (2), 321–329.

Schimank, U., and Lange, S. (2009) Germany: A latecomer to new public management. In C. Paradeise, E. Reale, I. Bleiklie, and E. Ferlie (Eds), *University governance: Western European comparative perspectives*, pp. 51–75. Dordrecht: Springer.

Shaw, M. (2014) Switchmen of reform: Competing conceptions of public higher education governance in Poland. Doctoral Dissertation. University of Minnesota.

Trow, M. (1996) Trust, markets and accountability in higher education: A comparative perspective. *Higher Education Policy*, 9(4), 309–324. doi:10.1057/palgrave.hep.8380051

van Vught, F. (1997) The effects of alternative governance structures: A comparative analysis of higher education policy in five EU member states. In B. Steunenberg and F. van Vught (Eds), *Political institutions and public policy: Perspectives on European decision making*, pp. 115–137. Dordrecht: Kluwer Academic Publishers.

Vîiu, G. A., Vlăsceanu, M., and Miroiu, A. (2012) Ranking political science departments: The case of Romania. *Quality Assurance Review for Higher Education*, 4(2), 79–97.

Vögtle, E. M., Knill, C., and Dobbins, M. (2011) To what extent does transnational communication drive cross-national policy convergence? The impact of the Bologna Process on domestic higher education policies. *Higher Education*, 61(1), 77–94. doi:10.1007/s10734-010-9326-6

Vukasovic, M., Jungblut, J., and Elken, M. (2017) Still the main show in town? Assessing political saliency of the Bologna Process across time and space. *Studies in Higher Education*, 42(8), 1421–1436. doi:10.1080/03075079.2015.1101755

World Bank (2004) *Tertiary education in Poland*. Washington, DC: World Bank.

9 Towards New Models of Decision Making within University Governance in Anglophone Nations

JULIE ROWLANDS

9.1 University Decision Making within Institutional Governance

Decision making involves choosing a course of action from a range of options; it forms the basis for much of the governance that takes place within higher education (Amaral et al., 2003). Within the context of academic governance, decision making generally involves the oversight of teaching and/or research and the protection and enhancement of their quality and standards (Austin and Jones, 2016). Academic governance sets the parameters around how teaching and/or research take place (Marginson and Considine, 2000) and is therefore central to their effectiveness and success.

Universities are large and complex organizations with multiple inputs to almost every decision. Much research and scholarship has been devoted to tracing how university decision making has changed in the face of developments such as the widespread adoption of management practices imported from the public and private sectors (Shattock, 2014), and requirements for increased autonomy and accountability (Ball, 2016), resulting in the dominance of corporate and managerial forms of governance over more traditional collegial forms (Middlehurst, 2013). However, contemporary universities are not fiefdoms, and even the most managerial is not a dictatorship (Shattock, 2006). Thus, although collegial and managerial governance can be characterized as being at opposite ends of a spectrum, some scholars have argued that multiple forms of governance are enacted simultaneously; new modes, such as network and entrepreneurial governance, do not replace old ones but are instead added to the mix, with the balance shifting between and among them in response to internal and external demands (e.g. Blackmore, 2011;

McNay, 1999; Rhodes, 1996). Recent empirical research has also highlighted the complex ways in which the asymmetries of power within university decision making are established and maintained under circumstances where many line managers were formerly academics and many professional staff undertake tasks that might formerly have been thought of as academic in nature (Rowlands, 2017, 2018).

Despite these more nuanced ways of understanding power relations within university decision making, this chapter reports data from a comparative study of academic governance within England, the USA, and Australia showing that, on average, opportunities for currently practising academics to contribute to decision making about matters that affect teaching and research have declined (Rowlands, 2017). Other studies highlight reduced opportunities for student participation in university decision making (Planas et al., 2013) and substantial gaps between those who support students and staff, and those who make decisions about what those support services should be and how they should be delivered (Johnson and Deem, 2003). Taken together, these shifts expose universities to what are largely unacknowledged but significant risks and negative consequences, leading to reduced efficiency and effectiveness and an increased risk of failure (Bolden et al., 2015). This chapter argues the case for new models of university decision making that minimize these risks and negative consequences. Such models should facilitate the development of trust and collaboration between university executives, academics, professional staff, and students, ensuring that there is adequate input from academics and students to decisions about academic matters. There must also be increased input from professional staff to decisions that they are expected to implement.

The chapter commences with a brief outline of university decision making within the context of institutional-level academic governance before discussing ways in which university decision making has changed in recent years (Section 9.2). The chapter then outlines the potential impact of these changes on the effectiveness of university decision making, highlighting four specific consequences and unanticipated risks (Section 9.3). Finally, Section 9.4 briefly explores two alternative models of university decision making and considers the extent to which

these models demonstrate some capacity to respond to these consequences and unanticipated risks.

9.2 How and Why Has Decision Making within University Governance Changed?

As an institution, the university has changed significantly in the past 40
years, continuing an evolution that began more than 1,000 years ago
(Burnes et al., 2014). Seen through the eyes of many governments
worldwide, but especially those within Anglophone nations, universities are now more like any other form of commercial entity rather than
the special organizations that they once were, to be protected and
cultivated (Marginson, 2013). At the same time, universities have
become central to goals related to knowledge economy and innovation
discourses, deployed as part of broader positioning strategies by nation
states in relation to global marketplaces (Jessop, 2017). Within the
United States, the United Kingdom, and Australia in particular, state
policies increasingly treat higher education as a personal benefit rather
than a public good, with a significant financial burden falling on
individual students (Marginson, 2014); in these three nations, student
fees are now among the highest in the industrialized world (OECD,
2017). These shifts have driven the changes in university governance
noted earlier. As a result, there is now faster and more externally
focused decision making, dominated by managerial and corporate
practices including quality assurance and internal and external
accountability (Stensaker and Harvey, 2011). In turn, these processes
both demand and enable a demonstration of return on public and
private investment in higher education (Blackmore, 2009).

There have also been organizational changes within universities that
have impacted on where and how decisions are made. For example,
academic areas have been consolidated to create mega schools and
faculties, centralizing some academic and administrative decision making (Shattock, 2014). The number of deputy and pro-vice chancellor
appointments has also burgeoned, consolidating power within the centre
of the university (Morley, 2015) and away from traditional academic
governance bodies such as the academic board or equivalent, especially
in universities in the United Kingdom and Australia (Rowlands, 2018).
The locus of power within most contemporary universities in
Anglophone nations is indisputably the vice chancellor (also known as

the president or principal) supported by his or her senior executive team, rather than elected academic first-among-equals, as may have been the case in the past (Blackmore and Sawers, 2015).

This has had a direct and profound impact on university decision making and governance processes. Some of these changes are perceived as positive. For example, in many universities, decision making has become faster, makes more efficient use of resources such as time and numbers of staff involved, and is more strategically aligned than was previously possible. As a result, the use of public resources is more transparent and responsive (Marginson and Considine, 2000). It is also argued that the introduction of professional managers to university organizational areas means that teaching and research academics are freer to concentrate on their core roles, and that this has been a necessary shift in what is now a highly competitive academic environment (Taylor, 2006). However, this is hotly contested: there are extensive and well-documented critiques of these recent changes in university governance. For example, managerialism is accused of prioritizing financial and strategic matters over students and academics (Filippakou and Williams, 2014; Robertson and Dale, 2013) and of introducing top-down decision making that emphasizes control and measurable outputs over democracy and trust (Broucker et al., 2018). At the same time, it cannot be assumed that all universities everywhere have experienced these changes in the same ways. For example, some universities in the United Kingdom and the USA have retained their collegial governance structures (Rowlands, 2017), while universities established in England and Australia in the 1990s and later may have been more managerial from the beginning (Rowlands, 2013).

So far this chapter has traced some of the best-known recent changes in university governance and their effects on decision making. The remainder of the chapter draws on a large cross-national comparative study of academic governance in the USA, England, and Australia to highlight some of the consequences of these changes and the risks they bring to universities' core business of teaching and/or research. These three countries are useful exemplars because while their governance systems have each evolved from the Anglo–American governance model, however differently, they have also pursued quite marketized approaches to public higher education, again however differently. In turn, these can potentially impact significantly on decision-making processes and practices (Rowlands, 2017).

The chapter draws principally on two data sets. The first comprises data from a purposively selected sample of 93 publicly funded doctoral-granting universities on a very wide range of characteristics of the academic board – or equivalent principal academic decision-making body – in each university. The sample included 37 comprehensive Australian teaching and research universities with data collected in 2010 and 2015 (enabling some comparison over time), as well as 29 universities in the USA and 27 in England, with data collected in mid-2015. In each country the universities were a mix of ages, sizes, geographic locations, and levels of research intensity. The publicly available data collected in respect of each university include the name, size, composition, and key powers or responsibilities of the academic board or equivalent body, information about the place of each academic board within the governance structure of its respective university, details of the basis upon which each board was established (e.g. the nature of the legislative instrument), and the number and name of academic board standing- and sub-committees. Data were drawn from institutional websites and were cross-checked against relevant policy and legislation to ensure accuracy and currency.

The second set of information was developed from five detailed case studies of institutional-level academic governance undertaken within Australia and the USA, with the sample comprising a purposively chosen mix of elite research, teaching-focused, and comprehensive teaching and research universities, all publicly funded. The case studies focused on university power and authority arrangements and decision-making structures. Data collection was undertaken in Australia from 2010 to 2012 and in the USA in 2016, and involved academic board (or equivalent) and committee-meeting observation; document analysis relating to current and historic agendas, minutes, and subsidiary attachments; and interviews with 46 executives, current and former academic board members, university chancellors, practising academics, and others. The same interview questions were used in all universities in the USA and Australia, subject to minor modifications to accommodate differences in terminology and university structure. Data analysis included both within- and cross-case comparison of data types (Miles and Huberman, 1994). The case study data were then compared and contrasted with the publicly available data reported earlier, and with published historical records.

It is noted that the case study data are limited to Australia and the USA while the publicly available data are from all three nation states. However, the English publicly available data are a very useful point of comparison for the Australian data, given the similarities between English and Australian higher education and university governance systems. A limitation of this study is the sample size of five cases and the gap of five years between the time of data collection in Australia and the USA. The publicly available data help to offset this limitation to some extent. This data can also assist in the identification of themes from the case study findings that might potentially be more broadly reflective.

One of the dangers of cross-national research involves comparing data which appear similar and which may be described using similar words but which in fact can mean quite different things (Bleiklie, 2014). This risk is heightened in relation to comparisons of divergent higher education systems such as the United Kingdom and the USA. However, even within nations, universities are as different as they are similar. Thus, common themes may manifest differently within nation states and within universities. Such differences add complexity and nuance to the following analysis.

A further issue in cross-national comparative research is terminology; similar words may mean completely different things in different contexts. For example, in the USA the word 'faculty' describes those who teach and/or research, whereas in England and Australia 'academics' or 'academic staff' are the more commonly used descriptors. The principal academic governance body is commonly described as a faculty senate or academic senate in the USA, whereas in England and Australia the names academic board or academic senate are most commonly used. In the USA, the chief executive of a university is generally known as the president, whereas in England and Australia the most common title is vice chancellor. In this chapter, titles most commonly used in England and Australia are used generically (that is, academics, academic board, vice chancellor) unless data specifically collected in the USA are being discussed in which case USA titles are used.

9.3 The Potential Impact of Changes on the Effectiveness of University Decision Making

Elsewhere I have reported findings showing that many of the changes in universities themselves and in university decision making have been welcomed, or at least accepted, as inevitable and necessary by academics undertaking teaching and/or research (Rowlands, 2017). Vice chancellors are expected to behave like chief executives, within reasonable limits, and are universally seen as the locus of power for their university (Rowlands, 2015). However, my research and that of others has also shown that there are some consequences arising from these current decision-making models. In the following sections I highlight four such consequences and the significant risks they bring. The first of these is a loss of academic voice.

9.3.1 Consequence 1: Loss of Academic Voice

In general, there has been a significant reduction in opportunities for practising teachers and researchers – those for whom teaching and/or research is their main job – to contribute to university decision making about academic matters. There are many reasons for this, but they include three key factors. First, within Anglophone nations in particular, there has been a significant reduction in the proportion of university staff who are practising academics due to the increase in administrators and administrative structures, often at the centre of the university (Bexley et al., 2011; Locke, 2014; Stromquist, 2012). In addition, fewer academics than was previously the case are tenured or in continuing positions. For example, recent Australian data show that casual and fixed-term academic appointments increased substantially between 1989 and 2013, with casual academics estimated to undertake somewhere between 50 and 70 per cent of all undergraduate teaching in Australian universities (Andrews et al., 2016). Casual or sessional academics are frequently ineligible for election or appointment to decision-making bodies such as university councils and academic boards (Locke et al., 2011).

Second, within many universities the drive for efficiency and centralization of decision making has resulted in consolidation of schools and faculties (Shattock, 2014). Many of the decisions about academic matters are made by bodies that are faculty- or school-based and so there are now proportionately fewer decision-making bodies to which practising academics can seek to contribute. Further, in the United Kingdom and Australia especially, academic boards, as the principal academic decision-making body, are generally smaller than they once were, with comparatively fewer places reserved for practising teachers and/or researchers (Rowlands, 2017; Shattock, 2014). For example, in the oldest two Australian case study universities considered for this chapter, where it was possible to examine shifts in academic board composition over time, the size of the academic board had reduced by approximately 30 members in each case between 1990 and 2010.

Third, in many Australian and United Kingdom universities, including the research elite, there may be many more appointed senior executives and senior managers on academic boards and their committees than there are elected academics. The publicly available data collected for this study show that in 2015, 45 per cent of the members of the academic boards from the Australian sample and 50 per cent of members of the academic boards from the English sample were there by virtue of a management position they held (most often as a member of the senior executive or as a dean) and therefore their primary role was not teaching or research.

The data also show that between 2010 and 2015 the percentage of members of the academic boards from the Australian sample who were *ex officio* increased from 42 per cent to 46 per cent. That is, in five years the proportion of Australian academic board members who were practising academics decreased by 4 per cent to a little over half of all members. The significant proportion of English and Australian academic board members who are senior managers reduces the proportion of voting members who are grassroots, practising academics. It also affects the power dynamic during meetings, impacting on the willingness of those who teach and/or research to engage in robust debate or even to ask questions (Rowlands, 2018).

Although many deans and senior executives were once teachers and researchers, there is increasing empirical data to show how difficult it is for those who hold these positions to remain in touch with what it is actually like, in the current moment, to teach and research – to have to implement the decisions that are being made (Blackmore and Sawers, 2015). As Australian research has shown, it is almost impossible to maintain a genuine involvement in either teaching or research (or both) while undertaking 70–80 hours per week of senior management work, including a heavy schedule of meetings (Blackmore and Sawers, 2015; Marginson and Considine, 2000). Yet there are significant risks to universities where there is insufficient academic input to key decisions that affect teaching and research, including as regards curriculum and assessment. Recent studies, including one by the UK Leadership

Foundation for Higher Education conducted in 2015, have shown that overly strong central control actively inhibits the development of an entrepreneurial culture, including within research (Bolden et al., 2015; see also Clark, 1998; McNay, 2015). In turn, this has significant negative implications for innovation, transformation, and the quality of research output – stated goals of many universities and nations (Bolden et al., 2015). It also limits the potential for network decision making, at least partly because networks are horizontal rather than hierarchical arrangements (Ferrare and Apple, 2017).

9.3.2 Consequence 2: Loss of Student Voice

Student participation in university decision making has declined overall within Anglophone nations, including within Australia, at least partly because there tend to be fewer places reserved for students within decision-making bodies (such as academic boards and councils) than there once were (Shattock, 2014). The consolidation of organizational areas to create mega schools and faculties, as described earlier, has meant that there are now fewer decision-making bodies to which students can seek to contribute. Many students must also work long hours in addition to their studies and so are less able or willing to spend time on campus than was the case in the past (Planas et al., 2013), inhibiting their capacity to learn about and contribute to university decision making.

Unfortunately, there is little current research in the area of student contributions to university decision making. However, one study conducted across 16 universities in the United Kingdom in the 2000s showed that although university policies often put an emphasis on students, the focus tended to be on the implications for the students rather than on what students themselves might need or what they could potentially contribute (Johnson and Deem, 2003). As the study reported: 'It is not that senior managers interviewed had no concern for the student. Rather it is ... that these preoccupations are predominantly driven by financial and resource issues, rather than by students' actual demands or needs' (Johnson and Deem, 2003, p. 310). The same study found that in their day-to-day work senior executives and senior manager academics such as deans were far removed from students and needed to become much more directly aware of student needs. The following quote from an interview with a student representative on the academic board equivalent body at a US university illustrates this very powerfully:

We're not consulted. Things that directly impact or affect us directly are not considered for consultation. (Elected student member of academic senate, US teaching-intensive university)

Among practising academics, the predominant view was that university executives saw students as objects to be measured, or counted, rather than as valued and contributing members of the university community:

You know all this measuring stuff? ... It doesn't make anybody a better student or a better teacher. (Elected member, state-wide academic senate, US teaching-focused university)

Student participation in university decision making is critically important. Despite this, students are largely absent from the most commonly implemented models of university governance or decision making except at the margins (Luescher-Mamashela, 2010). This has significant implications not only for students themselves but for universities more broadly, both in terms of the quality of decisions made and student engagement (Carey, 2013).

9.3.3 Consequence 3: Separation of Academic Strategy from Academic Work

The third consequence of changes in university decision making is the separation of academic strategy from academic work. Within many universities in Australia and elsewhere, long-term strategic planning in relation to academic matters (such as the development of university academic or research plans) is no longer part of the terms of reference of any committee of which students and practising academics can be members. Where this is not the case, these committees may lack the resources, time, or expertise for such a task, and they are often too far removed from the necessary inputs, such as shifts in government policy, market positioning, and market demand (Rowlands, 2017).

However, where academic strategy becomes separated from academic practice, or academic work, there is the potential for a split between the academic directions the university wants to take and what is desirable and even possible from a teaching and research perspective. Sometimes such a dichotomy might be part of a deliberate strategy to shift the university quickly in one direction or another, but there can also be negative consequences where practice does not or cannot meet the vision and strategic direction. One of the important roles of university decision-making structures is ensuring that there is ownership of and commitment to academic goals and plans, and that there is alignment between the priorities set out in plans and the messages that are purveyed through on-the-ground mechanisms such as academic workload models and academic development support structures. A generic example of the potential for a split between overall university goals and what is possible on the ground might involve a university whose education plan calls for teaching to have an increased focus on student engagement at the same time that the faculty-based academic workload model for teaching reduces time allocated to each academic for student consultation and feedback. Another example could be a university whose research plan calls for greater focus on producing quality publications (that is, quality over quantity) at the same time that the faculty-based workload model rewards all journal articles equally, regardless of the status or rank of the journal. Both of these examples are completely hypothetical, but it is possible to envisage them (or variations thereof) occurring in many universities in the United Kingdom, United States, and Australia, as elsewhere.

This lack of alignment between what the university as a whole says it wants to do and what deans or equivalent feel able or want to achieve through mechanisms available to them appears to be common in universities. In my own research, deans and heads of school consistently reported feeling deeply frustrated by a perceived lack of control over directives that came down from the top, but at the same time were expected to deal with everything that came up from the bottom with few or diminishing resources. This is reflected in the following comment from a dean in an Australian university when asked which groups were influential in university decision making:

Well the deans aren't. We're not part of the Vice-Chancellor's executive. We actually run the University but we are not part of the executive because it has just got so big that we are just not part of it. (Dean and ex-officio academic board member, elite research-intensive Australian university)

Other recent Australian research on higher education leadership and management has shown similar findings (Blackmore, 2014). However, data from elsewhere present a more complex picture. For example, Apkarian et al. (2014) examined academic decision making within US four-year colleges and universities between 2000 and 2012 and found little evidence of managerial control. Conversely, the results of the international study of the changing academic profession (CAP), based on a common survey across 18 countries and 5 continents, show that while some US academics may have a narrower role in university decision making than some colleagues elsewhere, they report feeling more informed about decisions being taken within their university and are less likely than academics from other nations to report lack of involvement in university decision making as being a problem (Finkelstein et al., 2011).

9.3.4 Consequence 4: Gaps between Decision Makers and Service Providers

The fourth unintended consequence involves gaps between those general and professional staff who support students and academics and those who make decisions about what support services should be and how they should be provided. Data from the United Kingdom and Australia show that many professional staff feel they have significant (and growing) workloads and responsibility, but little autonomy to influence those decisions (Szekeres, 2006). For example, one large study in the United Kingdom found that while few senior managers aimed to exclude those who deliver the services from decision making (indeed, many of the managers expressed a strongly inclusive philosophy), the end result was decisions that did not take sufficient account of the view of professional staff about what was needed and what would work (Johnson and Deem, 2003).

A further issue in relation to service delivery within universities relates to a tendency to focus on structural issues, such as reporting arrangements, role titles, position descriptions, policies, and procedures, and outputs, such as data, against key performance indicators and targets, rather than functional matters such as what service is required and how it can be provided, or even how the process might work. Research in the USA by Kezar and Eckel (2004) indicates that by focusing on structural approaches and outputs universities can improve efficiency but not effectiveness of service delivery. A more recent study at a large London university found that focusing on aspects of service delivery such as documented roles, operating procedures, and performance standards does not improve performance because relationships are more important than structures and processes (Greenhalgh, 2015). In terms of decision making, the same study found that 'it matters less what form the structures of governance take than the extent to which they allow effective deliberation on the numerous tensions and paradoxes that characterise contemporary university life' (Greenhalgh, 2015, p. 208).

So far, this section has highlighted some potential, and possibly unintended, consequences arising from current models of university decision making within nations such as the United Kingdom, the United States, and Australia. These potential consequences include a loss of academic and student voice in university decision making about academic matters, the separation of academic strategy from academic work, and gaps between decision makers and service providers such as professional and general staff. In turn, these consequences pose significant potential risks for universities that I would argue are, as yet, largely unacknowledged. First is a potential lack of ownership of new initiatives by those who must implement them, leading to an increased risk of failure (Cardoso et al., 2018). Second is the potential for reduced creativity and entrepreneurship within the university as a whole, including in research practice, arising from reduced academic and professional autonomy (McNay, 2015; Wardale and Lord, 2016). Third is reduced effectiveness of functional areas and services (Kezar and Eckel, 2004).

However, while these risks are of significant concern, I suggest that the situation is more complex than it might first appear. For example, although in recent years managerial and corporate modes of decision making have been widely dominant (Blackmore, 2011), it is also known that many academics have taken up line management positions through appointments at executive dean and pro- or deputy-vice -chancellor levels (Blackmore et al., 2010). This tendency has been more pronounced as the number and scope of senior executive level positions has increased (Rowlands, 2019). It is also the case that the nature of everyday academic work has changed and there is a now a need for teaching and research academics to undertake a broader range and greater number of tasks that might formerly have been thought of as administrative or managerial in nature (Bansel and

Davies, 2010). Professional staff in universities increasingly require high-level academic credentials and many undertake roles that have an academic component, such as course and career advice, support for the student experience, community partnerships and learning support. As a result, the divisions between academic and administrative work, and between academia and management, are increasingly blurred. Celia Whitchurch (2013) calls these 'third space' roles – that is, roles that sit in between the traditional academic and administrative divide. This means there is much less clarity about what were formerly clear-cut divisions between executive, academic, and professional roles within universities. The divide between what is 'academic' and what is not in terms of decision making is continuing to evolve.

9.4 Towards New Models of Decision Making in Universities

The substantial consequences and significant risks for universities arising from current models of decision making and the shifting nature of executive, academic, and professional staff roles within universities suggest that these current models are neither efficient nor effective. This raises the question of what alternative models of university decision making might exist. There are numerous published 'best practice' guides to improving university governance, and these have been extensively critiqued elsewhere for underplaying the impact of relationships and power distributions on governance effectiveness and for underestimating the impact of local context by erroneously assuming that what works well in one university will work well in all (see Rowlands, 2017). Additionally, these guides tend not to focus on the fundamental decision-making aspect of university governance. As a result, alternative models of university decision making are exceedingly rare.

One genuinely alternative approach is provided by the Mondragon University of Spain, established in 1997.[1] This university operates as a non-profit cooperative within which every staff member is an owner with a personal stake in the success of the institution through an investment of the equivalent of 12 months' salary (Wright et al., 2011). All members have an equal vote on the annual business plan, which includes investment decisions, remuneration to the worker-owners, and other central business matters (Wright et al., 2011). However, this is far removed from the structure and function of universities in many (especially English-speaking) nations, where approaches to higher education tend to be much more strongly corporatist than in some European countries. It is therefore almost impossible to imagine the Mondragon model being implemented in the Anglophone world.

A further alternative was developed by the UK Leadership Foundation for Higher education, described as 'shared leadership' (Bolden et al., 2015). Their empirical research has identified three common dimensions of a genuinely shared approach to leadership within universities. These can be summarized as follows:

1. Context and culture – where leadership relies less on positional power and control, and more on placing trust in knowledge, experience, and expertise;
2. Change – where leadership takes place at multiple levels of an organization, not only at the top, and functions as a mix of top-down, bottom-up, and middle-out contributions;
3. Relationships – where leadership arises from collaborations between individuals working together to create a collective identity (Bolden et al., 2015, p. 63).

In terms of governance, a shared leadership approach of the type advocated by Bolden et al. would first involve looking at which bodies (e.g. committees or individuals) make which decisions and who is part of the decision-making process. Within all of my research in Australia and abroad, the most frequently made comment from academic and professional staff is that they wished their university would rely more on in-house knowledge and expertise when facing challenges or crises. Contrary to popular perceptions, staff are not opposed to change and almost all are strongly committed to the success of their university – but they want to have a more meaningful and constructive role in decision making than they are currently 'allowed'.

The approach advocated by Bolden et al. is underpinned by the idea that decision making is more effective when more than the senior management group gets to participate. They go on to provide four criteria that universities can use when evaluating whether their current leadership model is genuinely 'shared':

1. People: the involvement of a broad range of staff from a range of roles, backgrounds, and levels, all contributing knowledge;
2. Processes: support for individuals sharing expertise across traditional organizational boundaries;
3. Professional development: the active development of both individual and collective skills and behaviours;
4. Resources: that enable collaboration, networks and partnerships (ibid.).

Bolden et al. indicate that fear is a key barrier to implementing this model. This fear potentially comes from two key sources: fear from senior managers and executives that they will lose their decision-making authority, and fear from grassroots academics and professional staff that they will either not be listened to, or that they will be landed with additional tasks and responsibilities for which they are not remunerated and which they don't have time to undertake properly. Lack of trust is central to these concerns (Bolden et al., 2015). Trust is needed at multiple levels within university decision making but is rarely directly addressed. This is significant given how frequently lack of trust is cited as a reason for failure or breakdown in university decision-making models or frameworks (Rowlands, 2017). Empirical data also show that where such trust exists, the effectiveness of university decision making is improved (Kezar, 2004).

Through my research I have identified a number of factors that can potentially contribute to both a lack of trust and to relationship difficulties that surround university decision making. The first of these relates to the immense financial pressures faced by many publicly funded universities in nations such as Australia. These pressures are especially extreme in universities that are not research-intensive or elite, where income is primarily drawn from large-scale teaching. The second relates to composition of key decision-making bodies in the committee structure. Where the memberships of these bodies are dominated by executives (and sometimes dominated to a very significant extent: in some Australian universities up to 80 per cent of members of the academic board or equivalent are there by virtue of a management position they hold and not because of their teaching and research) there are simply far fewer opportunities for grassroots staff to participate in university decision-making processes. As universities become more streamlined and bodies such as faculty and school boards are reduced and abolished, as is happening in many universities, these tendencies for exclusionary decision-making processes are enhanced.

A third factor arises from the tendency for the most powerful people in any decision-making body to speak most often. In my studies of decision making in Australian and US universities it was not unusual for me to observe meetings where both executives and grassroots staff were present but only the executives spoke. The fourth and related factor is the knowledge base and skill level of the grassroots staff. If staff from all levels are going to participate in university decision making, then they need to know enough about the university and the internal and external issues it is facing for that participation to be meaningful.

This chapter has shown that decision making within universities has changed markedly within the past 40 years and can be expected to continue to change into the future. Many of the changes in university decision making are perceived as being positive, resulting in reduced inefficiencies and less elitism. However, the chapter has also reported data showing that, on average, opportunities for those who actually teach and/or conduct research to contribute to decisions that affect teaching and research have reduced. I have also argued that there are fewer opportunities for students and professional staff to contribute to university decision making of any kind. These gaps have the potential to expose universities to significant risks and negative consequences, such as a loss of ownership of new initiatives, reduced creativity and entrepreneurship, and reduced effectiveness of services.

It is therefore time to think about new models of decision making within universities that provide for the development of trust and collaboration despite differences in roles and levels. Executives, academics, professional staff, and students must all play a part in university decision-making processes, and we must recognize the necessity, in particular, of meaningful academic input to decisions about matters such as academic and research planning, curricula, and assessment. However, this is not a problem for senior management alone. All staff at all levels of a university have a responsibility to contribute to decision-making structures and processes, even if it might not always be the most convenient or interesting way to spend one's time. This means putting up our respective hands to serve on committees and working parties, and undertaking our committee work constructively and conscientiously, rather than shutting our eyes and hoping someone else will do it so that we don't have to.

Notes

1. See the website of the MU Mondragon Unibersitatea: www.mondragon.edu /en/home

References

Amaral, A., Jones, G. A., and Karseth, B. (2003) Governing higher education: Comparing national perspectives. In A. Amaral, G. A. Jones, and B. Karseth (Eds), *Governing higher education: National perspectives on institutional governance*, Vol. 2, pp. 279–298. Dordrecht: Kluwer Academic Publishers.

Andrews, S., Bare, L., Bentley, P. J., et al. (2016) *Contingent academic employment in Australian universities*. Melbourne: LH Martin Institute.

Apkarian, J., Mulligan, K., Rotondi, M., and Brint, S. (2014) Who governs? Academic decision-making in US four-year colleges and universities, 2000–2012. *Tertiary Education and Management*, 20(2), 151–164.

Austin, I., and Jones, G. A. (2016) *Governance of higher education: Global perspectives, theories and practices*. New York: Routledge.

Ball, S. J. (2016) Neoliberal education? Confronting the slouching beast. *Policy Futures in Education*, 14(8), 1046–1059. doi:10.1177/ 1478210316664259

Bansel, P., and Davies, B. (2010) Through a love of what neoliberalism puts at risk. In J. Blackmore, M. Brennan, and L. Zipin (Eds), *Re-positioning university governance and academic work*, pp. 133–146. Rotterdam: Sense.

Bexley, E., James, R., and Arkoudis, S. (2011) *The Australian academic profession in transition: Addressing the challenge of reconceptualising academic work and regenerating the academic workforce*. Melbourne: University of Melbourne. Centre for the Study of Higher Education.

Blackmore, J. (2009) Academic pedagogies, quality logics and performative universities: Evaluating teaching and what students want. *Studies in Higher Education*, 34(8), 857–872.

Blackmore, J. (2011) Bureaucratic, corporate, market and network governance: Shifting spaces for gender equity in educational organisations. *Gender, Work and Organization*, 18(5), 443–466.

Blackmore, J. (2014) 'Wasting talent'? Gender and the problematics of academic disenchantment and disengagement with leadership. *Higher*

Education Research & Development, 33(1), 86–99. doi:10.1080/ 07294360.2013.864616

Blackmore, J., Brennan, M., and Zipin, L. (2010) Repositioning university governance and academic work: An overview. In J. Blackmore, M. Brennan, and L. Zipin (Eds), *Re-positioning university governance and academic work*, pp. 1–16. Rotterdam: Sense.

Blackmore, J., and Sawers, N. (2015) Executive power and scaled-up gender subtexts in Australian entrepreneurial universities. *Gender and Education*, 27(3), 320–337. doi:10.1080/09540253.2015.1027670

Bleiklie, I. (2014) Comparing university organizations across boundaries. *Higher Education*, 67(4), 381–391. doi:10.1007/s10734-013-9683-z

Bolden, R., Jones, S., Davis, H., and Gentle, P. (2015) *Developing and sustaining shared leadership in education.* https://uwe-repository.worktribe .com/output/828871/developing-and-sustaining-shared-leadership-in-highe r-education

Broucker, B., De Wit, K., and Verhoeven, J. C. (2018) Higher education for public value: Taking the debate beyond New Public Management. *Higher Education Research & Development*, 37(2), 227–240. doi:10.1080/ 07294360.2017.1370441

Burnes, B., Wend, P., and By, R. T. (2014) The changing face of English universities: Reinventing collegiality for the twenty-first century. *Studies in Higher Education*, 39(6), 905–926. doi:10.1080/03075079.2012.754858

Cardoso, S., Rosa, M. J., and Videira, P. (2018) Academics' participation in quality assurance: Does it reflect ownership? *Quality in Higher Education*, 24(1), 1–16. doi:10.1080/13538322.2018.1433113

Carey, P. (2013) Student engagement: Stakeholder perspectives on course representation in university governance. *Studies in Higher Education*, 38 (9), 1290–1304. doi:10.1080/03075079.2011.621022

Clark, B. R. (1998) The entrepreneurial university: Demand and response. *Tertiary Education and Management*, 4(1), 5–16. doi:10.1080/ 13583883.1998.9966941

Ferrare, J., and Apple, M. (2017) Practicing policy networks: Using organisational field theory to examine philanthropic involvement in education policy. In J. Lynch, J. Rowlands, T. Gale, and A. Skourdoumbis (Eds), *Practice theory: Diffractive readings in professional practice and education.* Oxford: Routledge.

Filippakou, O., and Williams, G. (2014) Academic capitalism and entrepreneurial universities as a new paradigm of 'development'. *Open Review of Educational Research*, 1(1), 70–83. doi:10.1080/23265507.2014.964645

Finkelstein, M., Ju, M., and Cummings, W. K. (2011) The United States of America: Perspectives on faculty governance. In W. Locke, W. K. Cummings, and D. Fisher (Eds), *Changing governance and* management in higher education: The perspectives of the academy, pp. 199–222. Dordrecht: Springer.

Greenhalgh, T. (2015) Higher education governance as language games: A Wittgensteinian case study of the breakdown of governance at the London School of Economics 2004–2011. *Higher Education Quarterly*, 69(2), 193–213. doi:10.1111/hequ.12064

Jessop, B. (2017) Varieties of academic capitalism and entrepreneurial universities. *Higher Education*, 73(6), 853–870. doi:10.1007/s10734-017-0120-6

Johnson, R. N., and Deem, R. (2003) Talking of students: Tensions and contradictions for the manager-academic and the university in contemporary higher education. *Higher Education*, 46(3), 289–314. doi:10.1023/a:1025377826704

Kezar, A. J. (2004) What is more important to effective governance: Relationships, trust, and leadership, or structures and formal processes? *New Directions for Higher Education, Autumn (Fall)*, 2004(127), 35–46.

Kezar, A. J., and Eckel, P. (2004) Meeting today's governance challenges: A synthesis of the literature and examination of a future agenda for scholarship. *The Journal of Higher Education*, 75(4), 371–399.

Locke, W. (2014) *Shifting academic careers: Implications for enhancing professionalism in teaching and supporting learning.* www.advance-he.ac.uk/knowledge-hub/shifting-academic-careers-implications-enhancing-professionalism-teaching-and

Locke, W., Cummings, W. K., and Fisher, D. (Eds). (2011) *Changing governance and management in higher education: The perspectives of the academy.* Dordrecht: Springer.

Luescher-Mamashela, T. M. (2010) From university democratisation to managerialism: The changing legitimation of university governance and the place of students. *Tertiary Education and Management*, 16(4), 259–283. doi:10.1080/13583883.2010.529161

Marginson, S. (2013) The impossibility of capitalist markets in higher education. *Journal of Education Policy*, 28(3), 353–370.

Marginson, S. (2014) *'Bonfire of the publics'? Rebuilding the social foundations of higher education.* Paper presented at the 2014 Clark Kerr Lectures, University of California, Berkeley. www.cshe.berkeley.edu/eve nts/2014-clark-kerr-lectures

Marginson, S., and Considine, M. (2000) *The enterprise university: Power, governance and reinvention in Australia.* Melbourne: Cambridge University Press.

McNay, I. (1999) Changing cultures in UK higher education: The state as corporate market bureaucracy and the emergent academic enterprises. In

D. Braun and F.-X. Merrien (Eds), *Towards a new model of governance for universities: A comparative view*, pp. 34–58. London: Jessica Kingsley.

McNay, I. (2015) Leading the autonomous university: Conditioning factors and culture of organisations in the UK, Ukraine and other European contexts. *International Journal of Universities and Leadership*, 1(1), 7–14.

Middlehurst, R. (2013) Changing internal governance: Are leadership roles and management structures in United Kingdom universities fit for the future? *Higher Education Quarterly*, 67(3), 275–294. doi:10.1111/hequ.12018

Miles, M. B., and Huberman, M. (1994) *Qualitative data analysis: An expanded sourcebook* (2nd ed.). Thousand Oaks: Sage.

Morley, L. (2015) Troubling intra-actions: Gender, neo-liberalism and research in the global academy. *Journal of Education Policy*, 31(1), 1–18. doi:10.1080/02680939.2015.1062919

OECD. (2017) *Education at a glance 2017: OECD indicators.* www.oecd.org/education/education-at-a-glance-19991487.htm

Planas, A., Soler, P., Fullana, J., Pallisera, M., and Vilà, M. (2013) Student participation in university governance: The opinions of professors and students. *Studies in Higher Education*, 38(4), 571–583. doi:10.1080/03075079.2011.586996

Rhodes, R. A. W. (1996) The new governance: Governing without government. *Political Studies*, 44(3), 652–667.

Robertson, S. L., and Dale, R. (2013) The social justice implications of privatisation in education governance frameworks: A relational account. *Oxford Review of Education*, 39(4), 426–445.

Rowlands, J. (2013) Academic boards: Less intellectual and more academic capital in higher education governance? *Studies in Higher Education*, 38 (9), 1274–1289. doi:10.1080/03075079.2011.619655

Rowlands, J. (2015) Turning collegial governance on its head: Symbolic violence, hegemony and the academic board. *British Journal of Sociology of Education*, 36 (7), 1017–1035. doi:10.1080/01425692.2014.883916

Rowlands, J. (2017) *Academic governance within contemporary universities: Perspectives from Anglophone nations.* Singapore: Springer Nature.

Rowlands, J. (2018) Deepening understandings of Bourdieu's academic and intellectual capital through a study of academic voice within academic governance. *Studies in Higher Education*, 43(11), 1823–1836. doi:10.1080/03075079.2017.1284192

Rowlands, J. (2019) The domestic labour of academic governance and the loss of academic voice. *Gender and Education*, 31(7), 793–810. doi:10.1080/09540253.2017.1324132

Shattock, M. (2006) *Managing good governance in higher education.* Maidenhead: Open University Press.

Shattock, M. (2014) University governance in the UK: Bending the traditional model. In M. Shattock (Ed.), *International trends in university governance: Autonomy, self-government and the distribution of authority*, pp. 127–144. London: Routledge.

Stensaker, B., and Harvey, L. (2011) Introduction and overview of the book. In B. Stensaker and L. Harvey (Eds), *Accountability in higher education: Global perspectives on trust and power*, pp. 1–6. New York: Routledge.

Stromquist, N. P. (2012) The provost office as key decision-maker in the contemporary US university: Toward a theory of institutional change. In H. Schuetze, W. Bruneau, and G. Grosjean (Eds), *University governance and reform: Policy, fads, and experience in international perspective*, pp. 25–45. New York: Palgrave MacMillan.

Szekeres, J. (2006) General staff experiences in the corporate university. *Journal of Higher Education Policy and Management*, 28(2), 133–145. doi:10.1080/13600800600750962

Taylor, J. (2006) 'Big is beautiful'. Organisational change in universities in the United Kingdom: New models of institutional management and the changing role of academic staff. *Higher Education in Europe*, 31(3), 251–273.

Wardale, D., and Lord, L. (2016) Bridging the gap: The challenges of employing entrepreneurial processes within university settings. *Higher Education Research & Development*, 35(5), 1068–1082. doi:10.1080/07294360.2016.1139549

Whitchurch, C. (2013) *Reconstructing identities in higher education: The rise of third space professionals.* New York: Routledge.

Wright, S., Greenwood, D., and Boden, R. (2011) Report on a field visit to Mondragón University: A cooperative experience/experiment. *Learning and Teaching*, 4(3), 38–56.

10 Governance in Public and Private Higher Education in Europe: Patterns, Divergences, and Convergences

PEDRO N. TEIXEIRA AND ROBIN
MIDDLEHURST

10.1 Introduction

Governance in higher education has been described as ambiguous (Keller, 2001) and an elusive and abstract concept (Austin and Jones, 2016). Both the concept and the practice of governance are also recognized as contested, given tensions between different levels of authority and constituency interests: lay or state, academic or institutional, faculty or students (Locke et al., 2011; Shattock, 2017; Stensaker and Harvey, 2011). Additionally, scholars have commented that studies of governance in higher education often lack explicit theoretical frameworks (Huisman, 2009). Despite these difficulties and shortcomings, the topic of higher education governance has gained in prominence, propelled to the fore by the modernization and reform agendas of governments from the 1980s to the present, themselves a response to new challenges in the operating environments of higher education systems and institutions. It is timely, therefore, to take a closer look at governance, using developments in 'public' and 'private' higher education to illuminate potentially contradictory trends of convergence and divergence in emerging governance arrangements. This chapter will also seek to plug a scholarly gap by drawing on a range of disciplinary and theoretical perspectives to assist in interpreting current governance arrangements in the field of higher education, or to point to gaps in our understanding.

There are sound reasons for describing governance in higher education as elusive and ambiguous since concepts and practices of governance are intricately linked to contexts, whether historical, geographical or cultural, and these contexts are fluid and dynamic. For example, governance arrangements in the medieval universities of Bologna or Paris differed markedly, given particular relationships between students and professors in Bologna and between the teaching faculty and the supervisory authority of the church in Paris (Austin and Jones, 2016). In the case of the United Kingdom, Shattock (2006) identifies four distinct models of governance that emerged at different historical periods, reflecting different cultural and political traditions: the Oxbridge model, the Scottish model (both medieval in origin), the civic university model from the nineteenth century, and the Higher Education Corporation, born in the late twentieth century. In the twenty-first century, new types of higher education provider exhibit different types of governance, as we will explore herein, again expanding the range of models and concepts of governance. English traditions are different from those in continental Europe, where two different types of university model with different forms of governance emerged in the late eighteenth and early nineteenth centuries: the Napoleonic model, with a pattern of strong administrative influence from the state over university life, and the Prussian or Humboldtian model, with distinctive academic influence aimed at protecting academic freedom (Neave and van Vught, 1991).

Over several centuries, dimensions of elusiveness and ambiguity in governance have also applied to notions of 'public' and 'private' higher education. In continental Europe, the universities grew to be part of a public higher education system, regulated by the state (at national or provincial levels), while in the United Kingdom, until the twentieth century the majority of universities were established as private institutions with more independence from the state. However, in both cases, relationships with the state have changed over time, affecting not only governance arrangements, but also classifications of institutions as 'private' or 'public'.

Another dimension of ambiguity is that the focus of governance theories and practices can be at different levels. Austin and Jones (2016, p. 2) distinguish three levels – the micro level of the academic department, the meso-level of the organization or institution, and the macro level of the higher education system – while others distinguish broadly between the system and institution levels (Middlehurst and Teixeira, 2012). These different levels interact with each other, and changes at the system level, for example, will likely have consequences for governance at the level of the institution. Economic and political changes in the operating environments for higher education have impacts on the governance of higher education institutions (Shattock, 2017) as well as systems; hence, relationships between these different levels of governance are also fluid and dynamic.

Finally, changes in governance may appear to be clear-cut when enacted through formal legislation or policy rubric. However, as researchers have demonstrated, there is often divergence between policy rhetoric and the reality of governance practices on the ground (Middlehurst and Teixeira, 2012; Musselin, 2005). This may be because of temporal issues, in that proposed changes in governance arrangements take time to embed in working practices; or it may be because such changes reflect differences in values or power relations between the different actors involved, so that proposed changes meet resistance and can be enacted only partially, or not at all. Further possibilities are that new governance arrangements do not displace earlier modes, but incorporate them in ways that make higher education governance multi-layered and complex. Alternatively, our explanations of how governance works in theory and practice may be overly simplistic, or may miss important dimensions and interactions. What is clear is that offering a single definition of governance, an all-embracing theory, or definitive assertions about converging or diverging trends in governance arrangements is neither feasible nor desirable. Instead, it is more useful to draw on different disciplinary and theoretical lenses to illuminate the landscape of governance in higher education.

The difficulties of pinning down 'governance' also apply to its setting of 'higher education', where definitions of the territory are neither static nor clear-cut. In international classifications (such as ISCED), higher education is part of tertiary education, covering different kinds of intellectual and practical domains: academic education, advanced vocational education, and professional education at four post-secondary levels of qualification (levels 5 to 8 inclusive). In different countries, higher education may include a wide range of types of providers and provision (as in the USA) or be divided into different categories of institution (as in the binary higher education systems of the Netherlands or Germany). If one adds other dimensions such as modes of delivery or types of learning space – open, distance, e-learning, on-campus higher education – or domains of practice such as research and education, then the forms of higher education institution or provider become even more diverse. With developments in technology, institutional boundaries are becoming increasingly blurred; they can also vary across jurisdictions. In many parts of the world, both higher education systems and institutions are changing as a result of changing operating conditions and legislative and policy reforms such as the 'modernization agenda' of the European Commission, initiated in the early twenty-first century. Our discussion of developments in public and private higher education is part of this dynamic and fluid picture just as much as shifts in governance. This chapter, then, needs to be viewed as a kaleidoscope of moving parts, wherein explanations of what is happening are likely to be partial, incomplete, and temporary – but also, hopefully, illuminating.

The chapter is organized into three main sections. Section 10.2 addresses the changing landscape of higher education and public–private distinctions in particular. Section 10.3 focuses on governance arrangements in the two arenas of public and private higher education and at the two levels of system and institutional governance. Section 10.4 discusses theories of governance and their application to public and private higher education domains. All three sections discuss divergence and convergence in theories and practices. The concluding section draws the analyses together, noting gaps and pointing to promising directions for further research.

10.2 A Changing Landscape: Convergences and Divergences between 'Public' and 'Private' Higher Education

Various studies in the United Kingdom, continental Europe, and the USA (Altbach et al., 2009; Fielden et al., 2010; Levy, 2009; Teixeira et al., 2014, 2016, 2017) have reported growth in recent decades in the number of private higher education institutions, in the number of students enrolled in these institutions, or in the relative share of the higher education market held by private rather than public providers of higher education. Kinser et al. (2010) have suggested that private sector growth is a global phenomenon, with certain regions expanding significantly. For example, by 2010 Latin America had a higher education system that was 49 per cent private, while Asia's private higher education share was 36 per cent private. These two regions exceeded the

Table 10.1 *Relative importance of the private HE sector* in Europe as percentage of total enrolments*

Country	1998	2012	2015	Country	1998	2012	2015
Austria[a]	0.0	0.0	0.0	Latvia	9.5	28.7	26.1
Bulgaria	10.0	18.5	15.4	Liechtenstein[b]	18.6	1.8	12.5
Croatia[b]	2.5	7.1	7.1	Lithuania	2.7	10.8	9.7
Cyprus[c]	53.3	62.3	61.3	Poland	19.6	29.6	25.4
Czech Republic[d]	0.0	12.2	10.0	Portugal	34.5	20.2	16.4
Denmark[e]	0.0	0.1	0.1	Romania	30.7	22.9	14.3
Estonia	22.1	11.0	7.5	Slovakia	0.0	17.9	15.5
France	10.2	17.3	17.3	Slovenia	0.4	7.5	7.4
FYROM[f]	5.7	15.7	14.8	Spain	10.5	13.0	15.6
Iceland[g]	0.0	0.0	0.0	Switzerland[d]	6.7	8.9	9.6
Ireland	5.5	2.2	0.0	Turkey[h]	3.2	5.2	7.4
Italy	12.8	9.4	10.3	United Kingdom	0.0	0.0	0.0

Notes

* we have used the definition of private government-independent institutions
[a] data end in 2005;
[b] data start in 2003;
[c] data start in 1999;
[d] data start in 2002;
[e] data start in 2006;
[f] data start in 2005;
[g] data end in 2007;
[h] data start in 2001.
Countries omitted due to lack of information on the private sector for a considerable number of years: Albania, Belgium (French and Flemish Communities), Finland, Germany, Greece, Hungary, Luxembourg, Malta, the Netherlands, Norway, and Sweden.
Source: Compiled from EUROSTAT data base, Education and Training: URL https://ec.europa.eu/eurostat/web/education-and-training/overview

private higher education share at that time in the USA (26 per cent), Europe (16 per cent), and Africa (15 per cent).

While data are often incomplete, Table 10.1 is nonetheless indicative of growth in continental Europe, which has been particularly pronounced in southern and eastern Europe and less so in western and northern Europe. The data also indicate that in recent years there has been some decline in the size of private sectors in those countries that experienced a stronger growth in previous decades, mainly due to the combination of demographic declines in the younger age cohorts and persistent expansion of public supply.

To understand this growth, including the drivers behind it and the implications arising from it in relation to system or institutional governance, it is first necessary to examine the categories of 'public' and 'private' higher education more closely. Whether an institution or system of higher education is categorized as public or private is typically related to sources of funding (the state through public taxes, or individuals through private investments); ownership and control of staffing or operations (by states or governments for public institutions, and individual entrepreneurs, families, or corporations in the case of private institutions); and the beneficiaries of higher education services (for example, the general public and society, or private individuals). Further distinctions have become prominent in recent decades – for example, between 'non-profit' private and 'for-profit' private higher education (Levy, 2009). These latter distinctions refer to the distribution of any surpluses made. In the case of non-profit private higher education institutions, surpluses are expected to be distributed back into the core functions of education and research; in the case of for-profit private higher education providers, profits can also be distributed to shareholders.

These distinctions (public, private, non-profit, for-profit) are not only crude, but also increasingly misleading. England provides a case study of how the boundaries between categories of higher education system and institution are blurring as the operating environment for institutions is changing. Types of higher education institution in England include universities (a legally controlled title), colleges and other institutions providing higher education programmes (including further education colleges), and 'alternative providers' (independent, private for-profit, and non-profit providers). English universities are typically described as 'independent and self-governing'. However, this status has not remained constant over the last century and the reality today is more nuanced than it may at first appear. A significant milestone was the takeover of university financing by the state in 1946; prior to this, the state provided only about one-third of universities' funding, the rest being raised from private sources (Shattock, 2017). This change in funding source shifted the universities, in policy and political terms, into the realm of public institutions, although their legal autonomy deriving from charters, statutes, or Acts of Parliament remained formally unchanged. Further policy and political shifts occurred in the 1980s and 1990s: the state first encouraged competition between universities by expanding student numbers on the basis of price; then, in 2012, it changed the funding of teaching virtually entirely from grants and contracts between the state and institutions to a consumer-based system of tuition fees supported by a student-loan system, where the 'teaching contract' lies between the institution and individual students. As Shattock comments: 'This radical inversion of the funding system placed the management of universities on a very similar basis to that of private enterprises, and was accompanied by the freeing up of the conditions for the establishment of private universities, although the state retained the ability to influence the market through its control of the financing of student loans' (2017, p. 11).

These policy developments, along with others that encouraged universities to diversify their income sources away from dependence on state funding sources, have led to an increasing 'privatization' or 'commercialization' of universities, which we will discuss in more detail. This privatization of public universities has been noted by researchers in several countries (Altbach et al., 2009; Bok, 2003; Brown, 2010). One aspect of privatization – and one that has supplied a significant element of diversified income for UK universities – has come from internationalization, both in the recruitment of international students to the United Kingdom and the export of programmes overseas in various forms of transnational education (TNE). The expansion of universities' TNE activities has brought a further twist to distinctions between 'public' and 'private' institutions in that English (and other UK) universities, when operating in other jurisdictions around the world, are typically defined in legal terms as private enterprises, and are thereby subject to the regulations applying to these types of organizations. Hence, universities can be perceived as public institutions at home, supported by public funding, while also operating as private enterprises abroad, supported by privately sourced income streams. Both these elements, privatization and internationalization, have resulted in a significant blurring (or convergence) across the categories of 'public' and 'private' higher education. This blurring of boundaries has consequences for governance structures, levels of authority between different actors involved in governance processes, and attitudes and behaviours at operational levels, as we discuss in subsequent sections.

While there is notable convergence across public–private boundaries, there is also divergence, as several studies have shown. A common observation is to note the degree of institutional diversity across the private sector of higher education by comparison with a more homogeneous public sector, as displayed in much of western continental Europe, reflecting the instrumental and regulatory reach of the state in relation to public institutions in areas such as funding, staff policies, and student recruitment. The heterogeneity of so-called private sectors of higher education (which are not 'sectors' in any meaningful sense of sharing a common mission and similar structural features) include a variety of types of institution with different missions, ownership, and funding structures. Fielden (2008) describe four different types of institution: identity institutions (religious, cultural, and specialist providers of higher education, typically non-profit), elite non-profit private universities (as in the USA) and semi-elite private universities (as in Latin America, Pakistan, Thailand, Poland, and Turkey), demand-absorbing non-elite private providers often serving working adult populations, and for-profit global education businesses (such as Laureate or Kaplan). Levy (2009) includes a fifth, hybrid category made up of public–private partnerships. Such partnerships feature in the recent growth of private higher education in England as well as in Australasia. They are also part of the privatization of public higher education institutions and systems, with consequences for governance. Teixeira et al. (2012a, 2012b, 2013) note that many private higher education institutions are not universities, but specialist providers of higher level training in one or a few fields of study. These authors comment that the model of the university as an institution with a research mission is largely absent across private higher education institutions (which may be colleges, not universities). A notable exception is the USA, where elite private universities such as Yale, Harvard, Stanford, and Princeton have gained legitimacy through their research with both public authorities and society. The focus of much private provision in Europe is at the level of undergraduate education (Bachelors' degrees) as well as specialist diplomas and certificates. The absence of research in many private institutions makes doctoral study typically the preserve of publicly funded and regulated universities.

Other areas of divergence between public and private 'sectors' include the size of institutions and range of fields of study. Private higher education providers typically have small numbers of enrolments (Levy, 2002). In recent research for the government in the United Kingdom (BIS, 2016) across a sample of 732 institutions, the size of privately funded institutions ranged from just 100 students to more than 5,000, with only 5 providers having more than 5,000 enrolled students. This contrasts with UK universities in receipt of public funds which have anywhere from 10,000 to 40,000 students, while others in continental Europe are larger still, with comprehensive universities in major cities such as Vienna, Madrid, and Rome having up to 100,000 enrolled students. In relation to fields of study, many publicly funded universities have a wide subject offering while privately funded institutions typically offer a narrower range of subjects, focusing on low-cost programmes with strong student demand, such as law, economics, and management (Fielden et al., 2010; Teixeira et al., 2012a, 2012b, 2013). The nature of the subjects offered by private providers relates (to an extent) to the reasons behind their expansion, namely rising demand for higher education which in many countries exceeds public supply. The increasing demand for higher education reflects demographic growth, economic expansion, a rising middle class, rising levels of educational attainment, increasing social aspirations, and expanding labour markets (Kinser et al., 2010; Shah and Nair, 2016). In such contexts, the need for business-related studies is clear.

10.3 Governance Arrangements in Public and Private Higher Education: System and Institutional Levels

Governance is concerned with the structures and processes for decision making at different levels of the higher education system. As Keller (2001) states, the term – bearing in mind the ambiguities outlined earlier – may refer to those who administer the affairs of an organization at an institutional level, to those who manage the number and range of institutions at the system level, and to levels of power, authority, and influence that different constituencies have within the decision-making structures and processes. Other researchers note that governance is concerned with institutional goals (strategy), purposes (mission), and values, hence the practice of governance is about determining what is important and what counts (Marginson and

Considine, 2000). Much of the research and debates about governance in higher education refer to publicly funded institutions and systems, and there is limited focus on the governance structures of the private 'sector' at the institutional or system level. Poor data collection systems with respect to private (compared to public) providers of higher education lead to a perceived lack of transparency concerning private sector motivations and operations and to potential suspicion and mistrust of private providers. The lack of data also produces a skewed depiction of the changing landscape of higher education which ignores or overlooks private sector developments. Lack of knowledge and insight has other governance implications. It may hinder the capacity to regulate or steer private aspects of the higher education system – perhaps towards delivering greater or different contributions to social and economic goals – or to control unacceptable behaviour among providers seeking profits at the expense of students or taxpayers, as recent scandals in the United States, the United Kingdom, Australia, and New Zealand have revealed (Fielden and Middlehurst, 2017). In this section we present the limited evidence from small-scale studies of governance arrangements in private higher education that are illuminating, but require wider validation.

In a paper on global trends in university governance, Fielden (2008) focuses on governance at the system level, described as the way that governments plan and direct their tertiary education sectors. The study notes that with the expansion and diversification of higher education systems, there has been a shift from an old model of central control of operational details delivered by a ministry of education to a more distant model based on forms of strategic direction from a central source accompanied by more sophisticated models of performance and review. These models have been described by Neave and van Vught (1994) as a continuum from a 'state control model' to a 'state supervising or steering model' where institutions have more autonomy over their governance structures and processes. Different countries continue to occupy different locations on this continuum with respect to system-level governance of both public and private sectors. In addition, as some of the detailed analysis in Fielden's study shows, there is not always a clear-cut distinction between system-level and institution-level governance in that some national legislation not only defines the constitutional status of institutions as legal entities (with certain obligations) but may also define the composition of institutions' governing boards, their terms of reference, and rules for the conduct of business, as well as the powers and responsibilities of institutional leaders and their relationship with the structures and processes of academic governance.

With regard to the regulation of private higher education institutions, system-level governance includes: decisions to allow or prevent a provider establishing a new institution or campus; authorization to issue or recognize awards and transfers of academic credit; financial arrangements such as the granting of operating incentives or collection of taxes, and the eligibility of students to access public loans and scholarships; and the collection of information on financial and academic performance. At a strategic level, regulatory frameworks may also include policy statements on the role of the private sector and its contribution to national higher education goals, perhaps linked to access and equity targets; and, at the more operational level, there may be directives on the composition of institutional governance arrangements as described earlier (Fielden and Varghese, 2009). If we shift the lens from system-level to institution-level governance, developments within publicly funded national systems have been investigated more fully than developments across private providers of higher education.

10.3.1 Developments in Governance in Public Institutions in Europe

As noted earlier, higher education has faced significant expansion in recent decades and this expansion has been linked to economic motivations and purposes. This economic discourse has prioritized the creation of an institutional context favourable to the development of innovation and entrepreneurship, strengthening the view that the accumulation of human capital can improve the economic prospects of different communities (Grubb and Lazerson, 2004). Changes of motivations as to the purposes and outcomes of higher education at both the individual and societal levels have had an impact on the external and internal governance of higher education institutions, notably by stressing this economic dimension and the potential of institutions to benefit individuals and to contribute to socio-economic goals. This has had particular significance for systems of public higher education, for example those in western continental Europe which had previously been more closely associated with wider dimensions of higher education such as social equality and opportunity, construction of the nation state, and the training of skilled professionals for service in the public sector.

This shifting view of the primary purposes of public institutions has required new conceptualizations and adaptations of the contextual framework in which these organizations operate. If we regard institutions as part of an industry, then the context in which they operate should promote a rational use of resources in order to maximize the social return relative to the resources allocated to the sector. Hence, we have seen a reconfiguration of the higher education sector along market lines, often through policy initiatives and government interventions actioned through funding mechanisms, with the goal of promoting closer interaction between public universities and industry. Such reconfiguration has been particularly noticeable in countries with a long-standing and well-developed higher education sector. Government policies have stimulated institutions to view students as consumers and have nurtured commercial links between universities and private companies.

A further economic issue is that the expansion of higher education has brought significant financial challenges for public expenditure; hence, the cost of the system has become a major issue in almost every country in Europe and beyond. The financial challenges faced by higher education have been exacerbated by an adverse financial situation within the wider public sector over much of the last two decades (Barr, 2004; Teixeira, 2009). As higher education has moved from being an expanding sector to a mature industry (Levine, 2001), political attitudes to it have altered. In its expansion phase, growth was seen as a sign of improvement and higher education managed to keep public and social actors satisfied by accommodating larger numbers of students. In its mature phase, external stakeholders have become more demanding in relation to institutional efficiency and responsiveness in the deployment of public funds (Birnbaum and Shushok, 2001). This has had important consequences for prescribed modes of internal governance, notably through more explicit participation of external stakeholders in formal and informal mechanisms of governance. These developments have made the governing boards of institutions more corporate in style, suggesting convergence with private sector modes of governance.

A parallel development associated with the pervasive economic dimension of institutions has been the rising influence of academic management (Gumport, 2001; Meek et al., 2010). This has challenged the traditional sovereignty of intellectual and professional expertise as the legitimate foundation for institutional decision making. The internal allocation of resources within higher education institutions has increasingly prioritized financial and economic criteria over intellectual and epistemological ones. Furthermore, the contribution of a subject, a programme, or a staff member to the ability to generate resources is increasingly used as an indirect measure to assess the social and economic relevance of that unit or individual and their effectiveness in responding to wider (national, regional, or international) social and economic needs.

These internal changes in governance in continental Europe have altered the balance of authority and control by the state over higher education institutions, shifting institutions towards greater levels of autonomy (although in England, similar operating pressures have led to contrasting trends towards less institutional autonomy and more government regulation). The policy rhetoric on the continent over the last 25 years has been about increasing levels of institutional autonomy (de Boer and File, 2009); however, autonomy has different meanings and this issue has fuelled substantial debate. Researchers describe various dimensions of autonomy: for example, 'substantive' (meaning control over academic and research policy, the award of degrees, curriculum design, student selection, and portfolio of programmes), and 'procedural' (meaning authority over financial management, human resource management, the deployment of physical and other assets) (Berdahl, 1990). Where institutions have gained more autonomy and authority from state direction and control, the first level has been concerned with institutional strategy development, typically within a broad mission determined by national authorities. Internal governance structures may also be determined through national legislation, but institutional leadership, academics and students, and, to an extent, external stakeholders are also typically involved. Financial autonomy has increased in terms of internal budgeting and resource allocation, but does not always include extensive income diversification as yet (with national exceptions, such as the United Kingdom). Determining tuition fee levels occurs at the institutional as opposed to the state level in a few countries. Human resource management, staff selection, and recruitment have also been devolved to institutions, typically within framework conditions set by governments. However, with regard to student selection and admissions and access policies, while there is a trend towards more autonomy, centralized national procedures and regulations are still largely in play.

Finally, in pursuing their own priorities and in responding to a more globalized and competitive environment, institutions have engaged in a variety of partnerships at several levels. In relation to organizational autonomy, while most countries have external regulations relating to the form and structure of decision-making bodies in universities, there is still a degree of independence available to institutions, with clear national variations (Estermann and Nokkala, 2009). Along with trends towards the inclusion of external members in university decision-making processes, especially where dual governance structures exist (such as a board/council and senate), there is also a clear shift towards 'CEO-type rectors', and where this is the case, it is associated with greater autonomy in the design of internal management structures. However, this is not universal, with a significant number of more traditional modes of governance existing where the rector is an academic 'primus inter pares', selected by the academic community from among the professors of the university.

Greater institutional autonomy has been accompanied by various forms of accountability so that institutions are required to report on and to be audited or inspected in relation to their funding and financial management, their quality and academic management, their overall performance, and their responsiveness to students and wider stakeholders. In a detailed study of accountability in different countries around the world and in transnational contexts (including across Europe) several common trends were identified, suggesting convergence across national systems (Stensaker and Harvey, 2011). First, there was increasing government interest in accountability and government was a key player in new initiatives, with external and upward forms of accountability (between institutions and the state) dominating. Second, in many countries, special agencies set up by governments have emerged, charged with producing information for accountability purposes for government, but also for prospective students, their parents, and future employers. A third trend was that accountability in most countries was increasingly associated with the quality assurance of educational provision. While there are a number of other accountability measures, including funding instruments, developmental contracts, research indicators, and legal obligations, educational quality assurance has become a core accountability instrument, mainly through accreditation schemes.

History matters, particularly for developments in governance, since the latter depends significantly on the timing of the creation of each higher education institution and the very particular development of each higher education system. Thus, older universities still tend to retain some aspects of governance that reflect their medieval origins. Likewise, universities created through state initiatives, and systems that were largely shaped by state intervention throughout the nineteenth and early twentieth centuries, reflect this state intervention in their modes of governance. These same institutions also evolve their modes of governance to reflect fashions and trends in higher education policy and regulation, and these quite often leave traces even after being displaced by subsequent modes of governance. Currently, therefore, there is a certain degree of eclecticism in university governance, with many institutions combining historical modes of collegial and bureaucratic governance with more recent corporate-like and market-oriented ones. The multi-layered nature of governance arrangements combining historical and modern influences has been described in symbolic terms as 'academic-expert', 'bureaucratic-civil society', and 'corporate-market' perspectives on governance (Middlehurst and Teixeira, 2012).

The eclecticism in governance arrangements also reflects a contemporary tension between an institutional leadership willing to assert its power and authority and a significant resistance from traditional academic sources of power and governance. This tension is often solved through degrees of compromise with joint committees and what some would call dual or shared governance (Keller, 2001; Shattock, 2006). This type of governance consists of sharing authority between various constituent groups and interested parties (Rosser, 2002). The ensuing balance is often regarded as a particular strength of university institutions, even in periods of change, since various stakeholders are involved in processes of transformation. However, this balance is under pressure as institutional leadership is strengthened in response to increasing external pressures towards greater market orientation for institutions. Despite criticisms about the ineffectiveness of more collegial modes of governance and oft-expressed fears about the crisis and replacement of collegiality, a recent study (Kaplan, 2004) has shown that the actual situation is far more positive. Faculty (and students) continue to play a significant role in governance in many institutions and their participation continues to be valued. Nonetheless, the same study also confirmed that the balance of power has been changing over time, with visible advances in the power of management in decision making. These advances have been more prominent in some institutions, especially in those with lower research intensity, where the prestige and symbolic power of faculty tends to be lower. In his recent overview of the impact of external and internal pressures on the distribution of authority in British universities, Shattock (2017) corroborates the pressures towards convergence of governance across the publicly funded institutions, but also points to divergence across types of institutions, with sharper variation between research-intensive and ancient institutions compared to more teaching-intensive and newer institutions.

10.3.2 Governance Arrangements in Private Higher Education

Knowledge about the private higher education sector in Europe and the way it operates has not yet caught up with the development and expansion of this (very heterogeneous) sector; it also lags behind research on publicly funded systems. Knowledge and practice vary across countries; in some cases, the private sector is more integrated within the higher education landscape, and is more strongly regulated and accountable, with data available about several of its major features. In other cases, the degree of knowledge about this sector is limited as it is not regarded as a relevant part of the higher education system. There are also significant variations in information disclosure and reporting between different types of higher education providers (Middlehurst, 2016). This limited knowledge is particularly acute when it comes to the internal organization, management, and distribution of power and authority.

One recent small-scale study (Fielden, 2014) has provided insights into the governance of a sample of privately funded higher education providers, focusing on their internal governance arrangements. The study firstly examined the ways in which 16 regulatory agencies in different parts of the world addressed the governance of private providers. Building on earlier work on governance of private providers at the system level (Fielden, 2008), the author argued that there were important aspects to which governments should give regulatory attention, including the role of board members with a personal or family financial interest in the organization, the controls exercised on a private provider by a parent body ('related entity') in terms of the influence that could be exercised on substantive decisions concerning the institution or its educational functions, and the role of faculty in decision making to ensure the integrity of the institution's educational programmes and effective consultation with students. In the regulations of many countries, it is expected that board members will not be involved in the day-to-day operations of the organization, that owners or investors will not hold executive positions, and that faculty members will have sufficient opportunity to participate in decision making on matters related to curriculum, assessment, and academic integrity. In several countries, the provision of education is considered to have a particular public and societal relevance so that even if providers are interested in private returns from the business, they also have societal obligations. This may be interpreted in different ways – for example, ensuring that students succeed in their studies, or expecting the provider to participate in the socio-economic activities of the community in which it is located.

Fielden's 2014 study also examined five areas of corporate governance at the institutional level as indicators of how governance worked in practice among a small sample of seven providers with a location in England, suggesting that these indicators might also have a bearing on what counts as 'good governance' among privately funded providers. The five indicators were legal forms of providers and strategic control exercised by the corporate board; board membership, size of boards, and frequency of board meetings; disclosure of information (including outputs and outcomes for students); adoption of particular governance codes; and the relationship between academic governance arrangements and the corporate board. The findings from this study illustrate considerable diversity of governance arrangements across providers. The majority of arrangements diverge somewhat from the expectations of the regulatory agencies investigated. For instance, as regards strategic control, very few providers had students involved in central decision-making bodies, let alone on the corporate board. Moreover, in no case was there a majority of independent non-executive members. Several providers had board members who were nominees of the owners, and there were even situations in which all the shares of the education company were owned by the executives who sat on the board. Respondents reported that there was unanimity about objectives and targets between corporate owners and the institution's board, with mutually agreed financial and educational targets and objectives. However, there was some (limited) evidence that a corporate parent could potentially steer the operations of an institution through informal meetings outside formal boards, could hide ownership structures through tax havens, or could create different corporate forms including charitable trusts. Notwithstanding these potential situations, respondents maintained that financial and academic sustainability were both mutually reinforcing and of parallel interest to all parties.

As regards board membership, size, and committees, there were other interesting findings. The size of boards varied between 12 and 26 members, and were not dissimilar to the size of traditional university governing bodies where the trend has been towards smaller boards, showing some convergence between public and private universities. The non-profit private providers also showed similar numbers and types of sub-committee structures as those of public universities, including audit and risk, remuneration, and nominations committees. From the small sample, and among for-profit and non-profit providers, it was clear that a close connection existed between the board and academic matters; key academic committees reported to or were closely linked to corporate boards and, in many cases, boards were directly involved in (or received reports on) academic performance.

In relation to academic governance with staff and student involvement, many of the privately funded providers in the sample had the main academic committee as a formal committee of the board (rather than having a binary system with a separate senate or academic board). This differs markedly from traditional public universities in Europe, suggesting that the executive boards of privately funded providers tend to be more closely involved in issues of academic and reputational risk. Where academic councils or committees report to the board, they may involve non-executives with strategic academic expertise as well as staff and student representatives.

Fielden's study noted the variety of different governance arrangements among providers and the divergence of practice from the typical expectations of higher education governance currently enshrined in the regulatory standards of many countries. However, some of the academic reporting arrangements were highlighted as of potential interest to publicly funded institutions, as they increased their own commercial activities, notably in transnational education. Governing bodies of traditional universities and colleges might in future expect to monitor academic quality, risk, and performance more closely and directly, rather than relying on the current dual and separated structures of academic board or senate and governing body or university council. The examples from 'alternative' providers may hold some useful lessons for efficiency, for mitigation of risk, and potentially for enhancing performance. Indeed, there are important signals from the already more market-oriented higher education systems of England and Australia, of areas of convergence (as well as the divergence described earlier) at the system level in terms of common regulatory frameworks across publicly and privately funded institutions, and more universal codes of governance at institutional level (CUC, 2014).

10.4 Theoretical Perspectives on Higher Education Governance: Illuminating Public and Private Sector Convergences and Divergences

While there is no single grand theory of higher education governance, Austin and Jones (2016, p. 23) argue that there are some leading theories that can help in understanding different conceptions of governance. In addition, given our focus on higher education, it is important to remember that these leading theories sometimes build on, but sometimes also ignore, the vast array of theoretical perspectives on governance beyond higher education (Ansell and Torfing, 2016). Given our topic of public and private higher education, we have been selective in choosing leading theories that can illuminate convergences and divergences of governance across these domains. The focus is principally on external influences on higher education and their impact on governance at the system and institutional levels and not on the internal dynamics of meso- and micro-levels of governance inside institutions. Theoretical perspectives include institutional theory (DiMaggio and Powell, 1983; Meyer and Rowan, 1977), itself derived from organizational theory (Egeberg et al., 2016); resource dependence theory (Drees and Heugens, 2013); agency and stewardship theories (Davis et al., 1997); and stakeholder theory (Seyama, 2015).

Important aspects of governance take place within an organization, hence institutional theory is concerned with organizational variables such as structures, processes, and activities within organizations. It is also concerned with the social environment of the organization – social rules, norms, and expectations – and how these act as pressures on institutions and individual actors to conform. This theory explains convergence across particular types or classes of institution (such as research universities) whereby environmental norms, values, and expectations shape structures and drive specific practices such as collegiality.

In addition to convergence of governance within classes of institution, theorists also contend that environmental pressures are felt by organizations in two key ways. First, technical, economic, and physical pressures are associated with the sale of goods and services in markets. Second, social, cultural, legal, and political expectations pressurize institutions to act in specific ways. Both pressures apply to public and private sectors of higher education. An organization that aligns itself favourably in relation to external expectations may be seeking acceptance and legitimacy through such conformity. Adopting the governance arrangements of publicly funded institutions, as non-profit higher education providers in Fielden's small sample have done, is one possible example of 'legitimacy-seeking' behaviour. Alternatively, the changing nature of governance in publicly funded institutions may be an example of 'coercive isomorphism', whereby conformity is achieved through the coercive pressure of governmental regulations. Variants of coercive isomorphism include mimetic isomorphism – or voluntary imitation of structures and practices adopted from other sectors in the face of uncertainty – and normative isomorphism, which involves professionally based conformance to conditions of work, values, and norms. Some of the tensions that exist between institutional-level and faculty-level governance can be explained in terms of the balance between normative isomorphism and coercive or mimetic isomorphism. Tensions and associated reframing of governance also derive from competition in a market-based and more economically driven higher education system. As Meyer and Rowan (1977) contend, organizations are social and cultural systems embedded in an institutional context where pressures come from the state, professional associations, interest groups, and public opinion as well as market forces. This social context leads institutions to incorporate rules and practices from elsewhere into their own structures, thereby creating the kinds of convergences, as well as divergences, discussed earlier within the field of higher education and across different types of provider. Further complexities are added when considering the boundary between institutions and their environments. Where institutional theory emphasizes the boundary between the organization and its environment, open systems theory (Scott, 2003) emphasizes the permeability of the institution's boundaries to external influences. As noted, the boundaries between privately and publicly funded institutions are blurring, suggesting such permeability, with implications for governance at the system and institutional levels. As institutions have been encouraged to become more closely connected to businesses and the corporate sector and to foster strategic partnerships nationally and internationally, new 'network type' governance models are emerging (Austin and Jones, 2016, p. 29).

Resource dependence theory is based on the assumption that organizations are dependent on their environment for critical resources, and at the heart of this dependency lies an exchange between different sets of interests with differential levels of power and dependency. Power lies in the control of resources, and the agent with power can restrict access to the resources needed or dictate how the resources are used. This exchange relationship creates a form of governance that is rooted in compliance and accountability, and there is much evidence of it in the modernization and reform agendas of publicly funded higher education systems since the 1990s (European Commission, 2011). The subsequent emphases on the exercise of institutional autonomy and the pursuit of diversified income sources are arguably targeted at minimizing the institution's vulnerability in accessing funding from a single (state) source. For privately funded institutions, the dependency lies in a different direction (on tuition-fee income or private investments) but the governance task remains the same: to track and manage the critical resource dependencies. Resource dependence theory goes some way towards explaining the changing composition of governing boards (with more external than academic members) as well as the growth of an academic management cadre capable of managing the relational dynamics of governance internally as well as externally.

Agency theory (or principal–agent theory) has become influential in organizational theory and strategic management, particularly in explaining governance in the corporate sector (Austin and Jones, 2016). The principals are the owners (shareholders in public corporations) and the agents are executives hired to manage the organization. At the heart of the theory lies the assumption that principals and agents will each seek to increase their individual utility. The theory presumes a hierarchical contractual relationship between the principal and the agent where there is a delegation of authority to agents and an expectation that agents will act in the best interests of the principal. However, agency theory allows for a (likely) divergence of interest and utility choices between principals and agents (known as 'the agency problem'); thus, when agents are hired by owners, both monitoring mechanisms and incentive schemes are used to reduce self-advancing utility-maximizing behaviours on the part of agents, which may act against the interests of owners. Governance structures are used to minimize misalignment between principals' and agents' goals, minimize agency costs, and keep agents' self-advancing behaviours in check (Jensen and Meckling, 1976). Boards of directors in privately funded institutions are an example of agency theory in operation and, increasingly, agency theory may help to explain government–university relationships. It may also help us to understand the changing internal governance structures of publicly funded institutions where the board of governors has gained power at the expense of 'the staff', both academic and professional, and where boards formally delegate authority to strengthened executive managers.

There is a further dimension of the 'agency problem' that may be illuminating. This involves understanding the nature of 'opportunism' in the behaviour of agents to act in their own or the principals' interests. While misalignment of interests can lead to negative outcomes, alignment of interests may be created by increasing opportunities for utility-maximizing behaviours on the part of institutions. Governance reforms that emphasize institutional autonomy (with accountability) suggest the potential for increasing opportunities to align the interests of government and institutions in relation to national or societal goals; the promotion of entrepreneurialism may also be seen as a utility-maximizing behaviour. An emphasis on autonomy and enterprise has been accompanied by a shift in governance from traditional hierarchical authority-based governance (as seen in traditional publicly funded universities in continental Europe) to contractual exchange-based governance, where contracts may be behaviour-based or outcomes-based. Where governments dictate the composition of boards and reporting mechanisms, including government-driven quality assurance and evaluation systems, behaviour-based contracts tend to be in operation; where governments instead reward institutions for delivering policy goals, outcomes-based contracts are likely to be in use. In different countries across Europe, both approaches are used.

Where agency theory assumes individualistic and self-serving behaviours on the part of agents, stewardship theory, originating in psychology and sociology, assumes that agents will act in the best interests of the collective, deriving greater utility from cooperative behaviours at the expense of self-interest (Davis et al., 1997). Stewardship theory resonates with the model of the university as a public institution; it is associated with governance models that grant large degrees of autonomy to universities on the basis of trust and delegate strategic leadership and management responsibilities from governing boards to university presidents. Underlying agency and stewardship theories are different sets of psychological assumptions. In agency theory, the expectation is that agents will be motivated by extrinsic rewards and control mechanisms are structured around this expectation. Stewardship theory, by contrast, assumes that stewards are motivated intrinsically, driven by the need for growth opportunities, achievement, affiliation, and self-actualization (Davis et al., 1997). Furthermore, where stewards identify with the institution, their relationship with the organization is as a member; they willingly pursue its mission, vision, and objectives, thus bringing them into positive alignment with the principal's views of organizational success. These two theories also have different underpinning expectations of the bases and uses of power. Where agency theory is based on reward power and legitimate power (that is, power linked to status and position), deployed through formal organizational structures and processes, stewardship theory assumes that authority and influence are gained through personal power, built and deployed through relationships. Both theories have cross-overs into the management and leadership literature (Middlehurst, 1993), and these intersections may be useful in understanding the changing internal dynamics of institutions.

Critics of agency and stewardship theories argue that they are based, at most, on a triad of relationships between principals (owners or shareholders), agents (managers), and the board of directors (representing the principals) (Clarke, 2005). This does not capture the full range and complexity of social obligations and third party interests – such as communities, businesses, and civic organizations – with whom higher education providers now interact. These stakeholders can have significant impacts on the organization and structures of governance, in practice, reflecting these stakeholder influences in the composition of governing boards and in the construction of other bridging or network governance structures. Stakeholder theory assumes a more interdependent governance relationship with the external environment for both public and private higher education institutions, reflecting the reality of both market-based influences and government policy objectives.

10.5 Concluding Remarks

In this chapter, we have reflected upon governance in public and private higher education institutions, with a particular focus on the European situation, albeit with reference to parallel developments across the world. We have highlighted that, although continental European higher education is still dominated by public provision, private institutions have become an important part of the system in many parts of Europe, and this needs to be taken into account when investigating existing governance mechanisms and their effectiveness in an increasingly diverse institutional landscape.

In our analysis, we observe that divergences in patterns of governance in public and private institutions are influenced by legal status, which shapes internal balances of power and decision making. These sectors also have different histories and, despite important waves of reforms in recent decades, governance is still influenced by that history. Given that publicly funded institutions tend to be older and associated with the structure of public administration, older forms of governance have predominated, not least those reflecting medieval types (or reconstructed types) and political and bureaucratic modes of governance. In the private sector, this situation is more diverse, with non-profit providers presenting similarities to their public counterparts and those emerging in more recent waves of privatization presenting a stronger business and managerial approach to internal governance. However, these legal and historical factors should not be regarded as the only ones when analysing possible differences in governance between public and private sectors. The dynamics of public institutions in many countries has blurred the boundaries between the public and private sectors in terms of funding structures and type, size, and composition of decision-making bodies. Governance arrangements also reflect the size and age of institutions, comprehensiveness of the range of subjects offered, qualifications and contracts of academic staff, and research intensity.

The range of challenges facing higher education – notably, financial and wider economic challenges – has arguably also led to convergences between public and private higher education institutions and their structures and processes of governance. There may yet be longer-term consequences at the system level, giving rise to new regulatory frameworks and potential challenges to existing quality assurance or accountability arrangements. At the institutional level, there is the potential for conflict between academic and commercial interests. Increasing complexity in university operations brings challenges for the exercise of governance as well as the selection of governors (academics, students, and lay people) capable of giving the necessary time and expertise to the role. The combination of universities becoming more permeable to external influences and the internal need to negotiate between different interests has increased tensions, and perhaps the ultimate challenge for governance will be to make this a creative rather than a destructive force.

A related issue concerns the balance between universities' economic and non-economic dimensions and the implications of this for institutional governance. Governmental tendencies to perceive publicly funded higher education institutions increasingly as quasi-economic organizations has overshadowed the view that these are a peculiar type of organization with roles beyond the purely economic (Weisbrod et al., 2008). Furthermore, we should not forget the fact that higher education institutions (particularly universities) are more than 'an organization'. Universities are institutions, with a mission, and not merely organizations (Gumport, 2001). A focus on the organization tends to (over)simplify the nature and social role of higher education institutions, devaluing the role of history, tradition, norms, and path dependency. It also contributes to a narrower view of the scope and legitimacy of higher education as a contributor to societal well-being and national and regional development.

We have examined a number of theoretical perspectives on governance that are relevant to publicly funded and privately funded higher education. We have also noted that both governance and higher education are complex, and therefore multilevel and multi-layered theories have more explanatory value than single-dimensional theories. In the theories discussed here, the main focus is on how governance is enacted and impacted when external influences and pressures are felt in higher education systems and institutions. There is more work to be done to explore the micro- and meso-levels of governance, particularly in terms of the internal dynamics of governance inside public and private higher education institutions. Examining governance from conceptual and theoretical perspectives is useful in understanding the changes and developments that are occurring; indeed, governance may be regarded as a lightning-rod for observing and interrogating the social, cultural, and psychological impacts of changes in the operating environments of higher education institutions, both public and private. A fuller understanding of governance across all kinds of higher education provider and provision should help to us appreciate both the different contributions that these providers make to a well-functioning system and how best to achieve efficiency and effectiveness at the system and institutional levels.

References

Altbach, P., Reisberg, L., and Rumbley, L. (2009) *Trends in global higher education: Tracking an academic revolution*. Paris: UNESCO.

Ansell, C., and Torfing, J. (Eds) (2016) *Handbook on theories of governance*. Cheltenham: Edward Elgar Publishing.

Austin, I., and Jones, G. A. (2016) *Governance of higher education: Global perspectives, theories and practices*. London: Routledge.

Barr, N. (2004) *Economics of the welfare state* (4th ed.). Oxford: Oxford University Press.

Berdahl, R. (1990) Academic freedom, autonomy and accountability in British universities. *Studies in Higher Education*, 15(2), 169–180.

Birnbaum, R., and Shushok, F. (2001) The 'crisis' crisis in American higher education: Is that a wolf or a pussycat at the academy's door? In P. Altbach, P. Gumport, and B. Johnstone (Eds), *In defense of higher education*, pp. 59–84. Baltimore: Johns Hopkins University Press.

BIS (2016) *Understanding the market of alternative higher education providers and their students in 2014*. London: Department of Business, Innovation and Skills, UK Government. https://dera.ioe.ac.uk/20959/1/he-alternative-providers-2014.pdf

de Boer, H. F., and File, J. M. (2009) *Higher education governance reforms across Europe*. Brussels: Center for Higher Education Policy Studies.

Bok, D. (2003) *Universities in the marketplace: The commercialization of higher education*. Princeton: Princeton University Press.

Brown, R. (2010) *Higher education and the market*. New York: Routledge.

Clarke, T. (2005) Accounting for Enron: Shareholder value and stakeholder interests. *Corporate Governance*, 13(5), 598–612.

Committee of University Chairs [CUC] (2014) *The higher education code of governance*. www.universitychairs.ac.uk

Davis, J., Schoorman, F., and Donaldson, L. (1997) Towards a stewardship theory of management. *Academy of Management Review*, 28(3), 371–382.

DiMaggio, P. P., and Powell, W. W. (1983) The iron cage revisited: Institutional isomorphism and collective rationality in organizational fields. *American Sociological Review*, 48(2), 147–160.

Drees, J. M., and Heugens, P. P. M. A. R. (2013) Synthesizing and extending resource dependence theory: A meta-analysis. *Journal of Management*, 39 (6), 1666–1698. doi:10.1177/0149206312471391

Egeberg, M., Gornitzka, A., and Trondal, J. (2016) Organization theory. In C. Ansell and J. Torfing (Eds), *Handbook on theories of governance*, pp. 32–45. Cheltenham: Edward Elgar Publishing.

Estermann, T., and Nokkala, T. (2009) *University autonomy in Europe 1: Exploratory study*. Brussels: European University Association.

European Commission (2011) Communique on modernisation. MEMO/11/613. Brussels: EC.

Fielden, J. (2008) Global trends in university governance. Education Working Paper Series No. 9. Washington, DC: World Bank.

Fielden, J. (2014) The governance of private HE providers in the UK. *A research report for the Leadership Foundation*. London: Leadership Foundation.

Fielden, J., and Middlehurst, R. (2017) *Alternative providers of higher education: Issues for policy makers*. London: Higher Education Policy Institute.

Fielden, J., and Varghese, N. V. (2009) Regulatory issues. In S. Bjarnason, Kai-Ming Cheng, John Fielden, et al. (Eds), *A new dynamic: Private higher education*, pp. 71–89. Paris: UNESCO

Fielden, J., Middlehurst, R., Woodfield, S., and Olcott, D. (2010) *The growth of private and for-profit higher education providers in the UK*. London: Universities UK.

Grubb, W. N., and Lazerson, M. (2004) *The education gospel: The economic power of schooling*. Cambridge, MA: Harvard University Press.

Gumport, P. (2001) Built to serve: The enduring legacy of public higher education. In P. Altbach, P. Gumport, and B. Johnstone (Eds), *In defense of American higher education*, pp. 85–109. Baltimore: Johns Hopkins University Press.

Huisman, J. (Ed.) (2009) *International perspectives on the governance of higher education: Alternative frameworks for coordination*. London: Routledge.

Jensen, M. C., and Meckling, W. H. (1976) Theory of the firm: Managerial behaviour, agency costs and ownership structure. *Journal of Finance Economics*, 3(4), 305–360.

Kaplan, G. (2004) How academic ships actually navigate. In R. Ehrenberg (Ed.), *Governing academia*, pp. 165–208. Ithaca: Cornell University Press.

Keller, G. (2001) Governance: The remarkable ambiguity. In P. Altbach, P. Gumport, and B. Johnstone (Eds), *In defense of American higher education*, pp. 304–322. Baltimore: Johns Hopkins University Press.

Kinser, K., Levy, Daniel C., Casillas, Juan Carlos Silas, et al. (2010) *The global growth of private higher education*. ASHE Higher Educations Report 36/3. Hoboken: Wiley Subscription Services for Jossey-Bass.

Levine, A. (2001) Higher education as a mature industry. In P. Altbach, P. Gumport, and B. Johnstone (Eds), *In defense of American Higher Education*, pp. 38–58. Baltimore: John Hopkins Press.

Levy, D. C. (2002) Unanticipated development: Perspectives on private higher education's emerging roles. PROPHE Working Paper No.1. New York: The Program for Research on Private Higher Education. http://prophe.org/en/working-papers/unanticipated-development-per spectives-on-private-higher-education39s-emerging-roles/

Levy, D. C. (2009) Growth and typology. In S. Bjarnason, Kai-Ming Cheng, John Fielden, et al. *A new dynamic: Private higher education*, pp. 7–27. Paris: UNESCO.

Locke, W., Fisher, D., and Cummings, K. (2011) *Changing governance and management in higher education: The perspectives of the academy*. New York: Springer.

Marginson, S., and Considine, M. (2000) *The enterprise university*. Melbourne: Cambridge University Press.

Meek, L. G., Santiago, R., and Carvalho T. (Eds), (2010) *Deans – Higher education middle management in an international perspective*. Dordrecht: Springer

Meyer, J. W., and Rowan, B. (1977) Institutional organizations: Formal structure as myth and ceremony. *American Journal of Sociology*, 83(2), 340–363.

Middlehurst, R. (1993) *Leading academics*. Milton Keynes: SRHE/Open University Press.

Middlehurst, R., and Teixeira, P. (2012) Governance within the EHEA: Dynamic trends, common challenges and national particularities. In

A. Curaj, P. Scott, L. Vlasceanu and L. Wilson (Eds), *European higher education at the crossroads: Between the Bologna Process and national reforms. Part 2: Governance, financing, mission diversification and futures of higher education*, pp. 527–551. London: Springer.

Middlehurst, R. (2016) Privately funded higher education providers in the UK: The changing dynamic of the higher education sector. In M Shah and C S Nair (Eds), *A global perspective on private higher education*. Oxford: Chandos Publishing Elsevier Ltd.

Musselin, C. (2005) Change and continuity in higher education governance? Lessons drawn from twenty years of national reforms in European countries. In I. Bleiklie and M. Henkel (Eds), *Governing knowledge: A study of continuity and change in higher education*, pp. 65–79. Dordrecht: Springer.

Neave, G., and van Vught, F. (1991) *Prometheus bound: The changing relationship between government and higher education in Western Europe*. Oxford: Pergamon Press.

Neave, G., and van Vught, F. (1994) *Government and higher education relationships across three continents*. Oxford: Pergamon Press.

Rosser, V. (2002) Governance. In J. Forest and K. Kinser (Eds), *Higher education in the United States: An encyclopedia*, Vol. 1, pp. 279–284. Santa Barbara: ABC-CLIO.

Scott, W. R. (2003) *Organizations: Rational, natural and open systems*. Upper Saddle River: Prentice-Hall.

Seyama, S. M. (2015) Amenable performance management in higher education: Integrating principles of agency and stewardship theories. *Africa Education Review*, 12(4), 664–679. doi:10.1080/18146627.2015.1112157

Shah, M., and Nair, C. E. (Eds) (2016) *A global perspective on private higher education*. Cambridge: Chandos Publishing.

Shattock, M. (2006) *Managing good governance in higher education*. Maidenhead: Open University Press.

Shattock, M. (2017) University governance in flux. The impact of external and internal pressures on the distribution of authority within British universities: A synoptic view. Working Paper No. 13. London: UCL, Centre for Global Higher Education.

Stensaker, B., and Harvey, L. (Eds) (2011) *Accountability in higher education: Global perspectives on trust and power*. London: Routledge

Teixeira, P. (2009) Economic imperialism and the ivory tower: Economic issues and policy challenges in the funding of higher education in the EHEA (2010–2020). In B. M. Kehm, J. Huisman, and B. Stensaker (Eds), *The European higher education area: Perspectives on a moving target*, pp. 43–60. Rotterdam: Sense Publishers.

Teixeira, P., Biscaia, R., Rocha, V., and Cardoso, M. F. (2016) What role for private higher education in Europe? Reflecting about current patterns and future prospects. In M. Shah and C. S. Nair (Eds), *A global perspective on private higher education*, pp. 13–28. Cambridge: Chandos Publishing.

Teixeira, P., Kim, S., Landoni, P., and Gilani, Z. (2017) *The changing public–private mix in higher education: Patterns, rationales and challenges*. Rotterdam: Sense Publishers.

Teixeira, P., Rocha, V., Biscaia, R., and Cardoso, M. (2012a) Competition and diversity in higher education: An empirical approach to specialization patterns of Portuguese institutions. *Higher Education*, 63(3), 337–352.

Teixeira, P., Rocha, V., Biscaia, R., and Cardoso, M. (2012b) Myths, beliefs and realities: Public–private competition and higher education's diversification. *Journal of Economic Issues*, 46(3), 683–704.

Teixeira, P., Rocha, V., Biscaia, R., and Cardoso, M. F. (2013) Competition and diversification in public and private higher education. *Applied Economics*, 45(35), 4949–4958.

Teixeira, P., Rocha, V., Biscaia, R., and Cardoso, M. F. (2014) Public and private higher education in Europe: Competition, complementarity or worlds apart? In A. Bonaccorsi (Ed.), *Knowledge, diversity and performance in European higher education: A changing landscape*, pp. 84–105. Cheltenham: Edward Elgar Publishing.

Weisbrod, B., Pallou, B., and Asch, E. (2008) *Mission and money: Understanding the university*. Cambridge: Cambridge University Press.

PART III

Geographies of Governance

11 | *Higher Education Governance in North America*

GILIBERTO CAPANO AND JUN JIE WOO

11.1 Introduction

The process of ongoing change that has characterized systemic governance in Higher Education (HE) around the world over the last three decades (Capano 2011; Shattock 2014) has involved federal countries as well as non-federal ones. Even in federal countries, governments have attempted to readdress the whole higher education system in an effort to circumvent or supersede previous governance modes and the existing distribution of vested interests (especially the tendency of higher education institutions to be self-referential). Additionally, in federal countries, both governmental levels have wanted the higher education systems to better serve their respective societies and have pursued this systemic goal by trying to address them in different ways with respect to the past (less direct command; more evaluation, accountability, and performance funding).

This common process of redesigning governance is particularly interesting in federal countries since the presence of two levels of strong government has rendered the governance shift process particularly complex but, above all, extremely fascinating. The process is more complex for scholars than for policy makers since the composite nature of federal states makes it difficult to generalize any specific trend: the multilevel institutional system and the fragmented nature of such countries make it inherently difficult to reason in terms of a national system of higher education while what exists are federal state-level systems. This complexity is accompanied by the intriguing fact that in countries such as Canada and the USA, while the constitutions clearly provide for granting exclusive powers regarding higher education to federated units, federal governments have nonetheless constantly disregarded said constitutional design.

From this point of view, Canada and the USA are interesting not only due to the conflicting nature of each country's federalism, but also because the two are often considered more similar than they truly are. From a general, systemic point of view, this similarity is a stereotype, and this is true also regarding higher education. From a systemic point of view, the significant political and cultural differences between Canada and the USA have been masterfully sketched by Lipset (1989), who has underlined the political and cultural reasons for the deep divide between the two societies: anti-statism, egalitarianism, individualism, and populism characterize the USA; elitism, statism, collectivism, and particularism characterize Canada. Then, there is a difference in the form of government (presidentialism vs. parliamentarism). Finally, there is a different type of federalism because Canada includes Quebec, thereby showing a linguistic cleavage not present in the composition of US federalism. Notwithstanding the fact that the two federalisms are considered to be quite similar (usually the two countries are both considered part of the so-called competitive federalism model), the real ways these two federalisms work are very different, as we will show in the following paragraph.

As the two countries are so different, we should expect significant variations in their higher education policies. The reality is that not only are the structures of their respective higher education systems differentiated to a greater degree than expected, but the ways in which their state/provincial higher education systems are organized, ruled, and funded are also considerably different. Furthermore, their federal policies differ significantly and overlap only to a limited extent.

However, this diversity can be better understood by focusing on how the two levels of government have acted to pursue the worldwide common trend through which the systemic governance modes have been significantly changed in many countries.

Grasping the nature of this shift in federal countries is somewhat complicated due to the two levels of political power and the fact that every member state has its own policy legacy. Thus, we assume that the above-sketched diversity between the two countries must be seriously taken into consideration when analysing how the USA and Canada have interpreted the common template that has characterized the uniform shift in systemic higher education.

This shift has been characterized by a specific governmental emphasis on evaluation, institutional accountability, accreditation, competition, changes in the allocation of public funding, and increased pressure on universities to behave like corporate organizations (Capano and Pritoni, 2019; Dobbins and Knill, 2014; Lazzaretti and Tavoletti, 2006; Maassen and Olsen, 2007; Shattock, 2014).

This governance shift has also meant that all countries have experienced the rise of 'New Public Management' (NPM) policy practices, such as the privatization, outsourcing, and contracting out of public services (Bleiklie, 1998; Braun, 1999; Broucker and De Wit, 2015; Deem and Brehony, 2005). Such shifts towards NPM have been accompanied by the increasing use of regulatory tools as a means of governing and managing the higher education sector (Robertson, 2010). As with the NPM movement, this shift towards a 'regulatory state' has much to do with policy makers' desire to introduce greater accountability and increase the performance of higher education institutions, even as these institutions become imbued with a greater degree of autonomy (Blackmur, 2007; Enders et al., 2013; King, 2007; Moja et al., 1996; van Vught, 1988, 1989).

In light of this general trend, we adopt a narrower understanding of the concept of higher education governance, which focuses on a government's ability to guarantee that higher education institutions perform their key functions of education and research. In doing so, we do not delve into issues pertaining to the internal governance of universities and higher education institutions (although some of these will be present in our discussion of overall higher education governance). However, it has to be underlined that the other side of the systemic governance reforms has been, in the USA and Canada, as well in the other countries, the adoption of New Public Management techniques and tools, especially in governing institutions. Finally, in complex systems such as federal ones, it should be expected that the multilevel structure of policy making could be a kind of structural incentive to develop networks among the different actors to allow them to play more effective roles in multilevel policy dynamics (and thus networks could be considered a specific dimension of systemic governance).

Therefore, to grasp the characteristics of governance and accountability in the higher education systems of Canada and the USA, we need to focus on the systemic characteristics of such systems (the types of institutions are distinguished by their respective missions and ownership), on the role of and eventual changes to the state/provincial and federal governments across time, on the impact of NPM in the activities of the systems, and, finally, on the characteristics and roles of policy networks.

By focusing on these four dimensions, it is possible to better describe and understand how systemic governance works in the USA and Canada, and how those countries have been changing by remaining quite diversified.

11.2 Higher Education Governance in Federal Countries: A Conceptual Overview

The problem of governance in higher education in federal countries is fascinating because of the joint presence of two different centres of political authority – the federal government and the state government – and, consequently, because of the presence of different systems of administration, reporting, and accountability requirements that often vary between states.

The joint presence of two governmental levels also matters in cases such as the USA and Canada, where the constitutions exclude the exercising of any formal powers by the federal state over higher education. The exclusion of the federal level with respect to the matter of higher education does not mean the absence of the federal power in the real world of policy making. In fact, federal policy and political dynamics often reveal attempts by the federal government to interfere in matters that are the exclusive preserve of the state/provincial government. Thus, the presence of a federal structure of political power requires a specific analytical focus when systemic governance and institutional accountability in higher education are the objects of study. While the question of who determines the priorities, strategic direction, and operations of a country's higher education system, and how they do so, lies at the heart of higher education governance, federal countries are complicated cases when the issues of who and how are being analysed. In federal countries there is usually a clear constitutional separation of powers between the two levels of government regarding higher education: there is not just one national mode of systemic governance in higher education, there are as many such modes as there are units constituting the federation, and the federal government attempts to play some role in addressing/coordinating the overall system.

However, before focusing on higher education, we need to grasp the characteristics of federal dynamics as the way by which formal constitutional provisions are interpreted according to actual intergovernmental relationships, thus assuming that policy making in federal systems is

Table 11.1 *Varieties of federalism according to formal framework and federal relations*

		Formal framework	
		Disintegrated	Integrated
Federal relations	Centripetal	*Balanced*	*Unitary*
	Centrifugal	*Segmented*	*Accommodating*

Source: Colino (2013)

characterized not only by the formal constitutional framework but also by the patterns of intergovernmental relations. This double focus (on the formal framework and on intergovernmental relations) can facilitate an understanding of how federal dynamics influence the actions of governments (at both levels) in redesigning public policy governance arrangements.

This perspective – which echoes Elazar's (1987) distinction between the structure and process of federal systems, Friedrich's (1962) emphasis on the processual nature of federalism, and those studies that have focused on the structural interdependence between the two levels of government in federal countries (Bolleyer and Thorlakson, 2012; Braun, 2011; Erk, 2008; Erk and Koning, 2010; Thorlakson, 2003) – has recently been further developed by Colino (2010, 2013) in order to construct a typology of federal systems that helps frame the empirical analysis of governmental dynamics and interaction in policy making. This typology is based on the dichotomization of the aforementioned two dimensions: the formal framework (which can be integrated or separated to a greater or lesser degree), and federal relations (which may be more or less centripetal or centrifugal). The result is a four-fold typology based on four ideal types of federalism – or rather, federal dynamics (see Table 11.1). According to Colino (2013):

1. *Balanced federalism* derives from the aggregation of previously existing political communities or states. The constitutional pact guarantees the original powers of the founding members of the federation. The main value is thus the balance of powers. The constitutional design is normally interstate, while the intergovernmental structure of decisions and resources is independent. The strategies of governmental actors tend to be self-assertive, with conflict lines and

intergovernmental coalitions being more of a partisan type, although they are sometimes also territorially driven. The cases closest to this ideal type are those of the USA, Brazil, Australia, and Switzerland.

2. *Unitary federalism* usually originates from the decentralization of a previously centralist state or from the renewal of a federal tradition abandoned in the past as a result of a phase of totalitarian or authoritarian rule. Since unitary federalism originates in times of crisis, its value is that of guaranteeing agreement and cooperation among units. This is the type of federalism usually adopted by culturally homogeneous societies. The intergovernmental structure of decisions and resources is usually interdependent, based on shared competencies and aimed at guaranteeing similar conditions for the lives of all citizens. The intergovernmental rules of decision-making are usually of a hierarchical nature, dominated by federal initiatives but mitigated by certain mandatory joint decisions. Intergovernmental relations are normally based on a cooperative approach, and conflict lines and coalitions are partisan rather than territorial. Germany, South Africa, Austria, and, to a certain degree, Spain are closer to this ideal type.

3. *Segmented federalism* is characteristic of those federations where two different cultural communities coexist, one being in the majority. The typical executive–legislative configuration of this subsystem is parliamentarianism. The constitutional design is interstate, in which agreements between the leaders of the culturally diverse communities and intergovernmental institutions prevail. The intergovernmental structure of decisions and resources is highly independent because powers are mainly exclusive and separated. Intergovernmental decisional rules are usually negotiated between the two orders of government, and interaction tends to be of a competitive character, while the strategies of governmental actors tend to be self-assertive, with conflict lines and intergovernmental coalitions being predominantly of the territorial type. This ideal type is reflected in the fundamental evolution of federalism in both Canada and Belgium.

4. *'Accommodating' federalism* originates in societies with a certain degree of cultural heterogeneity, through a process of devolution or disaggregation of a centralist state as a means of preserving a common state. The values of accommodating federalism are usually the autonomy of the various units and cultural affirmation,

which is usually associated with asymmetric arrangements that are designed to satisfy different self-government aspirations. The 'accommodating' type system usually has a constitutional design of an interstate nature, with weak second chambers and the devolutionary process being controlled by the centre, which traditionally determines the pace and scope of the devolution. The intergovernmental structure of decisions and resources is usually characterized by the interdependence of the levels, reflected clearly in the dependence of the units on central funding. Intergovernmental decisional rules are of the hierarchical type, and, in practice, interaction styles may be either cooperative or quite competitive, depending on the nature of the constituent units. Conflict lines and intergovernmental coalitions may be both territorial and partisan. This ideal type is reflected in the federal dynamics of India and, to a certain extent, Spain.

Thus, thanks to this typology, we can understand not only how different federal political systems can be, but also that the two federalisms under analysis here are quite different. In fact, according to Colino's typology, the USA represents a balanced type of federalism, while Canada can be considered an example of segmented federalism. Unlike the more commonly adopted classificatory distinction in which the USA and Canada are grouped in the same family of competitive federalism (Elazar 1987), the distinction proposed here places the two countries in different categories, which is helpful when trying to understand certain peculiar characteristics of their higher education policies and of the roles of the federal governments in regard to such. Indeed, we argue that the different forms of federalism should be taken into consideration when analysing the shift in the systemic governance of higher education over the last three decades.

11.3 An Overview of Higher Education Systems: Historical and Structural Aspects

11.3.1 Historical Organizational and Institutional Legacies

Canada and the United States differ to a greater degree than is commonly believed. Not only do they have different political-institutional arrangements (presidential system vs. Westminster-type system) and, as we have already noted, different federal dynamics, they also differ in terms of certain important features of higher education:

1. the substantial lack of any private higher education sector in Canada, or of church-affiliated institutions;
2. the lack of hierarchical stratification and differentiation in Canada, whereas in the United States these can be considered a structural characteristic of the country's higher education system;
3. the limited number of higher education institutions in Canada (in relative terms);[1]
4. the absence of a Canadian federal department of education – the only such case in a federal country (Berdahl, 1971; Jones, 2014; Skolnik and Jones, 1992).

These structural differences are a legacy of the different historical paths the two countries have followed, but they need to be taken into consideration nevertheless. This is because while the two levels of government in Canada steer, or try to steer, their respective higher education systems, in the United States the large number of private universities does not allow the government to fully address the corresponding systems. As Lipset notes (1989), the Canadian experience is characterized by the historical emergence of a statist ideology that has institutionalized a collective belief that education, including higher education, should be considered a public good and is thus subject to a regime of quasi-monopoly. On the other hand, in the United States, HE is considered to be an important aspect of individual freedom, and thus while still a good, it can be treated as a private good.

A further institutional difference that merits examination is the way in which higher education systems have been coordinated or steered at the provincial/state level. While in Canada the coordination of the provincial system has always been the responsibility of the provincial government, and no intermediate body has ever had any real steering power (Fisher et al., 2014), in the United States each state has established a specific organization (board) mandated with the task of steering that state's higher education system. These boards may have different roles: there are 'state-wide/consolidated' governing boards that possess direct control over the organizational, fiscal, and employment aspects of all campuses, and there are 'coordinating' boards that are only in charge of monitoring campus policies and making recommendations to the legislature or government, depending on what is provided for by the states' respective constitutions (McGuinness, 2003; McLendon, Heller, and Young, 2005; SHEEO, 2009). Thus, from a governance point of view, a substantial difference between the two countries at the sub-federal level has been emerging and institutionalizing over time.

Despite these two differences, both countries have dealt with the massification of higher education starting from the same historical watershed moment – namely, the end of World War II. In both countries, veterans were encouraged and given help to enrol at university, and the federal governments established programmes favouring university education (Cameron, 1991; Cohen and Kisker, 2010).

In Canada, the federal government has been directly involved in funding universities for almost 20 years, but this has led to a degree of political unrest because while universities were happy to receive funds directly from the federal government, some provinces began to argue that this behaviour was unconstitutional (Quebec, for example, has prohibited its universities from accepting federal money since 1952). This issue has been resolved through a new system of indirect funding (by means of provincial grants and allocations). Thus, the federal government's direct involvement has consisted of financial support offered to students (together with, of course, the funding of research) (Jones and Noumi, 2018).

The end of World War II also witnessed the advent of a new activism on the part of the US federal government in addressing and/or influencing the functioning of the state higher education system, especially in three main policy domains: financial aid to students, research, and social justice (Schmidtlein and Berdahl, 2011). This intervention was institutionalized through the Higher Education Act, approved in 1965 and variously amended thereafter. This act aimed to strengthen the educational resources of US colleges and universities and to provide financial aid to post-secondary students. Furthermore, starting in 1958 and continuing during the Cold War, the federal government channelled a significant amount of money into universities for the purpose of applied research (Antonio et al., 2018).

Overall, following the historical watershed represented by the massification of higher education that began after World War II, both countries have witnessed signs of their respective federal government's interest in becoming involved in higher education, albeit in different ways and to different degrees.

11.3.2 *The Structure of the Two Higher Education Systems*

The two higher education systems have different origins and have developed in dissimilar ways. The US higher education system is highly differentiated and hierarchically diversified, while the Canadian one is much simpler and is characterized by a very limited degree of differentiation.

The incredible variety of US higher education has not been represented by any official typology; however, thanks to the Carnegie Classification of Institutions of Higher Education, it is now possible to categorize institutions within the complex US American HE system. The Carnegie classification categorizes American universities and colleges according to the types of degree programmes they offer (Carnegie Classification of Institutions of Higher Education 2017). This is shown in Table 11.2.

The complexity of the system also lies in the significant percentage of private universities and colleges. In fact, out of more than 4,000 institutions, only 38.2% are public, while 40.3% are private non-profit organizations, and 21. 5% are private for-profit institutions. Furthermore, the majority of research universities are public: of 130 higher research institutions, 97 are public. The large number of private institutions is unique to the US higher education system and represents the structurally highly competitive nature of the American HE system, which makes it unlike those of other Western nations. This structural and historical characteristic thus makes the US system more prone to marketization dynamics than other HE systems elsewhere are.

Public institutions receive a certain annual allocation of state funding, they sometimes stand on publicly owned land, and they may be subject to state regulations; private institutions, on the other hand, are free from state control, although they may sometimes receive state operating funds to provide public services, such as publicly funded academic programmes (US Department of Education, 2008). Regardless of whether they are public or private institutions, higher education institutions in the USA are generally organized and are licensed or chartered as non-profit or for-profit corporations. As with most corporate entities, American higher education institutions are governed by a board of trustees; the board members of public universities are appointed by a governor or legislature, while those of private institutions are generally elected by the board itself (US Department of Education, 2008). One very important fact is that, starting in 1990, the nation's states have gradually reduced public funding for their

Table 11.2 *Distribution of US institutions and enrolment by classification type (2017)*

Types of Institution	Institutions		Enrolment		
	Number	Per cent	Total	Per cent	Average
Doctoral Universities: Very High Research Activity	130	3.0%	3.797.803	19.0%	29.214
Doctoral Universities: High Research Activity	134	3.1%	1.915.536	9.6%	14.295
Doctoral/Professional Universities	159	3.7%	1.504.472	7.5%	9.462
Master's Colleges & Universities: Larger Programmes	346	8.0%	2.972.624	14.8%	8.591
Master's Colleges & Universities: Medium Programmes	192	4.4%	604.310	3.0%	3.147
Master's Colleges & Universities: Small Programmes	134	3.1%	322.540	1.6%	2.407
Baccalaureate Colleges: Arts & Sciences Focus	241	5.6%	381.761	1.9%	1.584
Baccalaureate Colleges: Diverse Fields	333	7.7%	514.020	2.6%	1.544
Baccalaureate/Associate's Colleges: Mixed Baccalaureate/Associate's	157	3.6%	432.885	2.2%	2.757
Baccalaureate/Associate's Colleges: Associate's Dominant	112	2.6%	887.990	4.4%	7.928
Associate's Colleges: High Transfer–High Traditional	300	6.9%	2.758.404	13.8%	9.195
Associate's Colleges: High Transfer–Mixed Traditional/Non-traditional	30	0.7%	143.012	0.7%	4.767
Associate's Colleges: High Transfer–High Non-traditional	13	0.3%	37.314	0.2%	2.870
Associate's Colleges: Mixed Transfer/Career & Technical–High Traditional	245	5.7%	1.486.961	7.4%	6.069
Associate's Colleges: Mixed Transfer/Career & Technical–Mixed Traditional/Non-traditional	53	1.2%	389.715	1.9%	7.353

Table 11.2 (cont.)

Types of Institution	Institutions			Enrolment		
	Number	Per cent	Total	Per cent	Average	
Associate's Colleges: Mixed Transfer/Career & Technical–High Non-traditional	12	0.3%	45.993	0.2%	3.833	
Associate's Colleges: High Career & Technical–High Traditional	265	6.1%	672.603	3.4%	2.538	
Associate's Colleges: High Career & Technical–Mixed Traditional/Non-traditional	58	1.3%	156.557	0.8%	2.699	
Associate's Colleges: High Career & Technical–High Non-traditional	24	0.6%	76.192	0.4%	3.175	
Special Focus Two-Year: Health Professions	268	6.2%	123.455	0.6%	461	
Special Focus Two-Year: Technical Professions	67	1.5%	33.649	0.2%	502	
Special Focus Two-Year: Arts & Design	31	0.7%	5.938	0.0%	192	
Special Focus Two-Year: Other Fields	68	1.6%	23.279	0.1%	342	
Special Focus Four-Year: Faith-Related Institutions	304	7.0%	91.241	0.5%	300	
Special Focus Four-Year: Medical Schools & Centers	35	0.8%	47.633	0.2%	1.361	
Special Focus Four-Year: Other Health Professions Schools	287	6.6%	291.178	1.5%	1.015	
Special Focus Four-Year: Engineering Schools	7	0.2%	10.440	0.1%	1.491	
Special Focus Four-Year: Other Technology-Related Schools	15	0.3%	21.615	0.1%	1.441	
Special Focus Four-Year: Business & Management Schools	79	1.8%	89.985	0.4%	1.139	
Special Focus Four-Year: Arts, Music & Design Schools	121	2.8%	106.311	0.5%	879	
Special Focus Four-Year: Law Schools	36	0.8%	18.791	0.1%	522	
Special Focus Four-Year: Other Special Focus Institutions	46	1.1%	41.581	0.2%	904	
Tribal Colleges	34	0.8%	16.424	0.1%	483	
All Institutions	4.336	100.0%	20.022.212	100.0%	4.618	

respective higher education systems. In 2015, such funding was half what it had been 25 years earlier (Antonio et al., 2018). At the same time, average tuition fees have almost doubled.

The Canadian system is much less complicated, and there is no real distinction between universities (in terms of 'teaching' or 'research' missions). However, as in the USA, it is somewhat difficult to classify Canadian institutions, particularly given the number of colleges that actually exist. According to the CMEC (2019), there are 163 universities in Canada, 96 of which are public. However, it must be emphasized that there are almost 200 colleges (including two-year degree-granting institutions that are mainly vocational – though in some provinces, such as Alberta and British Columbia, such institutions also have a university-transfer function). It must also be emphasized that universities receive two-thirds of the enrolment, while colleges receive one-third of enrolment. In 2017, universities enrolled approximately 1,100,000 FTE students, while colleges enrolled almost 600,000 FTE students (Usher, 2018). The distribution of public universities per province is shown in Table 11.3.

Table 11.3 *Provincial distribution of public universities in Canada*

Provinces and Territories	Universities
Alberta	9
British Columbia	10
Manitoba	6
Nova Scotia	11
New Brunswick	5
Newfoundland and Labrador	1
Ontario	32
Prince Edward Island	1
Quebec	19
Saskatchewan	2
Northwest Territories	
Nunavut	
Yukon	
Total	96

The private sector plays a marginal role within the system due to the low number of students enrolled in private universities in Canada. Public universities are considered 'public', although they are not public enterprises. In fact, they operate as autonomous non-profit corporations created by provincial acts or charters (Jones et al., 2001). Within each province, public universities are legally chartered as private not-for-profit corporations, even though they serve public interests (Jones, 2002, p. 215). From a policy perspective, there is little by way of federal-level authority or control over the higher education system, with higher education policy and governance delegated to provincial governments. For example, Ontario's Ministry of Training, Colleges and Universities is responsible for:

- Developing policy directions for universities and colleges of applied arts and technology.
- Planning and administering policies related to basic and applied research among higher education institutions.
- Authorizing universities to grant degrees.
- Distributing provincial funds to colleges and universities.
- Providing financial assistance to post-secondary school students.
- Registering private career colleges.

(Ministry of Training, Colleges and Universities, 2018)

It should be pointed out that vis-à-vis provincial government, Canadian universities have been granted considerable institutional autonomy, which was reinforced through the introduction of bicameralism in Canadian university governance by the 1906 Royal Commission on the University of Toronto. This aimed to reduce direct political interference in universities by their respective provincial governments and to prevent universities from becoming an 'arm of the state' (Jones, 2002, p. 216). Under this bicameral system, provincial government interests are restricted to a 'governing board' that is responsible for the administrative and operational affairs of the university, while academic decision makers form a 'senate' that oversees academic affairs. As Jones has noted:

Bicameralism represented a governance structure that attempted to balance the need for external accountability to the state which financially supported the institution with the need for the participation of the professoriate in decisions that focused on academic standards. (Jones 2002, p. 216)

As Kirby notes, '[i]n the Canadian context, national post-secondary education policy is in essence represented by the amalgamation of the common interests across postsecondary education policy in each province' (Kirby, 2007, p. 3). However, this is not to suggest a complete lack of federal governmental involvement in Canada's higher education system, as we shall see.

It is important to observe that although there is no national system, universities play an active role at the national/federal level. Universities Canada – formerly known as the Association of Universities and Colleges of Canada – serves to advocate for Canadian universities at the federal level, as well as to foster collaboration among universities, governments, the private sector, local communities, and international partners (Universities Canada, 2018). Like the various university and college associations in the American higher education landscape, Universities Canada plays a crucial role in influencing higher education policy and providing policymakers with the necessary policy feedback and input.

11.4 Key Themes and Shifts in Higher Education Governance in Canada and the United States

11.4.1 Federal and State/Provincial Governance Arrangements

11.4.1.1 The Federal Role

Over the last 30 years, these two North American countries have witnessed not only a process of change in the state/provincial systems of higher education coordination and governance, but also a close degree of interaction between the state and federal levels, with the latter attempting to increase its influence in various ways.

With regard to the federal level of governance in the United States, the Higher Education Act of 1965 and its subsequent reiterations constitute a cornerstone of the institutionalized role of the federal government in higher education. In fact, thanks to this act, the US federal government is able to implement various programmes that have a significant impact on the system. The most important such programmes concern financial aid for students and families (grants and loans), institutional aid (especially for historically black colleges), and teacher quality enhancement. Regulations have been continuously introduced to oblige higher education institutions to be transparent with regard to all aspects of university activity – including, for example, criminal acts of violence committed on university campuses (and the 2008 Higher Education Act provides for the withdrawal of federal funding in cases of non-compliance) (Maes, 2015). Furthermore, the Federal Department of Education is responsible for accrediting almost 100 organizations acting as accreditors for nearly 3,000 institutions. It is important to note here that starting with the Obama presidency, there has been a specific focus on developing a federal system of university monitoring to provide US citizens with due information about university activities.

However, while the US federal government has been trying to regulate several aspects of higher education, it has not been entirely capable (and neither have state governments) of preventing the private costs of higher education from rising. These increasing costs are the result not only of significant government cuts to higher education that have characterized state policies over the last 15 years, but also of extreme institutional competition; together, these factors have led to the accumulation of an incredible amount of collective debt by students and their families.

Two data points can be noted here regarding state appropriations to higher education systems: a decrease of 10% from 2000 to 2008, and an additional 20% from the beginning to the 2008 crisis until 2012 (SHEEO, 2016). This 30% decrease has been slowly recovered in the seven subsequent years (Center for the Study of Education Policy and SHEEO, 2019). These 15 years of financial difficulties have deeply influenced the system: universities have increased tuition fees, reduced faculty, and reorganized their campuses. These effects will not be easily reversed now that state funding has returned to the situation of 2008 (Mitchell et al., 2018). Here, it must be emphasized that in 2008, 30% of the revenue of public institutions came from tuition fees, while this percentage grew to 46% in 2017. Regarding the high level of student debt, in 2006 this amounted to 0.5 trillion dollars, while in 2018 it reached 1.5 trillion dollars – almost

45 million Americans have educational debt, and almost 10 million have educational debt higher than 100,000 dollars (Federal Reserve Bank, 2018).

Finally, it should be noted that federal funding represents one of the main sources of income for research universities (in 2015, the federal transfer of funds for research was 70 billion dollars, representing approximately 55% of the total research income of research universities).

In Canada, the role of the federal government has been less intrusive, following years of direct funding of the country's universities. To better understand the Canadian federal government's role, one needs to consider the fact that in 1967, the Council of Ministers of Education, Canada (CMEC) was established specifically to facilitate intergovernmental coordination and relations with pan-Canadian education organizations. This measure resulted in subsequent intergovernmental declarations and the launch of the Pan-Canadian Assessment Programme based on the voluntary participation of Canada's provinces, with the aim of providing a uniform measure of student proficiency. This attempt to create a national education policy, while respectful of the dualistic, segmented structure of Canadian federalism, was clearly inspired by the desire to design a results-based system of HE governance.

However, the real change has been seen in the federal government's policy on the funding of higher education. While on the one hand there has been a reduction in the standard transfer of funds to the provinces for higher education spending, on the other hand this has been accompanied by an increase in the specific funding of research activities and infrastructure (starting with the 'Network Centre of Excellences' launched in 1998, followed by other measures such as the Canadian Foundation for Innovation, set up in 1997; the Canadian Research Chair programme, established in 2000; and the so-called New Innovation Agenda). The federal government's policy of funding research has directly influenced the strategic planning adopted by many universities, especially the more research-oriented ones, while simultaneously creating the prerequisites for greater institutional diversity (Jones 2006). Thus, even if institutional governance has not been formally modified, the government's dual strategy (provincial/federal) has meant the presence of stronger ties, more targets to be met, more substantial funding, and a greater degree of targeted accountability to be taken into consideration, and ultimately proven, by the institutions themselves. Furthermore, this strategy has meant the increased marketization of higher education policy, due to both the need to compete for federal funding and the pressure to market research findings (Kirby, 2007). All of these changes have forced universities to adopt more managerial, verticalized internal governance modes; however, the expected results have yet to be seen, and the pre-existing consensual legacy remains important (Boyko and Jones, 2010).

11.4.1.2 State/Provincial Governance
In the United States, the method of governing public higher education at the state level has been a matter of ongoing reform and partisan politics. From this point of view, what emerges is a constant process of changing governance arrangements in addition to changes to the ways of funding state higher education systems. Regarding state governance arrangements, since 1980, for example, most states have changed their governance arrangements in higher education at least once (McLendon et al., 2007; Smith and Fulton, 2013). This process of change has seen swings to and fro between centralization and decentralization, and these fluctuations often depend on the dynamics of specific local politics. However, there has undoubtedly been considerable pressure exercised at the state level to increase the efficiency and accountability of universities, which would account for the growing shift towards consolidating state-wide bodies (Tandberg, 2010). Furthermore, there is empirical evidence pointing to the fact that not only has the role of governors in leading state higher education systems been strengthened, but also that there is a clear partisan divide in the way in which governors exercise their powers when they have to decide on how the state's HE system should be governed (McLendon and Ness, 2009; Tandberg and Anderson, 2012).

As far as funding is concerned, there is also evidence that the amount of money put into higher education, as well as the way this is distributed and spent, strongly depends on the specific economic context (Weerts and Ronca, 2006). Furthermore, many states have introduced performance-based funding, although this policy has not been as effective as expected (Rutherford and Rabovsky, 2014).

In Canada, a significant redesigning of provincial governance began with radical cuts in federal funding between 1995 and 1997. The reactions to these cuts by Canada's different provinces varied considerably, although certain common trends may be observed (Fisher et al., 2014). First, there has been a strong tendency to reinforce the direct relationship between provincial governments and higher education institutions by, among other things, abandoning the pre-existent intermediary advisory bodies (Jones and Noumi, 2018; Shanahan and Jones, 2007). Moreover, soft-competitive strategies regarding public funding (and, in all the English-speaking provinces, substantial increases in tuition fees) have also been gradually adopted; institutional accountability has been pursued in all of the provinces, in particular through the stipulation of contracts and agreements between universities and the nation's provincial governments. In some provinces, such as Ontario, for example, government policy has benefited from the advice of an agency established in 2005: the Higher Education Quality Council of Ontario. However, generally speaking, provincial governments, unlike similar bodies in other Western countries, have not developed policy sets that are focused on the assessment of institutional performance. From this point of view, the case of Canada's provinces is an exception since pressure for institutional accountability and effectiveness has not been exercised through those policy instruments that have generally been adopted in other countries. Indeed, it seems that there is a common value shared at both the political and social levels that assumes that access to higher education should be a prominent objective; it is no coincidence that in Canada 40% of the share of GDP invested in education (2.5%) is allocated to tertiary education.

11.4.2 New Public Management

From as early as the 1960s, American universities and higher education institutions have sought to 'rationalize' their managerial and operational processes, with a desire for greater efficiency in resource allocation, which has driven a shift towards what was previously known as 'scientific management' (Rourke and Brooks, 1964). This predisposition towards 'scientific' modes of management and accountability was an effort to encourage a subsequent 'managerial revolution' among American universities and higher education institutions, with these institutions often adopting New Public Management (NPM) approaches involving the extensive privatization, outsourcing, and contracting out of managerial functions and decisions (Amaral et al., 2003; Dunleavy and Hood, 1994; Hood, 1995; Keller, 1983; Osborne and Gaebler, 1993; Pollitt and Bouckaert, 2011; Rourke and Brooks, 1964).

The shift towards NPM in higher education governance has also been attributed to shifts in state–university relationships, with the massification and internationalization of higher education, the growing power of experts and the private sector, and the economization and democratization of society all leading to greater managerialism in higher education, together with the decentralization of regulatory and policy authority away from governments and towards higher education institutions (Amaral et al., 2003; Maassen, 2003; McDaniel, 1996).

The impact of introducing NPM into higher education management can be far-ranging. For instance, Slaughter and Rhoades (2003, 2004) have found that the privatization of knowledge and the growing emphasis on profit-making among higher education institutions have given rise to an 'academic capitalist knowledge regime' that places institutional and corporate interests above public interests. Such privatization has also been associated with a gradual decoupling of the public and private missions and interests among American universities (Morphew et al., 2018).

This has, in turn, impacted higher education policy and regulatory practices. For instance, states moved from minimal policies to more expansive approaches as universities' intellectual property activity grew between the 1970s and the early 2000s, with the laws on conflicts of interest amended so that universities and their faculties could hold equity positions in private corporations (even those that are in business relations with the university) (Slaughter and Rhoades 2003).

The introduction of NPM practices to the higher education sector has been similarly prevalent in Canada. For instance, Kirby (2007) argues that Canadian higher education policy reforms in the mid-2000s were aimed at incorporating NPM practices such as privatization, marketization, quality assurance, and internationalization into the higher education institutions of several major Canadian provinces. Ironically, this shift in higher education policy and management towards NPM has also been associated with greater government power over the establishment of the priorities and directions of higher education institutions. This is often achieved through the linking of provincial higher education funding to performance and the erosion of public sector monopolies on degree granting through the introduction of more private degree-granting institutions and higher education providers (Kirby, 2007,

p. 19). However, this increasing number of private institutions has not been very successful in terms of attracting students (Jones, 2014).

In short, the introduction of NPM into North American higher education has served two key purposes. First, NPM practices were introduced to ensure greater transparency and competitiveness among higher education institutions, often in response to the needs of stakeholders as well as those of an increasingly competitive and globalized higher education landscape. Second, this introduction of private sector incentives and managerial practices and prerogatives into higher education institutions has also allowed governments to strengthen their ability to determine the goals and directions of higher education institutions. Overall, even in its rhetorical usage, NPM has been useful from the governmental point of view to reinforce the corporate behaviour of HE institutions. The more that HE institutions, and especially universities, act as corporate actors, the more likely it is that they will react as expected to governmental policies. It is clear that this consequence of NPM adoption and rhetoric happens to the detriment of the power of the faculty and deeply impacts the principle of shared governance (on the dynamics of this and its evolution, please see Chapter 4 in this book).

By linking higher education funding to institutional performance and by introducing greater private sector involvement, governments have been able to dilute the autonomy and influence of traditional higher education institutions by reducing their sectoral monopoly and limiting the scope of their activities. However, this is not to say that HE institutions are powerless in the face of such pressures. As we will discuss in the next section, the North American higher education landscape is also characterized by a third major policy shift: the formation of influential policy networks.

11.4.3 Policy Networks

While the widespread adoption of NPM in the North American higher education landscape has introduced a significant degree of transparency and managerialism to higher education governance and university management, and while the government has changed the boundaries and instruments of sectoral governance arrangements, there has also been an ongoing process of institutionalization of policy networks. In fact, both the Canadian and American higher education systems are characterized by the presence of powerful policy networks, which are defined as an actor-centric set of structured interactions that includes both state and non-state actors (Atkinson and Coleman, 1992; Benner et al., 2003; Howlett 2002). This process of networkization, and thus the presence of structured persistent interactions among various actors, is not unexpected. Networks, as is well known, are a way through which policy actors try to coordinate with each other and find allies for pursuing common interests. In federal higher education systems, these networks are 'necessary' because policy actors need to act in a multilevel governance system and thus in a very complex environment. Hence, networkization could be very useful in terms of gathering continuous information and organizing political and policy strategies.

In his study of the Canadian higher education system, for example, Jones found that university governance tends to be dominated by a policy network comprising the governing board, senate, central university administration, and student and faculty associations. Typically nominated by the provincial government, the governing board is particularly influential in terms of university administration, possessing the ability to appoint university presidents and other senior staff, approve major institutional policies and financial decisions, and even lobby for change in broader government policies (Jones, 2002).

The presence of a policy network in Canadian university governance suggests a greater extent of state control and politicization than is initially obvious. For instance, the strong role of the state-appointed governing board in determining key institutional policies and decisions suggests the continued ability of the provincial state to influence, and even control, higher education institutions. Like any other policy network, Canada's higher education policy network also allows interest groups to articulate the interests of their members and influence both institutional and state policy processes through their lobbying activities (Jones, 2002, p. 231).

Furthermore, the application of a policy network heuristic in understanding Canadian higher education also reveals the presence and influence of the federal government through its role in funding university research (Jones and Oleksiyenko, 2011). Hence, while provincial governments are in charge of governing and regulating higher education institutions, the federal government continues to play a key role in funding university research and providing the resources needed for establishing research infrastructure.

However, this presence of a policy network is also tempered by efforts to introduce institutional diversity into the higher education system, with the Ontario government formally adopting a policy framework aimed at introducing greater institutional diversity in its public higher education system – that is, greater diversity and competition among higher education institutions (Piché and Jones, 2016). Such endeavours are also evident in other Canadian provinces, such as Alberta, British Columbia, Newfoundland, and Labrador (Kirby, 2007).

In the USA, higher education policy networks tend to be much more institutionalized in the form of associations at the federal level, while they are more diversified and informal at the state level (according to the specific context). Broadly speaking, key institutional representatives that make up the American higher education policy network at the federal level include the Directory of State Higher Education Agencies (EROD), which provides contact information and links for all state and territorial higher education commissions; the State Higher Education Executive Officer Network (SHEEO), a national network of state post-secondary education officials who head state higher education boards and post-secondary agencies; and the Association of Community College Trustees (ACCT), a national association representing specialized boards of trustees that oversee public community colleges and two-year associate degree programmes.

Associations representing public (state) higher education institutions include: the American Association of State Colleges and Universities (AASCU), a national association representing state-funded and state-affiliated higher education institutions in the United States; the Association of American Colleges and Universities (AACU), a national association of higher education institutions, including both public and private institutions as well as universities offering graduate studies, that are committed to undergraduate (bachelor's level) education in the traditional liberal arts; the Association of American Universities (AAU), a national association of comprehensive research universities that focus on doctoral studies in a wide variety of subjects and are concerned with issues of scientific research, research funding, and related policy issues; the Council of Independent Colleges (CIC), a national association of private higher education institutions, especially independent undergraduate colleges and small to mid-sized universities, that focus on undergraduate teaching as well as research; the National Association of Independent Colleges and Universities (NAICU), a national association of private higher education institutions of all types that focus on both teaching and research; and the National

Association of State Universities and Land-Grant Colleges (NASULGC), a national association of state colleges and universities established and partially funded under the American Government's First and Second Morrill Acts (1862 and 1890), together with other state higher education institutions. All of these national associations participate in the continuous lobbying through which universities and colleges try to influence federal higher education policy (Cook, 1998)

Furthermore, at the state level, public colleges and universities are affiliated with state governments, and occasionally municipal governments, through agreements, charters, budget allocations, state-appointed boards of trustees, state regulations of various types, and sometimes the state oversight of facilities. These relations underlie the strong pluralism that characterizes policy making in higher education at the state level, which has been little studied by scholars due to the fact that the states appear to be in quite a strong position in terms of their power to fund and address higher education institutions and thus seem substantially impermeable to the influence of external actors or dynamics (Ness et al., 2015).

However, the policy field of higher education is replete with diverse actors, and it is quite clear that a formalistic reading of policy making cannot be considered realistic. In many cases, local networks are significant at the state level, depending on the context. There is still insufficient empirical evidence in regard to this, although the activism of many actors is clear: not only institutional actors (such as state higher education agencies, politicians, and governing boards) but also individual lobbyists, university heads, chambers of commerce, faculty organizations, student associations, and political action committees are involved (Ferrin, 2005; Goodall, 1987; Hines, 1997; Ness, 2010). This plethora of actors would suggest the need for further research into the dynamics of networking, although it is a clear sign of the *networkization* of the field.

11.5 Conclusion

The governance of higher education has undergone significant changes in both the USA and Canada over the last few decades. These changes, although apparently inspired by the same general policy ideas, have followed different paths and have produced different outcomes. We have adopted the theoretical assumption that the differences between the two cases are related to the way in which the federal dynamics and the characteristics of the higher education systems have interacted with one another. This assumption has been confirmed by our analysis.

In fact, in the USA, balanced federalism has allowed the federal government to regulate various aspects of higher education policy, and the federal government is considered the political point of reference when certain problems require an aggregate response (as in the case of students accumulating massive debt, or with regard to the issue of transparency and the disclosure of correct information about the quality of universities). In Canada, on the other hand, segmented policy dynamics that are due particularly to the role of Quebec have only allowed the federal government to use specific financial tools to encourage universities to produce innovations and high-quality research.

Thus, there are more 'national' guidelines in higher education in the USA than in Canada. At the same time, however, the structural characteristics of the American system (its incredible diversity and the presence of a strong private sector) have continued to result in highly competitive dynamics whereby the role of the federal government is substantially weak (except when market failures call for the federal government's direct involvement). However, it is quite clear that the marketized dynamics of US higher education tend to create negative social effects. For example, there is a clear risk of the increasing cost of higher education resulting in more limited access to such education, and if this negative effect is not dealt with by the states, then the federal government will have to intervene (Antonio et al., 2018).

Thus, the American federal government can be considered to be more likely to intervene in higher education when a specific problem extends beyond the borders of an individual state to become a national problem. In contrast, the Canadian federal government is not allowed to do so. This is where the different types of federal dynamics truly matter.

Regarding the role of state/provincial governments, in both countries there has been intense activism in recent decades, aimed at regulating the two higher education systems. One characteristic regarding this governmental level that is common to both countries is the financial dimension of both state and provincial efforts to redesign the systemic governance arrangements in higher education. This financial dimension has been particularly evident in the United States, while in Canada it appears to have been less pronounced (except during the period 1995–1997) but has nevertheless contributed towards increased tuition fees in a country where such fees had always been very low.

There are also clear differences in the ways the two countries' respective higher education systems are steered: in the United States most states have adopted frequent and partisan governance reforms, and, generally speaking, after two decades of decentralization beginning in the late 1990s, there has been a more recent tendency towards the recentralization of state HE system steering. Canada has followed a very different path as governance reforms have been characterized by bi-partisan dynamics and substantial trust in higher education institutions, and have been favoured by the public's deep-rooted belief in the importance of education to quality of life for all concerned. Overall, while in the United States there is a perception that governmental intervention at both the federal and the state level is needed to guarantee the required minimal accountability of higher education institutions, in Canada there is less pressure in terms of this dimension of governance.

These two North American countries thus continue to differ in a period characterized by the deep redesigning of governance in higher education, and it does appear that the two countries are not converging at all towards more similar governance arrangements and policies.

Notes

1. Obviously it is difficult to compare two systems that are structurally so different. However, it emerges that there is a more capillary presence of higher education institutions in the USA than in Canada (due to the strong presence of private institutions as well as the typical tripartition of public/ state systems in research universities, state universities, and community colleges). Both countries have a high percentage of enrollment rates in higher education – in fact, the rates are higher than the OECD average (OECD, 2018)

References

Amaral, A., Meek, V. L., Larsen, I. M., and Lars, W. (2003) *The higher education managerial revolution?* Dordrecht: Springer Science & Business Media.

Antonio A., Carnoy M., and Nelson R. (2018) The United States of America: Changes and challenges in a highly decentralized system. In M. Carnoy, I. Froumin, O. Leshukov, and S. Marginson (Eds) 2018. *Higher education in federal countries*, pp. 37–95. Berkley: Sage.

Atkinson, M. M., and Coleman, W. D. (1992) Policy networks, policy communities and the problems of governance. *Governance*, 5(2), 154–180.

Benner, T., Reinicke, W. H., and Witte, J. M. (2003) Global public policy networks: Lessons learned and challenges ahead. *The Brookings Review*, 21(2), 18–21.

Berdahl, R. O. (1971) *Statewide coordination of higher education.* Washington, DC: American Council on Education.

Blackmur, D. (2007) The public regulation of higher education qualities: Rationale, processes, and outcomes. In D. F. Westerheijden, B. Stensaker, and M. J. Rosa (Eds), *Quality assurance in higher education: Trends in regulation, translation and transformation*, pp. 15–45. Dordrecht: Springer Netherlands.

Bleiklie, I. (1998) Justifying the evaluative state: New public management ideals in higher education. *Journal of Public Affairs Education*, 4(2), 87–100.

Bolleyer, N., and Thorlakson, L. (2012) Beyond decentralization: The comparative study of interdependence in federal systems. *Publius*, 42(4), 566–591.

Boyko, L., and Jones, G. A. (2010) The roles and responsibilities of middle management (Chairs and Deans) in Canadian universities. In V. L. Meek, L. Goedegebuure, R. Santiago, and T. Carvalho (Eds). *The changing dynamics of higher education middle management*, pp. 83–102. Dordrecht: Springer.

Braun, D. (1999) Changing governance models in higher education: The case of the new managerialism. *Swiss Political Science Review*, 5(3), 1–24.

Braun, D. (2011) How centralized federations avoid over-centralization. *Regional and Federal Studies*, 21(1), 35–54.

Broucker, B., and De Wit, K. (2015) New public management in higher education. In J. Huisman, H. de Boer, D. D. Dill, and M. Souto-Otero (Eds), *The Palgrave international handbook of higher education policy and governance*, pp. 57–75. London: Palgrave Macmillan UK.

Cameron, D. M. (1991) *More than an academic question: Universities, government and public policy in Canada.* Halifax: Institute for Research on Public Policy.

Capano, G. (2011) Government continues to do its job: A comparative study of governance shifts in the higher education sector. *Public Administration* 89(4), 1622–1642.

Capano, G., and Pritoni, A. (2019) Varieties of hybrid systemic governance in European higher education. *Higher Education Quarterly*, 73(1), 10–28.

Carnegie Classification of Institutions of Higher Education (2017) Basic classification [online]. *Carnegie classification of institutions of higher education*: http://carnegieclassifications.iu.edu/classification_descrip tions/basic.php

Carnoy M., Froumin I., Leshukov O., and Marginson S. (Eds) (2018) *Higher education in federal countries*. Berkley: Sage.

Center for the Study of Education Policy and SHEEO (2019) *Grapevine, Fiscal Year 2018–19*. https://education.illinoisstate.edu/grapevine/

CMEC (2019) Education in Canada: An overview. Ottawa: Council of Ministers of Education, Canada: www.cmec.ca/299/Education-in-Canada-An-Overview/index.html#04

Cohen, A. M., and Kisker, C. B. (2010) *The shaping of American higher education: Emergence and growth of the contemporary system* (2nd ed.). San Francisco: Jossey-Bass.

Colino, C. (2010) Understanding federal change: Types of federalism and institutional evolution in the Spanish and German federal systems. In J. Erk and W. Swenden (Eds), *New directions in federalism studies*, pp. 16–33. London: Routledge.

Colino, C. (2013) Varieties of federalism and propensities for change. In J. Broschek and A. Benz (Eds), *Federal dynamics: Continuity, change, and varieties of federalism*, pp. 48–69. Oxford: Oxford University Press.

Cook, C. E. (1998) *Lobbying for higher education: How colleges and universities influence federal policy*. Nashville: Vanderbilt University Press.

Deem, R., and Brehony, K. J. (2005) Management as ideology: The case of 'new managerialism' in higher education. *Oxford Review of Education*, 31(2), 217–235.

Dobbins, M., and Knill, C. (2014) *Higher education governance and policy change in Western Europe*. Basingstoke: Palgrave Macmillan.

Dunleavy, P., and Hood, C. (1994) From old public administration to new public management. *Public Money & Management*, 14(3), 9–16.

Elazar, D. S. (1987) *Exploring federalism*. Tuscaloosa: The University of Alabama Press.

Enders, J., de Boer, H., and Weyer, E. (2013) Regulatory autonomy and performance: The reform of higher education re-visited. *Higher Education*, 65(1), 5–23.

Erk, J. (2008) *Explaining federalism*. Routledge: London.

Erk, J., and Koning, E. A. (2010) New structuralism and institutional change: Federalism between centralization and decentralization. *Comparative Political Studies*, 43(3), 353–378.

Federal Reserve Bank (2018) *Report on the economic well-being of US households in 2017–May 2018*. www.federalreserve.gov/publications/20 18-economic-well-being-of-us-households-in-2017-student-loans.htm

Ferrin, S. E. (2005) Tasks and strategies of in-house lobbyists in American colleges and universities. *International Journal of Educational Advancement*, 5(2), 180–191.

Fisher D., Rubenson K., Shanahan T., and Trottier C. (Eds) (2014) *The development of postsecondary education systems in Canada.* Montreal: McGill University Press.

Friedrich, C. J. (1962) Federal constitutional theory and emergent proposals. In A. W. Macmahon (Ed.), *Federalism: Mature and emergent*, pp. 510–533. New York: Russell and Russell.

Goodall, L. E. (Ed.). (1987) *When colleges lobby states: The higher education/state government connection.* Washington, DC: American Association of State Colleges and Universities.

Hines, E. R. (1997) State leadership in higher education. In L. F. Goodchild, C. D. Lovell, E. R. Hines, and J. I. Gill (Eds), *Public policy and higher education* (ASHE reader series), pp. 376–409. Needham Heights: Simon & Schuster.

Hood, C. (1995) The 'new public management' in the 1980s: Variations on a theme. *Accounting, Organizations and Society*, 20(2–3), 93–109.

Howlett, M. (2002) Do networks matter? Linking policy network structure to policy outcomes: Evidence from four Canadian policy sectors 1990–2000. *Canadian Journal of Political Science/Revue canadienne de science politique*, 35(2), 235–267.

Jones, G. A. (2002) The structure of university governance in Canada: A policy network approach. In A. Amaral, G. A. Jones, and B. Karseth (Eds), *Governing higher education: National perspectives on institutional governance*, pp. 213–234. Dordrecht: Springer Netherlands.

Jones, G. A. (2006) Canada. In J. J. F. Forest and P. G. Altbach (Eds), *International handbook of higher education*, pp. 627–645. Dordrecht: Springer.

Jones, G. A. (2014) An introduction to higher education in Canada. In K. M. Joshi and Saee Paivandi (Eds), *Higher education across nations* (vol. 1), pp. 1–38. Delhi: B. R. Publishing.

Jones, G. A., and Oleksiyenko, A. (2011) The internationalization of Canadian university research: A global higher education matrix analysis of multilevel governance. *Higher Education*, 61(1), 41–57.

Jones, G. A., Shanahan, T., and Goyan, P. (2001) University governance in Canadian higher education. *Tertiary Education and Management*, 7(2), 135–148.

Jones G., and Noumi C. (2018) Canada: Provincial responsibility, federal influence and the challenge of coordination, In M. Carnoy, I. Froumin, O. Leshukov, and S. Marginson (Eds) 2018. *Higher education in federal countries*, pp. 96–125. Berkley: Sage.

Keller, G. (1983) *Academic strategy: The management revolution in American higher education.* Baltimore: The Johns Hopkins University Press.

King, R. P. (2007) Governance and accountability in the higher education regulatory state. *Higher Education*, 53(4), 411–430.

Kirby, D. (2007) Reviewing Canadian post-secondary education: Post-secondary education policy in post-industrial Canada. *Canadian Journal of Educational Administration and Policy*, 65, 1–24.

Lazzaretti, L., and Tavoletti, E. (2006) Governance shifts in higher education: A cross national comparison. *European Educational Research Journal*, 5(1), 18–36.

Lipset, S. M. (1989) *Continental divide: The values and institutions of the United States and Canada.* Toronto and Washington, DC: C. D. Howe Institute (Canada) and National Planning Association (USA.).

Maassen, P. (2003) Shifts in governance arrangements. In A. Amaral, V. L. Meek, and I. M. Larsen (Eds), *The higher education managerial revolution?*, pp. 31–53. Dordrecht: Springer Netherlands.

Maassen, P., and J. Olsen. (2007) *University dynamics and European integration.* Dordrecht: Springer.

Maes, J. (2015) US Higher Education Governance: New Public Management Reforms and Future Predictions. *Working Papers in Higher Education Studies*, 1(1), 90–113: www.wphes-journal.eu/

McDaniel, O. C. (1996) The paradigms of governance in higher education systems. *Higher Education Policy*, 9(2), 137–158.

McGuinness, A. (2003) *Models of postsecondary education and governance in the states.* Denver: Education Commission of the States.

McLendon, M. K., Deaton, S. B., and Hearn, J. C. (2007) The enactment of reforms in state governance of higher education: Testing the political instability hypothesis. *The Journal of Higher Education*, 78(6), 645–675.

McLendon, M. K., Heller, D. E., and Young, S. P. (2005) State postsecondary policy innovation: Politics, competition, and the interstate migration of policy ideas. *The Journal of Higher Education*, 76(4), 363–400.

McLendon, M. K., and Ness, E. C. (2009) The politics of state higher education governance reform. *Peabody Journal of Education*, 78(4), 66–88.

Ministry of Training of Ontario, Colleges and Universities (2018) Ministry of Training, Colleges and Universities [online]. *Ministry of Training, Colleges and Universities*: www.ontario.ca/page/ministry-training-colleges-universities

Mitchell, M., Leachman, M. Masterson, K., and Waxman, S. (2018) *Unkept promises: State cuts to higher education. Threaten access and equity.* Washington: Center on Budget and Policy Priorities.

Moja, T., Cloete, N., and Muller, J. (1996) Towards new forms of regulation in higher education: The case of South Africa. *Higher Education*, 32(2), 129–155.

Morphew, C. C., Fumasoli, T., and Stensaker, B. (2018) Changing missions? How the strategic plans of research-intensive universities in Northern Europe and North America balance competing identities. *Studies in Higher Education*, 43(6), 1074–1088.

Ness, E. C. (2010) The politics of determining merit aid eligibility criteria: An analysis of thepolicy process. *Journal of Higher Education*, 81(1), 33–60.

Ness, E., Tandberg, D. W. A, and McLendon M. (2015) Interest groups and state policy for higher education: New conceptual understandings and future research directions. In M. B. Paulsen (Ed.), *Higher education: Handbook of theory and research*, pp. 151–185. Dordrecht: Springer.

OECD (2018) *Education at a glance 2018*. Paris: OECD.

Osborne, D., and Gaebler, T. (1993) *Reinventing government: How the entrepreneurial spirit is transforming the public sector*. New York: Plume.

Piché, P. G., and Jones, G. A. (2016) Institutional diversity in Ontario's university sector: A policy debate analysis. *The Canadian Journal of Higher Education*, 46(3), 1.

Pollitt, C., and Bouckaert, G. (2011) *Public management reform: A comparative analysis – new public management, governance, and the neo-Weberian state* (3rd ed.). Oxford; New York: Oxford University Press.

Robertson, S. L. (2010) The EU, 'regulatory state regionalism' and new modes of higher education governance. *Globalisation, Societies and Education*, 8(1), 23–37.

Rourke, F. E., and Brooks, G. E. (1964) The 'managerial revolution' in higher education. *Administrative Science Quarterly*, 9 (2), 154–181.

Rutherford, A., and Rabovsky, T. (2014) Evaluating impacts of performance funding policies on student outcomes in higher education. *The Annals of The American Academy of Political and Social Science*, 655(1), 185–209.

Schmidtlein, F. A., and Berdahl, R. O. (2011) Autonomy and accountability: Who controls academe? In P. G. Altbach, P. J. Gumport, and R. O. Berdahl (Eds), *American higher education in the twenty-first century: Social, political, and economic challenges*, pp. 69–87. Baltimore: John Hopkins.

Shanahan, T., and Jones, G. A. (2007) Shifting roles and approaches: Government coordination of postsecondary education in Canada from 1995 to 2006. *Higher Education Research and Development*, 26(1), 31–43.

Shattock, M. L. (Eds) (2014) *International trends in university governance*. London: Routledge.

SHEEO – State Higher Education Executive Officers (2009) *State budgeting for higher education in the United States*. Boulder: SHEEO.

SHEEO – State Higher Education Executive Officers (2016) *State higher education finance*. Boulder: SHEEO.

Skolnik, M., and Jones, G. (1992) A comparative analysis of arrangements for state coordination of higher education in Canada and the United States. *The Journal of Higher Education*, 63(2), 121–142.

Slaughter, S., and Rhoades, G. (2003) Contested intellectual property: The role of the institution in United States higher education. In A. Amaral, V. L. Meek, and I. M. Larsen (Eds), *The higher education managerial revolution?*, pp. 203–228. Dordrecht: Springer Netherlands.

Slaughter, S., and Rhoades, G. (2004) *Academic capitalism and the new economy: Markets, state, and higher education*. Baltimore: The Johns Hopkins University Press.

Smith, M., and Fulton, M. (2013) Recent changes to postsecondary governance in states: 2011–13. Education Commission of the States: www.ecs.org/clearinghouse/01/09/33/10933.pdf

Tandberg, D. A. (2010) Politics, interest groups and state funding of public higher education. *Research in Higher Education*, 51(5), 416–450.

Tandberg, D. A., and Anderson, C. K. (2012) Where politics is a blood sport: Restructuring state higher education governance in Massachusetts. *Educational Policy*, 4(26), 564–591.

Thorlakson, L. (2003) Comparing federal institutions: Power and representation in six federations. *West European Politics*, 26(2), 1–22.

Universities Canada (2018) About us [online]. *Universities Canada*: www.univcan.ca/about-us/

US Department of Education (2008) *Organization of US education: Tertiary institutions*. Washington, DC: International Affairs Office, US Department of Education.

Usher, A. (2018) *The state of post-secondary education in Canada, 2018*. Toronto: Higher Education Strategy Associates.

van Vught, F. (1988) A new autonomy in European higher education? An exploration and analysis of the strategy of self-regulation in higher education governance. *International Journal of Institutional Management in Higher Education*, 12(1), 16–26.

van Vught, V. (1989) *Governmental strategies and innovation in higher education*. London: Jessica Kingsley Publishers.

Weerts, D. J., and Ronca, J. M. (2006) Examining differences in state support for higher education: A comparative study of state appropriations for Research I universities. *The Journal of Higher Education*, 77(6), 935–967.

12 | Governance Trends in European Higher Education

HARRY F. DE BOER AND JEROEN HUISMAN

12.1 Introduction

This chapter focuses on developments in governance in European higher education, with a focus on Western Europe. It presents an overview of the literature on this topic, including the various modes of governance as well as the changes in European higher education in recent decades. Our point of departure is to understand governance broadly as a system of 'authoritative direction and control'. All over Europe, policy makers and other stakeholders have been reconsidering the rules of the game to encourage higher education institutions to deliver high-quality services in an effective and efficient way (de Boer and Jongbloed, 2012; Broucker and de Wit, 2015). In recent decades, '[c]hanges have taken place in the forms and mechanisms of governance, the location of governance, governing capacities and styles of governance' (van Kersbergen and van Waarden, 2004, p. 143), in higher education as well as in other public sectors.

In continental Europe, the traditional 'bureaucratic-professional' approach, in which the coordination of higher education systems was driven by governments and academic oligarchies, has gradually shifted towards governance systems in which the logics of markets and networks are prominent (e.g. Bleiklie et al., 2011; Paradeise et al., 2009). There have been a number of reasons, applying in varying degrees to many European countries, for reconsidering the traditional modes of governance (de Boer et al., 2007; de Boer and Jongbloed, 2012; Pierre and Peters, 2000). First, economic recessions, combined with a growing demand for higher education, presented governments with fiscal pressures. There was a general belief that the emerging welfare state model, in which the state plays a key role in the protection of the socio-economic well-being of its citizens, was becoming unaffordable. Second, there was growing disillusionment and distrust in the potential

333

of governments to solve societal problems centrally. One of the consequences of this was an ideological turn towards the market as the superior mode of coordination. Government failures paved the way for neoliberal values, including market preference for the allocation of goods and services and the restructuring of public sectors known as New Public Management (NPM). Third, globalization, internationalization, and Europeanization caused governments and other national higher education stakeholders to reconsider their position and action potential. Increasingly, higher education and research became a dynamic global 'industry', with new actors entering the scene. Finally, there has been a growing awareness of the importance of having a strong and competitive higher education sector in the emerging knowledge society, calling for new rules of the game.

The structure of this chapter is as follows. We start by describing different conceptual models used to address and analyse higher education governance (Section 12.2). Next, based on these conceptualizations, we present general tendencies with regard to governance (Section 12.3). This section demonstrates that states have been delegating some of their powers to other levels in the higher education system, in four directions: an upward shift to the supra-national level, a horizontal shift to 'independent' agencies, a downward shift to the institutions ('autonomy'), and an outward shift ('privatization, contracting'). As a result of these shifts, often cited as a move from government to governance, the modes of system steering and coordination have become more complex and dynamic, including more stakeholders at different policy levels (Pierre and Peters, 2000; Rhodes, 1996). The shift from government to governance is seen as one of the more noteworthy developments in (studying) public sectors (Sundström and Jacobsson, 2007). It concerns, in general terms, the transition from hierarchical to network-based forms of steering, the overlapping of roles of political and societal actors, and a blurring of boundaries between the public and private domains. In higher education systems the new configurations of authority distribution can be seen as multi-level, multi-actor, and multi-domain. The latter refers to the increasing interconnectedness of the higher education, research, and innovation domains.

While it has been argued that in these new configurations state authority has been hollowed out, we will argue that 'steering from a distance', to characterize the state's new philosophy towards higher education, or the state stepping back, is not identical to the state stepping out. In fact, we will argue that a state-centric view still prevails in the new governance modes, although in certain areas (such as appointment of staff, spending matters, managing buildings and campus infrastructure, engaging in contracting with external partners) higher education institutions have gained more autonomy. Despite all the policy initiatives and changes to empower other stakeholders, such as the institutions or students in demand-driven systems, the state continues to determine the rules of the game to a large extent ('meta-governance'), even if the tools that it uses differ from those of previous decades. It has been argued that the shift from government to governance is overestimated, indicating, as we will also argue, the persistence of hierarchy, or at least the prominence of government in steering public sectors (Koch, 2013).

We follow this with a discussion of how structural reforms impact governance (Section 12.4). Many governments have taken forceful initiatives and introduced reforms to change the higher education landscape in their countries. Such structural reforms (e.g. mergers, excellence initiatives, redefining institutional mandates) illustrate our view that in governing contemporary higher education, despite NPM, marketization, and the like, the government remains a key player; its interventions seriously affect the higher education institutions and other stakeholders, and the interactions among them. We will then argue that governance configurations in European higher education not only have some similarities but also differ from each other in various ways: these European variants will be addressed in Section 12.5. Section 12.6 summarizes the key points of the chapter.

12.2 Higher Education Governance Conceptualized

Governance is a highly contested concept and is closely related to such terms as 'organization and management', 'steering', and 'coordination' (OECD, 2008, p. 69). In our eyes, it concerns the exercise of collective control towards common goals (de Boer and File, 2009, p. 10). Following Eurydice (2008, p. 12), we define governance as 'the formal and informal exercise of authority under laws, policies and rules that articulate the rights and responsibilities of various actors, including the rules by which they interact'. There have been several attempts to develop useful classifications and conceptualizations of governance for description and analyses. We present a few that have garnered much attention in studying higher education governance.

In higher education, Clark's triangle of coordination (1983) is the most well-known example and is regularly used as a point of departure to study higher education governance. Clark distinguished three dimensions forming a triangular space: state authority (varying from centralized to limited state intervention), the market (different degrees of market forces), and academic oligarchy (the different degrees of impact of the academic profession and communities). This triangle of coordination was conceptualized in the 1970s and early 1980s, before reform movements swept across higher education systems globally. Since then, the coordination triangle has been adapted by several authors (see Salazar and Leihy, 2013). Instead of a triangle, Braun and Merrien (1999) developed the cube of governance, also based on three dimensions: the procedural, the substantive, and the political culture dimensions. The procedural dimension concerns the degree of administrative control of higher education institutions by administrators, ranging from tight to loose. The substantive dimension relates to the goal-setting capacity for teaching and research by the government, also ranging from tight to loose. As regards the third dimension, Braun and Merrien make a distinction between utilitarian and non-utilitarian belief systems, referring to the role of higher education in the public service system.

Another widely used governance conceptualization is van Vught's (1989, 1995) distinction between two classic models of coordination: the state control model and the state supervision model. The state control model, derived from the model of rational planning and control, portrays the government as a hierarchical actor that micro-manages the higher education system. In its ultimate form, the government is fully informed and has complete control over higher education. The state supervision model, by contrast, relies heavily on the self-regulating capabilities of the higher education institutions. The government's role is far more modest, acknowledging its limited capacity to control the sector. It sets the rules of the game in such a way that the higher education sector itself is able to make fundamental decisions about missions, goals, services, and activities.

In between the poles of state control and state supervision, hybrid models can be conceptualized, such as the 'state contract model', which is based on Williamson's transaction cost reasoning (de Boer and van

Vught, 2016; van Vught and de Boer, 2015; Williamson, 1991). The state contract model focuses on the 'attempt to achieve some level of central coordination and protection for specific investments while retaining the high-powered incentives of market relations' (Klein, 2005, p. 438). Key elements of the state contract model are also clearly visible in the concept of market-based governance, which encompasses not only the delegation of state authority to other (private) actors, but also the introduction of market-style management and mechanisms of accountability in public organizations (de Boer and Jongbloed, 2012, p. 555). It represents a combination, or compromise, between the benefits of central coordination and control and the advantages of decentralized decision making. In the context of higher education, the model respects the autonomy of higher education institutions without denying the existence of government coordination by means of setting conditions and framing the game hierarchically ('meta-governance'). Cooperation between government and institutions, by means of agreements of mutual consent, is the core mechanism and provides opportunities to pursue self-interest conditionally: agreements allow for discretion but are not free of rules.

The last conceptualization of governance that concerns us here is the governance equalizer, developed by de Boer et al. (2007). These authors assume that governance configurations are made up of a specific blend of five dimensions at a particular point in time. These dimensions are: i) state regulation (the degree to which central actors such as the state prescribe institutional behaviour in detail); ii) stakeholder guidance (the degree to which external stakeholders set and guide directions for institutional behaviour); iii) academic self-governance (the role and impact of academic communities in higher education systems such as peer-review-based self-steering); iv) managerial self-governance (the role and impact of university leadership in steering the higher education system); and v) competition (coordination based on competition among institutions for scarce resources). Although the five dimensions are interrelated, the equalizer assumes that these dimensions are, to a large extent, independent. For instance, less state regulation does not automatically lead to more competition or more academic self-governance. As de Boer and Jongbloed (2012, p. 555) argue, the choice between markets and hierarchies is not a zero-sum game. The relative independence of the five dimensions implies that many different governance configurations are possible. This seems to hold in practice, as demonstrated in Section 12.5, which discusses European variants.

12.3 The General Picture

Based on studies on higher education governance in the last two decades, an overarching picture can be painted – or, at least, some general tendencies can be observed. Obviously the role of the state towards higher education has changed, often referred to as the shift from government to governance. Governance has become more complex and dynamic and involves more participants from different levels. Governance as exercise of authority increasingly concerns interconnected policy levels, with multiple actors influencing different parts of the decision-making process and shaping its outcomes. Traditional state authority over higher education in Europe has been redistributed across various policy levels.

In fact, there have been shifts in four different directions. There has been an upward shift, moving state authority to the supra-national level. The Bologna Process and its consequences may serve as a clear example here; decisions of the European Court (see, e.g., van Wageningen, 2015) have also affected national policies (among others, in the area of policies for student support). We have seen a tendency of 'moving out' – a transfer from state to market (marketization, privatization, contracting). The rise of private higher education and the introduction of pricing systems serve as examples of this. There has also been a tendency to transfer state authority to national bodies at arm's length from the state ('agencification') – in other words, 'moving sideways'. We observe, for example, the introduction of new accreditation bodies or greater responsibilities for funding agencies in system coordination. And finally, as part of political deregulation and liberalization agendas, we have seen the devolution of authority towards higher education institutions ('moving down') – enhancing organizational autonomy and encouraging institutional strategic actorhood (Whitley, 2012). There have been numerous reforms across Europe which aim to enhance organizational autonomy with different objectives. In some countries, universities have achieved a legally independent status (e.g. Portugal, Finland). In other countries, universities have acquired the role of employer, giving them more authority in staff matters, or have gained ownership over property and buildings (e.g.

the Netherlands). And in many countries new public funding schemes have given universities more discretionary powers in allocating and spending budgets.

This redistribution of authorities does not imply that the government is stepping out, rolling back, or hollowing out. In Europe, governments still play a pivotal role in this 'network of governance' by establishing frameworks, objectives, and priorities in and for the system. In steering higher education systems, governments – facing market as well as government failures (Dill, 1997; Jongbloed, 2003) – found themselves in a position to develop hybrid steering models, blending characteristics of central steering and 'spontaneous ordering' through marketization. In these hybrid situations, governments still shape the rules of the game to a large degree, but in a different way and by using new devices, which fit general tendencies in public sector management that stress the demand for performance, including obligations to publicly demonstrate performance (Bolton, 2003; Broucker and de Wit, 2015; Fryer et al., 2009). New funding schemes (output- and/or competition-based), mandatory quality assurance and accreditation systems, and explicit contractual obligations serve to maintain or improve system performance, seen as the primary task of the state. They embody both a changed government role and a continued one. This state contract model, characterized by bargaining, reciprocity, and mutual consent, indicates both the government's responsibility and the institutional autonomy of higher education institutions. It provides the government with the possibility to attach conditions, in the form of outputs to be realized and other (reporting) obligations, in return for public funding and other facilities.

The prominence of government in European higher education governance is also illustrated by various studies on institutional autonomy (e.g. Bennetot Pruvot and Estermann, 2017). The empowerment of higher education institutions through the devolution of authorities and decision-making capacities from the state to the institutions assumes that power balances are tilted towards the institutions at the expense of the state. Such a conclusion, however, would be both premature and too simplistic. De Boer and Enders (2017) argue that enhanced formal autonomy does not automatically correspond with the actual space that an institution has to make its own decisions. Organizational autonomy is a relational concept, which implies that external influences – state policies, for example – affect the decision-making space that institutions have. Based on the data from an eight-country study, de Boer and Enders conclude that most universities experience strong to medium levels of influence from the government and its agencies on their internal decision making, regardless of the degree of formal autonomy they possess. While the role of the state has changed, universities continue to operate in the shadow of hierarchy. As a result of funding, regulation, audit, and normative pressures, in reality institutions cannot escape from government interference and the government remains a key actor in governing the system. Moreover, it is important to note that governments, apart from fine-tuning their governance architectures over time, do – once in a while – significantly 'shake up' their higher education systems.

12.4 Big Reforms

The prominence of government is visible not only in the day-to-day steering arrangements, but also in what we term 'big reform' projects. The comparisons of governance arrangements in previous studies do highlight some dynamics over time, but often do not reveal the ways that (other) structural reforms in higher education systems impact governance. That is, by focusing on relatively stable policy areas (funding, quality assurance, institutional governance, programme provision, etc.), these studies offer significant insights in changes in key policy areas. But at the same time, such a focus does not pay sufficient attention to bigger reform projects that may – directly or indirectly – impact governance arrangements. In this section, we address a couple of these reforms and explore how they impact governance arrangements.

In their study on structural reforms, de Boer et al. (2017) investigate system-wide policy change, with specific attention to government policies that intend to metaphorically 'change the landscape' by bringing less/more horizontal or vertical differentiation into the system, or to change the (inter)relationships between higher education institutions. In themselves, these reforms cause governance changes, for the government clearly sets the 'rules for the game' and supplements the policy ideas and changes with instruments such as regulation, funding, and information (see also de Boer and van Vught, 2016). Examples of horizontal differentiation are the introduction of a private higher education sector in Poland and non-university higher education institutions in Croatia. The possibility to 'upgrade' colleges in Norway also fits this category. With vertical differentiation, governments intend to increase (performance) differences between higher education institutions, for example through excellence initiatives, such as the UNIK (Investment Capital for University Research) reform in Denmark, the CEI (International Campus of Excellence) reform in Spain, and a combination of similar policies in France. Reforms pertaining to interrelationships include merger processes in Finland and Wales, but also the setting up of associations (collaborative arrangements between universities and non-university *hogescholen*) in Flanders.

The Finnish case may serve to illustrate governance dynamics. Nokkala and Välimaa (2017) focus on merger initiatives in the Finnish higher education system and stress that Finnish higher education policies have been characterized for decades by gradual and slow change. In line with the Nordic welfare state model, governments were key stakeholders in setting strategies and policies for higher education, based on the idea of all higher education institutions being equal. The context of globalization and increasing international competition caused the government to rethink the landscape and to introduce various measures to increase efficiency and competitiveness. Mergers (i.e. creating larger, more efficient units that would be able to compete with universities abroad) were seen as a major instrument to achieve the government's goals. While it may be tempting to see these reforms as stand-alone landscape changes, implemented in parallel to the more stable policy areas, there were clear implications for the latter areas. In line with, or as a consequence of, the 'upscaling' of higher education institutions, many other governance changes were brought about. For instance, a minimum size was introduced for departments and other organizational units, alongside a minimum overall size for all higher education institutions. The legal foundation of higher education institutions was changed. Institutional governance structures were adjusted to make room for the involvement of external stakeholders in decision making, and executive powers of the rector were strengthened. Finally, and just as controversial as the changes to the institutional governance structures, academics' civil service status was changed into a contractual relationship, with higher education institutions as employers (Nokkala and Välimaa, 2017). Measured against either the governance equalizer (de Boer et al., 2007) or the dimensions of institutional autonomy (Bennetot Pruvot and Estermann, 2017), it is clear that 'one-off' structural reforms like the one in Finland have enduring impacts on the exercise of authority and control, and thus on governance arrangements.

Although the Finnish case is an extreme one (compared, for example, to mergers in Wales that did not entail many accompanying governance changes), the widespread occurrence of structural reforms across Europe suggests that in many other countries structural reform processes are having significant repercussions for governance regimes (see de Boer et al., 2017; Paradeise et al., 2009; see also Dobbins, 2011, on reforms in Central and Eastern Europe, and Huisman et al., 2018, on reforms in post-Soviet states).

12.5 European Variants

In this section we first offer theoretical views on why similar or different governance trends might be expected, and then present a number of empirical examples. The last sub-section reflects on the question of whether there are any (regional) patterns discernible between divergence and convergence.

12.5.1 Convergence and Divergence?

As already noted, some countries have moved quickly and others more slowly in governance changes. Some started early and others were late adopters (see Kehm and Lanzendorf, 2006). And changes are not always unidirectional. Dobbins and Knill (2014, p. 186) conclude in their four-country study that:

Great Britain ... has pulled back on several market-oriented policies, for example in the area of quality assurance, while the state is also increasingly exerting its leverage over academic content. And along these lines, there are few indications the HE governance in any of the four systems will become more market-oriented in the foreseeable future. For example, Germany is also in the process of retracting some market-oriented instruments, most notably tuition fees.

That said, the previous sections have demonstrated that there is indeed a broad governance trend in European higher education that can be summarized under the heading 'from government to governance'. It has been argued that this broad trend, observable in so many countries, is the result of the adoption of international and global

pressures. Higher education systems, traditionally organized nationally, are exposed to common reform agendas and global scripts
(Gornitzka and Maassen, 2014). The agendas, policy positions, and
ideas of supra-national and international organizations travel across
national and sectoral boundaries and, it is argued, produce similar
reforms and policies for national higher education systems. In the last
two decades, for example, many national governance reforms have
entailed elements of governance approaches that have been advocated
by the EU's modernization agenda for higher education or reflect the
views of the OECD on governance. The impressions of NPM as
a 'global script' to organize public sectors are clearly visible and have
been reported widely (Pollitt and Bouckaert, 2004).

Nevertheless, studies on governance in higher education reveal that,
next to similarities, differences across higher education governance
persist. As Gornitzka and Maassen (2014, p. 26) argue, '[a]lthough
national reform agendas for higher education have become more alike,
the reform outcomes can be argued to show many diverging tendencies'. Various authors have offered explanations for the differential
governance developments (Ferlie et al., 2008; Gornitzka and
Maassen, 2014; Jungblut and Vukasovic, 2013; Perellon, 2005): they
suggest that the key factor in countering the converging effect of global
scripts is the existence of national and sector-specific filters that interpret and modify these scripts. Agents such as national policy makers
and institutional leaders do not share the same beliefs systems, nor are
they passive recipients of new ideas. They have their own beliefs and
preferences and try to translate external pressures accordingly. The
likely outcome of the dynamic interactions among various agents
within a national higher education system is a system-specific response
to global scripts. This implies that within the big picture, portrayed in
the previous sections, variety flourishes.

The convergence hypothesis can be challenged in other ways as well.
First, change may not materialize as intended. Cerych and Sabatier
(1986) noted this phenomenon, and other authors have offered the
same explanations for implementation failures and unintended consequences. Higher education institutions are known for relatively high
levels of organizational and professional autonomy (including a belief
in academic freedom). The nature of higher education institutions,
characterized by unclear technologies, many uncertainties, and goal
ambiguity, means that external control is hard to achieve (van Vught,

1989). Deviations from intentions are to be found particularly when those who are to implement the changes do not fully subscribe to the reform intentions. As Gornitzka and Maassen (2014, p. 29) put it, '[s]ector specific characteristics and issues lead to variations in how major public-sector reforms are enacted'.

To take this argument further, agents can by definition exercise discretion. Global scripts do not prescribe action in detail. They also may carry internally conflicting norms or elements that are valued differently. Whereas there may have been support for some aspects of new governance approaches (such as more organizational autonomy), other aspects of governance (e.g. marketization) might be met with scepticism and resistance. New governance modes may also conflict with existing logics. New governance elements are implanted into existing institutions and policy areas and do not necessarily fit well (Gornitzka and Maassen, 2014). The room for interpretation and the potential conflict that this creates are sources for agency. Paraphrasing Scharpf (1997, p. 42), new ideas on governing a system 'will define repertoires of more or less acceptable outcomes of action that will leave considerable scope for the strategic and tactical choices of purposeful actors'. It is highly unlikely that this 'considerable scope' will be used in the same way in each country and, therefore, variation in governance modes seems self-evident.

A second challenge to the convergence hypothesis comes from path dependency. This overlaps to some degree with the previous explanation, for it alludes to existing power configurations and to the firmly and historically rooted institutionalized structures within higher education systems. In fact, the argument goes back to the emergence of the nation state (Neave, 2001). Although governments addressed similar aspects of the fabric of higher education – for instance, funding, certification, and academic employment – there were important differences between countries, resulting from their specific histories and domestic points of departure. There is general acknowledgement that contemporary governance developments are to some extent institutionally path-dependent (Krücken, 2003). Even if there would be convergence to – for example – a state supervision or market-type model of governance, significant differences would still remain because of the deeply ingrained and persisting norms, values, and interests that shine through in current governance arrangements (de Boer, 2003). A variant of this argument, rooted in Scandinavian institutionalism (Czarniawski and Sevón, 1996), is that many governance reforms are translated, filtered, converted, or adjusted because of particular institutional heritages and hence lead to new governance configurations that deviate from the global models (see, e.g., Dobbins and Knill, 2014) or are a combination of old and new configurations through a process of layering (Mahoney and Thelen, 2010).

Besides these two major factors, the literature also points to conflicting institutional logics (e.g. the market logic versus the bureaucracy logic) that play out differently in different national contexts (Jungblut and Vukasovic, 2013). This leads to crises or punctuated change (Gornitzka and Maassen, 2014), or to temporal sorting, where policy and governance developments are determined not so much by means–ends arguments, but rather by the coupling of policy problems and solutions (see Gornitzka and Maassen, 2014; Jungblut and Vukasovic, 2013).

Reviewing the recent literature on policy and governance change, the balance tilts towards the importance of agency as well as contextual and situational factors that may have a significant impact on the direction, pace, and nature of governance change. There are good reasons to assume that behind generic trends considerable variety looms. In the next section we will address a number of studies that support our claim of the establishment of governance arrangements in higher education across European countries that have both similarities and differences. We will then explore whether there are specific governance configurations emerging in response to global scripts.

12.5.2 Comparative Studies on Higher Education Governance across European Countries

It appears safe to say that most European higher education systems have picked up elements of new governance approaches. De Boer et al. (2007), using the governance equalizer, noted that England, the Netherlands, Germany, and Austria were all moving, generally speaking, towards a NPM model (see also Kehm and Lanzendorf, 2006). Nevertheless, striking differences were visible, particularly in the dimension of 'competition'. With strong competition for students, and research funding based on performance, England was a clear outlier in this dimension and it is therefore worthwhile to juxtapose this governance mode with the one in Austria at that time. In Austria, there was very limited competition between institutions. When universities were invited to develop specific profiles, the key driver was not so much competition, but the government's wish for country-wide educational planning. Likewise, performance did not play an important role, either in university–government relations, or internally in relations between rectors and deans (de Boer et al., 2007, p. 145).

In a study across 32 European countries, including Central and Eastern European countries and the Baltic states, the CHEPS Consortium (2006) note similarities in terms of governmental attention to changing funding arrangements, increasing institutional autonomy, introducing market mechanisms and quality assurance mechanisms, and changing internal governance structures, but stress that 'the range of governance reforms across Europe not only differs in terms of content but also in terms of timing' (p. 27). De Boer and File (2009, p. 15) echo this – again based on a comparison of governance trends in Europe – by summarizing that governance reforms are complex and target different areas of the higher education fabric, and that many governments 'have developed their "own versions" of the very same tidal wave'. Zooming in on institutional autonomy, Estermann and Nokkala (2009) make an inventory of how European governments shape aspects of autonomy (e.g. financial autonomy and academic autonomy). They conclude that there is a general trend towards more autonomy, but they emphasize differences across countries and even report some cases where autonomy has decreased. Their follow-up report (Bennetot Pruvot and Estermann, 2017, p. 41–52) offers scorecards for various dimensions of institutional autonomy and gives examples of significant differences. For instance, on the dimension 'organizational autonomy', the United Kingdom ranks first among 28 countries (and is therefore allocated a score of 100 per cent), Lithuania is ranked fifth (88 per cent), Hungary 23rd (56 per cent), and Luxembourg at the bottom (34 per cent). But in another dimension, the pattern is different: for 'academic autonomy', Estonia leads with 98 per cent, the United Kingdom is in the third position (89 per cent), as is Luxembourg (89 per cent), and Lithuania is ranked 26th (42 per cent).

Dobbins (2011) analyses governance reform in the Czech Republic, Poland, Romania, and Bulgaria and arrives at the conclusion that convergence towards the market has taken place. It is important to note that this study mapped the governance arrangements (as a mixture of state steering, market steering, and academic self-rule) through the recent history of these countries, from pre-communist to current times, with the Bologna Process being an important driver for change. While there is undeniably a trend towards the market, the author acknowledges that there are significant differences in how exactly marketization has taken place, and how close governments have come to the market model. The Czech Republic and Poland – with roots in the Humboldtian model – have moved far less in the direction of the market model than Bulgaria and Romania. The latter countries showed more signs of entrepreneurialism in university management, a stronger third-party funding basis, and a clearer move towards the introduction of student tuition fees. Huisman et al. (2018) analysed structural reforms in higher education in post-Soviet countries and reached similar conclusions: indeed, Bologna, internationalization, and marketization were important drivers of change, and, consequently, similar policy developments in these systems, while at the same time local institutional conditions produced convergence.

A recent encompassing comparative approach to governance in higher education is provided by Broucker and de Wit (2015). This study looks at NPM developments in the area of market(ization), budgetary policies, institutional autonomy, and institutional management in England, Portugal, the Netherlands, and Finland and concludes that 'NPM has found its way in HE and HEIs, but at a different speed and with varied intensity . . . Governments use the "toolbox" of NPM as they see fit' (p. 70). Leisyte and Kizniene (2006), analysing NPM developments in Lithuania, illustrate that instruments may actually also be lacking, with policies largely – at the moment of their analysis – being rhetoric.

Based on these studies, it seems safe to conclude that there is a general trend: many countries have introduced reforms in the same areas. Nevertheless, one has to be cautious in declaring convergence. While at first sight there may appear to be increasing similarity across European countries, two caveats lead us to be hesitant regarding a firm claim. First, most research – however sophisticated some of the studies may be – has not comprehensively compared the situations pre- and post-reform (Dobbins, 2011, and Dobbins and Knill, 2014, being noteworthy exceptions). Rather, trends have been identified in a rather interpretative way. Moreover, these trends are often based on the formal governance arrangements, which do not necessarily reflect actual implementation let alone reveal the perceptions of those experiencing the reforms. Second, the studies show that assessments very much depend on the object of focus and the level of detail being sought. For example, there has been a development towards stronger executive leadership, but if one zooms in on how university leaders are elected or selected and the composition of boards, there is an enormous variety of arrangements across Europe (e.g. de Boer et al., 2016).

12.5.3 Specific Configurations?

Not only in relation to governance reform, but also to higher education systems in general, there is often reference to the historical background of the systems (see also our reflections on the role of path dependency), with particular attention to elements of the political-administrative system (Bleiklie and Michelsen, 2013). This explains why notions such as the Anglo-Saxon, Napoleonic, Humboldtian, and Nordic models figure prominently in the discussion on the emergence and evolution of European higher education systems (see, e.g., Neave, 2001). While such labels are generally helpful as sensitizing devices, there are limits to their application. They may aptly describe a model at the time of its emergence (e.g. Humboldtian and Napoleonic models at the beginning of the nineteenth century), but not necessarily reflect contemporary governance arrangements. There may also be a considerable contrast between the model and reality. Whereas the Humboldtian model appears to have some clear and tangible elements (freedom in teaching, learning, and research; unity of teaching and research; university education as cultivation of the self – *Bildung*), some analysts prefer to speak of the Humboldtian model as a Weberian ideal type (see, e.g., Scott and Pasqualoni, 2016); others are more outspoken in calling it a myth (Ash, 2006). In a similar vein, Antikainen (2016) – citing Rinne (2012), but also referencing Esping-Andersen's (1990) notions of the welfare state – is able to list distinctive elements of the Nordic higher education model (e.g. lack of institutional hierarchy, the provision of higher education free of charge, fostering social equality), while at the same time stressing that recent reforms go against the traditional model. In their in-depth analysis of reforms in Scandinavian higher education, Gornitzka and Maassen (2010) emphasize that the 'result is that even in a region with a high level of policy integration and convergence, with similar traditions, and values and norm systems, the reform instrumentation gets a very specific national flavour and colour' (p. 36).

We therefore have some reservations as to whether specific models can be detected in Europe. For some aspects of higher education, it clearly makes sense to speak of such models: for example, Pechar and Andres (2011), using OECD data on expenditure, participation, tuition, and financial aid for students, convincingly show the continuing relevance of welfare regimes (conservative, liberal, social-democratic). On the other hand, there is much variation which cannot be explained by European models (Dobbins and Knill, 2014; Gornitzka and Maassen, 2010) and there are many outliers and counter-examples in the studies discussed so far (even Pechar and Andres, 2011, found the United Kingdom and Finland to be out of step with expectations; Huisman et al., 2018, also found much variation across post-Soviet countries), strongly suggesting that the usefulness of ideal typical models is decreasing. This has led some authors to speak of hybridization of models. The notion of hybridity is already implicit in the title of one of the early analyses of governance – 'An intriguing Janus-head' (Maassen and van Vught, 1988) – which analyses how the Dutch government of the mid-1980s showed elements of steering from a distance but at the same time demonstrated traditional features of state steering. Gornitzka and Maassen (2000), using Olsen's notion of state models, pick up the theme of hybridity and argue that it applies to many European countries. Subsequent research has confirmed the relevance of the notion of hybridity (e.g. Jungblut and Vukasovic, 2013), but has not advanced the mapping of (hybrid) governance models.

12.6 Conclusions

Using different conceptual models to address change in higher education governance in Europe, we have illustrated the shift from government to governance. At first glance, this development appears to represent a change from a combination of government control and academic oligarchy in coordinating higher education, towards a network- and market-based governance approach, characterized by a dynamic, interdependent mixture of multiple levels, actors, and domains. In the new governance configuration that we are witnessing in Europe, the relationship between state and institutions has changed, among other things by empowering institutions, and by giving a more visible role in system coordination to other stakeholders, including agencies which operate at arm's length from the government, institutional leaders, and students.

There are, however, three important qualifications to be made. First, more organizational autonomy does not mean that the state is actually 'stepping back'. Governments retain ultimate authority, despite higher education institutions having more organizational autonomy. Market forces may offer institutions opportunities for self-directed strategic action, but with governments still deciding on the rules of the game, real autonomy will be limited (de Boer and Enders, 2017). Second, like other reforms in public sectors (see, e.g., Pollitt and Bouckaert, 2004), change comes in different shapes. Our analysis has confirmed this for higher education, showing important differences across systems and time. Third, the many attempts to 'map' governance are often snapshots, largely overlooking the extent to which different governance models and instruments overlap and impact on each other, and also ignoring the fact that, besides their regular governance mode, governments often intervene by embarking upon large reform projects. We deem these qualifications to be important for those analysing future governance change in higher education.

References

Antikainen, A. (2016) The Nordic model of higher education. In J. E. Côté and A. Furlong (Eds), *Routledge handbook of the sociology of higher education*, pp. 234–240. London and New York: Routledge.

Ash, M. G. (2006) Bachelor of what, Master of whom? The Humboldt myth and historical transformations of higher education in German-speaking Europe and the US. *European Journal of Education*, 41(2), 245–267.

Bennetot Pruvot, E., and Estermann, T. (2017) *University autonomy in Europe III: The scorecard 2017*. Brussels: EUA.

Bleiklie, I., and Michelsen, S. (2013) Comparing higher education policies in Europe: Structures and reform outputs in eight countries. *Higher Education*, 65(1), 113–133.

Bleiklie, I., Enders, J., Lepori, B., and Musselin, C. (2011) New Public Management, network governance and the university as a changing professional organization. In T. Christensen and P. Laegreid (Eds), *The Ashgate research companion to New Public Management*, pp. 161–176. Farnham: Ashgate.

de Boer, H. (2003) Who's afraid of red, yellow and blue? The colourful world of management reforms. In A. Amaral, V. L. Meek, and I. M. Larsen (Eds), *The higher education managerial revolution?*, pp. 89–108. Dordrecht: Kluwer.

de Boer, H., and Enders, J. (2017) Working in the shadow of hierarchy: Organisational autonomy and venues of external influence in European universities. In I. Bleiklie, J. Enders, and B. Lepori (Eds), *Transforming universities in Europe*, pp. 57–83. Basingstoke: Palgrave.

de Boer, H., Enders, J., and Schimank, U. (2007) On the way towards New Public Management? The governance of university systems in England, the Netherlands, Austria, and Germany. In D. Jansen (Ed.), *New forms of governance in research organizations: Disciplinary approaches, interfaces and integration*, pp. 137–154. Dordrecht: Springer.

de Boer, H., and File, J. (2009) *Higher education governance reforms across Europe*. Brussels: ESMU.

de Boer, H., File, J., Huisman, J., et al. (Eds) (2017) *Policy analysis of structural reforms in higher education: Process and outcomes*. Basingstoke: Palgrave Macmillan.

de Boer, H., and Jongbloed, B. W. A. (2012) A cross-national comparison of higher education markets in Western Europe. In A. Curaj, P. Scott, L. Vlasceanu, and L. Wilson (Eds), *European higher education at the crossroads: Between the Bologna Process and national reform*, pp. 553–571. Dordrecht: Springer.

de Boer, H., Kolster, R., and Vossensteyn, H. (2016) Bestuursbenoemingen over de grens. Hoe is de procedure in andere landen geregeld? [Appointments of leaders across borders. What are the procedures in other countries?]. *TH&MA*, 5–15:81–85.

de Boer, H., and van Vught, F. (2016) Higher education governance in the Netherlands: From a Janus-head to a Trimurti. In N. Cloete, L. Goedegebuure, Å. Gornitzka, J. Jungblut, and B. Stensaker (Eds), *Pathways through higher education research: A Festschrift in honour of Peter Maassen*, pp. 25–32. Oslo: University of Oslo.

Bolton, M. (2003) Public sector performance measurement: Delivering greater accountability. *Work Study*, 52(1), 20–24.

Braun, D., and Merrien, J. X. (Eds) (1999) *Towards a new model of governance for universities? A comparative view*. London: Jessica Kingsley.

Broucker, B., and de Wit, K. (2015) New Public Management in higher education. In J. Huisman, H. de Boer, D. D. Dill, and M. Souto-Otero (Eds), *International handbook of higher education policy and governance*, pp. 57–75. London: Palgrave Macmillan.

Cerych, L., and Sabatier, P. (1986) *Great expectations and mixed performance: The implementation of higher education reforms in Europe*. Stoke-on-Trent: Trentham Books.

CHEPS Consortium (2006) *Funding higher education: A view across Europe*. Brussels: European Centre for Strategic Management of Universities (ESMU).

Clark, B. R. (1983) *The higher education system: Academic organization in cross-national perspective.* Berkeley: University of California Press.

Czarniawski, B., and Sevón, G. (Eds) (1996) *Translating organizational change.* Berlin and New York: Walter de Gruyter.

Dill, D. D. (1997) Higher education markets and public policy. *Higher Education Policy,* 10(3–4), 167–185.

Dobbins, M. (2011) *Higher education policies in Central and Eastern Europe: Convergence towards a common model?* Basingstoke: Palgrave Macmillan.

Dobbins, M., and Knill, C. (2014) *Higher education governance and policy change in Western Europe.* Basingstoke: Palgrave Macmillan.

Esping-Andersen, G. (1990) *The three worlds of welfare capitalism.* Cambridge: Polity Press.

Estermann, T., and Nokkala, T. (2009) *University autonomy in Europe I: Exploratory study.* Brussels: EUA.

Eurydice (2008) *Higher education governance in Europe: Policies, structures, funding and academic staff.* Brussels: Eurydice.

Ferlie, E., Musselin, C., and Andresani, G. (2008) The steering of higher education systems: A public management perspective. *Higher Education,* 56(3), 325–348.

Fryer, K., Antony, J., and Ogden, S. (2009) Performance management in the public sector. *International Journal of Public Sector Management,* 22(6), 478–498.

Gornitzka, Å., and Maassen, P. (2000) Hybrid steering approaches with respect to European higher education. *Higher Education Policy,* 13(3), 267–268.

Gornitzka, Å., and Maassen, P. (2010) Governance reforms, global scripts and the 'Nordic Model'. Accounting for higher education policy change? Paper presented at the conference 'Welfare state traditions, education and higher education policy. Comparing welfare state dimensions of education regimes', 5–7 May 2010, University of Konstanz, Germany.

Gornitzka, Å., and Maassen, P. (2014) Dynamics of convergence and divergence: Exploring accounts of higher education policy change. In P. Mattei (Ed.), *University adaptation in difficult economic times,* pp. 25–41. Oxford: Oxford University Press.

Huisman, J., Smolentseva, A., and Froumin, I. (Eds) (2018) *25 years of transformations of higher education systems in post-Soviet countries.* Cham: Palgrave Macmillan.

Jongbloed, B. W. A. (2003) Marketisation in higher education: Clark's triangle and the essential ingredients of markets. *Higher Education Quarterly,* 57(2), 110–135.

Jungblut, J., and Vukasovic, M. (2013) And now for something completely different? Re-examining hybrid steering approaches in higher education. *Higher Education Policy*, 26(4), 447–461.

Kehm, B. M., and Lanzendorf, U. (2006) *Reforming university governance: Changing conditions for research in four European countries.* Bonn: Lemmens.

van Kersbergen, K., and van Waarden, F. (2004) 'Governance' as a bridge between disciplines: Cross-disciplinary inspiration regarding shifts in governance and problems of governability, accountability and legitimacy. *European Journal of Political Research*, 43, 143–171.

Klein, P. G. (2005) The make-or-buy decision: Lessons from empirical studies. In C. Menard and M. M. Shirley (Eds), *Handbook of new institutional economics*, pp. 435–464. Dordrecht: Springer.

Koch, P. (2013) Overestimating the shift from government to governance: Evidence from Swiss metropolitan areas. *Governance*, 26(3), 397–423.

Krücken, G. (2003) Learning the 'new, new thing': On the role of path dependency in university structures. *Higher Education*, 42, 315–339.

Leisyte, L., and Kizniene, D. (2006) New Public Management in Lithuania's higher education. *Higher Education Policy*, 19(3), 377–396.

Maassen, P. A., and van Vught, F. A. (1988) An intriguing Janus-head: The two faces of the new governmental strategy for higher education in the Netherlands. *European Journal of Education*, 23(1–2), 65–76.

Mahoney, J., and Thelen, K. (2010) *Explaining institutional change: Ambiguity, agency, and power.* Cambridge: Cambridge University Press.

Neave, G. (2001) The European dimension in higher education: An excursion into the modern use of historical analogues. In J. Huisman, P. Maassen, and G. Neave (Eds), *Higher education and the nation state: The international dimension of higher education*, pp. 13–73. Amsterdam and London: Pergamon Press.

Nokkala, T., and Välimaa, J. (2017) Finland: Mergers in the context of continuity. In H. de Boer, J. File, J. Huisman, et al. (Eds) *Policy analysis of structural reforms in higher education: Process and outcomes*, pp. 225–244. Basingstoke: Palgrave Macmillan.

OECD (2008) *Tertiary education for the knowledge society (2 volumes).* Paris: OECD.

Paradeise, C., Reale, E., Bleiklie, I., and Ferlie, E. (Eds) (2009) *University governance: Western European comparative perspectives.* Dordrecht: Springer.

Pechar, H., and Andres, L. (2011) Higher education policies and welfare regimes: International comparative perspectives. *Higher Education Policy*, 24(1), 25–52.

Perellon, J. F. (2005) Path dependency and the politics of quality assurance in higher education. *Tertiary Education and Management,* 11(4), 279–298.

Pierre, J., and Peters, B. G. (2000) *Governance, politics and the state.* Basingstoke: Macmillan.

Pollitt, C., and Bouckaert, G. (Eds) (2004) *Public management reform: A comparative analysis* (2nd ed.). Oxford: Oxford University Press.

Rhodes, R. A. W. (1996) The new governance: Governing without government. *Political Studies,* 44, 652–667.

Rinne, R. (2012) The Nordic university model from a comparative and historical perspective. In J. Kauko, R. Rinne, and H. Kynkäänniemi (Eds), *Restructuring the truth of schooling: Essays on discursive practices in the sociology and politics of education,* pp. 85–112. Jyväskylä: Finnish Education Research Association.

Salazar, J., and Leihy, P. (2013) Keeping up with coordination: From Clark's triangle to microcosmographia. *Studies in Higher Education,* 38(1), 53–70.

Scharpf, F. W. (1997) *Games real actors play: Actor-centered institutionalism in policy research.* Boulder: Westview Press.

Scott, A., and Pasqualoni, P. P. (2016) Invoking Humboldt: The German model. In J. E. Côté and A. Furlong (Eds), *Routledge handbook of the sociology of higher education,* pp. 211–222. London and New York: Routledge.

Sundström, G., and Jacobsson, B. (2007) *The embedded state. From government to governance: The case of Sweden.* Stockholm: SCORE.

van Vught, F. (Ed.) (1989) *Governmental strategies and innovation in higher education.* London: Jessica Kingsley.

van Vught, F. (1995) *Policy models and policy instruments in higher education: The effects of governmental policy-making on the innovative behaviour of higher education institutions.* Vienna: Institute for Advanced Studies.

van Vught, F., and de Boer, H. (2015) Governance models and policy instruments. In J. Huisman, H. de Boer, D. D. Dill, and M. Souto-Otero (Eds), *Handbook of higher education policy and governance,* pp. 38–56. London: Palgrave Macmillan.

van Wageningen, A. C. (2015) The legal constitution of higher education policy and governance of the European Union. In J. Huisman, H. de Boer, D. D. Dill, and M. Souto-Otero (Eds) *International handbook of higher education policy and governance,* pp. 95–113. London: Palgrave Macmillan.

Whitley, R. (2012) Transforming universities: National conditions of their varied organisational actorhood. *Minerva,* 50(4), 493–510.

Williamson, O. E. (1991) Strategizing, economizing, and economic organization. *Strategic Management Journal,* 12(2), 75–94.

13 | Governance and Corruption in East and Southeast Asian Higher Education

Close Cousins, Close Encounters

ANTHONY WELCH

Fighting fraud is like the woodpecker:

always pecking at the tree, and digging out the pest.

WAN Gang, Minister of Science and Technology, China *(2010)*

13.1 Introduction

No analysis of governance in East and Southeast Asian higher education could be complete without treatment of its close cousin, corruption. As illustrated in this chapter, of the countries of East Asia – China, (including Macao and Hong Kong), Taiwan, Korea, and Japan – and Southeast Asia (the 10 member states of ASEAN), all suffer from the taint of corruption, albeit to substantially differing degrees. The selected examples herein chart cultures of corruption pervading higher education in the region, which are closely linked to system and institutional governance.

What is the link between governance and corruption? Good governance consists of far more than simple administrative efficiency (Farazmand, 2015): it promotes transparency and ethical behaviour, emphasizes and implements behavioural norms and associated practices, and sanctions transgressors. Poor governance, by contrast, licences various irregularities, both financial and organizational. As the recent IIEP/CHEA 'Advisory Statement for Effective International Practice' underlines, there are clear links between poor governance and corruption: nothing less than the integrity of academic governance and institutions is imperilled by the 'malignant tumour' of corruption (IIEP/CHEA, 2016; Yang, 2008). Defined as the abuse of entrusted power for private gain (personal or material), corruption includes nepotism and cronyism, fraud, theft, bribery, collusion, extortion, cheating, plagiarism, misrepresentation, and sexual harassment, among others (Heyneman, 2004).

The analysis herein initially reviews the literature on governance in higher education and posits the close, if complex, link between governance and corruption – notably, the ways that corruption is antithetical to good governance. Subsequently, the chapter details instances and forms of corrupt behaviour in China and several ASEAN member states, in both public and private sector higher education, revealing the close connection of governance to corrupt practices, and underlining the force of what is, in effect, 'a wake-up call to higher education worldwide . . . HEIs, governments, employers and societies generally, in both developed and developing countries, are far too complacent about the growth of corrupt practices, either assuming that these vices occur somewhere else, or turning a deaf ear to rumours of malpractice in their own organisations' (IIEP/CHEA, 2016, p. 2).

13.2 Government, Governance, and Higher Education

As the role of government has changed in recent decades, so too has governance, including in higher education. In an era of globalization, the role and reach of the nation state has been problematized, although in East Asia in particular the dominance of the developmental state model ensured that a major role persisted for government, and also in higher education (Carroll and Jarvis, 2017; Green, 2013; Welch, 2017). However, some have claimed that there are limits to the developmental state model. China, for example, has been argued to present something of a paradox: dramatic economic growth and progress have been achieved without 'good governance', a trend which to some extent parallels the dramatic rise of Chinese universities in various global ranking schemes over the past decade or so (Khan, 2015; Levin, 2010; Welch, 2016; Welch and Cai, 2011; Yang and Welch, 2012).

Debates around this claim raise the issue of what the constitutive elements of good governance are, and how they might be measured. International agencies have paid close attention to notions of good governance, particularly in recent times. This has included, for example, making certain 'structural adjustment' strictures a requirement – a condition for receipt of development loans (Farazmand, 2015). But in practice, what is commonly invoked in the name of good governance is very much of a neoliberal form: 'market approaches with emphasis on market-like competition among public organizations, results-oriented outputs, performance measurements, empowering managers to fire and hire temporary employees, privatization, efficiency, steering government versus rowing government, and getting rid of bureaucratic rules and regulations' (Farazmand, 2015, p. 14).

This, in turn, raises two questions. Firstly, do the elements listed here actually constitute good governance? Many have argued that the fissiparous effects associated with their implementation contradict any such claims. Data from the USA which show that the bottom 90 per cent of workers endured income stagnation over the past three decades, while the top 1 per cent were the major beneficiaries, is paralleled to a greater or lesser degree in East and Southeast Asia, where although hundreds of millions have been lifted from poverty over recent decades, most spectacularly in China, the gap between rich and poor has nonetheless widened. The current rise of right-wing populist nationalist movements both in Europe and in parts of Asia speaks, at least in part, to a rejection of capitalist globalization that, contra the claims of neoliberal economists, has not lifted all boats. In practice, while increasing economic growth overall, capitalist globalization has at the same time widened the gap between rich and poor, and left too many (women, indigenous minorities, rural dwellers, the less educated, and urban poor) on the margins, or simply left out (Atkinson, 2015; Held et al., 1999; Piketty, 2014; Sassen, 1998; Sklair, 2001, 2002, 2016; Stiglitz, 2002, 2016). Even such stoutly economic organizations as the World Bank have acknowledged its limitations (Robertson et al., 2009).

If, as is argued here, market-like, capitalist globalization yields such highly unequal results, there is a need for a more inclusive model of globalization. It is for this reason that the notion of sound governance has been put forward. This can include both indigenous governance traditions (powerful versions of which, for example, were evident in ancient times, in both the Persian and Chinese empires) and the contemporary role of global agencies (such as UNESCO, ILO, UNDP, and UNICEF), as well as NGOs in areas such as the environment, migration, health, education, and women's empowerment, that represent, in various ways, inclusive, counter-capitalist forms of globalization. Rather than an emphasis on social control, cheap labour, and profit, the focus here is on transparency, cooperation around capacity development, democracy, equity, legitimacy, and resistance to predatory, capitalist forms of globalization (Sklair, 1999, 2001, 2002). While there is no one version, such models of governance are more about 'concertation, cooperation and alliance formation rather than the traditional processes of coercion, command and control [that are more reflective of traditional models of government]' (van Kersbergen and van Waarden, 2004; Levi-Faur, 2012, 2013). Given the above account, then, the link between good governance and capitalist globalization is not tenable.

Secondly, are the above models of globalization, with their associated forms of governance, universal or another Western import? East Asia suggests an alternative, with the state traditionally closely involved in all aspects of national development, governance, and institution building. This includes the higher education sector, which has often been seen as both a pillar of economic growth and human capital development, and as a major repository of national history and culture. There is widespread consensus as to the key contribution that education has made to the overall development of East Asia, and even today, in both East and Southeast Asia, universities are seen as having 'played a remarkable role in the accelerated process of state formation' (Green, 2013, p. 305).

One point on which most analysts would agree is that governance is not coextensive with government (Capano et al., 2015). As an early report indicated, 'governance transcends the state to include civil society organizations and the private sector, because all are involved in most activities promoting sustainable human development' (UNDP, 1997, p. 11). This certainly includes higher education, particularly in Southeast Asia, and to a lesser extent some parts of East Asia. Even this wider concept, however, still omits key international dimensions – both the phenomena of growing regionalism and of globalization, the latter of which, in particular, is argued to be having a greater and greater impact on the state, including forms of governance: 'Governance in developing nations is more dominated by these global forces, and less domestic dynamics' (Farazmand, 2015, p. 17). Equally, governance is dynamic, with modes shifting according to changing circumstances. In education, for example, this could result in either greater institutional autonomy or more intrusion by the state (Capano et al., 2015). At times, in the name of accountability, the rhetoric of the former is paralleled by the reality of the latter: the so-called steering from a distance at times results in more steering, with less distance.

13.3 Governance in East and Southeast Asia

Context, however, is critical. While much of the literature on higher education governance still stems from the West, the allusion to distinct forms of governance in East and Southeast Asia makes an understanding of this context indispensable to any assessment of prevailing patterns. The extraordinary diversity evident in East and Southeast Asia makes this no easy task. Reforms include moves towards market socialism (Viet Nam and China); limited decentralization of university governance (Indonesia, Malaysia, and China); distinctions between public and private higher education sectors (China and ASEAN); massification outstripping regulatory capacity (China, Viet Nam, Indonesia, and Thailand); the selection of some leading universities for pilot projects featuring greater, if still limited, administrative autonomy (Thailand, Indonesia, and Malaysia); efforts to transform at least a few universities into 'world-class' institutions (China, Malaysia, and Viet Nam); devolution of the administration of the large majority of universities to provincial or municipal levels (China); privatization and corporatization of public universities (Malaysia, Indonesia, and Thailand); the spread of more or less radical forms of Islam in higher education (Indonesia, Malaysia, Thailand, and Philippines); incipient higher education regionalism (ASEAN and ASEAN-China); a greater emphasis on competition, rankings, and league tables (ASEAN and China); and recent steps towards greater regulation of certain functions within Chinese universities.[1]

As will be seen, this diversity of context also includes notable elements that undermine good governance in the sector: cronyism in senior higher education appointments (Malaysia and Viet Nam), and various forms of entrenched corruption in higher education governance (China and ASEAN). In China and several ASEAN states, leaders of HEIs are effectively selected by government/the ruling party, either explicitly or in practice. Equally, quality assurance processes are by no means always independent of government. In some cases, as elaborated below, reforms to license greater autonomy in at least some universities have only been partially implemented, as, despite proclamations of 'empowered governance', governments have proved reluctant to cede centralized power, or have implemented the schemes poorly, or very slowly (Aminudin and Welch, 2012; Malaysian Education Blueprint, 2015; Wan and Ahmad, 2015; Welch, 2012b, 2016). Such controls are poor guards against cronyism or corruption of governance through political interference.

13.3.1 Governance in Chinese Higher Education

China provides a good example of both powerful indigenous governance traditions from the past, some of which have left a powerful legacy, and contemporary forms that impart a distinctive character to governance, including in higher education. The two terms *zizhiquan* and *zizhuquan* describe two different concepts of autonomy, only one of which is more commonly used in Western governance discourse. The former term refers to the notion of autonomy as independence (connoting, in Chinese, a form of political sovereignty), while the latter refers to a concept of autonomy as self-mastery. It is this latter term that best captures the notion of university governance within China, that, in setting overall institutional goals as well as managing academic, personnel, and financial matters, 'focuses not only on the possession of power but also on the ability and skills of using that power to create conditions for universities to fulfil their historical goal of meeting the needs of society' (Zhong, 1997, p. 7; see also Zhong and Hayhoe, 2001).

Effectively, this is a form of power-sharing between universities and the Chinese government, whose recent re-assertion of ideological and administrative control over Chinese universities has arguably altered the balance. The dual system of university leadership, comprising the University President on the one hand, and the Party Secretary on the other, is another important element, echoed at individual Faculty level and in administrative departments such as Human Resources, or the ubiquitous International Office. In key universities under direct control of the Ministry of Education (MoE), the President and Communist Party Secretary are appointed by the MoE. Vice-Presidents and Vice-Party Secretaries are also appointed by the Ministry, but in consultation with the President and the Party Secretary (Li and Yang, 2014, pp. 32–33).[2]

There is no linguistic equivalent within the Chinese language for the notion of university autonomy as it is understood in English. This has shaped a different governance tradition in Chinese higher learning institutions. Ancient China had two sets of institutions of higher learning (for which there are some parallels in proximate East Asia). On the one hand, there were institutions at the provincial and prefectural level that supported the 'ladder of success' that led ultimately to the imperial examination system and institutions such as the Hanlin Academy, *Guozijian* (college for the sons of the Emperor), and *Taixue* (Institution of Supreme Learning) (He, 1967).[3] Such institutions were effectively 'an arm of bureaucratic power' (Hayhoe, 1996, p. 41). On the other hand, there were the *Shuyuan* (scholarly academies, or societies), often headed by a famous scholar, whose scholarship attracted acolytes and colleagues (Hayhoe, 1996; Zhong, 1997). The important point here is that, as Hayhoe highlights, neither of the two sets of institutions 'were characterized by the kind of autonomy enjoyed by the European university'. The former institutions 'were clearly an arm of the state for the recruitment and training of civil officials', while the experience of the latter varied between 'fragile autonomy' and ruthless suppression, 'on the grounds that they were subversive to imperial authority' (Hayhoe, 1996, pp. 11–12; see also Cheung, 2010).

Much the same was true after the revolution of 1949. The current governance system, outlined initially in the 1950s and 1960s, accorded little autonomy to universities. It was 'one-way and top-down', covering such fields as teaching, syllabi, and textbooks (Li and Yang, 2014, p. 22). The later 'Decision on the reform of the educational system' (1985) featured autonomy as a priority, and was followed in 1993 by the 'Programme for Education Reform and Development in China' that saw government as a facilitator, ceding more autonomy to universities. The subsequent 'Higher Education Law of the PRC' (1998) brought into being the 'President responsibility system' (校长负责制) and specified seven domains in which HEIs were to exercise autonomy: student admissions, specialized establishment, teaching affairs, research and service, international exchange and cooperation, administrative structures and personnel management, and financial affairs, including property management (PRC, 1998, Articles 30–38). A subsequent survey found, however, that autonomy was lacking in all domains, with the exception of academic staff recruitment (Li and Yang, 2014, p. 24), while national 'buffer agencies' such as the Centre for Degree and Graduate Education or National Evaluation Committee remain affiliates of the MoE. Quality assurance, too, remains in practice effectively under the control of the MoE, with only limited transparency (Raza, 2010).

The contradictions found between policies of enhanced autonomy on the one hand and 'the reality of constraints that universities continue to experience' (Yang et al., 2007; see also Raza, 2010, pp. 8, 11), on the other, have been exacerbated in recent years by government-imposed guidelines that are limiting research access and affecting academic staff recruitment and evaluation, as well as curriculum and pedagogical content. The so-called *Document 9*, for example, reasserted the central role of the Party, and party ideology, explicitly warning of the dangers from foreign influences (such as constitutional democracy, universal values, freedom of the press, and civil society), including in higher education (ChinaFile, 2013; Xi, 2017, p. 7). Subsequent government orders banning the use of VPNs (virtual private networks) led to public expressions of concern about the effects on research by members of the Chinese Academy of Sciences, as well as of the National People's Congress (UWN, 2017). Issued by organs such as the Central Committee of the CCP's General Office and the State Council General Office, the tenor of recent guidelines to HEIs has been to consolidate Party leadership and control and strengthen ideology (China Copyright and Media, 2015; Xi, 2017).[4] A further document – 'Strengthening and improving propaganda and ideology work in higher education' (2015) – re-emphasized building higher education into 'a strong battlefield for studying, researching and propagating Marxism', and strengthening ideology, by ensuring that the theoretical system of Socialism with Chinese characteristics suffused textbooks, classrooms, and minds (China Copyright and Media, 2015).[5] Reinforced in President Xi's speech to the 19th Party Congress in late 2017 (Xi, 2017), its implementation has affected a range of staffing processes in higher education, including recruitment, regular performance appraisal (conducted by relevant Party Secretaries), and promotion procedures, albeit thus far in the absence of precise metrics. Without checks and balances, this increasing extent of political control can be exploited at system and institutional levels, and has been associated with forms of cronyism and corruption.

A further key feature of Chinese governance patterns, including in higher education, is *guanxi*. In Chinese institutions, which are relationship oriented, rather than rule oriented, *guanxi* – defined as building personal relationship networks – is a long-standing, basic building-block of Chinese culture, referring to connections or relationships between people, including in higher education. It implies preferential treatment given to the partners in an exchange, via easier access to limited resources, increased access to controlled information and grants, and protection from external competitors. In the current highly competitive situation in Chinese universities, it is widely acknowledged to often operate in perverse ways: 'Naturally, if someone has a good *guanxi* with the official in charge, the official could interpret the rules in the way that is favorable for that person' (Guan, 2011 p. 2; see also Yang, 2002). As such, it can undermine merit-based appointments and promotions in Chinese universities, as well as proper access to research grants. Chinese scientists, both at home and abroad, regularly complain about the extent of political interference and *guanxi* that is often important for successful grant applications. As will be shown, it 'encourages researchers not to devote their time on research but on schmoozing with those in power. In some cases, bribery and corruption also take place' (Qiu, 2014, p. 162; see also Welch and Hao, 2014; Yang and Welch, 2010). While *guanxi* is basic to an understanding of Chinese society, its effects in higher education are not always consonant with transparency and good governance.

It has been widely argued that *guanxi* operates along lines of superior–subordinate relations, which value 'hierarchical obedience' (Shin, 2012; Tu, 1993, 1996; Zhai, 2017). In Chinese culture, 'deference to supervisor can be viewed as a typical behaviour and an important outcome' (Liu and Shi, 2017, p. 600). As part of their socialization, Chinese individuals 'learn to be deferential to superiors in higher statuses'; in both social interactions and in the workplace, 'people show respect for seniors and consult them when making decisions' (Zhai, 2017, p. 122). The seniority-based promotion system that dominates the workplace is at times exploited, denying opportunities to more junior talent. Within higher education, and more generally, internalized values of deference to authority ultimately support the reproduction of a hierarchical, paternalistic workplace culture that, along with obedience to family (filial obedience) and teachers, emphasizes obedience to seniors in the workplace. Such a paternalistic workplace governance culture may leave talented younger staff accepting unfair treatment, and feeling vulnerable and impotent; it has also been associated with values of political deference in China, which, in a patriarchal society, are more strongly evident among women than men (Zhai, 2017, p. 132). Such a culture of deference to one's superiors, and the associated legitimation of power, is open to abuse and corruption, including exploitation of younger staff, often female. 'Supervisor's power in the Chinese context expands subordinate's attachment to supervisor and strengthens subordinate's deference to supervisor' (Liu and Shi, 2017, p. 604).

13.3.2 *Governance in Southeast Asian Higher Education*

In Malaysia, too, the above-mentioned promise of devolved governance has not been entirely fulfilled. In 2012, five research universities were formally vested with autonomy: Universiti Malaya (UM), University Sains Malaysia (USM), Universiti Kebangsaan Malaysia (UKM), Universiti Putra Malaysia (UPM), and Universiti Teknologi Malaysia (UTM). But the fact that universities fall within the category of *Badan Berkanun Persekutuan* (Federal Statutory Bodies) means they are effectively semi-government entities, whose activities are 'closely monitored and controlled by the respective ministries' (Saleh and Aiman, 2015, p. 38). As will be shown, in practice this means that institutional leaders are effectively appointed by the ruling party (or coalition), and tend to be aligned with that party/coalition. Cronyism is one alleged outcome.

Indonesia has also displayed a parallel arc of moves towards greater university autonomy being later supplanted by proposals to withdraw it. In the onset of post-1998 democracy, which included significant moves to decentralize education, Indonesia introduced a scheme to reform its higher education system. Of the more than 3,000 higher education institutions across the archipelago, four were selected for a pilot programme that gave greater academic freedom and financial autonomy. Universitas Indonesia (UI), Institut Teknologi Bandung (ITB), Institut Pertanian Bogor (IPB), and Universitas Gadjah Mada (UGM) were accorded the status of *Badan Hukum Milik Negera* (BHMN), or 'state-owned legal institution'. The system proved robust enough for two further institutions to be added in 2004: Universitas Sumatera Utara (USU) and Universitas Perdidikan Indonesia (UPI), Bandung. Later, in 2006, Universitas Airlangga in Surabaya became the seventh institution to be granted BHMN status, which gave universities 'greater power to decide on academic programmes, including curriculum and staffing matters, including promotion of academics, as well as the autonomy to elect university leaders, from the Rector to heads of departments' (Aminudin and Welch, 2012). The substantial reform, however, did not last, and was replaced by a proposal that saw universities revert to the pre-2000 status of *Perguruan Tinggi yang*

Diselenggarakan Pemerintah (PTP), or Government-Administered Universities. Effectively, public universities returned to the status of a 'unit of a government agency under the direction of the Department of National Education' (Kusumadewi and Cahyadi, 2013). Widespread bribery and corruption were associated with Indonesian civil servants, including in the higher education sector (Prabowo and Cooper, 2016).

13.4 The Scope and Role of Corruption

While corruption is by no means new in East and Southeast Asia, three contemporary trends in regional higher education have opened the door more widely to corrupt practices. While governments, agencies, and ministries of (higher) education in the region have been chary of loosening the reins over HEIs, the opposing trend towards decentralization, with its diffusion of authority, has increased opportunities for engaging in illicit behaviour – it has at times been characterized as the decentralization of corruption. A second and widespread trend, towards greater privatization of higher education, has been argued to have a Janus face (Welch, 2007a, 2007b, 2011). An artefact of the increasing mismatch between spiralling demand and limited government resources, one face has overseen the swift growth of private higher education, which often outpaced the growth of public higher education. The often poorly regulated quality of this expansion has licensed various corrupt practices, including over entry procedures, at times with the collusion of government officials. Rapid expansion and massification, including of the private sector, 'puts great demand on admissions processes', as the Advisory Statement put it, somewhat coyly (IIEP/CHAE, 2016, p. 4). Meanwhile, the gaze of the second Janus face focuses on the increasing privatization of *public* HEIs, numbers of which, across the region, have established private for-profit arms, aimed at boosting institutional bottom lines. As illustrated below, however, such ventures have often been associated with inadequate transparency, both financial and organizational.

Lastly, the widespread and ongoing pressure across the region to lift research productivity, especially in (S)SCI journals in English, has helped stimulate an increase in various corrupt research practices in the region, including plagiarism, misrepresentation of students' research as being that of the professor, payment for publication, misuse of research funds, and falsification of research results. Now more subject to the unrelenting pressure of global competition, HEIs have been, at times, too willing to turn a blind eye to such malfeasance in the relentless quest to boost their institutional rankings (Hunter, 2015). Individually and collectively, the three trends not only enhance options for corrupt practices in higher education, but also serve to underscore the close connection to evolving governance norms and practices.

13.4.1 Corruption in East and Southeast Asia

The publication by Transparency International (TI) (2015a) of the corruption ratings of various ASEAN member states was both revealing and hotly contested by some of the listed countries. Nonetheless, the widespread, impressive array of corruption scandals across ASEAN in 2015 made the overall assessment of the region hard to deny (The Diplomat, 2015). They included Malaysia's massive and ongoing 1Mdb scandal,[6] another embracing the Indonesian parliamentary Speaker, charges against the Vice President of the Philippines, and corruption allegations against Thailand's military junta (The Diplomat, 2015, 2016). In East Asia, the ongoing anti-corruption campaign of China's President Xi unearthed spectacular cases involving vast sums of illegal money, abuse of power, nepotism, illegal property dealings, and even murder.[7] High-flying leaders brought down to earth included some from higher education, where practices of using bribery to gain promotion, and the buying and selling of positions in public organizations such as universities, had long been widespread (Xinhuanet, 2015b). Beyond the corrosion of public trust, exacerbation of inequalities, and the weakening of institutions and governance more generally, such practices have been estimated to represent about 8 per cent of total budget spending (Pei, 2007).

Overall corruption ratings for a range of ASEAN member countries, and China, as measured by Transparency International's Corruption Perception Index (CPI), reveal that only Singapore ranks high on transparency (TI, 2014), while the explicit link between governance and corruption in the World Bank's Control of Corruption index again singles out Singapore (World Bank, 2014).

13.4.2 Regionalism

In an era of galloping globalization, however, corruption is by no means limited to the nation state; increasingly, it is a cross-border phenomenon (Welch, 2016, 2017, 2018). As the recent Advisory Statement highlights, 'the steadily developing sophistication and borderless nature of information and communications technology has expanded the opportunities for fraudsters in all walks of life' (IIE/CHAE, 2016, p. 4). Moreover, the growth of cross-border corruption has outpaced the responses of many nation states in East and Southeast Asia, who have been slow to act to counter such flows: 'where cross-border trade, cultural exchange and regional peace and stability will be so vital, it is worrying that so little effort has been made to tackle corruption at the regional level' (TI, 2015a, p. 4). Links between cross-border corruption, governance, and achieving both national and regional goals was a focus of TI's charter document 'ASEAN Integrity Community': 'the current AEC mission will not achieve its stated goal of creating a single competitive market unless we improve governance structure and practices' (TI, 2015a, p. 10; see also TI, 2015b).

In practice, however, regionalism extends well beyond ASEAN, embracing substantial cross-border flows between several ASEAN member states and parts of southern China, notably Yunnan, Guizhou, and Guanxi.[8] What makes such regional cross-border flows significant is that so much is corrupt and illegal: trafficking of young women as wives or prostitutes; selling of babies; smuggling of jade, vehicles, and drugs; gambling; illegal logging; and mining (Shen, 2011). These activities are sustained by significant levels of bribery, corruption, and collusion (see Chan, 2013, pp. 89–105, 108–115; China Daily, 2014; Eimer, 2014, pp. 186ff, 200, 225–231; Evans et al., 2000; INYT, 2015a, 2015b; NY Times, 2015a; SMH, 2015, Welch 2016, 2018).

Each of these cases highlights governance as an issue, with both borders and distance from the centres of governance being longstanding issues, as the traditional Chinese idiom emphasizes: 'The Mountains are High and the Emperor Far Away' (*Shan gao, huangdi yuan*). Indeed, this irregular, illegal quality of regional cross-border flows has significant implications for conventional theories of governance, in particular for contemporary debates regarding regulatory regionalism (Jayasuriya, 2003, 2010; Robertson, 2008). For both intra-ASEAN and China-ASEAN flows, irregular regionalism might well be a better characterization of such cross-border currents (Scott, 2009; Welch, 2016, 2018).

13.4.3 Defining Corruption

As indicated, a broad definition of corruption, according to TI, is the abuse of entrusted power for private gain, either material or personal. As the above definition implies, the CPI is limited to public sector corruption, involving public officials, civil servants, or politicians. But when, in the private sector, someone is appointed to an academic position as a result of nepotism or cronyism, a bribe is paid to secure a place in a private university, or individuals pocket funds to which they were not entitled, this is clearly no less corrupt than similar occurrences in the public sector.

As instanced herein, using definitions and examples of corruption that are confined to the public sector is inadequate in two senses. Firstly, corruption is no respecter of arbitrary lines between public and private; in practice, it is at least as evident in private HEIs. While this is acknowledged by TI in framing their CPI – 'Private sector corruption is characterized by groups from this sector influencing decisions and actions that lead to abuses of entrusted power' (TI, n. d.) – the definition is rather weak, and does not embrace several forms of corruption detailed below. Secondly, the extension of private higher education over the past decade or two has increased both the potential for and the level of corruption. Again, the implications for governance are substantial. As governments in the region increasingly resiled from previous levels of support for public higher education, if not in absolute terms then at least in per-student funding, public HEIs moved to diversify their income streams. In East and Southeast Asia, a common resort has been to establish private sector, for-profit arms. Hence, it is proving to be increasingly difficult to draw clear lines between public and private, including in higher education.

That this has clearly been the case is evident in both ASEAN member states and China. Data from China illustrate the problem starkly: while enrolments rose more than fivefold in a matter of years, state support increased by a much smaller amount (Xinhuanet, 2010).[9] Effectively, from 1998 to 2003, enrolments rose by

230 per cent, while state funding rose by only 140 per cent (Sun and Barrientos, 2009, p. 192; Wu and Gao, 2010; Zhao and Sheng, 2008).[10] In Viet Nam, a similar gap opened up: student numbers rose 13-fold between 1987 and 2009, but higher education teaching numbers rose only three-fold. Largely as a result of the resultant cost squeeze, the financial condition of numerous HEIs in ASEAN member states and in China has become fragile: more face financial difficulties, and/or substantial levels of debt. In China, significant numbers are 'in the red' (Wu and Gao, 2010), while in a recent survey, few public HEIs in Thailand were assessed as financially solid (Welch, 2012a). The effects on institutional governance can be profound, as the President of an Indonesian university lamented some years ago: 'My main task is to raise funds and obtain money' (Jakarta Post, 2006). The potential for corruption is consequential.

The growing gap between spiralling enrolments and limited state support forced public sector HEIs to diversify income sources, often resorting to establishing parallel private programmes or institutions. The effect is to substantially blur the line between public and private in higher education (Welch, 2011, 2012b). As detailed below, the implications for corruption are substantial, if not always visible: data regarding such new income streams are often neither complete nor transparent, giving rise to numerous complaints and charges, including of fraud. Hence, one effect of the blurring of the distinction between public and private is to create more opportunities for corruption.

13.4.4 Measuring the Effects of Corruption

How important is it to measure the diverse effects of corruption? Corruption erodes public trust, makes it increasingly difficult to deliver basic services (by wasting scarce resources), and weakens good governance and civil society. Beyond these important effects, surveys and analyses of corruption among ASEAN member states also provide some measure of its economic effects (Wescott, 2003). It was estimated by Thailand's National Counter Corruption Commission (NCCC), for example, that up to 30 per cent of government procurement budgets could be lost due to corruption, an amount which, at the minimum, almost equalled the entire budget of the Ministry of Agriculture. At the upper end, it would exceed the combined budgets of Agriculture and Public Health (Wescott, 2003). Data from Viet Nam revealed that in

1998, nearly one-third of Viet Nam's public investment expenditure – around 5 per cent of GDP – was lost to fraud and corruption, a situation which had not improved during the following five years (Wescott, 2003). As elsewhere in ASEAN, the situation in Viet Nam is not helped by poor public sector pay and the associated widespread practice of moonlighting. In China, it has been estimated that bribery, kickbacks, theft, and misspent funds (including in higher education) amounted to at least 3 per cent of GDP (Pei, 2007). Since 2013, President Xi's ongoing anti-corruption campaign has unearthed bribery on a massive scale, including in the military, railways, power industry, and higher education.

13.4.5 Academic Corruption

The above forms of corruption translate to higher education in a range of ways, embracing behaviour that is illegal, unprofessional, or both. As numerous analyses have shown, corrupt practices in higher education take various forms. These can include issuing fraudulent certificates (for payment); distortions in procurement (regarding new university buildings, or maintenance contracts); accepting or paying bribes, or exploiting students for sex, in return for entry into university, passing a course, or granting a degree; offering or accepting payments for higher grades; levying private payments for additional tuition, without which the student will not pass the exam; claiming fake qualifications; engaging in cronyism/nepotism; engaging in plagiarism; falsifying research results; passing off students' research as that of the professor; misusing research funds; or paying bribes to secure academic posts, get promotion, or gain programme or institutional accreditation (Bakhari and Leach, 2009; Caixin, 2013, 2016a, 2016b; China Daily, 2010a, 2010b; Hallak and Poisson, 2007; Heyneman, 2004, 2009, 2011; ICAC, 2015; IIEP/CHEA, 2016; qq.com, 2014; TI, 2005, 2013; Xinhuanet, 2015a, 2015b; Yang 2008, 2016). Such practices weaken higher education by lowering quality overall, degrading public and employer confidence in the abilities of graduates and qualifications of HEIs, and undermining the strength of qualifications and quality of governance. Many such forms of corruption relate directly to institutional governance, as captured in the traditional Eastern idiom 'An open door to the safe is an invitation to thieve' (Hallak and Poisson, 2007, p. 6).

This has broader implications for society: if an education system is seen to be based on corruption and cronyism, there is a loss of trust not only in educational qualifications and expertise, but in governance more broadly and the political system as a whole (Heyneman, 2011). In addition, the loss of economic efficiency can be substantial: it has been estimated by some that, in extreme cases, rates of return to education can be reduced by as much as 70 per cent, and life-time earnings of individuals by as much as 50 per cent (Heyneman et al., 2008).

Academic corruption is not limited to (South) East Asia, of course, or even Asia (Mohanty, 2015; TI, 2013). It occurs in every environment, and is complicated by increasing global mobility, and underpinned by a move towards charging high fees, most notably for international students. In even the wealthiest systems, the incentive to enrol students into such high-fee-paying programmes, whether or not the student actually attends, and whether their entry qualifications have been rigorously checked – and at times by falsely promising a level of infrastructure that, upon arrival, the student finds sorely lacking – has often proved to be too tempting (ICAC, 2015).[11] The links to lax governance were highlighted by the Colby Nolan case in Pennsylvania in 2004. It centred on a student who paid US$ 299 for a Bachelor's degree, but was subsequently granted an MBA on the basis that he had 'work experience', including baby-sitting and retail management. That the 'student' was ultimately outed as a cat (named Colby Nolan), underlined the failure to adequately regulate the spread of degree mills that, in the USA and elsewhere, were very willing to corruptly grant bogus degrees for cash (NBC News, 2004). But research malpractice is also more widespread than was supposed (Martinson et al., 2005), while in Germany at least two federal Ministers have resigned in recent years over allegations that their PhDs were plagiarized. A third was ultimately cleared, after review (BBC, 2015b; The Guardian, 2013; Reuters, 2016; see also IIEP/CHEA, 2016, p. 2). Together with other examples, such as the suspension of the President and two top aides of the University of Toulon on charges of accepting bribes (Washington Post, 2009), these cases highlight issues of the adequacy of governance, at both institutional and national levels.

Nonetheless, although corruption may be ubiquitous, the levels found in (South) East Asia are so pervasive that they are accepted by some as routine. As an acting rector of a substantial university in Thailand explained recently, 'Ramkhamhaeng University considers cheating in exams by students to be trivial. It is common in all exams' (Young, 2013, p. 1). The same is true in Viet Nam (McCornac, 2009, 2012). The following section charts major contours of academic corruption in China and Southeast Asia, revealing both its pervasiveness and its multiple forms.

13.5 Charting Corruption in East and Southeast Asian Higher Education

It is hard to overstate the importance of understanding the forms and extent of corruption in higher education in the region, and their links to governance. Such corrupt practices involve lowering entry standards, selling of posts, bribery, other illicit financial gains, and collusion, inter alia. One index of growing concern is seen in Figure 13.1, which reveals a major rise in Chinese journals of articles devoted to the twin themes of academic misconduct and academic integrity.

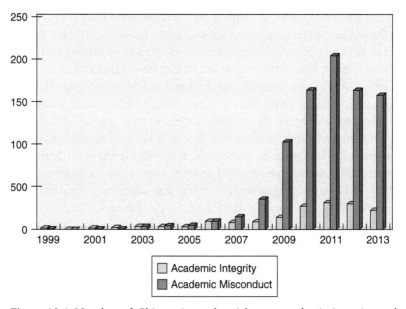

Figure 13.1 Number of Chinese journal articles on academic integrity and academic misconduct (1999–2013)

In Indonesia, too, concerns have been growing, including with regard to the practice of *Jalur Khusus* ('Special Path'), whereby places in high-demand programmes such as Engineering are reserved and then sold to wealthy families at very high rates – from 150 million Rupiah (US$ 17,650) to 225 million Rupiah (US$ 26,470). At the highly reputable *Gadjah Madah* University, 28 per cent of 34,000 applicants for places in 2008 were found to have paid large 'brokerage' fees to middlemen, in return for a guaranteed place (UWN, 2008; Welch, 2011, p. 43). While institutional leaders claim that such guaranteed places are limited to about 10 per cent of the current student intake, and that they cross-subsidize places for poorer students, it is often much less clear whether such cross-subsidization indeed takes place, and, if so, how many students benefit. In the absence of full transparency, critics allege that the proceeds of such sales have at times been diverted into the pockets of institutional leaders (Jakarta Post, 2004, 2005; Tempo, 2003; UWN, 2008). It was suspected that *Jalur Khusus* schemes, too, have benefitted individuals from the same HEIs (Jakarta Post, 2005).

Other forms of corruption in Indonesian higher education relate to the national quality assurance process, upon which individual HEIs' reputations depend. A poor rating by the national accreditation agency Badan Akredtitasi Nasional (BAN), for example, would make it difficult to recruit students and secure income. In one such case, a private HEI's Faculty of Engineering, faced with an upcoming evaluation of its facilities by BAN, knew all too well that its engineering infrastructure was inadequate. The Faculty thus approached local engineering firms to borrow numerous items of major equipment. The day after the inspection, which ultimately yielded a satisfactory B rating, all items of equipment were promptly returned to the local firms. Such stories are not uncommon: 'Many private schools provide engineering education without sufficient equipment to support the curriculum and end up compromising the quality of their graduates' (Buchori and Malik, 2004, p. 261). The system, which depends on bribery of and collusion with relevant officials, underscores the need for improved governance, in particular a more effective regulatory regime, against a background where the widespread and persistent culture of corruption (widely known in Indonesia as KKN – *Korupsi, Kolusi, Nepotisme*) can undermine the effectiveness of quality assurance procedures, and the quality of higher education more generally

(IIEP/CHEA, 2016, p. 4; Monocolumn, 2012; Siaputra and Santosa, 2015; Welch, 2011).

Corruption involving bribery and collusion in Viet Nam has been exacerbated by the growth of private higher education, which, although still relatively small, is targeted to grow to 40 per cent of total higher education enrolments by 2020 (HERA, 2010). Serious problems at two private HEIs – which, as non-state institutions, were ineligible to receive public funds – related to over-enrolment, in a context where the Ministry of Education and Training (MOET) legally defines enrolment limits for such institutions. Dong Do University was found by MOET to have over-enrolled its quota by 280 per cent. Accusations that Dong Do officials were themselves profiting from the practice were allegedly part of a wider pattern of corruption involving, inter alia, 'score trading, diploma fabrication, title purchasing, deceptive reporting, plagiarism and misuse of funds' (Tuoitrenews, 2012; see also McCornac, 2009, 2012; Viet Nam News, 2002a).

A second issue – that of entry standards – involved Dong Do leaders accepting bribes by students or their families, in order to secure entry. This, too, was strictly illegal, but allegedly occurred in an effort to boost numbers of enrolments and income levels (Overland, 2006; Welch, 2011). The practice, also common in Cambodia (Dawson, 2009), exacerbates inequalities, since poor students cannot afford the bribes. As Seila, a 21-year-old from a poor family of rice farmers, lamented in response to a government crackdown that saw pass rates at the Grade 12 exam (which are critical to university entrance) plummet from 87 per cent the year before to just 26 per cent: 'I think if I could have cheated I could have passed, ... but ... I couldn't get the answer sheet' (The Guardian, 2014).

Official investigations uncovered substantial breaches linked to bribery and corruption: papers were given inflated grades, at times by unqualified markers; several dozen students were enrolled without even being on the list, or without upper secondary graduation certificates (Welch, 2011, pp. 143–144). As a result, Dong Do's 2002 enrolments were cancelled and the university was given strict instructions to end such illegal practices. Ha Noi police were called in to investigate, and, if necessary, to prosecute the Rector and other senior staff responsible. The Deputy Chair of the university's board of management was subpoenaed 'for his involvement in one of the biggest scandals to date in the education sector' (Viet Nam News,

2002a, 2002c). The former director of its training department was also subsequently charged.

Such incidents clearly raise questions of governance – but also of government. Of major concern is that, at times, gamekeeper has turned poacher: the very officials responsible for ensuring standards and transparency were themselves part of the corruption. In a separate case in 2002, two senior MOET officials, each at Deputy Minister level, were reprimanded or sacked after involvement in the 'Asian International University (AIU)' scam. Both officials were linked to a 'bogus university, which ... enrolled thousands, awarding worthless paper degrees' (Viet Nam News, 2002b). After five years, AIU ceased operation, leaving more than 2,000 students stranded, and with collective debts of hundreds of thousands of dollars. In another incident, the so-called American Capital University (ACU) offered an MBA programme together with a partner, the variously titled Singapore (later Senior) Management Training Centre. Both institutions became defunct, again leaving substantial numbers of students thousands of dollars out of pocket (Ashwill, 2006).

Pressures for income diversification have also led to corrupt practices at times. In the face of the kinds of cost pressures alluded to above, institutional responses across ASEAN have been broadly similar: public HEIs in several countries mounted what are variously termed 'Extension', 'Diploma', or 'Executive' courses, for high fees. Purportedly developed in response to demand, the programmes have much lower entry criteria than regular courses; in some cases, they are open to anyone who can pay. Commonly, the same staff from the parent institution teach such 'Extension' courses, thereby lowering the quality of teaching and research programmes within the mother institution, since staff involved are less available to students and have no time to revise curricula or undertake research. Quality is also problematic within many such 'special' courses, where much the same qualification is offered, but with much less demanding academic standards.

As alluded to earlier, Thailand's Office for National Education Standards and Quality Assessment (ONESQA) estimated that no more than 10 universities, all public, were financially solid. But even those became increasingly dependent on high-fee parallel programmes: responding to the regional currency crisis of the late 1990s, public HEIs raised income from other sources by 450 per cent, leading to intense competition among public sector HEIs to offer 'Executive' programmes, of sometimes dubious quality, for substantial fees. Some public HEIs reported 60 per cent of their income as having derived from such commercial ventures, with individual faculties reporting as much as 75 per cent (Poapangsakorn, 2008). The resource squeeze drove public HEIs to compete vigorously with private HEIs, particularly by establishing fee-paying programmes at 'learning centres': 'Many of them are using shopping centres as their branches' (Bangkok Post, 2008). Lack of transparency in the dispersal of the significant additional income earned via such programmes has only fuelled charges that funds were at times being diverted to institutional leaders, and/or those leading the programmes. Weak governance processes at both institutional and national levels allowed such practices to continue.

Wider problems related to financial probity and transparency also surfaced. In Malaysia, rising numbers of complaints to Malaysia's National Consumer Complaints Centre in 2009 centred on 'Executive' courses offered by public HEI 'subsidiaries'. The CEO of the Malaysian Qualifications Authority indicated that most of the courses offered by commercial arms of public universities fell outside the Malaysian Qualifications Framework. Once again, poor financial transparency led to allegations that Deans and others were personally profiting from such exercises. Cases in which the nominal student allegedly paid someone else to complete academic work set for the degree underline the failure of adequate governance processes at both institutional and, arguably, national levels.

13.5.1 China: Academic Fraud, Bribery, Collusion, Fake Degrees

Financial transparency, while important, is by no means the only concern, however. Widespread academic corruption in China takes many forms, and undermines the strength of the undoubted and impressive rise of Chinese higher education and research in recent years (Yang and Welch, 2012).[12] The range and pervasiveness of academic fraud has led to it being characterized as 'an industry of plagiarism, invented research and fake journals that Wuhan University estimated in 2009 was worth $150 m, a fivefold increase on just two years earlier' (The Economist, 2013). Paying bribes to place one's article in a journal is a widespread, and growing, practice.

In response to a Chinese government survey, *Nature* reported in 2010 that 'a third of more than 6,000 scientific researchers at six leading institutions admitted to plagiarism, falsification or fabrication' (The Economist, 2013). A 2012 survey of the US *PubMed* database revealed that China led the world in retractions due to duplication.[13] In 2010, after finding that 70 papers submitted to an international journal by Chinese scientists had been fabricated, the leading British medical journal *The Lancet* urged the Chinese government to 'assume stronger leadership in scientific integrity' (The Economist, 2010). In addition, some mainland academic entrepreneurs fake scholarly articles which they then sell to academics, as well as marketing counterfeit versions of existing medical journals in which they sell publication slots. Placing an article in one of the counterfeit journals could cost as much as US$ 650, while buying a fake article is a comparative bargain, at perhaps US$ 250. In one such case, according to police, the racket had netted its creators several million yuan (US$ 500,000 or more) since 2009. Buyers of such services were generally medical researchers in quest of promotion (The Economist, 2013).

Bribery and corruption are not new, of course, having also been reported in the ancient imperial systems of exams, and sometimes resulting in the execution of perpetrators (He, 1967; Heyneman, 2009; Min, 2004; Miyazaki, 1981). In the fiercely competitive contemporary world of Chinese higher education, however, widespread reports of misuse of research funds are attributed to a culture in which 'sound research programmes are nothing compared with rapport with officials in charge. It is even more disgusting that some intellectuals and government officials collude to cheat, in the name of satisfying the country's strategic needs' (China Daily, 2010b).

As seen, the actual allocation of major research grants, too, is tainted: 'the connections with bureaucrats and a few powerful scientists are paramount ... To obtain major grants in China it is an open secret that doing good research is not as important as schmoozing with powerful bureaucrats and their favourite experts' (Shi and Rao, 2010, p. 1128). Other investigations have highlighted the practice of paying bribes to secure promotion, and buying and selling of positions, the money for which is recouped by on-selling other, lower-level positions (Caixin, 2016a, 2016b; CCTV, 2011; Huffington Post, 2014; qq.com, 2014; Xinhuanet, 2015a, 2015b). In 2015 alone, the Central Commission for Discipline Inspection (CCDI) listed 32 officials at

HEIs for investigation. Of these, 12 were suspected of severe disciplinary violations, and 20 of violations of Party rules and the law (Xinhuanet, 2015a).[14]

High-profile figures have been charged with listing fake degrees, part of a wider pattern of business leaders and party officials 'gilding their resumes with doctorates' (UWN, 2014a). Bribery to gain entry to well-known universities is also not uncommon, netting one admissions director some US$ 3.6 million from just 44 students (NY Times, 2015b). Collusion between businessmen and officials while jointly undertaking Executive MBA (EMBA) programmes has been alleged (UWN, 2014b), while a high-profile investigation of a leading university by the CCDI led to recent charges of 'misuse of research funds, safety problems related to the university's new campus construction projects ... and poor regulation of university-run enterprises including hospitals associated with the university'. This, it claimed, created a 'ripe condition for corruption' (UWN, 2014c). Misuse of research funds, in particular, is said to be endemic: 'Across academia, research funding is used for personal travel, meals, entertainment and lodging. Dinners with friends are written up as business meetings, and expenses for custom-made home furnishings are labeled "buying pencils for children"' (Caixin, 2013).

Regular incidents of fake scientific results and plagiarism continue to surface even at leading universities (with one president claiming to have dealt with more than 40 cases at his own university within two years). The high incidence has been linked to a publish-or-perish culture known as *jigong jinli* – the quest for quick success and short-term gain (Nature News, 2010). In 2008 a major Chinese scientific journal editor's scrutiny of submitted articles revealed 31 per cent of 2,233 articles contained examples of plagiarism (Nature News, 2012). A 2008 survey of 1,641 students at 10 universities revealed that more than one in five students admitted to changing data that didn't match expectations. More troublingly, while 60 per cent of PhD students reported that they sometimes witnessed misconduct, only 5 per cent would report it. At least as troubling was that students' tolerance of misconduct increased the longer they stayed in education. Once again, links to wider notions of governance were important, with one researcher pointing to 'a broader lack of honesty in governance [that] makes it tough to build a culture of honest research' (Nature News, 2012). Indeed, in a high-profile case, a Urology professor at the celebrated Huazhong University of Science and Technology in Wuhan was jailed for five and a half months after hiring thugs to beat up a critic and well-known exposer of academic fraud who had argued against his election to the august Chinese Academy of Science (CAS) (Chemistry World, 2010). In response to this corrupt culture, the CCDI announced a third round of inspections of university science and technology departments in 2014; despite this, 2015 yielded a further rich crop of convictions (UWN, 2014c, 2014d; Xinhuanet, 2015b). The effects on the system are profound and pervasive. Inevitably, such an entrenched culture of corruption 'wastes resources, corrupts the spirit, and stymies innovation' (Shi and Rao, 2010, p. 1128; see also ScienceMag, 2011).

13.5.2 Cronyism, Nepotism, 'Tuition Classes'

Cronyism in higher education appointments and promotions is a further troublesome element that undermines sound governance and weakens institutional and system efficiency. In China, the long-standing and powerful culture of *guanxi* means that at times, the strength of an individual's relationship network is more important than performance in determining promotions and results of job applications. In Malaysia, collusion and political interference have been alleged in the appointment of Vice Chancellors, and in action taken against academics whose independence is seen as a threat to the regime (IIEP/CHEA, 2016, p. 4). The effective termination of the respected Datuk Dr. Mohamad Redzuan Othman, the head of the University of Malaya's Centre for Democracy and Elections (UMcedel) in 2014 was one such instance. After polls conducted by Professor Redzuan's Centre revealed falling support for both the ruling UMNO party and its leader, he was instructed by the Education Ministry in mid-2014 to resign as UMcedel Director, and told that his tenure as Dean of the Faculty of Arts and Social Sciences in the university was also being revoked. The action provoked a former Deputy Education Minister (at the time a Senior Fellow at UM), to resign in protest at blatant political interference. Direct interference from the university's Board of Directors Chairman was alleged: 'UM is just like an UMNO branch to Arshad' (Malaysia Today, 2014a, 2014b, 2014c; see also Wan and Ahmad, 2015). In a further instance, two Deputy Vice Chancellors from the same university were removed in early 2015, amid allegations that their dismissals were politically motivated (Malaysian Insider, 2015).

Last, but not least, is the common practice of levying extra fees for what are called in Myanmar 'tuition classes'. While explained to some extent by low public sector salaries in the region, the practice nonetheless falls within the definition of corruption indicated herein. By no means limited to Myanmar, the practice there is common at all levels of education. By restricting the curriculum content covered in regular classes, the teacher ensures that students cannot pass without also enrolling in additional, fee-based classes, taught out of hours, by the same teacher. Students unable to afford the significant additional fees are condemned to fail. The practice is also common in Cambodia (The Guardian, 2014).

13.5.3 Countering Corruption: The Role of Governance

Better governance can certainly be a means to counter corruption in higher education. As demonstrated in this chapter, however, in some instances gamekeeper has turned poacher: the very officials charged with countering corruption have themselves at times proved to be perpetrators. Within HEIs, Deans and Deputy Presidents have on occasion been perpetrators. Corruption is no respecter of rank; indeed, the financial and other 'rewards' are often greater at higher levels.

A further barrier to effective regulation of corruption in the region is limited state capacity. This is of particular importance given the Janus face of privatization illustrated herein. On the one hand, the swift growth of private sector HEIs and enrolments in the past decade or two has, in a number of systems, outstripped growth in public sector HEIs. On the other hand, there has been increasing privatization of public sector HEIs, under pressure to diversify their income sources. The rise in demand from both trends has exceeded the regulatory capacity of related agencies, which has not kept pace with the swelling of enrolments, new HEIs, and parallel 'Executive' or 'Diploma' programmes.

Arguably most important, however, is the prevailing culture of governance that may limit the willingness of governments and HEIs to implement effective anti-corruption measures. Thus, the Advisory Statement's admirably clear list of forms of corruption, and accompanying measures that could be instituted to prevent them, fails to take into account the resilient local cultures, which in Asia feature patriarchy and paternalism, respect for authority, seniority, and age – all elements that militate against effective anti-corruption measures. Yet, it is these cultural values that often underpin governance norms and practices in many parts of the region, including in higher education. In cultures, systems, and HEIs where such values are still core, how likely is it, for example, that 'transparent processes for appointments to governing councils of all state bodies involved in the regulation and administration of higher education' would be effectively implemented, or that QA or accreditation panels 'exclude individuals [with] conflict of interest'? (IIEP/CHAE, 2016, p. 5).

13.6 Conclusion

While corruption in higher education is by no means restricted to East and Southeast Asia, the illustrations presented here show its effects there to be both profound and pervasive. Examples of all three of Indonesia's trinity of *Korrupsi, Kollusi,* and *Nepotisme* have been given. It is true that low public sector salaries throughout the region, with the exception of Singapore, and to a lesser extent Malaysia and Thailand, provide part of the explanation. As an academic from Cambodia explained in 2014: 'How can I live on $150 a month? If you divide my salary by 30? In the morning, I spend 10,000 riel ($2.50) on coffee and noodles alone. So how about parties? Or food? Or doctor's visits? Or toothpaste? Or haircuts?' (The Guardian, 2014).

Responses such as this underline that resilient local cultures of governance are not the only factors involved in sustaining corruption in higher education. In low-income systems such as Cambodia, Laos, and Myanmar, where public sector salaries are routinely insufficient to sustain a middle-class lifestyle, including high-quality education for one's children, should it come as a surprise that senior administrators such as Deans, Vice-Presidents, and Presidents of HEIs (those charged with implementing anti-corruption measures, but with the most to gain from their absence) are not uncommonly perpetrators? And that those in the lower echelons sell exam papers, or ensure that the reach of the conventional formal curriculum is insufficient to pass the exam, so that students are effectively compelled to attend 'tutorial' classes, after hours, for fees? (IIEP/CHAE, 2016, p. 7).

However, the practices analysed in this chapter reflect a wider culture of corruption and fraud, by no means restricted to the lower

echelons, that delivers rich rewards to some while depriving many more
of access to good-quality higher education. As seen, corrupt practices
are not restricted to those on low wages. On the contrary, corruption
on a massive scale is often perpetrated by those with substantial assets –
because they can, and because the gains are large. The link between
low-level corruption by those at the base of the system and large-scale
corruption by leaders, including in higher education, was explained by
a Cambodian lecturer in philosophy: 'They want to kill teachers for
corruption but why don't they target corruption in their own office
first?' (The Guardian, 2014). The link to governance, including in
higher education, is clear but limited. The absence of good governance
allows such practices to flourish, thereby weakening the quality of
higher education and exacerbating the gap between rich and poor,
weak and powerful. But, as this chapter has shown, other factors also
contribute.

Ultimately, the perpetuation of corrupt practices in universities
erodes trust in both these institutions and the wider society. On both
normative and economic grounds, societies need to nurture all the
available talent: male and female, rich and poor, rural and urban
(ADB, 2012). It is on both grounds, therefore, that the perpetuation
of corruption must at least be contained. While formal measures of
good governance are critical, they are insufficient without wider efforts
to change long-standing cultural practices that allow corrupt practices
to persist. Instituting transparency measures at institutional and
national levels, such as auditing and publishing HEI financial statements, publicly advertising Codes of Conduct, and publishing regular
reports on corruption at both HEI and national levels, can be an
important means to mitigate opportunities for corruption
(Heyneman, 2004). Nevertheless, as the quotation that prefaced this
chapter underlines, it is an ongoing task of considerable proportions.

Notes

1. For details, see: Dang (2017); Jayasuriya (2003, 2010); Ka (2007); Kaur
   et al. (2014); Malaysian Education Blueprint (2015); Norman and Aini
   (2015); Raza (2010); Taib and Abdullah (2015); Wan and Ahmad (2015);
   Welch (2012a, 2012b, 2015, 2016, 2017, 2018); World Bank (2007).
2. The same system applies in Viet Nam, where the Party Secretaries exist
   in parallel with Rectors, Deans, etc., and the Party 'plays the leading role

in all decision-making processes at every level of the system. Senior administration staff such as the Rector, have to be party members' (Hong, 2011, p. 256; see also Khanh and Hayden, 2010, p. 132). An early experiment by the Ministry of Higher Education (subsequently the Ministry of Education and Training [MOET]), whereby the University of Ha Noi – now part of Vietnam National University (VNU), Ha Noi – could elect its own Rector, was abandoned at the expiry of his term. The Ministry then resumed the right to appoint University leaders (Hong, 2011, p. 256).

3. During the period from the mid-fifteenth century, the Ming dynasty – under pressure from the Mongol invasion – sold titles of 'Student of the Imperial Academy' (He, 1967, p. 104).

4. The 'Opinions' in the 2015 document embraced seven domains: i) Strengthening and improving higher education propaganda and ideology work as a major and urgent strategic task; ii) Guiding ideology, basic principles, and main tasks; iii) Realistically promoting the entry of the theoretical system of Socialism with Chinese characteristics into textbooks, classrooms, and minds; iv) Forcefully raising the ideological and political quality of higher education teaching teams; v) Incessantly expanding higher education mainstream ideology and public opinion; vi) Striving to strengthen management of the higher education propaganda and ideology battlefield; vii) Realistically strengthening Party leadership over higher education propaganda and ideology work (China Copyright and Media, 2015).

5. Again, the Vietnamese system is not much different: 'Vietnamese education is socialist education that is popular, national, scientific, modern and founded on Marxism-Leninism and Hô Chi Minh Thought' (Hong, 2011, p. 227).

6. The 1 Malaysia Berhad (1Mdb) scandal erupted in 2015, when Malaysia's Prime Minister Najib Tun Razak was forced to admit that more than RM 2.67 billion (circa US$ 700 million) from the heavily indebted 1MDB (a national strategic development company) had been channelled into his personal bank account. Since then, the scandal has spawned investigations by the *Wall Street Journal*, the *Times of London*, the Attorney General of Switzerland, Hong Kong Police, the US Justice Department, and the United Kingdom's Serious Fraud Office.

7. The phrase 'tigers and flies' was used by President Xi to indicate that both large and small examples of corrupt officials would be targeted. No one was to be exempt. The anti-corruption campaign, initiated in 2013, has seen thousands of officials prosecuted, at the national level as well as at *Shĕng* (Province), *Xian* (county), *Chu* (Division), *Tin* (department), and *Ju* (Bureau) levels. Findings of bribery, embezzlement, and abuse of

power were made against some of China's most senior officials, including Bo Xilai, a member of the Standing Committee of the Politburo (China's Cabinet). (His wife, Gu Kailai, was charged with murder.) Zhou Yongkang, another former member of the Politburo, and Secretary of China's *Zhengfawei* Central Legal and Political Affairs Commission, was sentenced to life imprisonment in mid-2015, after being found guilty of bribery, abuse of power, and intentionally disclosing national secrets. Assets of more than US$ 14 billion were seized as part of the investigation (BBC, 2015a; Caixin, 2016a, 2016b).

8. The first two are Provinces; the third is designated an Autonomous Region, a status equivalent to other border regions of China, such as the Xinjiang Uyghur Autonomous Region, in China's Northwest.

9. Over several years from 1999, the Chinese government deliberately raised higher education enrolments by between 25 and 30 per cent annually, partly in response to the effects of the regional currency crisis, and partly to reform Chinese HEIs.

10. In this period, government subsidies declined from 14,902 *yuan* per student to 7,586 *yuan*, dropping further from 5,553 *yuan* per student in 2004 to 5,376 *yuan* in 2005. Operating expenditure per student declined from 2,297 *yuan* to 2,238 *yuan* over the same time period.

11. In one instance, international students considering enrolment in a tertiary college in Melbourne, Australia, were lured online with photos of large and impressive colonial era buildings, only to find upon arrival that the photos were of the central railway station.

12. As measured by their presence in the highly regarded Science Citation Index (SCI), the number of articles from mainland China grew from a negligible share in 2001 to 9.5% in 2011, second in the world to America. According to a 2017 report published by the Institute of Scientific and Technical Information (ISTIC) of China, more than 2 million Chinese papers were published in SCI journals from 2007 to 2017, ranking second only to the USA (in absolute terms), for number of publications and citations (Jia 2017). The respected journal *Nature* reported that in 2012 the number of mainland authored papers in the journal's 18 affiliated research publications rose by 35 per cent over the previous year (The Economist, 2013; see also CRI, 2011; Yang and Welch, 2012).

13. That is, the same article published in different journals. The extent of such corrupt practices led some mainland scientists to joke that SCI stands for 'Stupid Chinese Idea'.

14. The practices of paying bribes for promotion, and buying and selling of posts, have also been criticized in Viet Nam and elsewhere (Tuoitrenews, 2012).

References

ADB (2012) *Counting the cost: Higher education for inclusive growth in Asia*. Manila: Asian Development Bank. www.adb.org/sites/default/files/publication/29679/counting-cost.pdf

Aminudin, A., and Welch, A. (2012) What happened to autonomy? *Jakarta Post*, 23 June. www.pressreader.com/indonesia/the-jakarta-post/201206 23/281694021863456

Ashwill, M. A. (2006) US institutions find fertile ground in Vietnam's expanding higher education market. *International Higher Education*, 44 (6), 13–14.

Atkinson, A. (2015) *Inequality: What can be done?* Cambridge, MA: Harvard University Press.

Bakhari, S., and Leach, F. (2009) 'I invited her to my office': Normalising sexual violence in a Nigerian college of education. In S. Heyneman (Ed.) *Buying your way into heaven: Education and corruption in international perspective*, pp. 9–22. Rotterdam: Sense Publishers.

Bangkok Post (2008) Learning curve: Educators worry over lack of quality control. *Bangkok Post*, 28 July.

BBC (2015a) Cracking China's corruption: Huge hauls and long falls. BBC News, 18 January. www.bbc.com/news/world-asia-china-30808665

BBC (2015b) German defence minister denies plagiarism. BBC News, 27 September. www.bbc.com/news/world-europe-34376563

Buchori, M., and Malik, A. (2004) Higher education in Indonesia. In P. Altbach and T. Umakoshi (Eds), *Asian universities: Historical perspectives and contemporary challenges*, pp. 249–278. Baltimore: Johns Hopkins University Press.

Caixin (2013) Anti-corruption in the classroom. *Caixin*, 5 July. http://english .caixin.com/2013–07-05/100552275.html

Caixin (2016a) Legal expert warns graft will continue until political system fixed. *Caixin*, 20 January. http://english.caixin.com/2016–01-20/100901 823.html

Caixin (2016b) Fudan university chief fired over Lianing election-rigging scandal. *Caixin*, 18 September. http://english.caixin.com/2016–09-18/10 0989225.html

Capano, G., Howlett, M., and Ramesh, M. (2015) Rethinking governance in public policy: Dynamics, strategy and capacities. In G. Capano, M. Howlett, and M. Ramesh (Eds). *Varieties of governance: Dynamics, strategy and capacities*, pp. 3–24. London: Palgrave Macmillan.

Carroll, T., and Jarvis, D. (Eds) (2017) *Asia after the developmental state: Disembedding autonomy*. Cambridge: Cambridge University Press.

CCTV [BBS] (2011) Xian Jiaotong University buying and selling posts. CCTV, 5 April [in Chinese]. http://bbs.cntv.cn/thread-14686852–1-1 .html

Chan, W.-C. (2013) *Vietnamese–Chinese relations at the borderlands*. London: Routledge.

Chemistry World (2010) Academic Controversy Leads to Bloodshet [sic.], https://fangzhouzi-xys.blogspot.com/2010/12/

Cheung, A. (2010) Checks and balance in China's administrative traditions: A preliminary assessment. In M. Painter and B. Peters (Eds), *Tradition and public administration*, pp. 31–43. London: Palgrave.

ChinaFile (2013) Communiqué on the current state of the ideological sphere (Document 9). 8 November. www.chinafile.com/document-9-chinafile-translation

China Copyright and Media (2015) Opinions concerning further strengthening and improving propaganda and ideology work in higher education under new circumstances. 19 January. https://chinacopyrightand media.wordpress.com/2015/01/19/opinions-concerning-further-strengthen ing-and-improving-propaganda-and-ideology-work-in-higher-education-u nder-new-circumstances/

China Daily (2010a) Behind the fancy foreign diplomas. 7 December, www .chinadaily.com.cn/china/2010-07/15/content_10108627.htm

China Daily (2010b) Investing in science. 10 September. www .chinadaily.com.cn/opinion/2010-10/09/content_11387722.htm

China Daily (2014) Guangxi ready to crack down on drugs. 3 November.

China Weekly (2010) Elites accused of fabricating degrees. 12 July. www .chinadaily.com.cn/china/2010-07/12/content_10092166.htm

Dang, Q. (2017) Regionalising higher education for repositioning Southeast Asia. *Oxford Review of Education*, 43(4), 417–432.

Dawson, W. (2009) The tricks of the teacher: Shadow education and corruption in Cambodia. In S. Heyneman (Ed.) *Buying your way into heaven. Education and corruption in international perspective*, pp. 51–74. Rotterdam: Sense Publishers.

The Diplomat (2015) Corruption scandals hound ASEAN leaders in 2015. A big year for regional integration has been marred by troubling national corruption scandals. 11 December. http://thediplomat.com/2015/12/cor ruption-scandals-hound-asean-leaders-in-2015/

The Diplomat (2016) Cambodia now ASEAN's most corrupt country. The country records the region's worst score in Transparency International's annual corruption index. 2 February. http://thediplomat.com/2016/02/ca mbodia-now-aseans-most-corrupt-country/

The Economist (2010) Academic fraud in China. Replicating success. 22 July. www.economist.com/blogs/banyan/2010/07/academic_fraud_china

The Economist (2013) Looks good on paper. A flawed system for judging research is leading to academic fraud. 3 October. www.economist.com/news/china/21586845-flawed-system-judging-research-leading-academic-fraud-looks-good-paper

Eimer, D. (2014) *The emperor far away: Travels at the edge of China.* London: Bloomsbury.

Evans, G., Hutton, C., and Eng, K.-K. (Eds) (2000) *Where China meets Southeast Asia: Social and cultural change in the borderlands.* London: Palgrave.

Farazmand, A. (2015) Governance in the age of globalization: Challenges and opportunities for South and Southeast Asia. In I. Jamil, S. M. Aminuzzaman, and S. T. M. Haque (Eds), *Governance in South, Southeast, and East Asia*, pp. 11–26. London and New York: Springer.

Green, A. (2013) Postscript: Education and state formation in East Asia. In A. Green *Education and state formation*, pp. 305–385. London: Palgrave Macmillan.

Guan, J. (2011) Guanxi: The key to achieving success in China. *Sino-Platonic Papers*, 217, 1–11.

The Guardian (2013) German education minister quits over PhD plagiarism. 9 February. www.theguardian.com/world/2013/feb/09/german-education-minister-quits-phd-plagiarism

The Guardian (2014) Cambodia crackdown on corruption in schools scores low with exam cheats. 2 September. www.theguardian.com/global-development/2014/sep/02/cambodia-corruption-crackdown-exam-cheats

Hallak, J., and Poisson, M. (2007) *Corrupt schools, corrupt universities: What can be done?* Paris: UNESCO and International Institute for Educational Planning.

Hayhoe, R. (1996) *China's universities 1895–1995: A century of cultural conflicts.* New York: Garland.

He, B. (1967) *The ladder of success in Imperial China: Aspects of social mobility, 1368–1911.* New York: Columbia University Press.

Held, D., McGrew, A., Goldblatt, D., and Perraton, J. (1999) *Global transformations: Politics, economics and culture.* Stanford: Stanford University Press.

HERA (2010) *Higher education reform agenda.* Ha Noi: Ministry of Education.

Heyneman, S. (2004) Education and corruption. *International Journal of Educational Development*, 24(6), 637–648.

Heyneman, S. (2009) Educational corruption in international perspective. In S. Heyneman (Ed.), *Buying your way into heaven: Education and corruption in international perspective*, pp. 1–8. Rotterdam: Sense Publishers.

Heyneman, S. (2011) The corruption of ethics in higher education. *International Higher Education*, 62, 8–9.

Heyneman, S., Anderson, K., and Nuraliyeva, N. (2008) The cost of corruption in higher education. *Comparative Education Review*, 52(1), 1–25.

Hong, N. (2011) Challenges to higher education reform: A university management perspective. In J. London (Ed.), *Education in Vietnam*, pp. 237–258. Singapore: ISEAS.

Huffington Post (2014) How to bribe your way into the Chinese Government. www.huffingtonpost.com.au/entry/chinese-government-buy-of_n_6247742.html?section=australia

Hunter, M. (2015) It's time to put university research in Malaysia under the microscope. *Malaymail Online*, 12 October. www.themalaymailonline.co m/what-you-think/article/its-time-to-put-university-research-in-malaysia-u nder-the-microscope-murray

ICAC (2015) *Learning the hard way: Managing corruption risks associated with international students at universities in NSW*. Sydney: Independent Commission Against Corruption. https://intermediatescan.files.word press.com/2015/04/international_students_publication_-_web.pdf

IIEP/CHEA (2016) *Advisory statement for effective international practice. Combatting corruption and enhancing integrity: Contemporary challenge for the quality and credibility of higher education.* Paris: International Institute for Educational Planning (IIEP-UNESCO) and Council for Higher Education Accreditation (CHEA/CIQG). https://unesdoc .unesco.org/ark:/48223/pf0000249460/PDF/249460eng.pdf.multi

INYT (2015a) In China, few real victories in 'People's War' on drugs. *International New York Times*, 26 January.

INYT (2015b) Rebels kill dozens of soldiers in Myanmar. *International New York Times*, 14 February.

Jakarta Post (2004) State universities open door to the rich. 8 April.

Jakarta Post (2005) Halueleo uncovers admission scandal. 23 April.

Jakarta Post (2006) Schools with international orientation mushrooming. 26 January.

Jayasuriya, K. (2003) Introduction: Governing the Asia Pacific, beyond the 'new regionalism'. *Third World Quarterly*, 24(2), 199–215.

Jayasuriya, K. (2010) Learning by the market: Regulatory regionalism, Bologna, and accountability communities. *Globalisation, Societies and Education*, 8(1), 7–22.

Jia, H., (2017) China's Citations Catching Up, Nature Index (November). www.natureindex.com/news-blog/chinas-citations-catching-up

Ka, H. (2007) The search for new governance: Corporatisation and privatisation of public universities in Malaysia and Thailand. *Asia Pacific Journal of Education*, 27(3), 271–290.

Kaur, S. (2014) *Comparing selected higher education systems in Asia.* Penang: IPPTN.

van Kersbergen, K., and van Waarden, F. (2004) 'Governance' as a bridge between disciplines: Cross-disciplinary inspiration regarding shifts in governance and problems of governability, accountability and legitimacy. *European Journal of Political Research*, 43, 143–171.

Khan, A. (2015) The relevance of the concept of good governance: Revisiting goals, agendas and strategies. In I. Jamil, S. M. Aminuzzaman and S. T. M. Haque (Eds), *Governance in South, Southeast, and East Asia*, pp. 133–152. London and New York: Springer.

Khanh, D., and Hayden, M. (2010) Reforming the governance of higher education in Vietnam. In G. Harman, M. Hayden, and P. Nghi (Eds), *Reforming higher education in Vietnam*, pp. 129–142. New York: Springer.

Kusumadewi, L., and Cahyadi, A. (2013) The crisis of public universities in Indonesia today. International Sociological Association, Universities in Crisis Blog. http://isa-universities-in-crisis.isa-sociology.org/?p=1010

Levi-Faur, D. (2012) From 'big government' to 'big governance'? In D. Levi-Faur (Ed.), *The Oxford handbook of governance*, pp. 3–18. Oxford: Oxford University Press.

Levi-Faur, D. (2013) Levi-Faur on 'What is governance?'. https://governancejournal.wordpress.com/2013/03/10/levi-faur-on-what-is-governance/

Levin, R. (2010) Top of the class: The rise of Asia's universities. *Foreign Affairs*, May/June. www.foreignaffairs.com/articles/china/2010-05-01/top-class

Li, M., and Yang, R. (2014) Governance reforms in higher education: A study of China. IIEP Research Paper. Paris: UNESCO.

Liu, P., and Shi, J. (2017) Trust in the subordinate and deference to supervisor in China: A moderated mediation model of supervisor–subordinate guanxi and political mentoring. *Chinese Management Studies*, 11(4), 599–616.

Malaysia Education Blueprint (2015) Malaysia education blueprint 2015–2025 (higher education). Putrajaya: Ministry of Education. www.um.edu.my/docs/um-magazine/4-executive-summary-pppm-2015-2025.pdf

Malaysia Today (2014a) UM professor resigns following orders from Education Ministry. 30 June. www.malaysia-today.net/2014/06/30/um-professor-resigns-following-orders-from-education-ministry/

Malaysia Today (2014b) Saifuddin quits UM post in solidarity with UMcedel Director. 30 June. www.malaysia-today.net/2014/06/30/saifuddin-quits-um-post-in-solidarity-with-umcedel-director/

Malaysia Today (2014c) I did not resign, I was sacked, says UM's Prof Redzuan. 5 July. www.malaysia-today.net/2014/07/05/i-did-not-resign-i-was-sacked-says-ums-prof-redzuan/

Malaysian Insider (2015) 'UM deputy vice-chancellors removed for being too lenient, pro-opposition, say sources', https://sg.news.yahoo.com/um-deputy-vice-chancellors-removed-being-too-lenient-225902333.html

Martinson, B., Anderson, M., and de Vries, R. (2005) Scientists behaving badly. *Nature* 435, 737–738.

McCornac, D. (2009) Corruption in Vietnamese higher education. In S. Heyneman (Ed.), *Buying your way into heaven: Education and corruption in international perspective*, pp. 75–78. Rotterdam: Sense Publishers.

McCornac, D. (2012) The challenge of corruption in higher education: The case of Vietnam. *Asian Education and Development Studies*, 1(3), 262–275.

Min, A. (2004) *Empress orchid*. New York: Houghton and Miflin.

Miyazaki, I. (1981) *China's examination hell: The civil service examinations of Imperial China*. New Haven: Yale University Press.

Mohanty, S. (2015) Academic integrity practice: The view from India. In T. Bretag (Ed.), *Handbook of academic integrity*, pp. 1–5. Dordrecht: Springer.

Monocolumn (2012) The challenges of corruption in Indonesia. 30 April. https://monocle.com/monocolumn/2012/the-challenges-of-corruption-in-indonesia/

Nature News (2010) Publish or perish in China. *Nature*, 463, 142–143. www.nature.com/news/2010/100112/full/463142a.html

Nature News (2012) Zero tolerance: A university cracks down on misconduct. *Nature*, 481, 134–136. www.nature.com/news/research-ethics-zero-tolerance-1.9756

NBC News (2004) School that awarded MBA to cat sued. 7 December. www.nbcnews.com/id/6664906/ns/us_news-crime_and_courts/t/school-awarded-mba-cat-sued/#.VsVZqMd-q-J

Norman, M., and Aini, A. (2015) Changes and challenges in institutional autonomy. In F. M. Taib and M. N. L. Y. Abdullah (Eds), *Governance reforms in public universities of Malaysia*, pp. 36–58. Penang: Universiti of Sains Malaysia Press.

NY Times (2015a) The plunder of Myanmar. *New York Times*, 24 January. www.nytimes.com/2015/01/24/opinion/the-plunder-of-myanmar.html?_r=1

NY Times (2015b) Bribery confession in China calls into question integrity of college admissions. *New York Times*, 5 December. www.nytimes.com/2015/12/05/world/asia/china-renmin-university-admission-bribery.html?_r=0

Overland, M. (2006) Vietnam cracks down on corruption. *Chronicle of Higher Education* March 10.

Pei, C. (2007) Corruption threatens China's future. *Policy Brief 55*. Washington, DC: Carnegie Endowment for International Peace.

Piketty, T. (2014) *Capital in the twenty-first century*. Cambridge, MA: Harvard University Press.

Poapangsakorn, N. (2008) *Implications for financing higher education in Thailand. Paper presented at the conference, Financing Higher Education and Economic Development in East Asia*, DPU University, Bangkok.

Prabowo, H., and Cooper, K. (2016) Re-understanding corruption in the Indonesian public sector through three behavioral lenses. *Journal of Financial Crime* 23(4), 1028–1062.

PRC (1998) *Higher Education Law of the People's Republic of China*. People's Republic of China. www.china.org.cn/english/education/184667.htm

Qiu, J. (2014) China's funding system and research innovation. *National Science Review*, 1(1), 161–163.

qq.com (2014) Illustration: Where the money comes from to buy official posts – selling houses, getting loans and obtaining sponsorships [in Chinese]. http://news.qq.com/a/20141106/065711.htm

Raza, R. (2010) *Higher education governance in East Asia*. (Draft). Washington, DC: World Bank. http://siteresources.worldbank.org/INTE ASTASIAPACIFIC/Resources/HigherEducationGovernance.pdf

Reuters (2016) German defense minister cleared of plagiarism allegations. 9 March. www.reuters.com/article/us-germany-minister-plagiarism-idUSKCN0WB2C2

Robertson, R., Brown D., Gaëlle, P., and Sanchez-Puerta, M. (2009) *Globalization, wages and the quality of jobs*. Washington, DC: World Bank.

Robertson, S. (2008) Europe/Asia regionalism, higher education and the production of world order. *Policy Futures in Education*, 6(6), 718–729.

Saleh, N., and Aiman, A. (2015) Changes and Challenges in Institutional Autonomy, F. M Taib and M. N. L. Y. Abdullah (Eds), *Governance reforms in public universities of Malaysia*, pp. 36–58. Penang: Universiti of Sains Malaysia Press.

Sassen, S. (1998) *Globalization and its discontents*. New York: The New Press.

ScienceMag (2011) Piqued Chinese dean throws down the gauntlet. *Science*, 333, 1368. https://science.sciencemag.org/content/333/6048/1368

Scott, J. (2009) *The art of not being governed: An anarchist history of uplands Southeast Asia*. New Haven: Yale University Press.

Shen, H. (2011) *Trafficking in women across the Yunnan–Myanmar border in transnational migration-era China*. Washington, DC: The Brookings Institution. www.brookings.edu/~/media/events/2011/6/30-east-asia-trafficking/0630_shen_powerpoint.pdf

Shi, Y., and Rao, Y. (2010) China's research culture. *Science*, 329, 1128.

Shin, D. C. (2012) *Confucianism and democratization in East Asia*. New York: Cambridge University Press.

Siaputra, I., and Santosa, D. (2015) Academic integrity campaign in Indonesia. In T. Bretag (Ed.), *Handbook of academic integrity*, pp. 1–9. Dordrecht: Springer.

Sklair, L. (1999) Competing conceptions of globalization. *Journal of World Systems Research*, 5(2), 143–163.

Sklair, L. (2001) *The transnational capitalist class*. Oxford: Blackwell.

Sklair, L. (2002) *Globalization: Capitalism and its alternatives*. Oxford: Oxford University Press.

Sklair, L. (2016) The transnational capitalist class, social movements, and alternatives to capitalist globalization. *International Critical Thought*, 6 (3), 329–341.

SMH (2015) Chinese jade miners in overdrive in Myanmar. *Sydney Morning Herald*, 19 December.

Stiglitz, J. (2002) *Globalization and its discontents*. New York: Norton.

Stiglitz, J. (2016) Globalization and its new discontents. *Project Syndicate* 5 August. www.project-syndicate.org/commentary/globalization-new-discontents-by-joseph-e–stiglitz-2016-08

Sun, F., and Barrientos, A. (2009) The equity challenge in China's higher education policy. *Higher Education Policy*, 22(2), 191–207.

Taib, F. M., and Abdullah, M. N. L. Y. (Eds) (2015) *Governance reforms in public universities of Malaysia*. Penang: Universiti of Sains Malaysia Press.

Tempo (2003) Jalur khusus. Memenbus kampus ternama. 1 June.

TI [Transparency International] (2005) *Stealing the future: Corruption in the classroom – Ten real world experiences*. Berlin: Transparency International. www.transparency.org/whatwedo/publication/stealing_the_future_corruption_in_the_classroom_ten_real_world_experiences

TI (2013) *Global corruption report: Education*. Abingdon and New York: Routledge for Transparency International. www.transparency.org /gcr_education

TI (2014) Corruption Perceptions Index (CPI) 2014: Results. *Transparency International*. www.transparency.org/cpi2014/results

TI (2015a) ASEAN Integrity Community: A Vision for Transparent and Accountable Integration. *Transparency International*. www.transparency.o rg/whatwedo/publication/asean_integrity_community

TI (2015b) Why ASEAN needs to confront corruption in Southeast Asia. *Transparency International*. www.transparency.org/news/feature/ why_asean_needs_to_confront_corruption_in_southeast_asia

TI (n.d.) Private sector. *Transparency International*. www.transparency.org /glossary/term/private_sector

Tu, W. M. (1993) Confucian traditions in East Asian modernity: Exploring moral authority and economic power in Japan and the four mini-dragons. *Bulletin of the American Academy of Arts and Sciences*, 46(8), 5–19.

Tu, W. M. (1996) *Confucian traditions in East Asian modernity: Moral education and economic culture in Japan and the four mini-dragons*. Cambridge, MA: Harvard University Press.

Tuoitrenews (2012) Educator says Vietnam education infected with dishonesty. 10 October. http://tuoitrenews.vn/education/2616/educator-says-vietnam-education-infected-with-dishonesty

UNDP (1997) Reconceptualizing governance. *Discussion paper*. New York: United Nations Development Program.

UWN (2008) Indonesia: University admissions scandal. *University World News*, 27 April. www.universityworldnews.com/article.php?story=20080424153208204

UWN (2014a) Questionable qualifications of disgraced top official. *University World News*, 14 March. www.universityworldnews.com/article.php?story=20140314083027914

UWN (2014b) Business degrees affected by anti-corruption campaign. *University World News*, 3 July. www.universityworldnews.com/article.php?story=20140703142605689

UWN (2014c) Anti-corruption watchdog targets top university. *University World News*, 9 July. www.universityworldnews.com/article.php?story=20140709094127322

UWN (2014d) New targeted inspections in anti-corruption drive. *University World News*, 28 March. www.universityworldnews.com/article.php?story=2014032718583169

UWN (2017) Research could suffer as internet controls tightened. *University World News*, 13 July. www.universityworldnews.com/article.php?story=20170713140950894

Viet Nam News (2002a) Enrolment irregularities bring on suspensions at Dong Do University. 14 January.

Viet Nam News (2002b) Officials fall in school scandal. 7 October.

Viet Nam News (2002c) Police grill professor over Dong Do University scandal. 19 June.

Wan, C. D., and Ahmad, A. (2015) Governance of higher education in Malaysia. In K. Joshi and S. Paivandi (Eds), *Global higher education: Issues in governance*, pp. 339–379. Delhi: B. R. Publishing.

Wang, M.-M. (2012) All under heaven (*tianxia*): Cosmological perspectives and political ontologies in pre-modern China. *HAU, Journal of Ethnographic Theory*, 2(1), 337–383.

Washington Post (2009) Scandal erupts at French University over alleged Chinese bribes. www.washingtonpost.com/wp-dyn/content/article/2009/10/19/AR2009101902272.html

Welch, A. (2007a) Blurred vision? Public and private higher education in Indonesia. *Higher Education*, 54(5), 665–687.

Welch, A. (2007b) Governance issues in South East Asian higher education: Finance, devolution and transparency in the global era. *Asia Pacific Journal of Education*, 27(3), 237–253.

Welch, A. (2011) *Higher education in Southeast Asia: Blurring borders, changing balance*. London: Routledge.

Welch, A. (2012a) *Counting the cost: Financing higher education for inclusive growth*. Manila: Asian Development Bank.

Welch, A. (2012b) The limits of regionalism in Indonesian higher education. *Asian Education and Development Studies*, 1(1), 24–42.

Welch, A. (2015) Universities must promulgate a message of Muslim moderation. *The Australian*, 6 May. www.theaustralian.com.au/higher-education/opinion/universities-must-promulgate-a-message-of-muslim-moderation/news-story/a4319a1056ca932c845efc4783a6e611

Welch, A. (2016) Irregular regionalism? China's borderlands and ASEAN higher education: Trapped in the prism. In S. Robertson, K. Olds, R. Dale, and Q. A. Dang (Eds), *Global regionalisms and higher education: Projects, processes, politics*, pp. 166–190. Cheltenham: Edward Elgar Publishing.

Welch, A. (2017) Higher education and the developmental state: The view from East and Southeast Asia. In T. Carroll and D. Jarvis (Eds), *Asia after the developmental state: Disembedding autonomy*, pp. 359–387. Cambridge: Cambridge University Press.

Welch, A. (2018) China's southern borderlands and ASEAN higher education: A cartography of connectivity. In P. Meusburger (Ed.), *Geographies of the university*, pp. 569–603. Dordrecht and New York: Springer.

Welch, A., and Cai, H. (2011) Enter the dragon: The internationalisation of China's higher education system. In J. Ryan (Ed.), *China's higher education reform and Internationalisation*, pp. 9–33. London: Routledge.

Welch, A., and Hao, J. (2014) Hai Gui and Hai Dai: The job-seeking experiences of high-skilled returnees to China. In K.-H. Mok and K.-M. Yu (Eds), *Internationalization of higher education in East Asia: Trends of student mobility and impact on education governance*, pp. 90–114. London: Routledge.

Wescott, C. (2003) Combating corruption in Southeast Asia. In J. Kidd and F.-J. Richter (Eds), *Fighting corruption in Asia: Causes, effects and remedies*, pp. 237–269. Singapore: World Scientific Press.

World Bank (2007) *Malaysia and building a knowledge economy: Building a world class higher education system*. Washington, DC: World Bank.

World Bank (2014) Control of corruption (Worldwide Governance Indicators). http://info.worldbank.org/governance/wgi/index.aspx#home

Wu, D., and Gao, Y. (2010) In the red? Debt levels at higher education institutions in China. *Procedia Social and Behavioural Sciences*, 2(2), 5855–5863.

Xi, J. (2017) Secure a decisive victory in building a moderately prosperous society in all respects and strive for the great success of socialism with

Chinese characteristics for a new era. Speech to 19th Party Congress, 18 October.

Xinhuanet (2010) China's quiet educational revolution. www.chinadaily.com .cn/opinion/2010-04/21/content_9755578.htm

Xinhuanet (2015a) China's graftbusters hit more SOEs. 12 February. www .ecns.cn/business/2015/02-12/154620.shtml

Xinhuanet (2015b) China's discipline inspectors target ivory tower corruption. 25 November. www.china.org.cn/china/Off_the_Wire/2015-11/25/content_37160754.htm

Yang, M. (2002) The resilience of guanxi and its new deployment: A critique of some new guanxi scholarship. *China Quarterly*, 170, 459–476.

Yang, R. (2008) Corruption in China's higher education system. A malignant tumor. *International Higher Education*, 39, 18–19.

Yang, R. (2016) Toxic academic culture in East Asia. *International Higher Education*, 84, 15–16.

Yang, R., Vidovich, L., and Currie, J. (2007) 'Dancing in a cage': Changing autonomy in Chinese higher education. *Higher Education*, 54(4), 575–592.

Yang, R., and Welch, A. (2010) Globalisation, transnational academic mobility and the Chinese knowledge diaspora: An Australian case study. *Discourse: Studies in the Cultural Politics of Education*, 31(5), 593–607.

Yang, R., and Welch, A. (2012) A world class university in China? A case study of Tsinghua. *Higher Education*, 63(5), 645–666.

Young, D. (2013) Perspectives on cheating at a Thai university. *Language Testing in Asia*, 3(6), 1–15.

Zhai, Y. (2017) Values of deference to authority in Japan and China. *Journal of Comparative Sociology*, 58(2), 120–139.

Zhao, L., and Sheng, S. (2008) Fast and furious: Problems of China's higher education expansion. *EAI Background Brief No 395*. Singapore: East Asia Institute.

Zhong, N. (1997) University autonomy in China. Unpublished PhD thesis, University of Toronto.

Zhong, N., and Hayhoe, R. (2001) University autonomy in twentieth-century China. In G. Peterson, R. Hayhoe, and Y. Lu (Eds), *Education, culture and identity in twentieth century China*, pp. 265–296. Ann Arbor: Michigan University Press.

14 | Fixing the System?
Trends in African Higher Education Governance

ROSE AMAZAN AND KASSAHUN KEBEDE
DAWO

14.1 Introduction

This chapter focuses on the higher education sector and some policy reforms in Africa, looking particularly at the area of university governance. It situates the trends in African higher education governance reform within the broader context of international, continental, national, and institutional policy shifts. It highlights a range of factors, control mechanisms, and challenges that continue to impede the progress of university reform in African higher education.

To this end, the chapter begins by contextualizing the issues around higher education governance in African universities, detailing some of the central policy challenges and the impact of recent policy initiatives. This will be followed by an examination of the various issues relating to the diversity of governance in higher education in Africa. The section goes on to explore the interplay of policy, the market, and state/government involvement, while paying due attention to the historical and political specificities of the continent; namely, colonization, extensive state involvement in higher education, economic vicissitudes, the rapid expansion of higher education, and two decades of state neglect of the higher education sector.

Having painted the global picture of higher education governance in Africa, the chapter then focuses on the governance of Ethiopian higher education as an illustrative case. Drawing on empirical data, the aim here is to explore the academic governance of public universities in Ethiopia within the context of the higher education reform introduced through the Education and Training Policy (FDRE-ETP, 1994) and the Higher Education Proclamation No. 650/2009 (FDRE-HEP, 2009).

Although the case of Ethiopia cannot be wholly representative of the situation of higher education governance in Africa, it allows for a fully contextualized analysis of the way in which the shifts in governance seen across parts of the continent are enacted in a highly mediated way.

It is important to note the existence of some common, underlying geopolitical assumptions, although it is beyond the scope of this chapter to examine these in detail. For example, any discussion of higher education governance in Africa as a whole must take into account various structural differences between regions. While there is no agreed term for the subdivisions of countries and regions discussed here, we might think about the differences, for example, between Southern Africa and Northern Africa, including their specific histories of development and colonization. Imported styles of government can also be grouped to differentiate countries and their forms of higher education systems: for example, one might contrast Francophone centralism with Anglophone heterogeneity. These have an impact on the scope and reach of the analysis herein.

14.2 Contextualizing the Issues

The revitalization of Africa's higher education (HE) system is critical to the continent's development. To some extent we can agree with those economic analyses that see capacity building and human resource development as a way to propel growth and development. This vital source of hope has been recognized by the African Union's development framework strategy, Agenda 2063, in achieving its set objectives. These objectives include building 'a prosperous Africa based on inclusive growth and sustainable development, an Africa whose development is people-driven, relying on the potential of African people … [an] Africa as a strong, united and influential global player and partner' (African Union, 2015, p. 2).

This transformative potential of education is both a challenge and an engine of change, but it places huge demands upon the sector. Higher education in Africa has undergone some dramatic changes in recent decades, including the rapid expansion of both the public and the private systems, an increase in fee-paying student schemes, the increased enrolment of women and other groups, and a drop in public expenditure from state governments and funding from international donors. The effects of these changes are still being felt today in tertiary institutions across the continent. These issues make institutional governance and leadership crucial to success.

Generally speaking, African HE systems have experienced some extreme difficulties in dealing with these changes and demands. The 1980s and 1990s saw a massive decline in most aspects of HE in Africa. Over the last two decades, access to HE in Africa has remained at 5 per cent, which is one-fifth of the global average of 25 per cent (Mba, 2017). Women are still significantly underrepresented, especially in the STEM subjects (science, technology, engineering, mathematics), as well as in the fields of agriculture and health. The brain-drain phenomenon, coupled with the Structural Adjustment Programmes (SAPs) which reduced the role of the state while introducing market ideology in the 1980s, exacerbated the situation and continue to impede many parts of the African HE system. More recently, factors associated with globalization and marketization have impacted on the HE sector. Some argue that the sector's failure to respond to the pressures of the market are responsible for the migration of skilled labour (Teferra, 2010; Varghese, 2013). At the same time, many university graduates who remain in their own countries are unemployed and unable to secure good prospects. These issues can compound each other.

Due to the increased demands on HE, and the challenges that universities in Africa face in providing quality education, university governance has become more of a focus. Higher education governance debates often go hand in hand with a country's interest in improving its national productivity (El-Khawas, 2012). According to Jaramillo et al. (2012), HE institutional governance is one of the most important factors affecting the quality of tertiary education. Similarly, Hénard and Mitterle (2010, p. 15) argue that 'governance has become a major leverage tool for improving quality in all aspects of higher education'.

Fundamental to the issue of governance is the relationship between governments and higher education institutions themselves. Across Africa, governments control all aspects of their countries' HE systems and seek to regulate the functions of HE. This state control model is prevalent in many developing countries. According to the Task Force on Higher Education and Society (TFHES, 2000, p. 53), 'state control has tended to undermine many major principles of good governance. The direct involvement of politicians has generally politicized HE, widening the possibilities for corruption, nepotism, and political opportunism'. This state control reduces the autonomy of HE institutions, a trend we see across the continent. According to Oanda and Sall (2016, p. 62), 'political interference in leadership and management of universities infringed on institutional autonomy in a manner that compromised academic freedom'.

The World Bank (1988, 2000) has acknowledged governance as a major constraint to the efficiency of African universities. The establishment of buffer organizations between governments and universities, and new institutional governing bodies, are signs of a move away from direct government control in the context of the increasing demand on the HE sector to be more accountable, efficient, and productive. How these reforms/policies have impacted the governance and management of HE will be discussed herein.

14.2.1 Challenges Facing Higher Education Governance in Africa

Modern HE in Africa was mainly imported from Europe and is relatively young (Beverwijk, 2005; Varghese, 2004), with the majority of first-generation African universities being established in the 1950s. Public universities flourished after African countries achieved their independence from their colonial governors. The monopoly of the public HE institutions, however, came to an end in the closing decades of the twentieth century when private sector institutions emerged as viable alternatives. Reforms initiated by the 'structural adjustment programs, the deregulation policies and the financial crisis of the state created an encouraging environment for the emergence of the private higher education sector in Africa' (Varghese, 2004, p. 4). Nevertheless, in spite of competition from the ever-expanding private higher education institutions (PRHEIs), the public higher education institutions (PUHEIs) still account for a large segment of students. For instance, within the sub-Saharan African (SSA) region, public institutions account for 72 per cent of the total student enrolment, while the remaining 28 per cent goes to private institutions (Mouton and Wildschut, 2015, p. 4).

The massive growth in student enrolment numbers in both public and private universities over the past 50 years contributes a great deal to the numerous challenges that the African HE sector is currently facing. These include: quality assurance issues; inadequate funding;

lack of human resources, in the sense of both inadequate and
unqualified staffing; poor facilities; pressures to expand; poor governance; and leadership and management demands (Aina, 2010;
Pillay, 2010; Yizengaw, 2008). Increased demand for access to
higher education has led to the rapid expansion of HE institutions,
which has compromised the quality of the education on offer as
well as curricular relevance – the alignment of higher education
with the needs of the labour market (UNESCO, 2012; Varghese,
2016). Lack of opportunities for regional and international collaboration and partnership has also impacted on the quality and
relevance of teaching and research, leaving many graduates unable
to match their skills to labour demands (Aina, 2010; Pillay, 2010;
Yizengaw, 2008).

Arguably, most countries in Africa suffer from a shortage of
human resources, especially in the STEM fields (Mba, 2017). At
the same time, many university graduates are unemployed and have
difficulty securing suitable positions. According to Oanda and Sall
(2016), there are two factors which contribute to the continuation
of these two crises. They point to the lack of a holistic and strategic
policy, compounded by increased enrolments that the universities
cannot easily handle. This disconnect between market supply and
demand on the one hand, and national development needs and
graduates' skills on the other, continues to slow economic development and growth in many African countries. It is of course important to recall that this tension/mismatch is a problem for the West
too, and is not unique to Africa or indeed other parts of the developing world. However, the focus here is on the situation as it affects
Africa.

According to a report by the Inter-University Council (IUCEA) –
a body created to regulate HE in East Africa[1] – at least half of
graduates of East African universities lack skills which would
enhance employability, including technical mastery and basic work-
related capabilities (IUCEA and EABC, 2014). Uganda has the least
qualified graduates, with 63 per cent lacking the necessary skills,
followed closely by Tanzania at 61 per cent, Burundi at
55 per cent, Rwanda at 52 per cent, and Kenya at 51 per cent
(IUCEA and EABC, 2014). This problem stretches beyond East
Africa: South Africa is one of the most developed nations in this
region, and yet here too there are more than 800,000 vacancies in the

private sector alone, while 600,000 university graduates are unemployed (The Economist, 2012). Global shifts in the nature of work also play a role. The idea that rapid developments in the new economy might further complicate the relationship between current university qualifications and actual job requirements is a challenge for governments and social theorists alike.

Funding represents another major challenge. The decision of the World Bank to concentrate on policies supporting basic education, and neglecting HE, had dire consequences for funding. Most universities on the continent struggled to meet demand even with government support; when state funding failed to keep up with the expansion of the HE system, the result was a decline in teaching standards/quality of education and a depletion of research facilities (Varghese, 2016). In Ethiopia, for instance, 'the rate of expansion of public provision in HE has been so rapid that capital expenditure absorbed 65 per cent of the total HE budget during 2003–08' (Ravishankar et al., 2010, p. 20); as a result, the government found it difficult to keep up with this recurrent need.

This touches upon a series of interlocking arguments that will be evident throughout this chapter. Governments want their education systems to be efficient (defined partly in terms of helping to produce 'good' human capital). However, in order to make this happen, states have had to intervene very directly in university structures and forms of governance. As with economic liberalism in the nineteenth century, governments are considerably less laissez faire than the classical ideology might suggest. Thus, we often see the state using the market ideology as a cover to dictate to universities how they want things done.

Furthermore, the introduction of fee-paying students in the 1990s (to compensate for lost revenue) was quite damaging (see Mamdani, 2007; Oanda and Sall, 2016), setting back the public HE sector which was still dealing with the consequences of the SAP era. As is often the case, a squeeze on public expenditure effectively promotes the private. Private HE was able to flourish and become one of the fastest growing sectors in Africa (Mouton and Wildschut, 2015). For instance, within the SSA region alone, the public HE sector comprises 109 universities and 526 polytechnics/colleges, while there were 456 private universities/colleges in 2012 (Mouton and Wildschut, 2015, p. 4; see also SARUA, 2012).

14.2.2 The Impacts of Higher Education Policies/Reforms on Governance in African Higher Education Institutions

The competing political discourses operating behind reform changes in Africa can be attributed to market-driven approaches and struggles for autonomy from state interference. Evidence shows that many reform measures in HE in Africa are triggered by the realization that expansion cannot be supported solely with public resources and funding (Varghese, 2013, 2016). Thus, African universities are effectively forced to take on market-friendly reforms, which in turn demand changes to the institutional governance structure. This neoliberal approach cherishes certain kinds of business models and strategies which focus on deployment of the concept of 'good governance' through market-oriented reforms. These reforms include deregulation; adoption of flatter management structures; establishment of semi-autonomous agencies to replace public service departments; performance-based accountability; and adoption of market-based leadership and management strategies, principles, and techniques (Kebede, 2015).

While these market-driven reforms were an attempt to substitute state control and reduce reliance on state funding, government influence over HE has not in fact declined. Rather, the role of the state in HE has been redefined – some would say strengthened – in order to enforce/regulate accountability measures (Varghese, 2016). As Capano et al. (2015, p. 319) argue, 'governments are still very much in charge, in every governance mode'. To make sense of this, it might help us to think about the state in terms of its remit. Unlike individual agencies in the private sector, the state implicitly has a necessary relation to the concept of the public interest and a responsibility for the whole country. This can be seen more in terms of the development of a framework for operating and regulating the system than in terms of financing, managing, and controlling institutions of HE (Varghese, 2016, p. 38).

A study by the International Institute for Educational Planning which analyses the impacts of reform measures on the governance of HE in five African countries (Ethiopia, Kenya, South Africa, Ghana, and Nigeria), found that, on the whole, reform measures such as the establishment of a governing board, institutional autonomy, funding, and reorganization of university structures and operations, facilitated a move away from direct government control (Varghese, 2016). However, as previously mentioned, this has not been successful. Saint

(2009), having reviewed the legal frameworks of 49 African countries, identified only 15 out of 42 SSA countries where semi-autonomous buffer bodies had been established. Such bodies are more commonly found in Anglophone African countries; Francophone countries have tended to create separate ministries of HE. For instance, in Ethiopia, the change of the socialist government in 1991 and the resultant shift in the political and economic condition of the country forced the incumbent government, the Ethiopia Peoples' Revolutionary Democratic Front (EPRDF), to introduce a series of reforms in the education system in general, and in HE in particular (Weldemariam, 2008). These reforms in the HE governance and management system were precipitated especially by the urgent need to ensure 'the academic freedom and accountability of the HEIs [higher education institutions] as well as their administrative autonomy' (FDRE-MoE, 2005, p. 13). The introduction of the Education and Training Policy (ETP) in 1994 focused on the idea that Ethiopia's education system needed to transform from the previously elitist configuration to an open-to-all approach. This policy was instrumental in the reform of the HE sector. The ETP clearly outlined the rights and duties of all involved in education, as well as stating the duties of educational management – that is, to create the necessary conditions to expand, enrich, and improve the relevance, quality, accessibility, and equity of education and training (FDRE-ETP, 1994, Articles 3.8.1–3.8.5).

However, according to some authors (Nega, 2012; Saint, 2004; Varghese, 2013) the situation on the ground is quite different from that which was originally intended. Varghese (2013, p. 20) argues that 'the success of reforms' in Ethiopian HE is 'still debatable'. Many studies (Ashcroft and Rayner, 2011; Mehari, 2010; Nega, 2012; Saint, 2009) have tried to identify the general governance problems and challenges facing HE institutions in Ethiopia. Very few, however, have addressed the issues of HE governance adequately.

14.3 Trends in Governance, Leadership and Management in African Higher Education

In 2002, Dearlove warned that the governance of African HE had become a recognized cause for concern. Further evidence is provided in a study on the overhaul of governance, leadership, and management in Ethiopia's HE system, which concluded that there are 'three central problems related to governance, management, and leadership that lead to a range of other related problems that could threaten the reform of higher education in Ethiopia' (FDRE-MoE, 2004, p. 5). These three problems referred to a lack of readiness on the part of HE institutions, the government, and its agencies to embrace the new 'situation of autonomy and accountability'. In this vein the authors of the study also stressed the failure to establish a mature institutional culture (FDRE-MoE, 2004, p. 5).

These issues are common across the continent. Many African governments have attempted to mitigate some of the challenges they face by trying to implement reforms and policies that alter the nature of their relationship with universities. For instance, in South Africa the government launched several policies and initiatives to address HE governance issues (often referred to by the new term 'cooperative governance'). The trail can be followed through a 1996 report of the National Commission for Higher Education, a 1996 Green Paper, a 1997 White Paper and Bill on Higher Education, and the Higher Education Act of 1997 (see Mouton and Wildschut, 2015). However, Sayed (2000) thinks the state of HE governance in South Africa is better viewed as an outcome of the politics of policy contestation. He argues that, while the idea of cooperative governance may have a seductive appeal, unfortunately 'it masks a number of tensions and contradictions regarding the balance between control and regulation, the nature of decision making, the balance between consultation and co-decision making, the relationship between the state and civil society, and the policy mechanisms employed to steer the system' (Sayed, 2000, p. 488). These debates and discussions revolve around questions relating to 'the purpose(s) of higher education, the tension between university autonomy and public accountability, the balance between self-regulation and governmental intervention and control, and the nature of academic freedom' (Sayed, 2000, p. 477).

The bottom line is that state involvement in university affairs is the norm in many African universities, which can create tension between the government and the institution (Mouton and Wildschut, 2015; Saint, 1992). Typically, the head of state is the ultimate authority in appointing the executive body (e.g. vice chancellors, members of council) (Mouton and Wildschut, 2015; Teferra and Altbach, 2004), making political interference in university affairs an inevitable reality. The manner in which these leaders are appointed (not necessarily based on merit or calibre) creates challenges for achieving harmony in the sector.

African HE institutions are increasingly under the influence of 'state driven higher education policy and the constantly increasing intervention of external quality assurance' (Hénard and Mitterle, 2010, p. 2). These increases in auditing are best seen in a relational way: for example, reductions in funding have left some institutions starved of ongoing funds. As Hénard and Mitterle (2010, p. 2) point out, there are 'losses of billions of dollars to individual universities because of decreasing support from donors and possible future cuts in government spending to counter-balance the subsidies'.

To an even greater extent than in developed economies, the relationship between the HE system and national governments in developing countries is often one of dependency and control. In some of its earlier reports, the World Bank took the view that there was too much government involvement in the HE sector in Africa (World Bank, 1988, 2000). It saw this involvement as hindering the dynamism of the education sector. However, in an apparent contradiction, the same organization also identified inadequate governance as a big limitation for universities in Africa. Following this logic, governance should be via private, not state, mechanisms. When the World Bank criticizes a national government (such as Ethiopia's) for excessive interference in an education sector, this might be seen as a predictable critique from an organization that appears to be ideologically committed to privatization. Is the World Bank open to the charge of being contradictory here? At the very least we can question its power to set agendas and priorities over the heads of national governments.

It can be argued that the World Bank's position should be viewed with some scepticism as it seems to be overly influenced by the prevailing neoliberal view that the market knows best, and that states should not 'bail out' or prop up institutions, or even seek to run them with government money. Irrespective of this, a number of initiatives by the World Bank were proposed to mitigate the alleged interference of the state, such as withdrawal of direct government involvement in accreditation processes and regulations; sharing governance with the ministries of education, faculty, and university management; and securing external funding to assure financial stability of institutions (Oanda and Sall, 2016; World Bank, 1988, 2000).

A lot of work has gone into theorizing how governments govern, and much of this could be related to the specifics of university governance. As Capano et al. (2015) point out, we would need, at the very least, to distinguish between govern*ance* and govern*ment* (the latter referring to purposive use of power, usually by a nation state, and the former being a wider concept connoting the accumulation of relations between government and non-government bodies). Maybe we need to think of the way the state rules in a changed field of devolved functions and relations as 'new governance'. However, as Capano et al. suggest, it would be dangerous when discussing policy formation or new ways of 'ordering reality' to think that states have been devolved out of existence or that they do not desire to be the ultimate arbiters and decision makers. Notions of 'de-governmentalization' may be premature or over-played: 'there is plenty of evidence suggesting that while the role of the state may indeed have changed to adapt to and accommodate more complex and rapidly changing environments, the dominant role of government in these new governance arrangements remains intact' (Capano et al., 2015., p. 3).

14.3.1 *Marketization of Higher Education Governance in Africa*

The shift to opening up the university sector to the market is a general trend both in developing countries and the West. The market-driven/neoliberal ideology in HE governance postulates that leaders elected from the academic community cannot meet today's demands. As a result, the top leadership of universities are appointed from outside the university system and are expected to bring with them 'prestigious contacts, research achievements, or knowledge of competitors' (El-Khawas, 2012, p. 1). Thus, the traditional academic-driven governance model is no longer acceptable, and the corporate governance model has taken its place.

Trends in decision making or governing bodies have also moved away from the traditional academic-led model. Currently there is a shift to new governance models which include shared governance (participatory or stakeholder decision making), corporate governance (an entrepreneurial approach in which the state plays a supervisory role while policy and strategy are delegated to institutions), and flexible governance (open to enhanced learning and adaptation to an increasingly dynamic environment and market) (Kebede, 2015, p. 19). As institutions move towards more market-oriented, cost-effective, entrepreneurial models, governance will be concentrated in the hands of the top management, and administration will move towards professional management with a New Public Management slant (Krug, 2011).

In the context of Ethiopia, Solomon (2010) argues that the shift from the traditional approaches of academician-led decision making to a government-controlled governance system resulted in a deterioration of educational quality in HE institutions. Arguably, this has led to a lack of trust in the ability of the current (government-dominated) HE sector to bring about economic growth and development. However, others contend that the reforms that have taken place in the country have facilitated a number of improvements in HE governance and management (Varghese, 2013; Yizengaw, 2003). They argue that the changes have been positive in many ways, and that the universities are now more autonomous financially, with concomitantly less intervention on the part of the government in their affairs. The rest of this chapter will focus on the case of Ethiopia.

14.3.2 Methodology

The main empirical data discussed here are drawn from a larger study (see Kebede, 2015) on the academic governance system of public and private universities centring upon Ethiopia. The focus of that study was the academic governance of public and private HEIs with regard to organizational structures and functions of academic units and their governance structure, and their openness and transparency, as stipulated in two documents: the Education and Training Policy of 1994 (FDRE-ETP, 1994) and the Higher Education Proclamation No. 650 of 2009 (FDRE-HEP, 2009).

Using cyclical processes of collecting and analysing data (following Johnson and Christensen, 2012, p. 514), an in-depth investigation of the problem was conducted through a comparative case study approach using a qualitative research design. This design was selected because it allowed the case to be viewed through 'a wide- and deep-angle lens', and facilitated an analysis of academic governance in the case study universities (Johnson and Christensen, 2012).

The data set for the larger study consisted of 20 participants: these included HE officials (2), quality assurance officers (5), department and faculty heads (5), and teachers and students (8), all purposely selected from two university cases, one public and one private. The cases were selected based on: (i) year of establishment; (ii) whether the university is being audited by the Higher Education Relevance and Quality Agency (HERQA) for institutional performance; and (iii) the status of the university in terms of total student enrolment. Findings were also drawn from document analysis of secondary data such as academic legislation, proclamations, regulations, and guidelines produced by the case study universities, HERQA, the Education Strategy Centre (ESC), and the Ministry of Education (MoE). It should be noted that since the focus of this chapter is on public universities in Ethiopia, only data from the public university case will be discussed here.

14.4 Higher Education in Ethiopia

14.4.1 Background and Legislative Framework

Public higher education institutions in general, and public universities in particular, are a recent phenomenon in the history of Ethiopia. Perhaps unlike some other African countries, Ethiopian HE has its roots in traditional church education (Amare, 2005; Saint, 2004), which was offered by the Orthodox Church at elementary, secondary, college, and university levels (Amare, 1967). Modern HE in Ethiopia began in the nineteenth century with the arrival of Christian missionaries who thought providing educational facilities would win hearts and minds and make new converts. Many scholars believe that Addis Ababa University, founded in 1950, was the country's first public university, but Amare (2005) dates modern HE in Ethiopia back to the establishment by the government of the first technical school at Gafat, near the town of Debretabor, in Amhara Region, to produce weapons and to defend the country from the then European colonizers. However, HE demonstrated little progress, even after the establishment of Addis Ababa University, as this 'remained the only higher learning institution in the country for over half a century' (Solomon, 2010, p. 96). It was only after the EPRDF government came to power in 1991 that the expansion of HE began in earnest.

From that period Ethiopia adopted a wide range of reforms of its education system, beginning with the introduction of the ETP which focused on the need to transform the education system from an elitist system. The HE sector went through three stages of reforms: the foundation of a legal framework, expansion of facilities, and the improvement and revitalization of the system (Higher Education Strategic Centre, 2012). The first phase was characterized by the preparation of major legal frameworks such as the ETP, the Education Sector Development Plans, and other relevant white papers; in the second and third phases, the government focused on the actual expansion of the education sector and reforms necessary to maintain quality and relevance within the expanding HE system (Higher Education Strategic Centre, 2012). At the same time, these measures created conditions 'to encourage and give support to private investors to open schools and establish various educational and training institutions' (FDRE-ETP, 1994, Article 3.9.6).

Article 3.8 and sub-articles 3.8.1–3.8.5 of the ETP, and the Higher Education Proclamation (HEP) No. 650/2009 (FDRE-HEP, 2009), provide the legal ground for developing autonomous, active, and internationally recognized public and private universities. The policy set out the necessity of a series of measures to reform the country's educational organization and management with the aim of ensuring that educational management is democratic, professional, coordinated, efficient, and effective, and to encourage the participation of women. The policy laid the ground work for educational institutions to be autonomous in their internal administration and in the design and implementation of education and training programmes. Further, overall coordination and democratic leadership by boards or committees now includes members from the community (FDRE-ETP, 1994, Article 3.8 and sub-articles 3.8.1–3.8.5).

Since these reforms, public universities in Ethiopia have been given the power to design and implement their own strategic plans, income diversification strategies, and ICT development. At the level of academic programmes, they can introduce new programmes in response to the anticipated labour market needs that underpin the nation's economic development strategy as well as initiate graduate programmes (Kebede, 2015). The university curricula have been upgraded and a new buffer agency (HERQA), which monitors both quality and relevance of academic programmes, has been established (FDRE-HEP, 2003; World Bank, 2003).

14.4.2 Expansion/Evolution

With the coming to power of the EPRDF in 1991, undergraduate enrolment grew rapidly. In 1971 there were only 4,500 students enrolled in HE out of a population of 34 million (Saint, 2004), which was far below the average for the region. Before 1986, Ethiopia had only 11 HEIs, 2 universities, and 7 colleges and institutes in various parts of the country (Wondimu, 2003). At the time of writing, the total number of public universities had reached 38, and is due to grow to 47 by 2020 (see FDRE, 2016; FDRE-MoE, 2017). The total number of undergraduates enrolled increased significantly between 2003/2004 and 2015/2016, from 56,072 to 778,766 (FDRE-MoE, 2017). The technical and vocational training (TVET) sector has also experienced a massive boom. The number of students enrolled in TVET institutions increased from 5,264 in 1999/2000 to 271,389 in 2014/2015 (Seid et al., 2015).

The private HE sector has also grown, almost trebling in size since 2003. At the time of writing, the total number of PRHEIs – universities, university colleges, and institutes – has reached 98, of which 4 hold university status (i.e. Unity, St Mary's, Admas, and Rift Valley Universities). In terms of student numbers, research sponsored by FDRE-MoE (2004) with the aim of overhauling higher education in the country predicted that the share of private higher education in terms of students' enrolment would reach 40–50 per cent of total HE enrolment by 2009. However, the 2017 MoE Education Statistics Annual Abstract showed that private HE institutions were enrolling only 118,577 of Ethiopia's 778,766 higher education students – a mere 15.2 per cent (FDRE-MoE, 2017).

The number of teaching staff in HE has also increased enormously. The total number of local and expatriate academic staff nearly tripled from 11,028 in 2008/2009 to 30,496 in 2015/2016 (FDRE-MoE, 2017). Along with this expansion, the type, complexity, and modalities of HE offered in the country have also increased hugely. There are now regular, distance, summer, evening, and cross-border modes of delivery in the system. The use of e-learning/virtual mode in HE institutions in Ethiopia is still in its infancy as universities grapple with challenges (e.g. lack of human resource and infrastructure, absence of policy, access, awareness) in using this mode (see Anberbir, 2015).

Despite this growth and expansion, HE institutions in Ethiopia (similar to the rest of Africa) have faced issues with the quality of the educational offering and with assuring that their graduates' abilities match the skills needed to enter the workforce. The expansion, coupled with the high population growth rate, has put tremendous pressure on the Ethiopian labour market (Seid et al., 2015). According to the World Bank (2007), approximately 600,000 individuals enter the Ethiopian workforce every year. Since the Ethiopian economy is unable to keep up with this demand for jobs, this represents a marked oversupply of labour, resulting in high unemployment rates and long-lasting unemployment, especially among young graduates (Seid et al., 2015). Some have argued that the Ethiopian government was previously too concerned with early schooling reforms to the detriment of supporting the university sector. The emphasis on lower-age-range education led to a long-term neglect in the production of highly skilled, fully employable graduates. However, holding government education and employment policies to account has proved difficult.

In part this relates to a perennial problem around education and national economic development in changing times. Universities (like schools) are not job agencies nor, crucially, do they 'make jobs'. They always have to play catch-up with the evolving employment scene. If there are not enough jobs waiting for their graduates they can say – with some justification – that it is not their fault. The government might argue that the universities should turn out better (job-ready) graduates, but the blame game at this point becomes circular. Nevertheless, some form of supply and demand relationship must exist. Labour and jobs are an integral element of market relations, and governments must take whatever actions they can.

14.4.3 Higher Education Governance in Ethiopia

The governance and management structure of PUHEIs in Ethiopia usually includes the board, the president, the senate, a managing council, university council, academic unit council, academic unit managing council, and department assembly, plus advisory or specialized committees or councils that may be established by the board, senate, or university council.

As the chief executive officer (CEO) – itself a position title redolent of the shift to corporate culture in HE – of the institution, the president is responsible for overall operations and substantive transactions. The board, which is the highest governing body in the institution, has responsibilities ranging from examining, approving, and following up the implementation of proposals for institutional reorganization, organizational plans, policies, administration, and academic programmes, to the issuing of directives regarding qualification requirements and procedures for nomination, appointment, and terms of office of the vice-presidents, other academic officers, and members of the senate (FDRE-HEP No. 650/2009, Articles 44: 1–4). Mintzberg (1983, p. 15) describes the CEO as the most powerful influencer both 'in and around the organization'. The presidents are indeed powerful within the universities; although accountable to their respective management boards, they are chief executive officers, heads of the university councils, and the senate. While this has given the presidents adequate executive power to get things pushed through the decision making bodies easily, there is also the danger of using their power to infringe the rights and independence of academic staff and units in the universities.

The senate is the leading body of the institution for academic matters. Some of the roles and responsibilities of the senate include determining the academic calendar, ensuring proper implementation of the institution's statutes related to all academic and research matters, and approving and nominating academic units as well as employment of academic staff with the rank of professor. The president is the chair of the senate. Another important governing or advisory body in relation to academic affairs in public universities is the university council. It is composed of members of the managing council, all deans, directors, members of the senate standing committee, the chief librarian, the registrar, other key academic officers, service department heads, academic staff, and student representatives. The role of the university council is to advise the president on matters such as plans, budget, organizational structures, academic programmes, agreements of cooperation, splits and mergers, and closures of academic units, as well as on the performance of departments (FDRE-ETP, 1994, Article 57: 1, 2).

14.4.4 Challenges Affecting Higher Education Governance in Ethiopia

According to Varghese (2004), PUHEIs are faced with a number of challenges. This is mainly because the expansion of public tertiary institutions 'has drained resources, overburdened faculty members, encouraged "faculty flight" (academic staff leaving a faculty) and reduced overall quality' (Hayward, 2010, p. 35). Since research at faculty level is a critical backbone of post-graduate education, this has hindered the development of programmes, and of institutions over-all (Hayward, 2010). The budgetary implications of the recent expansion of HE have also been enormous.

Quality audit reports published by HERQA from 2011 to 2015[2] identify the following challenges as prevailing in PUHEIs in Ethiopia: (1) lack of effective communication systems to reach internal and external stakeholders who could effectively participate in the realization of the visions, missions, and educational goals of the HEIs; (2) lack of participatory and transparent governance systems, which impacts on effectiveness in the assurance of quality and relevant education; (3) lack of adequate systems to update and maintain infrastructure and learning resources, with the result that most HEIs suffer from inferior quality buildings and inadequate mainte-nance practices; (4) shortage of effective staff development policies and strategies, with HEIs depending on the MoE to send academic staff for additional and long-term training; (5) lack of appropriate systems to provide guidance and counselling to students, especially those with special needs; and (6) for some of the audited universities, lack of an effective system for programme approval, monitoring, and evaluation (see also van Deuren et al., 2013; Tesfaye, 2015). Nor do these HEIs have mechanisms through which stakeholders – such as employers who are active in the labour market – can participate in the design and review of programmes.

At the time of writing, very few of the audited public universities have prepared policy guidelines for teaching and learning, or for stu-dent assessment. Classrooms are still dominated by a teacher-centred approach and norm-referenced types of student assessments. The main reason given for this is that a high student to staff ratio, and inadequate knowledge and skill on the part of the academic staff, make other approaches unachievable. The HERQA findings also show that none of the public universities has established alumni associations which could contribute to the development and review of programmes. In addition, there have been few efforts to foster or nurture national and international networks, to reduce attrition in funding, or to oversee research funds, leaving the HEIs underfunded and isolated.

There are other challenges too. In terms of staffing, there is a very high gender disparity in all public universities, with males dominating throughout, both in total numbers and in positions of authority. For instance, in the 2015/2016 academic year only 3,455 of 27,892 (14 per cent) of the teaching staff in public HE institutions were women (FDRE-MoE, 2017). This discrepancy between male and female academics is even more evident in qualification levels, with 2,595 male PhDs versus 221 female academic staff (9 per cent) (FDRE-MoE, 2017). In terms of research, there is no overall coordinating body to ensure that the research undertaken by the HE sector as a whole is meeting the country's developmental needs. A case study at Jimma University by Melese (2012) confirms that university teaching staff are minimally (or not at all) engaged in research, despite articles in university regulations stating that all teaching staff should devote 25 per cent of their work time to conducting research (van Deuren et al., 2013). Enforcing this requirement is not easy – a problem which is not unique to African universities.

According to van Deuren et al. (2013), weak leadership is another challenge in Ethiopian HEIs. Their study found that Jigjiga University, for instance, has a problem forming or communicating a common vision and translating that vision into practicable day-to-day activities. Top leaders spent the bulk of their time on routine activities, a problem compounded by a quick turnover of middle leadership. Weak communication among university communities, and unattractive financial incentive mechanisms, partly explain some of these challenges.

In our own study, one of the high-level academic staff participants (HU7) identified the incompatibility between the inputs on the ground (infrastructure, teachers, budgets, etc.), and the numbers of students coming to the university, as a challenge. This has forced some of the top leadership, such as the Academic Vice President (VPAR), to become involved in non-academic activities, including facilitating student catering, refurbishing student dormitories, and organizing the purchase and administration of facilities such as water, electricity, and other services. This, the respondent believes, diverts the attention of academic staff away from their core task – to produce skilled manpower through teaching, learning, research, and community services. Another issue raised by a participant (HU5) is that letters, documents, and other important guidelines on quality assurance and related matters sent by

HERQA to the university are usually addressed to the VPAR, rather than the offices of the quality assurance directorate. It seems that, in many cases, these documents never reach their correct destination.

Another challenge mentioned by participants is the lack of relevant content in courses, leaving thousands of young graduates with no real hope of securing jobs (see also Oanda and Sall, 2016). It is worth mentioning that Ethiopia has experienced some rapid economic growth, averaging 11 per cent between 2005 and 2011 (Seid et al., 2015). The most current available data suggest that, in general, there has been a drop in the national unemployment rate from 8.2 per cent in 1999 to 5.4 per cent in 2013. Urban unemployment has also dropped, from 26.1 to 21 per cent, in the same period (Seid et al., 2015). Despite these achievements, there is a disconnect between the demands of the labour market and the graduate skills being produced. According to Seid et al. (Seid et al., 2015, p. 10), 'anecdotal evidence suggests that a large increase in the number of college graduates following the expansion of tertiary education in recent years partly explains the high unemployment rate and long unemployment duration among new college graduates'. Serneels (2007) puts unemployment duration among new graduates in Ethiopia at 45 months. Additionally, our study found that 'duplication and proliferation of programmes in the universities' (HU7) also contribute to this trend. Thus, graduate unemployment is a real concern and should not be taken lightly. This is a reality for many young graduates, not only in Ethiopia but across the whole continent.

On a more optimistic note, the HERQA quality audit reports found that most of the public HEIs have organizational structures that are newly developed and that focus on effective and efficient service delivery and good governance. They are well structured, appropriate, and effective, and decentralized to college level, indicating the duties and responsibilities of the academic and support staff. Nevertheless, less than two-thirds (62 per cent) of the PUHEIs had transparent governance systems at the time of the audits; some of the audited universities did not have effective systems for programme approval, monitoring, and evaluation. Nor did they (as mentioned earlier) have any mechanisms through which stakeholders such as employers could participate in the design and review of programmes. A significant number of the HEIs (25 per cent) had no participatory governance system (Tesfaye, 2015).

14.4.5 The Higher Education Relevance and Quality Agency in Ethiopia

As implied, one of the factors that influences the academic governance of a university is the structure created by the institution to dispense quality education services. HERQA was established by HEP No. 650/2009 (FDRE-HEP, 2009, Article 22). At programme level, HERQA aims to support higher education institutions in providing information about the quality of a programme. HERQA undertakes institutional quality audits on government universities and procedures; it creates institutional quality audit reports which pinpoint some of the strengths and weaknesses of the universities regarding internal quality assurance systems and distributes these to major stakeholders. The objective of HERQA's institutional quality audit is to assess the appropriateness and effectiveness of a higher education institution's approach to quality assurance, its systems of accountability, and its internal review mechanisms. In addition, the opportunity is taken to recommend to the management specific ways of improving (Tesfaye, 2015).

However, HERQA faces some challenges of its own (relating to status, autonomy, credibility, staff shortages, and low salaries) that make it more difficult to do its job well. One such issue is its lack of authority. The institutional quality audits undertaken by HERQA are not mandatory and are mostly based on self-evaluations submitted voluntarily to the agency by the universities (HERQA1 participant). This means HEIs that are not willing to be audited are simply left out of the process. Further, the audit reports do not have any consequences, except for their dissemination to the public. While some HEIs implement the recommendations in the audit reports, and improve their quality assurance system, others ignore them. Unfortunately, there is no legal or procedural provision which makes public HEIs accountable if they do not follow HERQA's recommendations. Public universities in Ethiopia were largely established by regulations based on Article 5 of HEP No. 650/2009 (FDRE-HEP, 2009): they do not have to apply for accreditation or re-accreditation from HERQA or any other government bodies for their study programmes.

Additionally, although HERQA was mandated by HEP 650/2009, which spelled out its autonomy, the agency is still struggling with its status as an independent, autonomous, quality assurance agency. HEIs sometimes voice their concerns and doubts about the work of the agency because it is government funded and financially dependent on the MoE. Its autonomous status has also been weakened by the fact that decisions made by the agency have sometimes been reversed by ad hoc appeal committees of the MoE, irrespective of procedures and guidelines requiring an independent appeal process (see FDRE-HEP, 650/2009, Articles 82: 2 and 3). The current appeal procedure in action at the MoE is, however, ignoring the requirements for an independent process. HERQA finds itself in an unfortunate position: it is sometimes seen by the HEIs as a watchdog for the government, while at the same time the MoE sees it as a representative of the HEIs. Both perceptions lead to an undermining of the credibility, autonomy, and authority of HERQA.

To make matters worse, the MoE has recently established an inspection branch of its own – the Higher Education Inspection Directorate – engaging in the same activities as HERQA. Some of the HERQA officials interviewed (HERQA1 and HERQA3) see this newly established body as a duplication of HERQA and a waste of time and scarce resources. Participants in our study (HERQA1 and HERQA2) point to the overlap in the roles of HERQA and this new department; they believe that the new Directorate is doing more harm than good, leading to confusion in both the public and private HE sectors. Both bodies send experts and use more or less the same standards to assess the quality assurance status of universities, while universities have to report the same information to both bodies. Moreover, it could be argued that neither body contributes effectively to higher standards in universities. Nevertheless, an expert respondent from the MoE (MoE1) argues that the work of the Directorate is complementary to that of HERQA, and does not see any contradictions.

14.4.6 Transparency and Openness of Higher Education Governance in Ethiopia

In the light of the above, we might ask if PUHEIs in Ethiopia have the mechanisms to ensure openness and transparency – which, according to Olsen (2004, p. 20), represent a 'core strategic point in the organization of work on quality assurance'. For example, procedures and criteria used to promote academic staff to higher ranks and leadership positions lack adequate transparency. Some of the participants of our study believe that management uses some 'unclear and hidden' criteria – such as ethnicity – to pick their favourite candidate for academic positions. According to one respondent:

Unclear and hidden criteria such as ethnicity have been used to determine who should be elected by the management. Most of the criteria used by the management are subjective and unclear. ... You may have good documents, better peer evaluation results but the management may not allow you to take the position ... It is the management which determines who should be appointed, based on ethnicity and other unclear criteria who should be assigned in spite of your work and research experience. (HU8)

The government did attempt to add political considerations to staff evaluation criteria in 2002, but this was found to interfere with the process (Saint, 2004) and therefore was not implemented officially.

Overall, the study found that when staff witness individuals with little or no experience and/or educational background getting promotions and leadership positions, it creates doubts and lack of trust. This feeds into a work environment where staff are 'unhappy', 'dissatisfied', and have no confidence in the processes or the institutional governance. As a consequence, staff may develop negative attitudes towards the new or promoted persons and treat them as 'implants' because they think these people are chosen for their ethnicity or their political affiliation to the governing party. These sentiments are not uncommon. In a study on Ethiopian diaspora mobility, Amazan (2011) found that being affiliated with the ruling party does come with certain perks and privileges. Returnees who were interviewed felt that they were excluded from many opportunities because they were non-partisan or were not of the right ethnic group (Amazan, 2011).

A related issue is the selection of academic staff for scholarships. It is commonly believed that those who are favoured by the management are rewarded by receiving opportunities to pursue their education in Western countries such as Canada and Norway, while others are restricted to studying locally or in Indian universities:

[S]cholarships to Western countries are not open. Mostly they are open to the people in the management. These are people who have good affiliation with the political leadership. They themselves tell you that they are from a given ethnic group. If scholarship opportunities come from local universities, countries such as India, it is free for competition. ... They [management] tell you, of course, that it is open for everybody for competition but those who compete for the scholarship are those from the top management, not even from the middle management. (HU8)

It was also found that academic staff have different understandings regarding standards and criteria for promotion. Some felt that 'the standards are mostly abstract and vague'. The criteria are laid out in different legislative documents; however, when dealing with the actual process, something completely different occurs, echoing similar findings by Varghese (2013). In reality, if participants were not affiliated with the ruling party, opportunities for promotions were far more restricted (Amazan, 2011). Agreeing upon necessary standards and enforcing improvements is a complicated process and it is one that is easier to describe than to do. In the university sector the idea of improved quality is accepted as a common goal by universities, government, staff, and students. However, some would argue that despite all the increased oversight and new attempts to regulate and monitor the quality of education in Ethiopia, there has been only limited progress (e.g. in classroom practices and student learning experiences).

In Ethiopia, the problems of monitoring or auditing quality (by HERQA and other bodies) continue. Respondents suggested that audits are done but are not followed up. Since HERQA has no power to enforce the recommendations they make to universities, issues and problems may be identified repeatedly, but there seems to be little evidence of universities as a whole acting on the auditors' recommendations. There are other, equally sensitive issues that also remain unaddressed. These include the low salaries of some university staff, which may have the unintended consequence of promoting corruption as staff seek ways to supplement their income.

14.5 Conclusion

This chapter has discussed higher education governance in regions of Africa with an emphasis on Ethiopian higher education governance, including a reflective review and qualitative data on governance in HEIs in Ethiopia.

The first part of the chapter laid out some commonalities of university governance structures across Africa. It argued that university governance is always overdetermined. It is a complex area full of contradictions and the lags and discontinuities typical of applied policies. For example, universities are burdened by government scrutiny and regulation and are held to externally set targets while simultaneously being under-resourced in their efforts to achieve those targets. Although the focus of this chapter has been on Africa, it should be remembered that the same could be said of the HE sector in many Western countries. The second part of the chapter turned to the specific example of Ethiopia, which shows both particularities and generalizable patterns.

The roots of many of the governance issues of African HE are strongly grounded in politics and history and are marked by post-coloniality and the growing independence from colonial powers/rule. The governance, leadership, and management challenges that African universities currently face are due in part to the systems inherited from the days of colonization. However, as Sayed (2000) argues, these debates take on a whole new form in an age of financial austerity and neoliberalism. The increased reliance on market ideology as the solution in relation to both funding of the HE sector and university governance issues is a crucial ideological development, as is the drift towards neoliberal thinking and practice. At the same time, we have to be careful not to simply use neoliberalism as a catch-all phrase wheeled into the analysis like a deus ex machina. It is still an influential ideology/practice, but it has to be seen locally as composed of different strategies, with their own contradictions and unintended consequences.

It would be wrong to conclude that the situation cannot improve. There have already been some improvements and some individual success stories. Most importantly, there are academics who care about their jobs and teaching well, and the majority of stakeholders realize there is a lot to be gained from a healthy and well-run HE sector.

Notes

1. IUCEA covers five countries: Burundi, Kenya, Rwanda, Tanzania, and Uganda.
2. These documents are not available to the public. For a summary of them, please refer to Tesfaye 2015.

References

African Union (2015) *Agenda 2063: The Africa we want*. Addis Ababa: African Union Commission.

Aina, T. A. (2010) Beyond reforms: The politics of higher education transformation in Africa. *African Studies Review*, 53(1), 21–40. doi:10.1353/arw.0.0290.

Amare, A. (2005) Higher education in pre-revolution Ethiopia: Relevance and academic freedom. *The Ethiopian Journal of Higher Education*, 2(2), 1–45.

Amare, G. (1967) Aims and purposes of Church education in Ethiopia. *Ethiopian Journal of Education*, 10(10), 1–11.

Amazan, R. (2011) Mobilising the Ethiopian knowledge diaspora: How can the Ethiopian knowledge diaspora be mobilised into participating effectively in the tertiary educational process in Ethiopia. PhD thesis, University of Sydney, Sydney, Australia.

Anberbir, T. (2015) Survey of the use e-learning in higher education in Ethiopia. www.researchgate.net/profile/Tadesse_Anberbir/publication/3 18317502_Survey_of_the_Use_e-Learning_in_Higher_Education_in_Eth iopia/links/59636db00f7e9b81948eef17/Survey-of-the-Use-e-Learning-in -Higher-Education-in-Ethiopia.pdf

Ashcroft, K., and Rayner, P. (2011) *Higher education in development: Lessons from Sub-Saharan Africa*. Charlotte: Information Age Publishing Inc.

Beverwijk, J. M. R. (2005) *The genesis of a system: Coalition formation in Mozambican higher education, 1993–2003*. Enschede: University of Twente.

Capano, G., Howlett, M., and Ramesh, M. (2015) Bringing governments back in: Governance and governing in comparative policy analysis. *Journal of Comparative Policy Analysis: Research and Practice*, 17(4), 311–321. doi:10.1080/13876988.2015.1031977

Dearlove, J. (2002) A continuing role for academics: The governance of UK universities in the post-Dearing era. *Higher Education Quarterly*, 56(3), 257–275.

van Deuren, R., Kahsu, T., Ali, S. M., and Woldie, W. (2013) Capacity development in higher education: New public universities in Ethiopia. Working Paper No. 2013/24. Maastricht: Maastricht School of Management.

The Economist (2012) Education in South Africa: Still dysfunctional. Standards still leave a lot to be desired. *The Economist*, 21 January. www .economist.com/node/21543214

El-Khawas, E. (2012) Strengthening universities around the world. *International Higher Education* 67, 3–5.

FDRE (2016) Growth and Transformation Plan II (GTP II) 2015/16–2019/
    20. Addis Ababa: Ministry of Education, Federal Democratic Republic of
    Ethiopia.
FDRE-ETP (1994) *The education and training policy.* Addis Ababa: Federal
    Negarit Gazeta, Federal Democratic Republic of Ethiopia.
FDRE-HEP (2003) Higher education proclamation No. 351/2003. Addis
    Ababa: Federal Negarit Gazeta, Federal Democratic Republic of Ethiopia.
FDRE-HEP (2009) Higher education proclamation No. 650/2009. Addis
    Ababa: Federal Negarit Gazeta, Federal Democratic Republic of Ethiopia.
FDRE-MOE (2004) Higher education system overhaul (HESO). *Report of
    the committee of inquiry into governance, leadership and management in
    Ethiopia's higher education system.* Addis Ababa: Ministry of Education,
    Federal Democratic Republic of Ethiopia.
FDRE-MOE (2005) The Federal Democratic Republic of Ethiopia education
    sector development program III (ESDP-III) 2005/2006–2010/2011 (1998
    EFY–2002 EFY). Program action plan (PAP). Addis Ababa: Ministry of
    Education, Federal Democratic Republic of Ethiopia.
FDRE-MOE (2017) Education statistics abstract 2015/2016. Addis Ababa:
    Ministry of Education, Federal Democratic Republic of Ethiopia.
Hayward, F. (2010) Graduate education in Sub-Saharan Africa. In
    D. Teferra and H. Greijn (Eds), *Higher education and globalization:
    Challenges, threats and opportunities for Africa*, pp. 33–50. Maastricht:
    Maastricht University Centre for International Cooperation in Academic
    Development.
Hénard, F., and Mitterle, A. (2010) *Governance and quality guidelines in
    higher education.* Paris: OECD. https://search.oecd.org/edu/imhe/46064
    461.pdf
Higher Education Strategy Centre (2012) *A guideline of modularization for
    Ethiopian higher education institutions.* Addis Ababa: Ministry of
    Education.
IUCEA and EABC (2014) *Regional higher education qualifications gaps:
    Composite study. Vol II: East African community qualifications
    framework for higher education situation report.* Inter-University
    Council for East Africa and East Africa Business Council. www
    .percpaceinternational.com/uploads/1/6/0/2/1602844/east_africa_statu
    s_of_higher_education_composite_situation_report_april_2014.pdf
Jaramillo, A., Manuel, J. M., Demenet, A., et al. (2012) *Universities through
    the looking glass: Benchmarking university governance to enable higher
    education modernization in MENA.* Washington, DC: World Bank.
Johnson, B., and Christensen, L. (2012) *Educational research: Quantitative,
    qualitative, and mixed approaches* (4th ed.). London: Sage Publications.

Kebede, K. (2015) Academic governance in public and private universities in Ethiopia: A comparative case study. PhD thesis, Addis Ababa University, Addis Ababa, Ethiopia.

Krug, K. (2011) Towards changing higher education governance. A comparative study of North Rhine-Westphalian (German) and Lithuanian higher education. BA thesis, University of Twente, Enschede, The Netherlands. http://essay.utwente.nl/61089/1/BSc_K_Krug.pdf

Mamdani, M. (2007) *Scholars in the marketplace: The dilemmas of neo-liberal reform at Makerere University, 1989–2005.* Kampala: Fountain Publishers.

Mba, J. C. (2017) Challenges and prospects of Africa's higher education. Global Partnership for Education blog, 3 May. www.globalpartnership.org/blog/ch allenges-and-prospects-africas-higher-education

Mehari, Y. H. (2010) Governance in Ethiopian higher education system: State–higher education institutions relationship, the case of Mekelle University. MA thesis, University of Oslo, Norway, University of Tampere, Finland, and University of Averio, Portugal (joint degree). http s://tampub.uta.fi/bitstream/handle/10024/81780/gradu04446.pdf? sequence=

Melese, W. (2012) Research–teaching link in higher education institutions of Ethiopia: The case of Jimma University. *Basic Research Journal of Education Research and Review*, 1(6), 85–98.

Mintzberg, H. (1983) *Structure in fives: Designing effective organizations.* Englewood Cliffs: Prentice-Hall.

Mouton, J., and Wildschut, L. (2015) *Leadership and management: Case studies in training in higher education in Africa.* Cape Town: African Minds.

Nega, M. (2012) Quality and quality assurance in Ethiopian higher education: Critical issues and practical implications. PhD thesis, University of Twente, Enschede, The Netherlands.

Oanda, I., and Sall, E. (2016) From peril to promise: Repositioning higher education for the reconstruction of Africa's future. *International Journal of African Higher Education*, 3(1), 51–78. doi:10.6017/ijahe.v3i1.9637

Olsen, T. D. (2004) *Quality assurance at the University of Copenhagen: Internal evaluation component of the audit of the University of Copenhagen.* Denmark: University of Copenhagen.

Pillay, P. (2010) Introduction. In P. Pillay (Ed.), *Higher education financing in East and Southern Africa*, pp. 1–6. Cape Town: African Minds.

Ravishankar, V. J., Kello, A., and Tiruneh, A. (2010) *Ethiopia: Education public expenditure review.* Addis Ababa: Ministry of Education.

Saint, W. S. (1992) Universities in Africa: Strategies for stabilization and revitalization. World Bank Technical Paper No. 194. Washington, DC: World Bank.

Saint, W. (2004) Higher education in Ethiopia: The vision and its challenges. *Journal of Higher Education in Africa/Revue de l'enseignement supérieur en Afrique*, 2(3), 83–113.

Saint, W. (2009) Legal framework for higher education governance in Sub-Saharan Africa. *Higher Education Policy*, 22, 523–550.

SARUA (2012) *SARUA annual report*. Johannesburg: Southern Africa Regional Universities Association. www.sarua.org/?q=content/annual-report-2012

Sayed, Y. (2000) The governance of the South African higher education system: Balancing state control and state supervision in cooperative governance? *International Journal of Educational Development*, 20, 475–489.

Seid, Y., Taffesse, A. S., and Ali, S. N. (2015) Ethiopia: An agrarian economy in transition. Working Paper No. 2015/154. Helsinki: UNU-WIDER.

Serneels, P. (2007) The nature of unemployment among young men in urban Ethiopia. *Review of Development Economics*, 11(1), 170–186.

Solomon, A. (2010) Tension between massification and intensification reforms and implications for teaching and learning in Ethiopian public universities. *Journal of Higher Education in Africa/Revue de l'enseignement supérieur en Afrique*, 8(2), 93–115.

Teferra, D. (2010) Deploying Africa's intellectual diaspora: Potentials, challenges and strategies. In D. Teferra and H. Greijn (Eds), *Higher education and globalization: Challenges, threats and opportunities for Africa*, pp. 89–100. Maastricht: Maastricht University Centre for International Cooperation in Academic Development.

Teferra, D., and Altbach, P. G. (2004) African higher education: Challenges for the 21st century. *Higher Education*, 47(1), 21–50.

Tesfaye, T. (2015) *Higher education quality assurance in Ethiopia: Achievements, challenges and ways forward*. Terminal report (March 2005–January 2015). Addis Ababa: HERQA.

TFHES (2000) *Higher education in developing countries: Peril and promise*. Washington, DC: Task Force on Higher Education and Society. http://documents.worldbank.org/curated/en/345111467989458740/Higher-education-in-developing-countries-peril-and-promise

UNESCO (2012) *Youth and skills: Putting education to work*. EFA Global.

Varghese, N. V. (2004) *Private higher education in Africa*. Geneva: UNESCO, International Institute for Educational Planning (IIEP), Association for the Development of Education in Africa (ADEA) and Association of African Universities (AAU).

Varghese, N. V. (2013) *Governance reforms in higher education: A study of selected countries in Africa*. Paris: UNESCO. http://unesdoc.unesco.org/i mages/0024/002454/245404e.pdf

Varghese, N. V. (2016) *Reforms and changes in governance of higher education in Africa*. Paris: UNESCO, International Institute for Educational Planning (IIEP). http://unesdoc.unesco.org/images/0024/002 469/246939e.pdf

Weldemariam, M. D. (2008) Higher education quality audit in Ethiopia: Analyzing the methods and procedures. MA thesis, University of Oslo, Oslo, Norway.

Wondimu, H. (2003) Ethiopia. In D. Teferra and P. G. Altbach (Eds), *African higher education: An international reference handbook*, pp. 316–325. Bloomington: Indiana University Press.

World Bank (1988) *Education in Sub-Saharan Africa: Policies for adjustment, revitalization, and expansion. A World Bank policy study*. Washington, DC: World Bank. http://documents.worldbank.org/curated/ en/816101468009945118/Education-in-Sub-Saharan-Africa-policies-for- adjustment-revitalization-and-expansion

World Bank (2000) *Can Africa claim the 21st century?* Washington, DC: World Bank. http://siteresources.worldbank.org/INTAFRICA/Resources/ complete.pdf

World Bank (2003) *Higher education development for Ethiopia: Pursuing the vision*. Addis Ababa: World Bank. http://siteresources.worldbank.org/ INTAFRREGTOPTEIA/Resources/Ethiopia_Higher_Education_ESW .pdf

World Bank (2007) *Urban labour markets in Ethiopia: Challenges and prospects. Volume I: Synthesis report*. Washington, DC: World Bank. https://openknowledge.worldbank.org/handle/10986/8011

Yizengaw, T. (2003) Transformations in higher education: Experiences with reform and expansion in Ethiopian higher education system. Paper presented at the conference Improving tertiary education in Sub-Saharan Africa: Things that work, Ghana, Accra (September).

Yizengaw, T. (2008) Challenges of Higher Education in Africa and Lessons of Experience for the Africa–US Higher Education Collaboration Initiative. A Synthesis Report Based on Consultations Made Between March–April, 2008 and Review of Literature Related to Higher Education and Development in Africa. Washington, DC: National Association of State Universities and Land-Grant Colleges (NASULGC).

15 | Neoliberals versus Post-Neoliberals in the Formation of Governance Regimes in Latin America's Higher Education

MIGUEL ALEJANDRO GONZÁLEZ-LEDESMA
AND GERMÁN ÁLVAREZ-MENDIOLA

15.1 Introduction

A common idea in the literature on higher education in Latin America is that in the 1980s, neoliberalism began to bring about a radical change in policies: an almost absolute retraction of the state and generalized market predomination (Schugurensky and Torres, 2001). A few decades later, when various Latin American governments began steering toward the left, neoliberal policies were believed to have reached their end (Pulido, 2009; Sader, 2008; Sader and Gentili, 2003). However, as this chapter will show, neoliberalism did not eliminate the state, nor did the market replace the old, underlying logic of political exchange in traditional statist policies. Leftist governments, identified as *post-neoliberal*, not only did not dismantle the reforms implemented in the 1990s, they also adapted some of them to develop systems of higher education.

The literature shows increasing recognition of the differentiated governance of neoliberal and post-neoliberal governments, although they paradoxically share objectives such as increasing the supply and coverage of education, expanding financing, and improving quality (e.g. Bruner and Ganga, 2016; Oliveira and Feldfeber, 2016). However, the pre-eminence of ideological focuses still relegates to the background the analysis of differences and similarities among the concrete instruments and policies that are deployed in each nation to attain common objectives. In the same sense, research on HE policy is still scarce on the way the reforms implemented before the regional political changes have conditioned the selection of policies and instruments in regional systems of higher education since the second decade of this century.

Our hypothesis regarding the political/electoral upheavals in several nations since the late 1990s, in the sphere of public policies and the governance of higher education, has been expressed in terms of the *emphasis* placed on a certain type of policies, rather than on radical changes in the *steering* of educational systems. Therefore, the differences and similarities among systems of higher education would be determined by 1) the degree of conditioning of government action by the *policy legacy*; and, therefore, 2) the processes of change in the forms of system control and administration, in terms of the adjustment and adaptation of policies.

To analyse these topics, Section 15.2 discusses the neoliberal policies related to higher education in Latin America and the way these policies have produced systems with a public component (subject to market reforms), and a private component (with variable levels of state regulation). The Section 15.3 of the chapter, based on the models of privatizing education developed by Verger, Fontdevila, and Zancajo (2017), identifies three models of privatization in higher education. These models are based on: a) a structural reform of the state; b) the privatization of the supply and the reformation of public universities; and c) the expansion of low-cost institutions. Section 15.4 addresses the arrangements of governance that arise from processes that adjust and adapt policies, based on two forms of accumulation or overlap of policies, defined here as *linear* or *convergent*. In this respect, an analysis is made of the way governments – independent from their political orientation – have elevated their levels of coverage through the public or private supply, or a combination of both. In conclusion (Section 15.5), we propose a categorization of regional systems of higher education, based on three governance regimes. Formed by a combination of actors, instruments, and performance in terms of systemic objectives (enrolment, financing, and quality), these regimes are: a) *private integration*, b) *dual governance*, and c) *loose governance*.

15.2 Governance of Higher Education: Between Neoliberalism and Post-neoliberalism

Governance alludes to the ways the actors involved in a certain policy arena coordinate in solving collective problems. In the case of Latin

America's higher education, the evolution of these forms of coordination must be analysed from the perspective of how governments have directed change by conceding greater authority to market actors, along with greater autonomy in decision making to public-sector actors.

In the past three decades, the region's governments have structured governance, increasing or reducing actors' freedom as a function of medium- or long-term objectives. In this sense, 'governments design the systemic forms for the governance of higher education through a combination of strategic goals and means, and then establish the nature of the policy instruments to be adopted for the pursuit of said goals' (Capano, 2011, p. 1626).

This statement has relevance for our analysis because of the implementation of market-based policies from the 1980s up through 1998, without totally dismantling the traditional mechanisms of state control. Subsequent political shifts to the left in several countries of the region, and the conformation of neoliberal and post-neoliberal blocs, led to a reassessment of the state's role in education. The result, however, has not been processes of renewed state control of higher education or the abandonment of market policies and instruments.

Latin America's move toward neoliberalism has translated into the abandonment of a development model in which the state was a protagonist in the political and economic organization of society. The privatization of public assets and the liberalization of the profit motive in previously restricted settings (education, health, and other sectors) detonated a transformation process based on the state's assumed inability to promote goods and services in an efficient manner. According to Ball (1998, cited by Magalhães and Amaral, 2009, p. 184), 'reforms were driven by the suspicion that the state bureaucracy and government officials were major obstacles to the attainment of the public interest'.

With the economic crisis of the 1980s, a new generation of Latin American rulers, government officials, and academics promoted measures aimed at reducing state intervention and favouring market action. In the sphere of education in general, these actions led to the increased rationalization of expenditure, administrative decentralization, and the transfer of responsibilities to smaller regional units, along with a series of reforms focused on deregulating teaching and the entry requirements for private-sector providers of educational services (Bonal, 2002).

Higher education in Latin America underwent – in varying mode, scope, depth, and speed in each country – a general process of privatization: a broadening of the private sector and the increased use of private resources in system financing. In response to intense questioning about the efficiency, quality, and economic pertinence of higher education, a reform agenda was created to generate mixed systems of higher education. Such systems were characterized primarily by: a) growing private-sector participation in the supply of educational services; b) the implementation of quality assurance systems; c) the adoption of market behaviours among public institutions; d) the strategic administration of part of the government's budget; e) the operation of diverse systems of conditioned financing; and f) the implementation of forms of institutional administration based on new public management (González-Ledesma, 2014).

Enrolment in higher education in Latin America grew from 4 million students in 1980 to 10 million in 2000. A large part of this increase was due to the multiplication of the private-sector supply, especially in the 1990s. In 1995, 38.1% of the enrolment in higher education was in a private institution (García-Guadilla, 1996). The implementation of new forms of institutional governance and the Latin American state's strategic administration of public financing found counterparts in the developed nations of North America and Europe; however, the privatization of the supply is a distinguishing characteristic of the higher education systems of Latin America and other regions in the world, such as Asia, Eastern Europe, and Africa. The changes in systems of higher education in the 1990s have represented the emergence of a new order – a new order that has seemed to suggest that the state is no longer at the centre (Huisman, 2009, pp. 3–5), and that the government is limited to steering-at-a-distance through evaluation of results, discouragement/encouragement of behaviours, and the creation of broad margins for the entry of other actors (Neave and van Vught, 1991).[1]

However, the implementation of the plan of neoliberal reforms did not occur without setbacks. Starting in the late 1980s, protests of various sizes took place in universities to dispute the most polemical aspects of the reforms, particularly those linked to the transfer of educational costs to students and their families, and restrictions in access to university enrolment. Student movements in Mexico, Ecuador, Argentina, and Colombia expressed general ill will towards the consequences of reduced social spending and increased poverty;

additional concerns were political instability and the corruption of high government officials.

Social distress and the emergence of a new and unfavourable economic situation between 1997 and 2002 (known as the 'lost half-decade'), along with historic maximums of unemployment and stagnation (Ocampo, 2002; Carrera, 2004), established the conditions for the electoral victories of leftist parties and leftist movements in several nations.[2] The arrival of Hugo Chávez as the president of Venezuela (January 1999) marked the beginning of an unparalleled political swing to the left in Latin America. The economic upsets of the 'lost half-decade' (1998–2003), the exhaustion of the Washington Consensus, and social discontent were also determining factors in the change of government in Argentina (2000), Brazil (2003), Uruguay (2005), Bolivia (2006), Ecuador (2000), Nicaragua (2007), and El Salvador (2009). Thus, by 2015 more than 60 per cent of Latin America's population was living under leftist or central-left governments.

According to some researchers (Panizza, 2009; Segrera, 2016), this leftward swing divided the region's political map into two major blocs: one formed by the *post-neoliberal*[3] governments oriented to the 'state's return' and opposed to United States policy, and the other represented by *neoliberal* governments (Chile, Mexico, Colombia, Peru, Guatemala, Honduras, Costa Rica, and Paraguay[4]), which have maintained free-market policies.

The ideological positioning of these blocs appeared in different political programmes that openly confronted the Washington Consensus, compensating for the state's renewed role by not renouncing capitalism as an economic system or representative democracy as a political system. At the same time, liberal governments opted to accept more vigorous state participation, without losing sight of the needed efficiency of the economic system and government administration.

In nations that experienced administrative changes with a leftist orientation, according to Pulido, the 'point of inflection' in education was 'caused by the progressive consolidation of the focus on human rights, versus the mercantilist trend of neoliberalism' (2010, p. 3). These administrations promoted the public supply of higher education. On the other hand, with arguments centred on the economic importance of raising the population's educational levels, liberal governments returned to the expansive agenda of public high school and higher education, focusing at the same time on addressing the quality problems produced by unregulated expansion of the private sector. New agencies and agents came on stage in a context of revitalized democratic life and the relative economic bonanza resulting from the price of raw materials (Segrera, 2016).

The study of the governance of systems of higher education in Latin America, however, faces a dilemma that emerges from the combination of two situations linked to the *change, adjustment,* and *adaptation* of *policies.* The first situation has to do with the conditioning and lasting effect of policies that stimulate, on the one hand, the growth of the private sector's educational supply, and on the other, the adoption of the market's forms of administration and operation in public institutions of higher education. The second situation is related to the way that both neoliberal and post-neoliberal governments responded to such realities to attain common objectives such as increasing the supply, financing, and quality; this situation lasted until 2016, when the post-neoliberal cycle began to show signs of weakening.

15.3 Policy Change: Conformation of a Shared Background

Until 1998, Latin America's systems of higher education were differentiated by the forms national governments selected to increase private-sector participation in providing educational services, as well as by the promotion of reforms in the heart of public universities. Although the limited or null presence of rules for operating the market of private education was a common element of the expansive wave of the private sector in the 1990s, it became clear that while some countries had opted to delegate almost all of the increased enrolment to the private supply, other countries followed paths directed to the conformation of mixed systems.

The new policy instruments destined to reform public institutions of higher education were based on the principles of a rational budget, economic pertinence of professional formation, efficiency, merit, and competency among institutions and individuals. Yet applying these instruments was problematic due to the political conflicts that some aspects of the reform generated and the contradictions that arose from interaction with pre-existing instruments and practices. In the first case, we refer to measures of a structural nature, especially those of an economic type, such as the implementation of fees and service charges that encountered resistance in several countries in the region (mainly

Mexico, Colombia, and Costa Rica). In the second case, we refer to the coexistence of contradictory instruments, such as increased flexitime in administrative and teaching posts versus the contract signed with traditional unions.

From the accumulation of political obstacles and gradual measures, a mixed governance of systems of higher education was devised. Such governance combined various degrees of development in the administrative reform of the public sub-system with policies of involvement in market expansion. In this context, the privatization of supply was the most tangible result. This fact will help us to analyse the initial change of policies, since encouraging market participation was one of the solutions adopted to deal with the drastic cuts in social spending in the 1980s. It was also a way to meet the demand for educational services that public institutions could not satisfy. Because of projected growth in the sector, private education was a good option for attaining the objective of broadening the coverage of higher education, which had widely varying proportions in the countries in the region.

Taking into account the classification by Rama (2009) of the levels of coverage in Latin America, systems of higher education in the late 1990s can be divided into three groups: *elite* (from 8.8% to 13.1%), *minority* (from 16% to 28.5%), and *massive* (from 34.4% to 46%).[5] At the same time, each nation had levels of privatization of the supply that ranged from *low* (from 10.9% to 28.4%), *intermediate* (from 35.3% to 48.6%), and *high* (from 58.3% to 71.7%). The combination of both dimensions in each country illustrates the trajectories of the increasing coverage and the relationship with the systems' opening to the market – factors that correspond to three of the six models of privatization of education as identified at the international level by Verger et al. (2017).[6] These models are: a) *state structural reform*, b) *scaling-up privatization*, and c) *expansion of low-fee private schooling in low-income countries* (See Figure 15.1).

According to Verger et al. (2017), each model includes a set of 'contextual mechanisms, agents, and devices that operate in conforming visible trajectories of reform' (Verger et al., 2017, p. 2). In other words, the models give structure, based on meaning (in this case, privatization and expansion of coverage), to certain governance arrangements that can be evaluated according to their results.

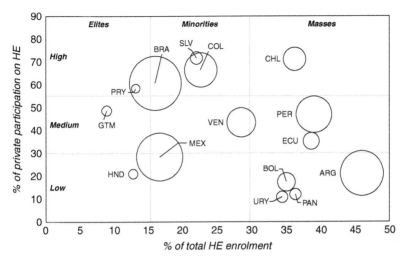

Figure 15.1 Systems of higher education in Latin America: privatization and enrolment after neoliberal shifts (1998)
Elaborated by Authors. Based on Rama (2009) and Verger et al. (2017). Data from UIS-UNESCO, World Bank Data, National Institute of Statistics (Bolivia).

15.3.1 Models of Privatization

The Product of a State Structural Reform. This is about a radical reconfiguration not only of the state's role in the educational setting, but also in the policies of education in legal, political, discursive, and ideological terms. Chile is the only country in the region that corresponds to this model. The reconfiguration of the Chilean state was possible thanks to a combination of extreme social discipline, imposed by the military dictatorship of Augusto Pinochet (1973–1990), and neoliberal policies. The restructuring of the educational system permitted the implementation of market instruments for administering schools, as well as mechanisms for the functioning of a highly integrated services market. Institutions of higher education functioned as private suppliers of a public service, in a market where some institutions could obtain state financing of various types, but where student possibilities to attain higher education rested almost entirely on their purchasing power (Fried and Abuhabda, 1991). The Chilean system is distinguished by its combination of a high degree of privatization with total coverage of the masses. However, Chile's higher education faced problems due to 1) the weaknesses of its structure of governance, specifically the difficulty of regulating the proliferation of low-quality private institutions under the protection of the liberalization of the 1990s; 2) the assignment of subsidies based more on historic (inert) criteria than on performance indicators; 3) persistent inequity in access to higher education; and 4) the absence of transversal mechanisms for quality assurance (Brunner, 2005).

A Result of the Gradual Expansion of Privatization. According to Verger (2017), this type of privatization, in contrast with the preceding model, advances through the accumulation of small, gradual changes that alter educational systems significantly over the long term. This is the case of the systems of higher education of Argentina, Bolivia, Brazil, Colombia, Ecuador, Mexico, Panama, Peru, Uruguay, and Venezuela. They have all promoted the growth of the private supply, as well as the implementation of reforms in the public sub-system. Their variations depend on 1) the accumulation of problematic results upon the implementation of polemical measures; 2) the interaction among new policies, pre-existing instruments, and system dimensions; and 3) the priorities of the neoliberal agenda, defined by the situations of national policy, which in various countries relegated higher education in the last place. The first two factors are included in the sphere of higher education and are therefore easier to identify. The last factor is difficult to attribute to specific governmental choices without making an exhaustive analysis of the historical trajectories in each case. However, it is possible to identify the way these dynamics operated and their consequences for educational systems through the priority financing of elementary education, and the incentives provided to self-financing and the recuperation of costs at public universities – matters recommended by international financial organizations (González-Ledesma, 2010).

In light of government cutbacks and student opposition to the collection of fees, public universities have been financially strangled. In addition to the loss of competitiveness and the deterioration of institutional quality, such events have translated into a severe contraction of the public supply. The result has been the exclusion of increasingly higher numbers of young people lacking in economic resources to pay a private institution or overcome barriers to entry, especially in public universities with greatest demand. Towards the end of the past century, the accelerated expansion of private higher education came to a halt. The supply had surpassed the aggregate demand for this type of service, and the state was beginning to reactivate its role as a provider of higher education – a phenomenon that appeared in full during the first decade of the current century, as in Mexico (Álvarez-Mendiola, 2011). In some countries with massive coverage, such as Bolivia, Panama, and Ecuador, the result was a significant loss in the capacity of public supply to meet the growing demand for higher education. This phenomenon is similar in Brazil, Colombia, and Peru, with coverage of minorities and masses, but with the difference that the private sector did not absorb the growing demand, since the elevated relative costs and the economic dynamics in each case prevented ulterior growth. In the case of Mexico and Venezuela, classified as systems for minorities, the restriction in growth was the product of combined deficiencies in the public and private subsystems.

Private growth in Argentina and Uruguay was limited by the difficulties associated with pre-existing policies and instruments. Both countries had strong public systems, with institutions of direct, unrestricted access and ample freedom for students and teachers in decision making. In this context, although the market for higher education broadened, the new institutions could not compete with the old institutions of a religious nature, which were not interested in expanding beyond the elites they traditionally served (Bernasconi, 2008). Therefore, in the late 1990s, Uruguay had the least private participation in the region (10.9%). Argentina, on the other hand, stood out for having the highest levels of coverage (46%), mostly by public institutions.

The problems of the mixed systems vary according to the emphasis placed on either increasing private supply or reforming public institutions. The principal problems include: 1) the exclusion of students due to economic reasons, available supply, or both; 2) evidence of low-quality/poor practices among the private institutions of higher education; 3) the absence of clear rules for operating private institutions of higher education; 4) the lack of public investment in higher education; and 5) reduction in the rate of growth of coverage.

The Result of the Expansion of Low-fee Private Institutions. This type of institution exists in low-income countries where the state's role is limited or non-existent and the demand for educational services is met almost exclusively through the market or through humanitarian aid. For Verger et al., the nations that correspond to this model are in Africa (Malawi, Nigeria, Kenya, and Ghana), southern Asia (India and Pakistan), and Central America. Most of the private institutions of higher education from the expansive phase of the 1990s in Latin America could fit the authors' description, especially because of the quality deficiencies in the course they offer, profitability as their first objective, and the assumed economic convenience for clients with limited resources. However, these elements assume unique characteristics in countries such as Guatemala, Honduras, and Paraguay, due to their low levels of coverage. El Salvador, with a high degree of privatization, dedicates a very low percentage of its GDP to public higher education (0.2%). In cases such as this one, although the coverage is of minorities, it is clear that the state does not have the will or the ability to encourage the development of a public supply.[7] In fact, the main characteristic of these systems of higher education is the government's decision not to expand or develop the public sub-system.

The problems this development model of higher education faces are similar to those of the private spectrum of mixed systems, while aggravated by the government's permissiveness toward expansion. With few exceptions, the educational supply consists of catch-all institutions that offer formative options not requiring major investment and directed to sectors of the population with low resources. In contrast with private elite institutions, the prestigious market in this type of institution of higher education is based on the mobilization of aspirational messages that do not reflect the quality of education offered (Álvarez-Mendiola and González-Ledesma, 2018). The owners and authorities at this type of institution sustain that they offer better quality (Tooley and Dixon 2005, cited by Verger et al., 2017, p. 16). Families choose them because access to the limited space available in public options is extremely competitive; in addition, they perceive public institutions as deficient, disconnected from the job market, and low in quality. On the other hand, most nations with systems of higher education of this type lack information systems that allow obtaining data on the number of institutions and their students, or the quality of private institutions of higher education.

15.4 Neoliberals versus Post-Neoliberals: Two Ways of Adjusting but One Way to Adapt

In the current decade, systems of higher education are distinguished by their forms of articulating *governance regimes* as they: a) confront the problematic results generated in the 1990s; b) establish the rules of the game for coordinating among educational actors; and c) make the necessary adjustments for increasing coverage, improving financing, and increasing the quality of higher education. In contrast with the stage of reform we addressed in the previous section, these arrangements arise from ideologically differentiated national governments, based on different diagnoses of the nature of the problems at hand, the identity of the actors that need to coordinate in their solution, and the type of policy instruments to attain their objectives.

Still controversial among scholars is the degree of relevance of these differences in explaining the evolution of systems of higher education in Latin America. The emergence of post-neoliberal governments motivated some scholars to announce the dismantling of the privatizing policies implemented in the 1990s (De Sousa, 2015, p. 88–153). Other scholars warned of a possible modification of the market's role in higher education in countries that had remained firm in implementing neoliberal reforms (Brunner, 2016). In general, as the left accumulated electoral wins, many authors attempted to establish an identity between the ideological profile of governments and their policies in higher education (Gentili, 1999). Yet according to our analysis, this division does not explain the maintenance, adaptation, or even implementation of policies of higher education based on market instruments in countries with post-neoliberal governments; nor does it account for the implementation of policies centred on state intervention in countries with neoliberal governments.

In the first place, the individuals, parties, and movements that led political change claimed power thanks to competitive elections. Once in power, they did not dispute representative democracy as a political system, or capitalism as an economic system, although they rhetorically rejected the policies of the Washington Consensus and neoliberalism in general. In second place, higher education was not among the political priorities of the new governments, as it was the recuperation of control of strategic resources (oil, minerals, and water). Lastly, the evidence accumulated in the past 20 years shows that the trajectories of regional systems of higher education are more coherent with the central ideas of the reform that began in the 1990s, rather than with any other alternative educational project.

Based on the classification of Rama (2009), no country analysed here has *elite* coverage, and the systems of higher education that boasted high levels of enrolment have moved toward *universal* and *absolute* coverage. From 2000 to 2014, the percentage of Latin American youth aged 18 to 24 and enrolled in an institution of higher education increased from 21 per cent to slightly more than 40 per cent. According to the World Bank (Ferreyra et al., 2017), this increase was due to: 1) the higher participation of young people living in poverty (which grew from 16 per cent to 25% of the enrolment); 2) the diversification of the supply of higher education and the rise in enrolment in existing public institutions of higher education; and, above all, 3) the growth of the private sector, whose average participation in the region reached 50 per cent.

During this period, the systems of higher education under analysis are divided into *minorities* (20.7–30.8 per cent), *massive* (35.1–47.2 per cent), *universal* (51.1–77 per cent), and *absolute* (86–88.4 per cent). To better understand the levels of privatization in the supply we have broadened the range of each group, so that the systems with a *low* level of privatization are from 18.1–34.4 per cent, the *intermediate* level is from 37–49.2 per cent, and those with a *high* level are from 68.8–84.6 per cent. The types of privatization led to processes of *policy adjustment and adaptation* that are linked to the ideological profile of the government in power, as well as to the nature of the processes of policy accumulation and policy instruments associated with the objectives of privatization.

With regard to the ideological profile of the government, neoliberal administrations can be considered a relatively homogeneous bloc. Their differences (in addition to the dimensions of their economies and degree of development) lay in the way they attempted to strengthen their models of privatization while correcting the errors of their emerging educational markets in order to improve the indicators of coverage, financing, and quality (Briseño Roa, 2013; Sader, 2008). Post-neoliberal administrations, on the other hand, were divided into governments of *agreement* (Argentina, Brazil, El Salvador, and Uruguay), which sought to establish a balance among the pre-existing market policies and a more active state, but were self-limiting in their actions, and governments of *rupture* (Bolivia, Ecuador, and Venezuela), which have looked to create an educational system in which the state reassumes the central role as provider and coordinator (Sader, 2008; Stefanoni, 2012). According to Pulido (2010), the post-neoliberal governments aimed at indicators of coverage, financing, and quality, with a focus on the 'expansion of rights'.

The processes of accumulation of policies of a *linear* type are characterized by the coherence of objectives and instruments, and although they are not lacking in conflict, they follow a logical route with previous policies. In processes of a *convergent* type, on the other hand, accumulation is through successive approximations, at times indirect or imprecise. The difference between one type and another lies in the degree of coherence of the projection of policy objectives and the instruments used to attain those objectives. In the case of Chile and Peru, the processes of accumulation were of a linear type, with a predominantly private impulse; and, in Argentina and Venezuela, a predominantly public impulse. The remaining countries, with reforms of *scaling up* and the *expansion of low-fee private schooling*, produced convergent processes of accumulation. In countries such as Chile and Argentina, coherence has historically been very high, while in Colombia, Brazil, and Mexico the processes of accumulation have been gradual, with low alignment between objectives and policy instruments, although meaningful due to their *political* and *policy-related* consequences (Verger et al., 2017, p. 8).

If an identity exists between the government's ideological profile and the type of policies implemented, this identity should be expressed as either an increase or a decrease in the privatization of the supply. However, of the seven countries identified as post-neoliberal, only Venezuela demonstrates a clear tendency away from privatization, with a decrease of 14.1 per cent in private enrolment. Argentina, Bolivia, and Uruguay experienced marginal growth (in contrast with the increase in public enrolment); El Salvador experienced a slight decrease (−1.5 per cent). In Ecuador, private enrolment rose by ten points and the nation retained intermediate levels of privatization, in spite of a government of *rupture*, while Brazil, with a government of *agreement*, is the only nation from the post-neoliberal bloc that has, for historical reasons, one of the most privatized systems of higher education in the region (73.4 per cent). Among the neoliberal nations, Paraguay, Honduras, Panama, and Peru boast levels of private growth between 11 per cent and 25 per cent, a trend clearly in agreement with their market opening. In Chile, the private sector strengthened its expansion with the implementation of broader instruments of indirect financing, with a positive response from demand. The low growth of coverage in Mexico, one of the most coherent nations with free-market policies in general, depended primarily on the public supply, as in Guatemala.

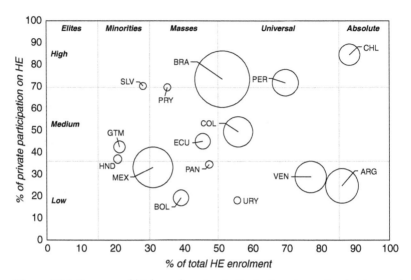

Figure 15.2 Systems of higher education in Latin America: privatization and enrolment after post-neoliberal shifts (2016)
Elaborated by Authors. Based on Rama (2009). Data from UIS-UNESCO, World Bank Data, National Institute of Statistics (Bolivia).

Colombia, however, is the most surprising case, since the years from 1998 to 2016 show a trend away from privatization greater than that of Venezuela (–17.3 per cent) (See Figure 15.2).

An analysis of the trend of coverage in the region clearly shows that during this second stage, the objective of increasing the participation of young people in higher education has been more relevant than the ideological coherence of the policies used to attain it. The ideological principles have an impact on the way the governments select a determined course of action, yet other factors also exist and at times are more powerful in influencing decision making. These factors may be linked to problematic results that appear during the first stage, such as low market performance in satisfying the demand for higher education. In addition, the pressures exerted by traditional actors (students, teachers, workers) to promote the growth of public universities counteract the trend towards privatization; while new actors (business leaders in education, economic sectors, agencies of evaluation) often react against government policies that endanger the processes of opening systems of higher education to the market, to the economic sector, or to evaluation.

Argentina (*agreement*) and Chile (*neoliberal*), for example, attained levels of *absolute* coverage in completely different ways. Argentina has maintained a growth policy sustained by the public supply and a minimum increase in public spending (0.3 per cent of GDP from 1998 to 2016), which assumes a reduced cost per student and low investment in research and development. In Chile, starting in 2005, the large amounts of public funds channelled through Credit with State Guarantee (CAE [Spanish acronym for Crédito con Aval del Estado]), a financing instrument that along with private loans and other economic aid, has allowed the nation to increase its coverage to almost 90 per cent. In the first case, the weight of co-governance and universities' autonomous tradition is a decisive factor for maintaining the status quo. In the second case, private-sector interests have been more in tune with the government, even when traditional actors have demanded the deprivatization of higher education.

Venezuela (*rupture*) and Peru (*neoliberal*) are examples of policies of differentiated attention for the public and private sectors. They showed notable dynamism in the period under analysis, both with processes of linear accumulation (although with more important public/private components than Argentina and Chile). Both nations have universal coverage, but while Peru implemented incentives for private expansion at the same time that it increased the financing of its traditional public universities, Venezuela – due to ideological reasons – created a third system of universities through *Misión Sucre*, to promote the growth of enrolment without becoming involved in (or supporting) the development of traditional autonomous universities. It did not regulate or prohibit the activity of private institutions, however.

In Ecuador (*rupture*), which has *massive* coverage, enrolment has increased to a large degree thanks to the private supply. However, the nation's ministry of education keeps strict control over private institution of higher education; for example, in 2012, with the help of the police, the ministry closed 14 universities, based on their low quality. This measure, which affected more than 40,000 students (not including alumni), represented strong encouragement for other institutions to accept the quality verification procedures as demanded by the state (El Espectador, 2012). Bolivia (*rupture*), with similar coverage, followed a policy of inertial growth, but increased subsidies for universities and research (from 1.4 per cent to 1.8 per cent of GDP).

The case of Mexico (neoliberal) shows a modest comparative increase in its percentage of coverage (lower than that of other nations with equivalent or lower levels of economic development), primarily through public institutions, yet with important participation from a loosely regulated private sector. Paraguay (neoliberal) has a higher rate of coverage (35.1 per cent), whose growth follows a dual logic of encouragement for both the public and private sectors.

The case of Brazil is unique. In the analysed period, the nation moved from a neoliberal government to a government of agreement, whose policies of expanded coverage attained, within a decade, the system's advancement from the coverage of elites to universal coverage (from 16 per cent in 1998 to 51.5 per cent in 2015). The means was predominantly private, with policies of positive discrimination to enable access for students from public schools and of African or indigenous origin (Lloyd, 2016). Colombia is also a special case since it encouraged, without relevant change in the ideological orientation of governments (neoliberalism), the expansion of coverage to a large scale; it advanced from a system of *minorities* to a *universal* system in the analysed period (from 22.6 per cent to 55.7 per cent), through the public sector. Growth in coverage was achieved primarily by expanding the non-university supply of higher education (Melo-Becerra et al., 2017) – which according to Ferreyra et al. (2017) is 'low range'.[8]

El Salvador, Guatemala, and Honduras form a separate group of nations because of their low level of coverage. Important differences are seen, however, in El Salvador's movement from a neoliberal government to one of agreement, which allocated support to the private sector and achieved growth in coverage from 22 per cent to 28.1 per cent. Guatemala, under neoliberal government, also backed the public sector, expending notorious effort on raising coverage from 8.8 per cent to 21.3 per cent. While also under neoliberal government, Honduras weakly promoted coverage through the private sector.

15.5 Politics and Policy: Different Governance Regimes of Higher Education in Latin America

According to Guy Peters, 'policy choices can be conceptualized as both a dependent variable for the political process … and an independent variable for explaining the steering capacity of the political system' (2012, p. 22). In the conformation of higher education governance regimes in Latin America, Peters' reasoning is relevant if we take into account the politically contingent character that prevails in the decision making at all times – that is, the dimension politics – or if we consider the way in which the policy mix affects the governance performance of the higher education systems over time – that is, the policy dimension. If we read the actions of governments with respect to the privatization of supply and the evolution of coverage in terms of the *adjustment* and *adaptation of policies*, rather than in terms of ideological positions, we can offer alternative interpretations of the dynamics produced by the combination of the dimensions of politics and policies.

On comparing the 'focus on rights' of the policies of post-neoliberal governments with the neoliberal governments' state intervention in 'market errors', what emerges is that the differences between them lay in the emphasis given to one or another type of policy. Post-neoliberal governments do not object to capitalism or to market participation in education. The proof is that the private supply has continued to grow and diversify, becoming the main engine behind the region's increased coverage. In any case, private actors' capacity for action varies from country to country. In some countries, private actors can access public funds, obtain earnings, open lines of credit, and even establish alliances with economic groups that operate in the educational markets of other nations. Such is the case for Chile, Peru, Brazil, and Ecuador. In certain countries, such as Brazil and Mexico, an important portion of the private supply corresponds to corporate groups that include various locations or campuses and even institutions with different names. Outstanding among these groups are the transnational suppliers, such as Laureate International.[9] In more restrictive contexts, such as Argentina, Bolivia, Uruguay, and Venezuela, institutions of higher education still operate as non-profit associations or foundations linked to religious groups; this situation has not represented an obstacle for conserving or even expanding their market niches (Altbach, 1999; Rama, 2017).

Except for systems consisting mainly of low-cost institutions, the public supply experienced dynamics of growth and diversification in almost the entire region. The autonomous universities and technical universities that appeared during this second stage were favoured by the increase in public spending, a result of international increases in raw materials prices, particularly oil. The backing for these institutions of higher education, however, was part of government policies designed to deal with the limits of growth of the private supply. In addition, the creation of technological universities was part of national development plans based on the training of human resources with high technical abilities. Found in this situation are the systems of higher education of Mexico, Paraguay, Brazil, Bolivia, and especially Colombia.

It is important to point out that both public and private institutions of higher education created or strengthened different types of associations of rectors (in some cases, simultaneously public and private), with the purpose of collectively negotiating government policies of higher education. This type of association frequently participates, proposes, or opposes government decisions with varying degrees of success. Among private institutions, on the other hand, membership in groups of this type is a relevant factor in accessing government resources, and thus attaining a privileged market position (Brunner and Miranda, 2016; Rama, 2017).

Agencies of evaluation and certification constitute another type of actor that can have considerable influence on systems of higher education and are present in all nations. Although such agencies evaluate increasingly more private institutions of higher education, their influence is greater in the public sub-system. Evaluating agencies can operate from the government – either as part of an area of the ministry of education or as autonomous public agencies – or perform as private organizations. The power of these agencies lies in their ability to define the access to economic and symbolic resources for institutions (universities and their programmes) as well as individuals (students who hope to enter a university, economic stimuli, and financing for teachers' projects).

Another common element in Latin American nations was the introduction of various instruments to promote the expansion of coverage of higher education. In many nations, this type of instrument is directed to students from both public and private institutions, and in some cases constitutes mechanisms of positive discrimination aimed at remedying unequal access. *Acción Afirmativa*, in Brazil, is perhaps the most notable example. The programme was first tested in the state of Río de Janeiro in 2003, and later spread to all public institutions of higher education and to hundreds of private institutions throughout the nation, ultimately becoming national policy through the Fees Federal Law of 2012 (Lloyd, 2016). As in Colombia, Brazil's institutions of higher education can grant loans to students with certain economic stipulations (interest rates, discounted fees, part-time work on campus) and academic conditions (merit- or fee-based), at prices always lower than market prices. In Argentina, Mexico, Uruguay, and Bolivia, scholarships are concentrated in the public sector (which offers practically free education) and consist of monthly stipends to support student living expenses. In Ecuador, Peru, and Chile, existing instruments are designed exclusively for private institutions of higher education whose end is to cover part or all of the cost of education.

15.5.1 Governance Regimes

For our purposes, *governance regimes* are based on three elements: a) the emergence of new actors who have various ends, interests, and capacity of action; b) combinations of instruments that oscillate between coherent configurations and problematic mixtures; and c) effectiveness in attaining common objectives. Governance regimes are the result of the ability to adjust or adapt policies to solve the problematic consequences of previous policies, which can become aligned with more or less effectiveness for attaining systemic objectives (Knill and Tosun, 2012). In some cases, the confluence of diverse actors occurs in a search for common objectives in the system, such as the growth of enrolment, forms of financing, and quality assurance, while adjustment and adaptation occur in decision-making processes with broad consensus. In other cases, the results of the governance arrangement reflect the interests of certain dominant groups in society, a situation that erodes the legitimacy of the system as other interests are ignored (Peters, 2008).

According to the characteristics and processes of development of the systems under analysis, we can identify three types of governance regimes:

a) Regime of Private Integration. The mixed character in the provision of educational services is, as we have seen, a feature of all regional systems of higher education. In this regime, however, governance occurs primarily through a process of public and private sector integration, with a predominance of market participation and organizational market forms. Actors, instruments, and policies are aligned through plans of systemic conduction aimed at privatization. 1) *Actors.* Ministries of education, associations of institutions of higher education, autonomous assessment agencies, private companies, credit institutions (in the case of Chile, student organizations). 2) *Instruments*. Incentives and disincentives, conditional financing, credit market, instruments of positive discrimination, competition among institutions, restricted access, general examinations to select and classify students. 3) *Objectives*. The systems of higher education in this regime are distinguished by having greater coherence between instruments and the objectives of the general arrangement. The differences among the countries that have this type of governance regime are related to degree and have to do with the absence or low performance of some instruments, as well as the degree of integration of the public and private subsystems in each case. According to their levels of coverage, the most successful systems of higher education in this group are Chile (88.4 per cent) and Peru (69.6 per cent), followed by Brazil (51.1 per cent), and Paraguay (35.1 per cent). The accumulation processes in the first two cases are linear, while those of the latter two cases are convergent. The main difference between Chile and the other nations consists of the structural character that it has shown since the beginning of its process of reform.

b) Regime of Dual Governance. Systems of higher education can be fundamentally public or private, but no trend towards integration exists. In most cases, the subsystems are governed with different criteria, although government actions promote the expansion of the supply according to the public-sector institutions on one the hand, and to the private-sector institutions on the other. Because of its characteristics, this regime has actors of greater diversity (and their resources and capacity of influence are asymmetrical), and instruments tend to combine in a contradictory manner. 1) *Actors*. Ministries of education, associations of rectors of private universities, assessment agencies (public and private), other actors (students, teachers, workers) with different degrees of participation (institutionalized) and influence; business leaders, credit institutions. 2) *Instruments*. Unrestricted or restricted access; incentives and disincentives; lump and conditional subsidies; selective or universal supports. 3) *Objectives*. Except for the case of Argentina and Venezuela, which have a degree of coherence based on processes of linear accumulation, the coexistence of subsystems tends to be problematic or contradictory in the remaining nations. In terms of coverage, the most successful country is Argentina (86 per cent), followed by Venezuela (77 per cent); both have linear processes of accumulation, although Argentina has maintained a more coherent policy in terms of the expansive model of the public supply. Colombia (55.7 per cent), Uruguay (55.5 per cent), Panama (47.2 per cent), and Ecuador (45.5 per cent) have shown better performance. Ecuador and Panama are outstanding, and their growth engine has been fundamentally the private sector. Bolivia (39 per cent) and Mexico (30.8 per cent) are the farthest behind in this group, although for different reasons. While Bolivia has opted to considerably increase its investment per student and has granted priority to developing elementary and secondary schools in general, Mexico has selected an inertial policy in coverage as well as in financing, which has resulted in more than a decade of stagnation in the nation's systems of higher education.

c) *Regime of Loose Governance.* The systems that form this group have been coherent with laissez-faire policies towards the private sector. 1) *Actors.* In all cases, the participation of government public entities is weak; public institutions, especially in El Salvador and Guatemala, operate under difficult conditions, although they are able to compete and remain afloat thanks to their dimensions and policies to recover costs. Private institutions of higher education concentrate most of the demand, but are not grouped into associations; within a permissive context, they are focused on winning market niches based on the territory and the characteristics of their academic supply, primarily in majors that require little investment. 2) *Instruments.* At the government level, except for sporadic financing (such as public infrastructure) and block resources for public institutions, the governments of these nations opt to *not-do*. The public universities, in contrast, have their own scholarship programmes for the economic sustenance of students or substantial discounts in fees; in addition, they channel international student support (such as the Carolina foundation scholarships from Spain). 3) *Objectives.* Due to historical issues, in addition to the development models of higher education that nations select following a neoliberal shift (*from privatization though low-cost institutions of higher education*), El Salvador (28.1 per cent), Guatemala (21.3 per cent), and Honduras (20.1 per cent) have the lowest levels of coverage and, in general, the lowest performance in the region.

15.6 Final Remarks

This chapter has shown that no causal relationship exists between the political/ideological orientation of Latin America's governments and the reform processes of their systems of higher education. In the neoliberal phase, governments established new governance arrangements based on market or market-like mechanisms to conduct institutions of higher education from a distance, under new rules of the game. In the public sector, the new rules consisted of assessment of individuals, programmes, and institutions to grant incentives and thus condition institutions' and actors' behaviours. In the private sector, greater freedoms were granted to open institutions and permit or tolerate educational profits. In some cases, private institutions of higher education were obligated to enter into processes of quality assurance.

In this phase, the systems' coverage grew, quite noticeably in some countries. In contrast, the private sector gained pre-eminence in almost all of the nations. Over the years, as actors' resistance was overcome, the types of evaluation, conditioned financing, and privatization of enrolment became the normal forms of conducting systems.

However, after two decades, the neoliberal systems began to show signs of exhaustion. Several countries made a leftward shift, and the state's role in providing education acquired renewed importance. Focuses based on rights and justice and expanding enrolment gained relevance, and the private sector faced severe questioning for its low quality and interest in profits. Thus, public financing in many countries tended to increase, encouragement was given to the growth of coverage, and pressure was placed on the control of private institutions of higher education. Nevertheless, all of these actions occurred in markedly different ways through processes to adjust and adapt policies. Both neoliberal and post-neoliberal governments kept instruments of market inspiration while using instruments of direct state intervention to finance systems and control them – a process we have called the *accumulation of policies*. In some cases, countries followed more or less *linear* processes of accumulation to expand systems; in other countries, thanks to gradual change and the expansion of low-cost institutions, policies have accumulated in a *convergent* manner, through successive, imprecise, and indirect approximations.

The specific form in which both neoliberal and post-neoliberal governments used market or statist policies results in three types of governance regimes. In some countries, actors and policies depended on the market and market-like instruments to take charge of most expanded coverage, system financing, and quality. This sort of integrating regime is predominantly private. However, other countries developed a different type of governance regime that is dual, in which the public and private sectors seem to develop on different paths: public policies and instruments intended for the public sector do not reach the private sector or only reach it in tangential form. The third type of governance is predominantly private, with low state interference, as experienced in Central American nations.

Notes

1. Almost all nations, regardless of the political orientation of their government, increased public spending and conditional financing, and continued using quality assurance policies in the public sector that were also promoted in the private sector. In various forms, all of the countries in Latin America encouraged programmes of positive discrimination and localization to expand traditionally marginalized sectors' access to higher education or support economically disadvantaged students. These countries also tended to conserve policies of efficiency in educational administration, inspired by the principles of New Public Management. In short, more than creating paradigms of totally statist or totally neoliberal policies, systems of policies have acquired mixed forms that combine elements of both, centred on justice and the right to education in the first case, and, in the second case, on economic considerations (conditional financing, competency instruments, and human capital).

2. 'In 1999, 9% of Latin America's population was unemployed and 43% was below the poverty line' (CEPAL, 2004). It is important to underline that in Latin America, government/opposition interaction tends to influence voter behavior more than voter identification with political parties on the left/right scale (Panizza, 2009, p. 77). As Stoessel indicates, 'the electoral victory of the left responds more to the antiparty stances that new leaders offer, than to their ideological stances' (Panizza, 2009, p. 130). This fact is fundamental for understanding how the discourse of personalities such as Hugo Chávez (Venezuela) or Lula da Silva (Brazil) was successful in linking the political exhaustion of the right in power with the need for a change in direction under their own leadership.

3. Regarding the debate on terms, see Stoessel, 2014

4. From 2008 to 2012, Paraguay was governed by Fernando Lugo, from the leftist Alianza Patriótica para el Cambio.
5. Martin Trow (1974) stated that the development of higher education can be analysed from the gross rate of enrollment, which he divides into *elite* (<15%), *massive* (from 15 per cent to 50 per cent), and *universal* (>50 per cent). For the case of Latin America, Claudio Rama proposes a different scale in search of 'more divisions that permit distinguishing more clearly ... the access of elites up to 15%, the access of minorities from 15% to 30%, of the masses up to 50%, universal access up to 85%, and absolute access with a higher percentage than universal access' (Rama, 2009).
6. The other models identified by Verger and colleagues are privatization in social democratic welfare states, historical public–private partnerships in education systems with a tradition of religious schooling, and privatization through catastrophe.
7. Verger et al. consider Peru to be part of the group of poor nations with a low-cost educational supply. While the nation undoubtedly has these characteristics, the dimensions of its system (more than 1 million students), the proportion of public–private supply in total coverage (47–53%), and the tradition of its public universities do not justify its inclusion in the category.
8. The shift toward extending coverage through the public sector is probably explained at least in part by the government's peace efforts and attention to social needs carried out in a political context of conflict and negotiation to disarm Fuerzas Armadas Revolucionarias de Colombia (FARC).
9. For the case of transnational suppliers and corporate groups of higher education in Mexico, see Álvarez-Mendiola, 2015 and Álvarez-Mendiola and Urrego-Cedillo, 2017.

References

Altbach, Philip, G. (1999) *Private Prometheus: Private higher education and development*. Westport: Greenwood Press.

Álvarez-Mendiola, Germán (2011) *El fin de la bonanza: la educación superior privada en México en la primera década del siglo XXI. Reencuentro. Análisis de problemas universitarios*, núm. 60, abril, México, UAM-Xochimilco, pp. 10–29.

Álvarez-Mendiola, Germán (2015) La educación superior transnacional en México. In Sylvie Didou Aupetit (Ed.), *Reflexiones de expertos sobre la internacionalización de la educación superior*, pp. 187–193. México: Cinvestav.

Álvarez-Mendiola, Germán, and González-Ledesma, Alejandro (2018) Marketing context and branding content of private universities in Chile and Mexico. In Antigoni Papadimitriou (Ed.), *Competition in higher education branding and marketing*. Cham: Palgrave MacMillan, pp. 37–62.

Álvarez-Mendiola, Germán, and Urrego-Cedillo, Fanny (2017) Los conglomerados de la educación superior privada en México: expansión, distribución territorial y predominio oligopólico. *Memoria electrónica del Congreso Nacional de Investigación Educativa*. México: Consejo Mexicano de Investigación Educativa, San Luis Potosí, México, 20–24 November. https://goo.gl/ARZjg3

Ball, Stephen (1998) Big policies/small world: An introduction to international perspectives in education policy. *Comparative Education* 34(2), 119–130.

Bernasconi, Andrés (2008) Is there a Latin American model of university? *Comparative Education Review*, 52(1), 27–52.

Bonal, Xavier (2002) Globalización y política educativa: Un análisis crítico de la agenda del Banco Mundial para América Latina. *Revista Mexicana*, 64(3), 3–35.

Briseño Roa, Julieta (2013) Youth, other ways of thinking, and the micro-geopolitics of knowledge between generations in the secundarias comunitarias indígenas schools of Oaxaca, Mexico. *Education Policy Analysis Archives*. https://epaa.asu.edu/ojs/article/view/3505

Brunner, José, Joaquín, (2016), 'América Latina y Chile: ¿hay salida del capitalismo académico?', *Distancia por tiempos, Blog Educación de Nexos*. https://goo.gl/D65HhT.

Brunner, José Joaquín, Elacqua, Gregory, Tillett, Anthony et al. (2005) *Guiar el mercado. Informe sobre la educación superior en Chile*. Chile: Universidad Alfonso Ibáñez.

Brunner, José Joaquín, and Ganga, Francisco Aníbal (2016) Reflexiones en torno a economía política y gobernanza de los sistemas nacionales e instituciones de educación superior en América Latina. 41(8), August. www.interciencia.net/wp-content/uploads/2017/10/573E-GANGA-VOL .-41_8.pdf

Brunner, José Joaquín, and Miranda, Daniel (2016) *Educación Superior en Iberoamérica. Informe 2016*. Chile: CINDA-Universia.

Capano, G. (2011) Government continues to do its job: A comparative study of governance shifts in the higher education sector. *Public Administration*, 89(4), 1622–1642. doi:10.1111/j.1467-9299.2011.01936.x

Carrera (2004) La deuda externa en América Latina, veinte años después: una nueva media década perdida. *Investigación Económica*, LXIII(247), 103–141.

CEPAL (2014)*The social inequality matrix in Latin America*. Santiago: United Nations. https://repositorio.cepal.org/bitstream/handle/11362/40 710/1/S1600945_en.pdf

De Sousa, Santos Boaventura (2015) *La Universidad en el siglo XXI*. México: Siglo XXI.

El Espectador (2012) Ecuador cierra catorce universidades por su 'pésima' calidad. Colombia. https://goo.gl/kZKUB9

Ferreyra, María Marta, Avitabile, Ciro, Botero Álvarez, Javier; Haimovich Paz, Francisco and Urzúa, Sergio (2017) *Momento decisivo: la educación superior en América Latina y el Caribe. Resumen*. Washington, DC: Banco Mundial.

Fried, B., and Abuhadba, M. (1991) Reforms in higher education: The case of Chile in the 1980s. *Higher Education*, 21(2), 137–149. doi:10.1007/ BF00137069

García-Guadilla, Carmen (1996) *Conocimiento, Educación Superior y Sociedad*. Caracas: Nueva Sociedad.

Gentili, Pablo (1999) El Consenso de Washington y la crisis de la educación en América Latina. *Revista Achipiélago*, 29, Argentina, 56–65.

González-Ledesma, Miguel Alejandro (2010) New modes of governance of Latin American higher education: The cases of Chile, Argentina and Mexico. www.academia.edu/16534575/New_modes_of_governance_of_ Latin_American_higher_education._The_cases_of_Argentina_Chile_an d_Mexico_draft_?auto=download

González-Ledesma, Miguel Alejandro (2014) New modes of governance of Latin American higher education: Chile, Argentina and Mexico. *Bordón, Revista Pedagógica*, 66(1), 137–150.

González-Ledesma, Miguel Alejandro (2017) Movimientos estudiantiles y reforma a la educación superior. Méxio (1999) y Chile (2011). In Renate Marsiske (ed.), *Movimientos estudiantiles en la historia de América Latina*, pp. 371–434. México: IISUE-UNAM.

Huisman, J. (Ed.) (2009) *International perspectives on the governance of higher education: Alternative frameworks for coordination*. London: Routledge.

Knill, Christoph and Tosun, Jale (2012) *Public Policy: A new introduction*. New York: Palgrave Macmillan.

Lloyd, Marion (2016) Una década de políticas de acción afirmativa en la educación superior brasileña: impactos, alcances y futuro. *Revista de la Educación Superior*, 45(178), 17–29.

Magalhães, Antonio, M., and Amaral, A. (2009) Mapping out discourses in higher education governance. In Jeroen Huisman (Ed.), *International perspectives on the governance of higher education: Alternative frameworks for coordination*, pp. 182–197. New York: Routledge.

Melo-Becerra, Ligia Alba, Ramos-Forero Jorge Enrique, and Hernández-Santamaría Pedro Oswaldo (2017) La educación superior en Colombia: situación actual y análisis de eficiencia. *Revista Desarrollo y Sociedad*, 78 (March), 59–111. https://goo.gl/SM495C

Neave, Guy and van Vught, Frans (Eds) (1991) *Prometheus bound: The changing relationship between government and higher education in Western Europe*. Oxford: Pergamon.

Ocampo, Jóse Antonio (2002) Media década perdida. *Notas de la CEPAL*, 24. https://goo.gl/jH3D5T

Oliveira, Dalila Andrade, and Feldfeber, Myriam (2016) The right to education in Latin America: An analysis of education policies in recent history of Brazil and Argentina. *Educació i Història: Revista d'Història de l'Educació*, 27, 107–133.

Panizza, Francisco (2009) Nuevas izquierdas y democracias en América Latina. *Revista CIDOB d'Afers Internacionals*, No. 85/86, Los retos de América Latina en un mundo en cambio (mayo 2009), 75–88. https://goo.gl/MtDjNc

Peters, Guy (2012) *Institutional theory in political science: The new institutionalism* (3rd ed.). New York: Continuum.

Pulido, Chaves Orlando (2009) Pos-neoliberalismo y educación: nuevos escenarios y desafíos en las políticas educativas en América Latina. *Boletín Referencias, n. 25, 6, febrero. Foro Latinamericano de Políticas Educativas – FLAPE*. https://goo.gl/mvaWJv

Pulido, Chaves Orlando (2010) 'Sobre el derecho a la educación en América Latina'. Mesa sobre los contextos regionales y el derecho a la educación. Preasamblea Latinoamericana de la Campaña Mundial por el Derecho a la Educación, Bogotá, Colombia. https://goo.gl/nPYfVJ

Rama, Claudio (2009) La tendencia a la masificación de la cobertura de la educación superior en América Latina. *Revista Iberoamericana de Educación*, 50, 173–195.

Rama, Claudio (2017) *La nueva fase de la universidad privada en América Latina*, Argentina: UIA/TESEO.

Sader, Emir (2008) *Refundar el estado: Posneoliberalismo en América Latina*. Buenos Aires: Instituto de Estudios y Formación de la CTA / CLACSO. https://goo.gl/Lc3e6y

Sader, Emir, and Gentili, Pablo (eds) (2003) *La trama del neoliberalismo: mercado, crisis y exclusión social*. Buenos Aires: CLACSO. https://goo.gl/MyxfRV

Schugurensky, Daniel and Torres, Carlos Alberto (2001) La economía política de la educación superior en la era de la globalización neoliberal: América Latina desde una perspectiva comparativista. *Perfiles educativos*, 23(92), 6–31. https://goo.gl/EU44qL

Segrera López, Francisco (2016) *América Latina: Crisis del posneoli-*
beralismo y ascenso de la nueva derecha. Ciudad Autónoma de Buenos
Aires: CLACSO.

Stefanoni, Pablo (2012) Posneoliberalismo cuesta arriba. Los modelos de
Venezuela, Bolivia y Ecuador a debate. Nueva Sociedad No 239, May–June.

Stoessel, Soledad (2014) Giro a la izquierda en la América Latina del siglo
XXI: Revisitando los debates académicos. In *Polis, Revista*
Latinoamericana, 13(39), 123–149. https://goo.gl/nSdfJB

Tooley J., and Dixon P. (2005) *Private education is good for the poor:*
A study of private schools serving the poor in low-income countries.
Washington, DC: Cato Institute. https://goo.gl/xM8yfV

Trow, Martín (1974) Problems in the transition from elite to mass higher
education. In OECD (ed.), *Policies for higher education: general report on*
the conference on future structures of post-secondary education, pp.
51–101. Paris: OECD.

Verger, Antoni, Fontdevila, Clara, and Zancajo, Adrián (2017) Multiple
paths towards education privatization in a globalizing world: A cultural
political economy review. *Journal of Education Policy*, 32(6), 757–787.
doi:10.1080/02680939.2017.1318453

Index

For EU product safety concerns, contact us at Calle de José Abascal, 56–1°, 28003 Madrid, Spain or eugpsr@cambridge.org.

www.ingramcontent.com/pod-product-compliance
Ingram Content Group UK Ltd.
Pitfield, Milton Keynes, MK11 3LW, UK
UKHW020404140625
459647UK00020B/2638